LIBERATION AND LIBIDO

Masculinity, Sexuality, and the Aesthetics of Gay Liberation in Canada, 1971–1987

Liberation and Libido delves into the vibrant, messy, and deeply political history of gay liberation in Canada, exploring how *The Body Politic* (*TBP*) shaped and challenged ideas of gay male masculinity – and gender more broadly – between 1971 and 1987. As one of Canada's largest lesbian and gay activist periodicals, *TBP* was a lively forum where people debated, defended, and dismantled notions of gender. It also shed light on the divergent representations of masculinity – some reinforced queer patriarchal ideas of whiteness, race, health, disability, and class, while others challenged and pushed back against the status quo.

Through an in-depth exploration of *TBP*'s images, advertisements, letters, classified ads, and editorial content, Hrynyk unravels how shifting attitudes toward masculinity, race, class, ability, and health played out on its pages. Two guiding frameworks underpin this analysis: queer patriarchy, which highlights the dominance of whiteness and masculinity within gay male spaces, and queer style, which captures the playful, rebellious manner in which queer culture appropriated and rejected mainstream gender and sexual norms.

This book presents *TBP* not simply as an activist newspaper but rather as a battleground where masculinity was contested, reshaped, and reimagined. From radical manifestos to steamy personal ads, every page of *TBP* reflected the push-and-pull between liberation and assimilation, activism and commerce. *Liberation and Libido* invites readers to reevaluate our understanding of masculinity, power, and desire in the context of queer resistance in Canadian history.

NICHOLAS A. HRYNYK is an assistant professor in the Department of Philosophy, History, and Politics at Thompson Rivers University, specializing in 2SLGBTQIA+ history, feminist and queer studies, and disability/mad studies.

Liberation and Libido

Masculinity, Sexuality, and the Aesthetics of Gay Liberation in Canada, 1971–1987

NICHOLAS A. HRYNYK

UNIVERSITY OF TORONTO PRESS
Toronto Buffalo London

Toronto Buffalo London
utppublishing.com
Printed in Canada

ISBN 978-1-4875-0707-7 (cloth)
ISBN 978-1-4875-2477-7 (paper)
ISBN 978-1-4875-3551-3 (EPUB)
ISBN 978-1-4875-3552-0 (PDF)

Library and Archives Canada Cataloguing in Publication

Title: Liberation and libido : masculinity, sexuality, and the aesthetics of gay liberation in Canada, 1971–1987 / Nicholas A. Hrynyk.
Names: Hrynyk, Nicholas A., author.
Description: Includes bibliographical references and index.
Identifiers: Canadiana (print) 20250197251 | Canadiana (ebook) 20250197278 | ISBN 9781487507077 (cloth) | ISBN 9781487524777 (paper) | ISBN 9781487535513 (EPUB) | ISBN 9781487535520 (PDF)
Subjects: LCSH: Gay liberation movement – Canada. | LCSH: Masculinity – Canada.
Classification: LCC HQ76.8.C3 H79 2026 | DDC 306.76/60971 – dc23

Cover design: Kristjan Buckingham
Cover images: Courtesy of Jearld Modenhauer

The manufacturer's authorised representative in the EU for product safety is Mare Nostrum Group B.V., Mauritskade 21D, 1091 GC Amsterdam, The Netherlands. Email: gpsr@mare-nostrum.co.uk

We wish to acknowledge the land on which the University of Toronto Press operates. This land is the traditional territory of the Wendat, the Anishnaabeg, the Haudenosaunee, the Métis, and the Mississaugas of the Credit First Nation.

This book has been published with the help of a grant from the Federation for the Humanities and Social Sciences, through the Awards to Scholarly Publications Program, using funds provided by the Social Sciences and Humanities Research Council of Canada.

University of Toronto Press acknowledges the financial support of the Government of Canada, the Canada Council for the Arts, and the Ontario Arts Council, an agency of the Government of Ontario, for its publishing activities.

Canada Council for the Arts   Conseil des Arts du Canada

Funded by the Government of Canada   Financé par le gouvernement du Canada   Canada

In memory of William Donald Tape

Contents

Illustrations

Acknowledgments

This book is the product of a ten-year journey through institutional archives and reading countless memos, briefing notes, articles, and organizational minutes about the tireless work of queer activists who have come before me. Like so many, I enjoy rights, freedoms, and protections as a gay man because of their perseverance, love, rage, compassion, and community building. I offer my sincerest gratitude to the former members of the *The Body Politic*'s editorial collective, some of whom provided me with much-needed insight into the daily workings of the paper. Gerald Hannon (in memoriam), Ken Popert, David Rayside, and Tim McCaskell, thank you for the fruitful and generative conversations. I would also like to extend my gratitude to Jearld Moldenhauer, a member of *The Body Politic* and an activist whose camera caught so many pivotal moments in queer history. His powerful work is featured on the cover of this book. Your generosity and work for future queer folks will always be remembered.

Thank you to my publisher, University of Toronto Press, and specifically my editor, Len Husband, who kindly helped guide me through each step of this process. Len's support and supervision were instrumental in transforming this manuscript into a book. Indeed, he saw this as a book project long before I did and continued to believe in it during every step. I also extend my deepest gratitude to my peer reviewers for taking the time to engage with my manuscript and for their thoughtful commentary and suggestions. Their enthusiastic support of this project as it evolved into a book will not be forgotten. I would also like to thank the Social Sciences and Humanities Research Council for generously funding this research, as well as the Canadian Federation for the Humanities and Social Sciences, which has also generously supported the publication of this book through their Awards to

Scholarly Publication Program (ASPP), funded by the Social Sciences and Humanities Research Council of Canada.

I am especially indebted to Dr. James Opp and Dr. Patrizia Gentile at Carleton University. Their belief in the possibilities of my research motivated me to continue working on this project even when I felt lost and demoralized. They have been wonderful companions, mentors, and friends on this journey. Other colleagues, and now friends, including Drs. Pauline Phipps, Renée Bondy, Pamela Walker, Audra Diptee, and Elspeth Brown have provided wisdom and guidance over the years, helping me find my voice as an academic, writer, and educator. More recently, Dr. Tina Block at Thompson Rivers University, where I now call home, provided thoughtful guidance and editorial advice as I finalized this monograph. My future endeavours will always be shaped by their generosity and friendship.

On a personal note, I express my deepest gratitude to my parents, Carol and Dan Hrynyk. They have supported me with every personal and professional decision I have made in my life. My brothers, Danny and Alex, I love you both. I also must thank my dear friends who have made this journey a memorable and enjoyable one. There are far too many names to mention, but you know who you are.

LIBERATION AND LIBIDO

Masculinity, Sexuality, and the Aesthetics of Gay Liberation in Canada, 1971–1987

Introduction

In December 1975, Ed Jackson, an editor for the ground-breaking newspaper in Toronto called *The Body Politic*, reflected on its homosexual consciousness-raising material and male erotic content. He argued that *The Body Politic*'s "images *may* have an unconscious impact on those who uncritically accept role playing relationships." His accentuation of "may" was an attempt to disassociate the newspaper from any insinuation that it was reinforcing a particular *image* or *ideal* of masculinity common in pornography at the time: white, butch, muscular, and enabled. In this heightened period of gay activism, there were disagreements among the newspaper's editorial collective about the artistic use of nudity, the sexism it arguably represented, and the commercial exploitation of bodies and "flesh" in a capitalist society.[1] Jackson admitted that there was a tendency to focus on male imagery at *The Body Politic,* which made the newspaper more "male-identified," but he believed that such images rectified centuries of men unable to see each other as sexual beings. It was the mention of sexism around an illustrative nude drawing, however, that shifted Jackson's attention to gender and, more specifically, masculinity.

Jackson suggested that only those "who worship at the altar of masculinity" were uncritical of their gender and would adhere to traditional notions of masculinity. His comment reflected the Marxist and libertarian attitudes of *The Body Politic*'s early members that desire was an individual's responsibility. Yet he added: "[M]asculinity, virility, butchness – call it what you will – many gay men are caught up by this image, their fantasies, and actions conditioned to imitate it."[2] His view that numerous gay men were "conditioned" to imitate a butch style of masculinity implies that images of masculinity, along with social and cultural attitudes, shaped gay male sensibilities around gender. While Jackson was one of many at *The Body Politic* who were quite sceptical of any "hegemonic" representation of gay male masculinity, he asked readers: "If they [male readers] buy the paper initially for the photos, and read the articles as well, are *The Body Politic* [emphasis added] editors exploiting the body for the sake of sales or for propaganda mileage? Is it identical to a steam bath selling itself with the promise of an illusory sexual bait?"[3] His questions were never concretely answered, but they do highlight that visualizing sexuality was an important element in legitimizing sexuality and, as an added benefit, helped sell gay liberation during the 1970s.

The Body Politic, hereafter referred to as *TBP*, exemplifies the entanglement of visual culture, queer patriarchal ideas of masculinity, and larger questions of what gay liberation meant during the 1970s and 1980s. Queer patriarchy involves the privileging of whiteness and patriarchal or "hegemonic" ideas of masculinity in the gay male community, particularly in the media.[4] As *TBP* member Robert Trow put it, erotic images were seen as part of a radical effort to visualize "problematic" sexual desire and claim pornography as a form of erotic art or, at the very least, a "specialized form of entertainment."[5] Activists' efforts to present gay sex and sexuality were extensions of a sexualized visual culture flourishing in the 1960s by homoerotic magazines such as Bob Mizer's *Physique Pictorial*. At this time, not being apologetic about gay pornography could be seen as a radical act in and of itself, as well as a rejection of heteronormative values around sex and the censorship of erotic content by the state. Queer activists believed that *any* type of sexual expression was central to "liberation" and thus any attempts to regulate sexuality or desire was an extension of state-sanctioned heteronormative oppression.

This book charts new territory in the history of gay liberation in Canada by exploring the complex relationship shared between representations of gay male masculinity (and gender more broadly) in *TBP* and the socio-cultural politics of gay liberation. Historians have tended to include *TBP* in histories of gay liberation as an engine of political activism.[6] These analyses have exclusively looked at the newspaper for its political messaging but not its cultural commentary. I contend that *TBP* is a key and hitherto underutilized source that helped shape a burgeoning gay and lesbian culture, particularly by legitimizing homosexual desires and providing material to fulfil those desires. *TBP* was particularly influential in the development, permeation, and mediation of how sexuality, gender, and, more specifically, masculinity, were stylized or visually coded. Each issue of *TBP* addressed the importance of representing same-sex desires, constructions of masculinity, and how these two might intersect with an increasingly commercialized gay culture that would benefit the financial demands of the *TBP* through advertising revenue.

There existed a tension between these Marxist and libertarian gay liberationists who aimed to disrupt heteronormative ideas of sexuality and the narrowing aesthetic of gay male masculinity over the 1970s that reflected a new form of what Heidi J. Nast calls "queer patriarchy."[7] The presentation or "style" of white, muscular, enabled bodies was driven in part by advertisements from bars and bathhouses, all of which provided financial support for a fledgling newspaper in the early 1970s. However, these ads brought with them questions as to how the paper was to accommodate a growing gay male consumer class who enjoyed this content and messages of gay liberation, which called for the dismantling of the gendered status quo. Changing depictions and subsequent discussions of gay male masculinity in *TBP* reflect a widening chasm between gay liberationist goals of representing and visualizing a variety of sexualities and genders, and a gay male culture being curated by paying advertisers.

I argue that the newspaper was a vital cultural platform in Canada through which the individual and collective imaginings of gay male masculinity were questioned, navigated, and linked to the ideals of gay liberation. Despite efforts to present a unified voice for gay liberation, *TBP* was home to diverse and varied perspectives among the editorial collective and readers alike. The active participation of readers through letters to the collective held the editorial team accountable for their content and opinions. The editorial collective appreciated this, stating in an internal memo that "letters should reflect diverse opinions, not necessarily one's [*sic*] that agree with *TBP* policy."[8] The dialogue between readers and collective members meant that *TBP*'s engagement with issues of masculinity was always intertwined with broader community politics.

Using critical discourse analysis informed by queer theory, I examine and deconstruct images, advertising strategies, letters, and articles found in *TBP* (provided by the ArQuives). These different components of the newspaper emerged out of (and in response to) shifting attitudes towards masculinity, race, class, ability, and health.[9] I find new meaning within these sources as I look at their interplay within the paper's classified ads, advertisements, news articles, readers' letters, and photospreads across different issues. This capacious approach reveals how representations and discussions of gay male masculinity were embedded in socio-cultural power relations that were re/produced, re/presented, or resisted over *TBP*'s lifespan. Social structures, such as race, gender, class, and sexuality, were both legitimized and challenged through the production and consumption of ideas of masculinity in *TBP*, often competing for the attention of the reader. Thus, each chapter explores different components of *TBP* to provide a new understanding of the ways in which masculinity was entangled with other categories of identity.

By examining the intertextual relationship between different sections of *TBP* (articles, advertisements, readers' letters, classified ads, coverage of the arts, etc.), I illustrate the deep intertwining of queer patriarchal notions of masculinity with the racial, sexual, spatial, and bodily politics of the 1970s and 1980s. For instance, images of men and masculinity in *TBP* weave together gender, race, and ability in both representation and performance for public consumption. The models are carefully curated and become, in the words of Elspeth Brown, a "human contact zone."[10] Models for bathhouse, bar, and fashion advertisements in *TBP* represent white imaginings of enabled butch masculinity by capitalist interests. These images rely on a "queer patriarchy" that commodifies and markets an aesthetic of gay masculinity while relying on traditional signifiers of masculinity as rugged, muscular, butch, and enabled. This was particularly true for subcultures of macho masculinity invested in bondage, domination, sadism, and masochism (BDSM). While I do not presume that queer patriarchy reflected the beliefs or ideologies of the newspapers' editorial collective or its readers, its presence in *TBP* was pronounced.

As such, I have three main objectives in this book: first, to demonstrate that *TBP* was an engine of queer cultural development in Toronto – it was a space for people to discuss, debate, challenge, and defend ideas of gender; second, to reveal how different representations of gay male masculinity were either bound up in or competed with larger queer patriarchal ideas of whiteness, race, health, disability, and class; and third, to compare and contrast competing representations of masculinity as evidence of the struggle to reconcile the personal politics of gay liberation with an increasingly commercialized queer culture. As Jackson's earlier comments highlight, the editorial collective had to balance their activist message with the practical financial demands of running a gay and lesbian political newspaper. However, placing consciousness-raising content next to images of white, muscular, enabled men worked to link a particular aesthetic of gender with gay liberation – a legacy that the contemporary queer community continues to reconcile with. In some ways, this book is a history of, and response to, the near-ubiquitous aesthetic of the white, muscular, enabled gay male and how he became the poster child of a modern gay liberation movement in Canada.

A Brief History of *The Body Politic*

To set the stage for an analysis of *TBP,* we must turn to its formation in 1971. *TBP* emerged out of the early years of the gay liberation movement in Canada. In Canada, incidents such as the arrest of George Everett Klippert and his classification as a "dangerous sexual offender" that came with an indefinite prison sentence in 1966 and the Supreme Court of Canada's denial of his appeal in 1967, galvanized gay men and women into protest. Klippert was the last person in Canada to be imprisoned for homosexuality before its partial decriminalization in 1969 with Bill C-150.[11] Historians Gary Kinsman and Patrizia Gentile call it a "partial" decriminalization because of the "exception" clauses for the offenses of gross indecency and buggery (a historical term for the act of sodomy), differences in age of consent (twenty-one years of age for homosexuals compared to fourteen years of age for heterosexuals), confining any homosexual acts to two adults and within private households.[12] Meanwhile, Tom Hooper describes the outcome of Bill C-150 as the "recriminalization" of homosexuality because of the continued anti-queer campaigns throughout the latter half of the twentieth century.[13] This ongoing discrimination and the campaigns of violence against gays and lesbians sparked a wave of protests in subsequent years, one of which was the "We Demand" demonstrations on Parliament Hill.

The "We Demand" protest was a watershed moment for radical queer organizing in the 1970s as it bolstered the agenda of its organizers, Gay Alliance for Equality (GATE), while inspiring new queer groups and publications such as *TBP* to mobilize queer Canadians. On 28 August 1971, over two hundred gay liberationists from a dozen gay and lesbian organizations descended upon Parliament Hill in Ottawa, Ontario. Organized by the "August 28th Gay Day Committee," the committee presented a brief to Parliament listing thirteen demands to the Canadian federal government, including that their sexuality be recognized as a legitimate expression of love and desire, that sexuality no longer constitute grounds for discrimination and violence, and that the Canadian federal government end its unofficial policy of carrying out such discrimination against queers within the civil service, RCMP, and Canadian military. *TBP* emerged when coverage of the protest by Jearld Moldenhauer in the underground newspaper *Guerilla* was altered by its editors. Historian Jaime Bradburn notes that Moldenhauer called this moment a "catalyst" for forming the newspaper because the community needed its own voice.[14]

TBP began out of the Toronto home of Moldenhauer. It is unclear who comprised its founding group, but by the third issue in 1972 it counted Ed Jackson, Herb Spiers, Hugh Brewster, Gerald Hannon, John Forbes, Paul Macdonald, Brian Waite, John Powers, Walter Klinger, and two individuals by the name of Brian and Doug among its ranks.[15] From the onset, *TBP* was built around an editorial collective, free from centralized control or bureaucracy. In many ways, the foundations of the paper reflected the Marxist and libertarian politics of the earliest members – a theme that will be touched on throughout this book.

TBP was first and foremost a newspaper focused on the political, social, and economic disenfranchisement of gays and lesbians in Canada.[16] It was constituted on six principles: to create a sense of gay community; to contribute to the growth of a consciousness that gay lifestyles are unique; to be a source of information about gay liberation; to provide a base for theoretical discussions concerning gay liberation; to provide a forum for current issues; and to encourage new gay imaginative writing.[17] In the words of historian David Churchill, *TBP* was one of North America's most "politically engaged and intellectually sophisticated lesbian and gay periodicals."[18] It never strayed from its original political agenda, but as its staff grew to include dozens of contributors, editors, and volunteers and as others left, the paper broadened to include book and film reviews, political debates, reflections on the arts, and guides to urban Canadian cities. These were topics and areas that arguably appealed to its largely middle-class male readership.

As a Toronto-based newspaper, *TBP* served as an important means of connecting the city's gay and lesbian community. It played a crucial role in unifying the flourishing gay community in the city, which had emerged in a population of 2.7 million in 1971. In many ways, *TBP* established a "counterpublic" among its readers.[19] The concept of "counterpublic," as used here, is based on Michael Warner's revisionist approach to public-sphere theory and queer theory, a counterpublic is an alternative, queer public for individuals who share a common ground and a distinct social imaginary, different from mainstream society.[20] In his words, it produces "the kinds of intimacy that bear no necessary relation to domestic space, to kinship, to the couple form, to property, or to the nation."[21] There was no formal "gay village" in Toronto during the 1970s and 1980s, and ongoing tensions between entrepreneurs and gay activists around the usefulness of a village as "a location of potential political and economic strength," in the words of geographer Catherine Jean Nash, stemmed from concerns that many bars and bathhouses were straight-owned businesses that financially exploited their gay and lesbian clientele.[22]

The newspaper's focus on Toronto also meant it catered to a primarily English Canadian audience. It did not reflect the gay and lesbian politics of French Canada in its formative years, nor did it extensively cover Québec and other francophone issues as the paper developed. While focused on political liberation, the paper would come to resemble more of a magazine with its edgy content and numerous images by the mid-1970s. The collective even described *TBP* as neither a newspaper nor a magazine, but rather a "newsmagazine."[23]

Inclusion of edgy content, including pornography, made *TBP* an important source for visualizing homosexuality at a time of strict media censorship around gay and lesbian content. For example, the Canadian Radio-television and Telecommunications Commission (CRTC) had strict rules on the representation of homosexuality on television and radio, and many gay and lesbian films and books were banned or restricted. The battle over censorship and depictions of erotic content persisted well into the 1980s, with *TBP*'s editorial collective frequently citing instances of state persecution of individuals in possession of "obscene" content – a term used to describe material that was deemed offensive to the mores of a heterosexual mainstream society.

Despite these obstacles, *TBP* quickly rose to become one of the most widely read and circulated English gay and lesbian newspapers in the country. By 1976, the newspaper was publishing issues with forty to fifty pages every month and had an estimated readership of 10,000 people both domestically and internationally.[24] This popularity was reflected by the wide availability of the newspaper in various locations across Toronto, such as the University of Toronto Bookroom, the York University Bookstore, Times Square Books, Olympia Books, the CHAT Centre, Glad Day Bookshop, and the Roman Sauna Baths.[25] As it gained national and international recognition, its reach and readership only expanded.

During its publication, *TBP*'s editorial collective lacked any consensual stance on gender. They seemingly all agreed that conventional gender roles were an extension of heteronormativity and, therefore, a contributing factor to homosexual oppression. Yet, even with the best intentions, the collective occasionally contributed to dominant discourses around masculinity and whiteness. The Marxist and libertarian politics of the collective members were central to the type of gay men's culture they promoted, but also the conflicts that came with some collective members justifying individual sexual tastes that others saw as racist, misogynistic, AIDSphobic, or simply the consequence of internalized homophobia. These differing viewpoints became more pronounced as the gendered and racial composition of *TBP*'s collective and contributors changed over time. While the collective viewed racism, misogyny, capitalism, and homophobia as interconnected oppressions stemming from a post-war, heteronormative, neoliberal world order, the imagery in *TBP* and subsequent discussions of desire on its pages did not always reflect this world view.

Writers and readers of *TBP* equally raised concerns that an increasingly homogenized aesthetic of gay male masculinity as butch risked carrying over the femme-phobia, misogyny, and internalized homophobia of mainstream culture. Gay liberation risked being bifurcated on issues relating to gender performance and expression. Lesbian firebrand and *TBP* collective member Chris Bearchell observed in 1978:

> Equally unjust assumptions of gay male activists are held by many lesbian feminists. One of the more common is that gay men believe that it is possible to change the definition of masculinity just enough to allow gay men to fit comfortably into a male-dominated society (this leaving women, including lesbians, holding the short end of the stick).[26]

The majority of *TBP*'s editorial collective were men, meaning questions of male masculinity were raised far more than those of female masculinity or femininity. Indeed, my own emphasis on gay male masculinity in this book is symptomatic of the editorial collective's male-dominated voice, although I highlight many instances in which lesbians addressed the male centrism of *TBP*. I will also return to this as a symptom of what Heidi J. Nast calls "queer patriarchy." The need for female-led consciousness raising efforts was an impetus for the creation of groups such as Lesbians Organization of Toronto (LOOT), Atlantic Provinces Political Lesbians for Equality (APPLE) in Halifax, Lesbians of Ottawa Now (LOON), and the Feminist Lesbian Action Group in Victoria, to name just a few. Liz Millward provides an exhaustive list of these organizations and informal groups based on the earlier work of scholars such as Becki Ross, Mariana Valverde, Cameron Duder, Joan Nestle, and Elise Chenier.[27]

By 1987, significant financial difficulties, a refocusing of energy on the HIV/AIDS crisis, and the belief that *TBP* could no longer effectively serve its purpose contributed to the demise of the newspaper. In the final issue of *TBP*, Rick Bébout explained to readers, "We're in a financial crisis. It isn't the first one we've faced, but it is not only worse than ever but somehow different."[28] Many of *TBP*'s volunteer members experienced similar financial pressures in the 1980s, given the rising cost of living under a burgeoning neoliberal economy. Members were increasingly forced to work in place of volunteering at the newspaper. Additionally, revenue and "personal" classified ads had dwindled – partly in response to men fearful of contracting HIV. Coinciding with dwindling subscription numbers, the holding company of *TBP*, Pink Triangle Press, chose to invest in its Toronto-focused tabloid *Xtra!*, formed in 1984. *TBP*'s original purpose to grow the gay liberation movement and build a gay consciousness had shifted to emphasize engaging gay men and lesbians "through a variety of means and media, offering them opportunities to support and participate in the development of ideas and in actions which promote liberating social change, focusing on sexuality in its social, political and cultural contexts."[29] These factors coalesced and resulted in *TBP* being put on an indefinite suspension after the February 1987 issue.

Methodological Approaches to Gay Male Masculinities

This book's primary analysis is of images, advertising strategies, letters, and articles. I critically interrogate the relationship between the various sections of the paper to better understand how representations and discussions of gay male masculinity were embedded in socio-cultural power relations that were re/produced, re/presented, or resisted. Images, for example, are rich with meaning and can communicate many different messages. According to French literary theorist Roland Barthes, images provide three types of messages: the linguistic message or written meaning associated with an image, the coded iconic message (which is the informational matter given by an image if all language and signs were removed), and finally, the non-coded iconic message, whereby individual perception shapes the meaning of an image.[30] Similarly, I approach images and their corresponding text as laden with multiple messages that spoke to gay male sensibilities, communicating codified meanings around masculinity, race, ability, and health.

Additionally, this book draws on oral interviews that I conducted in 2015 with former members of the *TBP* collective. Tim McCaskell, David Rayside, Ken Popert, and the late Gerald Hannon provide first-hand accounts of how political and divisive discussions of masculinity, race, the body, and HIV/AIDS were. Those interviewed for this monograph held extensive roles at *TBP* and were part of its daily operation. Some of them joined the collective relatively early, such as Hannon, while others, such as McCaskell, started after the newspaper had established a strong readership. I asked them questions ranging from their role at *TBP* to the collective's role in engaging with notions of masculinity, race, sexuality, disability, and HIV/AIDS. Their oral histories provide a more in-depth insight into the collective's decision-making process around editorial content and commercial and classified advertisements. I am grateful to the interviewees for sharing their knowledge, which has greatly informed my analysis of tensions within the collective.

The interviews conducted as part of this book also reveal how *TBP* engaged with constructions of gender within the gay community that have been previously repressed under an overarching political narrative. The history of *TBP* has been focused almost entirely on its efforts to galvanize gays and lesbians across Canada into political action during the 1970s and 1980s. It is important to note that while *TBP* was primarily a political newspaper, it also adopted the feminist principle that the personal is political. When asked how *TBP* approached masculinity, McCaskell argued that "the hegemonic notions of masculinity probably came up from the States rather than were generated here in Toronto."[31] The understanding that *TBP* had little influence in reinforcing or challenging styles of masculinity thus stems from a belief among some collective members that American cultural forces played a greater role in shaping Canadian content. Placing such importance on American content for the construction of gender and sexuality in Toronto's gay community signifies how interconnected gay cultural life was across North America, yet it does not consider the Canadian gay and lesbian individuals who engaged with and questioned what they saw in *TBP*. Indeed, there was no Canadian publication that was as far-reaching in scope and volume as *TBP*.

Framing my critical analysis of visual and textual content are two conceptual frameworks: queer patriarchy and queer style. "Queer patriarchy," as geographer Heidi J. Nast calls it, foregrounds the privileging of whiteness and patriarchal or "hegemonic" ideas of masculinity in the gay male community.[32] Nast argues that "images circulated of queer white male elites are unreal in that they represent a small fraction of gay men; yet they are also real in that they are produced for profit and pleasure, embodying material interests geared toward creating hegemonic queer identities and norms."[33] However, this book *does not* imply that the *TBP* collective or gay and lesbian liberationists at large were homonormative in the sense that they wished to operate within the structure of the state or state-sanctioned heterosexual ideas of "normalcy." Their Marxist and libertarian views sought to disrupt the state as an apparatus of oppression and violence against queer people. Nevertheless, examining *TBP* through the framework of "queer patriarchy" reveals an important tension between the editorial collective's aim at challenging traditional ideas of gender and the cultural developments that reaffirmed patriarchal notions of masculinity.

I also employ Adam Geczy and Vicki Karaminas's concept of "queer style" to approach and examine the aesthetic stylization of the male body in images, advertisements, and textual descriptions.[34] Geczy and Karaminas argue that whereas heterosexuality "is aligned to legible codes such as the suit for the male and the dress for the female, queer style is resistant to them. It does, however, have a set of consistent attributes such as non-functionality and exaggeration."[35] Queer style is both an aesthetic adoption and rejection of the sexual status quo, or using Adrienne Rich's term, "compulsory heterosexuality," to produce alternative sexual ways of being. I use this concept in tandem with queer patriarchy to explore the tension between the "exaggerated" stylizations of white, muscular, enabled macho masculinity and representations of queer people of colour, those with disabilities, and those affected by HIV and AIDS.

As a queer history that employs queer theory, I am aware of criticisms by scholars such as Cathy Cohen, who have taken issue with early queer theory's privileging of whiteness.[36] I take an intersectional approach in my engagement with race, disability, and other vectors of difference to create a more nuanced understanding of marginalization and the ways in which gay men of colour or men with a disability wrote about the politics of representation. I am also aware of "queer" as a historical term that comes into usage during the twentieth century to signify "odd" or "peculiar." However, its change in meaning as a derogatory word in the interwar years meant many gay men distanced themselves from the term.[37] Thus, I use the term "gay" and "lesbian" as signifiers for the traditional politics found in much of *TBP*. This does not mean trans and gender nonconforming individuals were not present in the paper, but the politics around masculinity were almost exclusively bound up in ideas of what it meant to be a *gay* man at the time.

I position gay men as actors who consciously and subconsciously perform their masculinity as a "style" with the understanding of desirability and physical appearance in mind.[38] "Style," in the words of Susan Sontag, is a "notion that applies to any experience (whenever we talk about its form or qualities)." While visual art, fashion, and music have a style in the conventional sense, Sontag argues that "[w]henever speech or movement or behaviour or objects exhibit a certain deviation from the most direct, useful, insensible mode of expression or being in the world, we may look at them as having a style, and being both autonomous and exemplary."[39] I take Sontag's understanding of style in its performative sense and apply it to how gay masculinity was imagined, played with, and undermined, but also the ways in which it spoke back to perceptions of masculinity in society at large.

Philosopher Maurice Merleau-Ponty approaches style as a lived phenomenon or expressive gesture.[40] Building upon this, Kelby Harrison argues that style is "not a mask, but instead an actual form of existence."[41] Rather than pursue style as an expression of the inner self, style is an integral linkage between an individual's purposeful identity and their engagement with the world. The relationship between style and gender resonates with Judith Butler's theory of performativity and the body. Butler argues that gender, assumed to be a natural internal essence, "is manufactured through a sustained set of acts, posited through the gendered stylization of the body."[42] As a result, movements, gestures, and acts of the body "constitute the illusion of an abiding gendered self."[43] Indeed, countless classified ads, readers' letters, and editorial columns in *TBP* testify to the ways in which mannerisms, behaviours, and tone of voice were all considered aspects of gay male style.

In the 1970s and 1980s (just as now), gay male masculinity was bound up in the duality of "passing" and "camp." The term "passing" has had significant weighting in the history of sexuality for scholars interested in understanding how "the closet" became a metaphor for passing as "straight" or conforming to traditional gender roles and behaviours.[44] Passing is a phenomenon that is not limited to sexuality, as Allyson Hobbs notes in her study of racial passing and race-making in America.[45] Indeed, racial or sexual passing relies on the indeterminacy of an individual's speech, clothing, mannerisms, behaviours, and life story. Preferring the term "closetedness," Eve Sedgwick defines the process of covering up one's sexual identity as "a performance initiated as such by the speech act of a silence – not a particular silence, but a silence that accrues particularity by fits in starts [*sic*], in relation to the discourse that surrounds and differentially constitutes it."[46] Passing not only masked gay men's homosexuality for protection from violence and discrimination but also articulated safety as an outcome of a passing performance or aesthetic. The consequence was a dichotomy within gay male culture between those who *could* pass and those who *could not*. Passing also serves as a reminder that performances of masculinity were (and remain) spatially contingent – the closet is one many oscillate in and out of based upon the meaning and nature of any given space.

In comparison to passing, "camp" is considered a safe eroticism of both the body and gender, based on images of desire endorsed by a society with heterosexual underpinnings.[47] Camp is a slippery term that has eluded critical definition. Fabio Cleto argues that camp has been "Tentatively approached as *sensibility, taste,* or *style,* reconceptualised as *aesthetic* or *cultural economy,* and later asserted/reclaimed as (*queer*) *discourse*."[48] For Sontag, camp is not a natural sensibility, but a "love of the unnatural: of artifice and exaggeration."[49] Richard Dyer, a contributor to *TBP*, viewed camp as a vital way of being human without conforming to the "drabness and rigidity of the het [heterosexual] male role."[50] Macho style, for example, involved clothing that drew on straight ideas of working-class masculinity while simultaneously making that same aesthetic homoerotic by turning the male body into the sexualized object to be gazed upon. To be macho meant dressing and displaying one's body in highly masculine ways that were ostentatious and somewhat theatrical to the point of exaggeration. It should be noted, however, that macho style was predominantly represented and donned by white men as a manifestation of queer patriarchy. Joseph Bristow argues that men who embraced the macho clone aesthetic could "adopt and subvert their given identities, appearing like 'real men' and yet being the last thing a 'real man' would want to be mistaken for: gay."[51] The duality between camp and passing was, and continues to be, reflected in *TBP*'s images of posed models, artistic renderings, or discussions on proper and improper displays of masculinity.

This book's analysis of gay male masculinity as a *style* inserts itself into a rich history of queer visual culture. In his writing on gay men's resistance to state policing and sexual regulation, historian Steven Maynard explores[52] how early twentieth-century Toronto men circumvented homosexual policing by engaging with codes to cruise and engage in public sex acts.[53] This use of codes for sex echoes Matt Houlbrook's analysis of queer life in twentieth-century London, England, whereby men seeking sex with men in public "exchanged recognition signals of movement, gesture, and gaze, in a complex spatial poetics that utilized the conventions of street life to simultaneously reveal and conceal their actions."[54] What has not been thoroughly explored, however, is how Canadian federal, provincial, and municipal police and intelligence agencies regulated gay men and lesbians in public through similar codes and practices. For example, in the 1970s, police donned plainclothes to enter gay bars, bathhouses, parks, alleyways, and lavatories; some even lured gay men with promises of sexual relations only to subsequently arrest them for gross indecency. The use of queer style by police officers demonstrates that queer visual culture could be weaponized against the very community which seemingly endorsed such aesthetics.

Queering visual culture has flourished since the 1980s, most notably in the extensive works of film scholar and critic Thomas Waugh.[55] Other historians such as Elspeth Brown have examined how queer individuals and sensibilities contributed to a new type of commercialized sexuality in twentieth-century marketing.[56] Models, photographers, agents, couturiers, and advertisers all played a role in developing an aesthetic language of fashion and luxury that has been central to modern consumer culture. Historian Jennifer Evans considers queer visual aesthetics in her article "Seeing Subjectivity: Erotic Photography and the Optics of Desire," whereby she queers the work of German photographer Herbert Tobias and the medium of photography to critically think about photographs as documents that are a part of an ongoing conversation about intimacy, pleasure, and desire.[57] Reflecting on this relationship between observer, subject, and medium further echoes Peter Geller's argument that visual images reveal the "power relationship inherent in the photographic encounter and to the struggle over representation lying beneath the surface."[58] The relationship between photographer and subject is critical when approaching images in *TBP* that present historicized values of sexuality, the body, gender, able-bodiedness, and race. Editors for *TBP* captured and carefully curated images in the paper, keeping in mind the politics of specific manifestations of queer style and masculinity and how they might sell issues.

When historian David Johnson looked at physique magazines in the 1950s, he found evidence of a burgeoning underground gay subculture centred on the admiration of the male body.[59] These images were not necessarily about visualizing "deviant" sexuality but appreciating the male form and, when viewed by gay men, helped to formulate early queer sensibilities. These early sensibilities and the importance placed on "visualizing" queer love and desire became part of the ethos of gay liberation: liberate sexuality by visualizing sexuality. Indeed, the muscular models of these physique magazines became enshrined in a more visible gay culture following the gay liberation movement of the early 1970s. For *TBP*, sexually appealing images appeared alongside consciousness-raising content, suggesting that the two were not irreconcilable or even antithetical.

Visual culture is a powerful medium in developing gender and sexual "regimes of truth," as Foucault would contend.[60] Evidence in *TBP* suggests that representations of masculinity were entangled in the struggle for social power.[61] However, I am mindful of David Ciarlo's question: "Is advertising a cultural mirror, or were advertisers the puppet masters of the popular mind?" He argues that this question is "irresolvable" and "remains a thorny crux of contemporary studies of visual culture." He does concede, however, that "[v]iewing imagery collectively and coherently, as a corpus over time, allows us to see the existence of patterns – of ways of crafting *and* of seeing imagery – that are mutually reinforcing."[62] In the context of *TBP*, once images are decoded, they may speak to broader visual patterns in conceptualizations of masculinity as a visual currency.

Historian Roland Marchand notes that the frequency with which cliché images appeared in advertising formed a visual vocabulary of the nation as well as, using Clifford Geertz's term, "the social history of the imagination."[63] Historian Kathy Peiss builds on Marchand's analysis when addressing beauty culture and gender as they relate to the creation of the self. For Peiss, visual culture is the by-product of a capitalist market that socializes people to consume a specific idea of gender normality, which, in turn, shapes their social image.[64] This means that images of American beauty culture and "making faces," a term Peiss uses to describe the performance of wearing makeup and posing with the ideal body, are visual indicators of gendered performances put on display solely for the public gaze.[65] Sharon Cook furthers this line of argument by contending that the observer "operates within a prescribed set of conventions and possibilities."[66] Photographs and visual advertisements are not only features of "the modern intellectual and emotional landscape," in the words of Cook, but captivate the gaze of young people and teach them to construct a visual identity through popular culture.[67] This book builds on this rich historiography by framing queer style as a phenomenon that was actively curated by advertisers and cultural producers, and subsequently consumed and embodied by gay men.

Situating This Analysis of *TBP*

Recent scholarship on sexuality and masculinity have problematized the assumed cohesiveness of lesbian and gay communities over the twentieth century, a narrative found in progressive LGBTQ histories of the 1970s and 1980s.[68] Contemporary analyses challenge the understanding that the gay and lesbian political and social culture was one of inclusion when it was, in fact, often fragmented and divided along the lines of class, race, gender performance, and sexual proclivity.[69] These points of critical insertion have positioned masculinity within frameworks that consider race, gender, sexuality, and the body using intersectional analyses.[70] Many critics, such as Elizabeth Jane Ward and E. Patrick Johnson, argue that these other registers (class, race, disability, and gender) do not complement an essential or definitive sexual identity, but rather constitute unique identities.[71] Similarly, I argue that *TBP* reflected the slow unravelling of a unified image of gay liberation during the 1970s and 1980s – if there was one to even unravel. Discussions around race and racism, HIV/AIDS, white macho masculinity, and the exclusionary practices of bars conveyed the disjointed experiences among gay men in Canada.

Themes in this book include representations of masculinity, gay men's journey through space and style, nuances of race and masculinity and efforts to address racist stereotypes, and finally, collisions of disability and HIV/AIDS. Mediations of masculinity in *TBP* suggest what Michel Foucault and Jay Miskowiec describe as a "heterotopia," a space that should but does not reflect everyday existence.[72] This book argues that *TBP* was a heterotopia in which advertisements, pornography, and photographic spreads portrayed the butch macho man as unrealistically ubiquitous in the gay male community. Meanwhile, *TBP*'s writers and readers alike took issue with the binary of the hetero/homosexual matrix, whereby male effeminacy was considered undesirable. The result: styles of gay male masculinity in the 1970s and 1980s were a response to culturally mandated ways of being masculine in a heteronormative society *as well as* politicized attempts to disrupt them.

The visibility of homosexuality as well as alternative expressions of gender were particularly important given the social climate of Cold War Canada. Paranoia around Soviet influence in politics, the economy, and social well-being saw homosexuality equated with communism and as antithetical to the heterosexual nuclear family. Historian Mary Louise Adams argues that it was during the 1950s and 1960s that heterosexuality took on a particular resonance and form as national and social security, resulting in the ostracism of those defined as sexually "abnormal" or "deviant."[73] As the dominant social order, heterosexuality was reinforced by the Canadian federal government, which drew on medical models of sexuality. Considering post-war medical and psychotherapeutic discourses, Elise Chenier argues that in addition to homosexuals, "other sexual 'outsiders' such as transvestites, transsexuals, and bisexuals, were culturally defined as mentally ill and pathologized to be a serious threat to the safety of others, including children."[74] The obsession with being considered "normal" persisted throughout the twentieth century, particularly as homosexuality became pathologized as a medical condition.[75]

Meanwhile, homosexual acts were not necessarily seen as markers of a politicized identity in the nineteenth and early twentieth centuries. George Chauncey demonstrates in his oft-cited work *Gay New*

York that men who engaged in sexual acts deemed "homosexual" did not necessarily identify as such, particularly if they performed a "normal" expression of masculinity. For example, the term *trade* referred to "straight-identified men who worked as prostitutes serving gay-identified men" but who nonetheless identified as masculine and heterosexual. In Chauncey's words, "So long as the men abided by the conventions of masculinity, they ran little risk of undermining their status as 'normal' men."[76] Conceptions of homosexuality changed, however, as sexology and psychology became fields of inquiry into sexuality and identity. These efforts at cognitive exploration linked sexual behaviours and gender performance with individual identity.[77] In response, gay and lesbian activists in the 1960s and 1970s, including those with *TBP*, challenged the medicalization of homosexuality and sexual deviance by shifting discussions of sexuality away from medicine towards an ethnic model that suggested gays and lesbians constitute a "people with a distinct culture," in the words of Christopher Nealon.[78] This early queer sexual culture offers a historical backdrop of Canadian lesbian and gay history that resonates with French philosopher Michel Foucault's argument that "where there is power, there is resistance."[79]

Patriarchal understandings of masculinity in North American gay communities partially emerged from child-rearing practices in heterosexual nuclear families in the post-war era. As John D'Emilio contends in *Sexual Politics, Sexual Communities* (1983), familial environments played a significant role in how gay men and women performed and understood gender. In his words, the heteronormativity of the American family created a framework whereby "homosexuals mechanically superimposed the heterosexual ethic on their own situation."[80] The repercussions of a heteronormative matrix informing gay culture were reductive understandings of butch masculinity while simultaneously regarding "marriage and the nuclear family as the linchpin of women's and homosexual oppression," in the words of Chenier.[81] Indeed, *TBP* collective member Herb Spiers argued that "[t]hrough institutionalized pressures like marriage, society attempts to dictate normal sexuality."[82] The early 1970s witnessed the early concerns around styles of masculinity and the adoption or presence of butchness, fearing that it was an extension of heteronormative masculinity in the gay male community, including some members of *TBP*.[83]

This book is informed by, and contributes to, histories of queer masculinity and sexuality. Jack Halberstam, Cameron Duder, Elizabeth Kennedy, Madeline Davis, and Liz Millward are just a few who have demonstrated how women could (and did) embody a variety of masculinities in the lesbian community, including the identity of "butch" or "dyke."[84] Meanwhile, Chauncy notes a relationship of power between men who performed acceptable masculinities and those, such as the "fairy" whose "violation of gender conventions served to confirm the relative 'normality' of other men."[85] Other historians of gay masculinities such as David Johnson, Murray Healy, Tim Edwards, Peter Hennen, E. Patrick Johnson, and Arturo J. Aldama and Frederick Luis Aldama, all disrupt conventional understandings of masculinity in queer communities as singular, one-dimensional, and without influence by larger heteronormative social systems.[86] However, R.W. Connell contends that while gay men and lesbians have blurred the boundary between masculine and feminine, "gay men also know the prevalence of homosexual desire among the apparently highly masculine (the gay jock, the warder who rapes, the army 'buddies')."[87] Building on and contributing to these works on masculinity, I contend that historical representations of masculinity in *TBP* reflected *and* refracted queer patriarchal ideas manifesting within the gay male community.

Masculinities, Gender, and Race

Drawing on the ideas of Bobby Noble, David Eng, and other queer scholars of colour, this book explores how *TBP* revealed the process of "othering" bodies that did not conform to white imaginings of masculinity. Noble argues that just as the multiplicity of masculinities in the queer community (including parodies) disrupt heteronormative male sexuality, they may simultaneously affirm "white notions of queer diversity."[88] As a prominent voice of gay and lesbian communities across Canada, *TBP* espoused many ideas and ideologies that highlight the centrality of whiteness in gay cultural life. However, voices from people of colour were also present among the collective – including Lloyd Wong, Richard Fung, Minh, and David Vereschagin. Additionally, women such as Mariana Valverde, Chris Bearchell, and Jane Rule were present in women's issues columns, readers' letters to the collective, and editorial articles by volunteers and contributors to the newspaper. These viewpoints were a critical counterbalance to the editorial collective's predominantly white male voice.

In the last few years, Canadian historians, activists, and thinkers have challenged *TBP* for not only centring white gay and lesbian voices but also ignoring the important work of gay men and women of colour or trans* members of the community. A critical consideration of queer sources is needed to avoid naturalizing a particular white, middle-class, enabled narrative of queer history, with particular actors at its centre.[89] In approaching *TBP* from this standpoint, I believe the newspaper remains an important opportunity to examine instances in which gay men of colour challenged white privilege and racism by using *TBP* as a platform. There are numerous instances in which gay men used *TBP* to rebuke colonial understandings of Asian docility, Black hypersexuality, Latino sexual insatiability, and Indigenous invisibility. These efforts were further galvanized with the formation of gay and lesbian groups focused on the advancement of racial issues, such as Gay Asians of Toronto (GAT) in 1980 and Zami, the first Canadian Black and West Indian gay and lesbian group, in 1984.[90]

A closer examination of masculinity in *TBP* therefore requires an analysis of whiteness and race.[91] Racialized understandings of the male body and masculinity were placed along a spectrum that saw white men as a benchmark for desirable performances of gender and sexuality. Jennifer Nash argues that intersectional theorists tend to "ignore the intimate connections between privilege and oppression."[92] In response, I trouble the assumption that white is "non-racialized"[93] or neutral because, in actuality, representations of white men in *TBP* are sites, or as Ruth Frankenberg puts it, "locations," of power that were – and arguably remain – tremendous undercurrents in the development and categorization of what is butch or effeminate, healthy and virile, enabled, or desirable.[94]

Keeping this in mind, I nuance the racialization of men and the politics of sexual liberation that coincided. For instance, the late Martin Levine argues that "black men had some visibility and currency in clone [ubiquitous macho bodies and attitudes] circles, but it was often because of the association with danger, and a rougher masculinity."[95] Meanwhile, Gordon Pon draws from Asian queer theorist David Eng to contend that, "Asian North American men are both materially and psychically emasculated by discourse such as orientalism."[96] Indeed, constructions of racialized masculinities in *TBP* were deeply rooted in Western conceptions of the "Orient," an artistic and literary place that separated Western neoliberalism and scientific enlightenment from the spiritual and mystic Global South, according to postcolonial scholar Edward Said.[97]

I also include these discussions to challenge overly simplistic narratives around Canadian sexual progressivism. Many white, gay narratives in Canada perpetuate the trope that social activism is a white activity and demarcate social and public spaces as inherently white spaces. As a result, gay liberation becomes a metonym for progressive whiteness. This book emphasizes that white retellings of Canada's gay and lesbian past all too often relegate gay men and women of colour to a "ghetto" within a ghetto, contributing to the contemporary exclusion and sexualized stereotypes of racialized gay men and women.[98]

Chapter Summaries

This book is structured around chronological and thematic lines to highlight how gay male political and cultural developments emerged simultaneously alongside a distinctive queer aesthetic. Between 1971 and 1987, for example, *TBP* charted styles of masculinity within discussions of the gay male body, bodybuilding, the movement of bodies across space and place, race, and the reverberations of HIV/AIDS and other debilitating diseases. By placing *TBP* at the centre of discussions around gay male masculinity and queer style, this book links cultural constructions of gender and sexuality with an active self-conscious gay community that had liberation as one of its objectives.

My first chapter, "Visualizing Sex to Sell Issues," charts the development of gay male erotica in the 1950s, 1960s, and 1970s to illuminate its appearance in *TBP*. I argue that stylistic representations of gay male masculinity and the gay male body in *TBP* demonstrate how nude and erotic images became parts of radical efforts to visualize "problematic" sexual desire and claim pornography as erotic art in the name of "liberation." These same images were also part of a commercially manufactured representation of gay male masculinity driven by advertisers and a growing gay male consumer class. The semi- or fully naked men that graced the pages of *TBP* thus heralded (served as a cultural reverberation of) the widening chasm between gay liberationist goals of visualizing sexuality and a gay male aesthetic being curated by those operating bars, bathhouses, and gyms. In essence, there was a fundamental relationship between flows of capital into the newspaper from advertisers and the narrowing of gay male style towards a homogenized aesthetic that was white, muscular, and enabled.

The second chapter, "Pin the Macho on the Man," examines the construction of macho style and the macho clone in Toronto's gay male community. A style that initially consisted of tight jeans, white shirts, moustaches, and a macho demeanour, the macho aesthetic became increasingly visualized in myriad ways by the mid-1970s. Macho style even included some leather by the 1980s, which was more closely associated with bondage and sadomasochism (BDSM) but not rooted in the reconciliation of pain as pleasure. The clone was a performance of queer style that played on themes of whiteness, able-bodiedness, Roman-Greco physiques, and clothing associated with a hypermasculine working-class identity. There also existed a concern among some within the gay community that macho style encouraged "passing" as heterosexual, whereby gay men could enjoy the pleasures of gay life and the privilege of hiding themselves in society by acting butch. Therefore, this chapter is a foundation for subsequent chapters that examine the consequences of macho style and the physical and social boundaries that appeared within Toronto's gay male community via *TBP*.

Chapter three examines the spatial relationship gay men had with Toronto and other large Canadian cities, as well as the ways in which masculinity was envisioned in gay bars, bathhouses, clubs, parks, alleyways, gyms, and public washrooms. Gay male style was a fundamental component in how gay men navigated sexualized spaces and resisted police/state violence. Spaces such as Toronto's Young Men's Christian Association (YMCA), for example, changed in meaning as gay men navigated the showers, changing facilities, and weight rooms. To inform readers of these particularities, *TBP* provided guides for readers to explore and navigate the city. Certain bathhouses and gyms became synonymous with different subcultures in the gay male community, attesting to the significance of style as an outlet for identities and the demarcation of masculinities along spatial lines. The newspaper also provided gay men with tips on how to circumvent police surveillance of said spaces, frequently reporting instances of entrapment and brutality. However, *TBP* was used by undercover police to entrap gay men or raid bathhouses while disguised in plainclothes. Such tactics on the part of police were responded to with public activism by gay men and lesbians, thus bringing in a third dimension to the relationship between sexuality, space, and place: resistance.[99]

The fourth chapter addresses discussions around race and masculinity in *TBP*, as well as the images and classified ads inspiring these conversations. Race proved to be a category of identity that upended white gay liberationists seeking to balance their manifesto of individual sexual freedoms with the racial politics of the community. The newspaper's white political message of sexual liberation exemplified the privileges afforded to white gay men in the community at the cost of racialized members. With the formation of anti-racist gay and lesbian organizations such as Gay Asians Toronto and Zami in the 1980s, there was a gradual development in the representation and discussion of race in *TBP*, particularly efforts to address the fetishization of gay men of colour. *TBP* reflected white racist imaginings, such as Black men as hypersexual, Asian men as effeminate, Latino men as straddling notions of white masculinity, and further marginalizing Indigenous men as invisible. While editors of *TBP* often pushed back against these racist stereotypes, these articulations of desire sparked debates regarding how gay men could and should express their sexual interests and how the politics of sexuality was mediated by the newspaper.

Finally, chapter five focuses on the changing rhetoric around masculinity during the AIDS crisis beginning in late 1981. After AIDS had become widely accepted as a "gay disease," queer style fundamentally transformed into a politicized statement around health and the viability of the gay male body. Fear of the unknown disease re-inscribed gay male bodies as sites of pollution, and gay men faced increasing levels of discrimination in public. This chapter draws parallels between the invisibility faced by men with disabilities and the ableist language used to describe the "debilitating" effects of HIV/AIDS in *TBP*. Queer style was performed by AIDS-afflicted gay men to both cover their bodies from the physical signs of disease and demonstrate that they were no less sexual beings. In a culture that championed the enabled macho male, masculinity became further intertwined with building beautiful and healthy bodies to confront stereotypes of AIDS, as well as the practice of "safe sex" through the use of condoms as prophylactics. Parts of this chapter formed the basis for the article "'No Sorrow, No Pity': Intersections of Disability, HIV/AIDS, and Gay Male Masculinity in the 1980s" in *Disability Studies Quarterly*.

Chapter One

A Sexualized Culture to Gay Liberation

In the January–February 1983 issue of *TBP*, former ArQuives (formerly the Canadian Lesbian and Gay Archives) archivist Alan Miller examined early bodybuilding publications *Physique Pictorial*, *Muscle Power: The Bodybuilder Magazine and Your Physique*, and *Demigods* as gay cultural texts. Titled "Beefcake with No Labels Attached," the article emphasized that physique magazines operated as erotic magazines for gay men under the guise of art or physical culture. Many homophile publications in the 1950s were "too political or too obvious (and of course not racy enough) for most gay readers," in the words of Miller.[1] In the case of *Physique Pictorial*, art director George Quaintance, a "painter/photographer of gay iconography (whose postcards of cowboys, sailors and Greek soldiers are now famous)," changed the magazine's visual content to include a playful use of bodybuilders, muscular models, and the boy-next-door type. As a result, "there was a definite parting of ways between 'physique' and serious muscle-building mags," according to Miller.[2] In many ways, Miller's observations of physique periodicals stressed both the importance of visual imagery in cultural constructions of gender and sexuality in gay cultural life and the intricate relationship between bodybuilding, muscularity, and gay male masculinity as a style.

This chapter situates *TBP* within a broader context of North American and Western European gay and lesbian magazines to provide context for discussion of macho style in chapter two. *TBP* and other prominent gay liberationist newspapers and magazines drew upon the seemingly naturalized relationship between the muscular body and masculinity in their effort to build up gay cultural life through homoerotic visual imagery. Amid the international newspapers examined in this chapter, *TBP* can be viewed as a Canadian outlet for this global trend towards macho aesthetics in sexualized imagery. *TBP* contained articles and images from other North American and Western European gay and lesbian papers, and many of them shared similar images of white, muscular, enabled men that circumvented Canadian censorship laws around straight and gay pornography. In addition to reflecting commercialized interests, these images reflect the early fascination of visualizing gay men's sexuality and the gay male body as a form of sexual liberation. As a result, the butch macho clone became closely associated with gay liberation.

Prior to *TBP*'s formation, Canadian magazines such as Alan B. Stone's *Physique Illustrated* (1962–3) and *Face and Physique* (1962–4) targeted consumers concerned about male health and virility; however, they were largely bought by gay men because they contained images of scantily clad muscular men. Historian David Johnson notes that the proliferation and consumption of physique magazines in the United States from 1945 to 1969 is evidence of a burgeoning gay consumer market that validated gay men's attraction to other men by encouraging readers "to identify with the models and see their homoerotic interests as natural."[3] In his book *Buying Gay* (2019), Johnson contends that the use of openly homoerotic images helped create the conditions of possibility for gay liberation because they helped create a gay public.[4] These images presented physique models as statuesque figures who embodied ancient Roman-Greco ideals of the male body and masculinity. Johnson argues that the "invocation of ancient Greece [has] had a long history in the gay community, dating back to the 1920s, as a way for gay men to create a folklore of a collective past and a way to legitimize and naturalize male admiration for the male body."[5] Gay and lesbian periodicals in the 1970s helped reproduce the muscular body as an ornamental style for gay men by showing it off in a similar manner to clothing.

For example, macho style frequently evoked a Roman-Greco style of male musculature, whiteness, and, during its formative years, a working-class aesthetic of Levi's denim jeans and white T-shirt. There were inclusions of cross-racial desire, including the fetishization of the Black "stud" and the "Indian Chief," but the dominant racial formation was whiteness. Indeed, correlations between masculinity and muscularity derived from a middle-class borrowing of working-class and Black muscularity in the nineteenth century. The desire for muscularity led to the "muscular Christianity" movement at the turn of the century, the introduction of athletic machines to Ivy League gyms, and were even seen as an antidote to neurasthenia and the decline of white civilization in the wake of industrialization, immigration, and urbanization.[6] To have muscles meant to be masculine, and to be masculine required muscles.[7] Thus, the macho body was fetishized as an object of beauty and source of pleasure for readers, one instinctively centred on its look. Appreciating macho style as an aesthetic resonates with film theorist Laura Mulvey's concept of "fetishistic scopophilia," whereby objects, bodies, and images in visual cultures can become pleasurable in and of themselves.[8] These homoerotic magazines exposed Canadian gay men to a burgeoning international market of gay male imagery and sexualized visual culture on an unprecedented level.

The tensions around sexualized images of gay male masculinity in *TBP* also speak to disagreements that existed among the editorial collective and gay liberationists at large with regard to capitalism. For many, capitalism was seen as inherently patriarchal and contributed to the social and economic oppression of gay men and women. Ken Popert cautioned other collective members at a meeting in 1980 that distinctions must be made between "businesses that cater to specifically gay purposes, and those that just want our money but sell lumber or bread or whatever."[9] He also urged them to consider the accumulation of wealth *within* the gay and lesbian community. Chris Bearchell echoed such concerns at that meeting and suggested economic alliance with business must also be political. However, as *TBP* and many other newspapers and magazines grew in size, so too did their operating costs and dependency on external sources of revenue.

A History to Gay Male Visual Culture

Part of the collusion of sexual content and gay liberation had to do with the prominence of early gay pornography according to film theorist and academic Thomas Waugh. Writing in to *TBP* in 1983, Waugh wrote about the importance of the pornographic genre in curating gay male sensibilities and desires. More specifically, he sought to validate or, at the very least, surmise why there was a desire for the butch white male. His academic work was – and remains – an important scholarly intervention in discussions and debates around pornography, gender, sex, and power; yet his work in *TBP* allowed readers at the time to join the conversation. Waugh destabilized the desire for butch muscular masculinity as "natural" or as an extension of heteronormative performances of masculinity while simultaneously exemplifying what *TBP* already demonstrated: representations of gay male style and masculinity were shaped and moulded by commercial interests.

Following his visits to the Kinsey Institute for Sex Research in 1982 and 1983, Waugh wrote "A Heritage of Pornography" in 1983 and "Photography, Passion, and Power" in 1984, both of which affirmed to readers of *TBP* that a white butch performance of masculinity was part of a longer historical project of visualizing gay men's sexuality. The Kinsey Institute in Bloomington, Indiana, was established in 1947 by entomologist and sex researcher Alfred Kinsey and became one of the largest archives of material pertaining to sex, gender, and reproduction in the world. After watching over one hundred underground gay films produced between the 1920s and 1970s and countless images, Waugh described the ways in which an underground gay culture flourished in the twentieth century along aesthetic lines. Warning that his findings should not be considered a comprehensive history of gay pornographic film, he nevertheless sought to validate pornography as an effective art form for shaping gay men's desires within the context of the ongoing "sex wars" during the early 1980s.

First, the presence of men – ordinary or modelesque – coded as heterosexual in pornography was testament to a growing culture of conformity in North America. Not only were butch performances of masculinity made to be desirable in many of the films Waugh studied, but a working-class masculinity becomes entangled with gay male sensibilities. For example, having a model perform "ordinary" actions, such as "the model as nude worker attacking rocks with a pickaxe" in the candid camera work of an individual named AT, creates an aesthetic reference of "ordinariness" for the audience. This style of a working-class, heterosexually coded masculinity is also found among AT's work featuring "sailors, the most common icon of pre-Stonewall gay mythology, who become walk-on extras in this first documentary of a gay cruising area," Waugh argued.[10] Use of models in narratives such as these creates an important visual marker for butch *performances* of masculinity.

The "beefcake" became a mainstay in homoerotic visual culture, including pornographic films such as *Greek Gods* (date unknown) or *Heat Wave* (date unknown) and valorized male statuesque models by the 1960s.[11] For Waugh, these films paved the way for more hardcore erotica such as *Boys in the Sand* (1971) and demonstrated the importance of pornography as a catalyst for styling gay male masculinity in the post-war period as muscular and white. While not all films were merely suggestive in their homosexuality or filled with white protagonists (Waugh provides the example of *Oh Doctor* and its Black protagonist, Iva Crusty Crotch), this limited example inadvertently suggests that racialized, explicitly homosexual protagonists were the exception rather than the norm for 1960s pornography.[12]

Waugh's analysis of pornography continued to unfold on the pages of *TBP* in March 1984. That month, he published "Photography, Passion and Power," in which he argued that "Fuck photos have always had to serve not only as our stroke materials but also, to a large extent, as our family snapshots and wedding albums, as our cultural history and political validation." Other types of photographs examined in his article included pictures of models having sex for "brothel photography," statuesque male models posing for magazines such as *Physique Pictorial*, and erotic images of both real military officers and show models dressed as soldiers. Reading these photographs, Waugh argued that "[I]t is images in interaction with the world, not images in isolation, that we must focus on when we talk about porn, when we talk about how we use images and how they use us."[13] Indeed, images, particularly photographs, play an important role in the construction of reality by acting as part of a "system of information, fitted into schemes of classification and storage," as Susan Sontag argues.[14] Like heterosexual pornography, gay pornography crafted a specific understanding and appreciation of the male body that operated within cultural frameworks around age, gender, class, race, and ability.

Without gender differentiation between male and female, Waugh saw power relations in homosexual content through body type, masculinity, and aesthetic style. In his words, "the iconography of cigarette, jean-jacket and 'drop dead' pose is still with us thirty years later, clonified [*sic*] into three million walking mirror images. In still photos, it is difficult to denote 'straight' precisely … so the macho body type is used as shorthand."[15] Waugh did not simply explore the ubiquity of gay male machismo but attempted to discover the phenomenon's roots and the power of visual culture in defining gender. When stressing the importance of "posing" as well as referring to clothing as "iconography," Waugh's analysis harks back to Erving Goffman's concept of sign-vehicles. The positioning and movement of the body, how the body is adorned with clothing, and what type of clothing is selected are all elements that make up Goffman's theory of sign-vehicles as extensions of the self. In this manner, Waugh invariably argues that gay male masculinity was intrinsically linked to the presentation of the self through style and performance.

Capitalism and Shifting Discourses Around Gay Male Masculinity

Stylistic presentations of gay male masculinity in *TBP* reflected broader trends among North American and Western European gay newspapers and magazines to raise the consciousness of gay men and women while meeting the financial demands that came with print publishing. *TBP* frequently featured male models or images from stock photography of butch, muscular men that were ubiquitous in international gay newspapers and magazines. The male models often evoked a butch masculinity rather than anything effeminate or explicitly queer. They were also nearly ubiquitous in their defined musculature and whiteness. This was partly the result of a growing commercial culture of gay male sex and the aforementioned prominence of white muscular butch men in gay male pornography and bodybuilding periodicals that had emerged over the twentieth century. As the following periodicals will demonstrate, there was an international network of gay male consciousness-raising periodicals that sought to mix activism with sexualized content in order to sell messages of equality and liberation and to build a gay public.

From its early years, *TBP*'s editorial collective complemented their content using imagery published across North America and Western Europe that often adhered to a white butch style of masculinity. In my interview with Tim McCaskell, the editor of the international news segment of *TBP* from 1974 until 1987, he argued that much of the explicit sexualized imagery found in *TBP* was a testament to the emergence of stock image banks in the 1970s:

> So what images appeared were images that appeared in advertising. And those tended to be stock images that permeated gay publications right around the world. I mean, I can remember saying to Gerald Hannon one day, I was reading the Italian paper and I think, "you know, this is exactly the same picture in this ad that people are using in Toronto … the exact one … what does this mean?"[16]

Stock photography banks, such as The Image Bank and Comstock, rented out high-quality, ready-made photographs based on standard American and European advertising practices. Their images of male models were standardized in musculature and whiteness, helping to unify Western European and North American understandings of gay male style. They combined fantasy and reality, making them "striking visual materializations of cultural stereotypes," according to communications scholar Paul Frosh.[17] These images were made for re-use and sold well because they connected a desire for the ideal male body with gay culture and the heritage of pornography and physique magazines.[18]

After Dark (1958–82) was one such American periodical to appeal to a gay male audience using buff, white macho men on its covers as a marketing ploy to lure gay male readers (Figure 1.1). An entertainment

Figure 1.1 Cover of *After Dark*, March 1972. Photographer: Kenn Duncan. The ArQuives, *After Dark* fonds.

magazine that covered cinema, stage plays, ballet, and performance art, *After Dark* was "a masterpiece of indirection, a magazine that was all insinuation, an elaborate dance around its unidentifiable subject, which emerged only in hints, winks, and nudges, in photographs of the muscular torsos of aspiring actors or sultry Adonises sprawled invitingly on satin sheets," in the words of author Daniel Harris.[19] Using images of semi-naked and fully naked dance troupes and muscular athletes with wry smiles, *After Dark* invited readers to not only enjoy their consciousness-raising content but to gaze upon the groins of their statuesque models.

The use of male models straddled the division between art and homoerotic pornography, but by no means were writers in *After Dark* uncritical or purposefully opaque about the extent to which white, muscular enabled men had become enshrined in society as the epitome of beauty and masculinity. In 1979, *After Dark* writer Nathan Fain openly acknowledged that:

> we find ourselves surrounded by a gigantic open-air exhibit of living, breathing – not to mention jogging, swimming, dancing, skating, weight lifting – human beauty, works of art to rival Tiepolo, Raphael, Veronese; art that works, votes, sweats, ruts, looks at itself in the mirror each morning and think, "Boy. Wow. If you aren't the most gorgeous *thing*!" An inundation, verily, of national narcissism, the likes of which we've never seen before.[20]

This muscular aesthetic that Fain referred to was also prominent in other magazines in the United States, such as general interest magazines *Christopher Street* (1976–95) and *The Advocate* (1967–), and more sexually explicit magazines such as *Queen's Quarterly* (1968–80), a national magazine "for gay guys who have no hangups," and its spin-off, *Ciao* (1973–80), a gay travel magazine that frequently contained images of nude white muscular men.

Christopher Street frequently portrayed muscular men throughout its pages. The magazine's emphasis on theatre, ballet, and other arts earned it "a budding reputation as a gay *New Yorker*."[21] However, the magazine also brought into question how gay men stylized their bodies and performed their sexuality with articles such as "Patterns of Aging Among Gay Men" by Douglas Kimmell, "Where Have All the Sissies Gone?" by Seymour Kleinberg, and Johnny Greene's "The Male Southern Belle" and "Gay Rites, Straight Style."[22] By mixing discussions of gender and artistic reviews with sexualized imagery in content such as "Butch: Gay Machismo, Illustrated" (Figure 1.2), *Christopher Street*

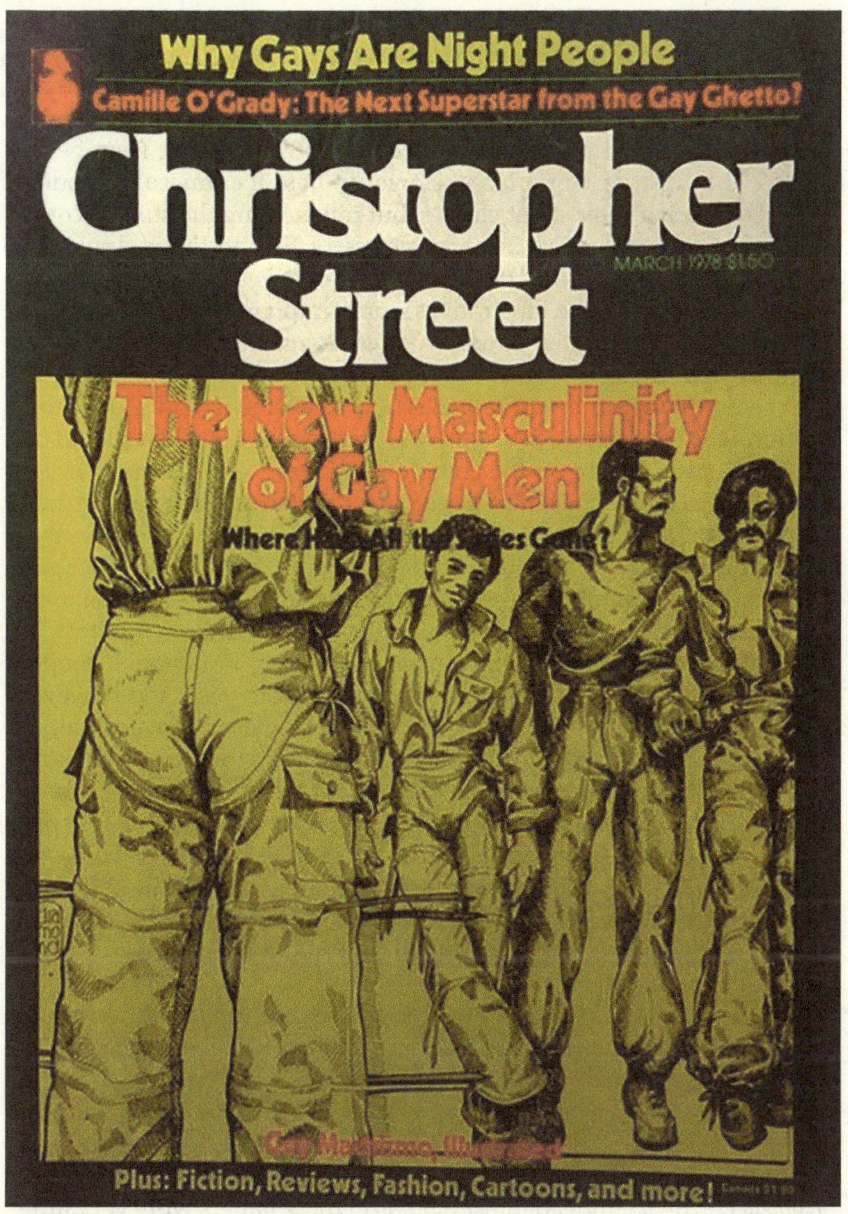

Figure 1.2 Cover of *Christopher Street*, March 1978. The ArQuives, *Christopher Street* fonds.

mediated the gendered aesthetics of gay artistry and gay cultural life in America.[23] This cover, for instance, presented the "new" masculinity of the gay community as one deeply informed by working-class masculinity. The boilersuits (sometimes referred to as coveralls) on the model on this cover were traditionally used to protect clothing from being soiled in industrial workplaces. However, here the muscular models are not covering their street clothes, but rather using the suits to cover their semi-naked bodies. The campiness of this aesthetic draws on working-class masculinity but adds a sexualized element by revealing the upper torso of these illustrative figures, implying a queer co-option of a predominantly heterosexual work environment. In doing so, these cartoon figures along with the text of "new masculinity" reinforce an association between a working-class butch aesthetic and a desirable performance of gender for gay men. Moreover, the emphasis placed on gay male masculinity on the cover of *Christopher Street* demonstrates the extent to which the aesthetics of queer patriarchal masculinity had become a cultural force worthy of recognition by the "gay *New Yorker*."

The purposeful presentation of the male body in *TBP* and other gay periodicals was similar to the *Playboy*'s "pin-up" girl in that the male muscular body was stylized in ways that mirrored the femininity of the voluptuous curves on the female playmate.[24] Emmanuel Cooper argues, "The naked male body, however artful the pose, and however much the direct external sexual characteristics are removed, cannot be divorced from the erotic implications of the nude body seen – by women or by homosexual men – as desirable."[25] Similar to the men of *Playboy*'s counterpart, *Playgirl*, however, portrayals of male models in *TBP* or other gay periodicals frequently exaggerated common perceptions of masculinity rather than challenge them. These images reinforced tropes of masculinity as white, muscular, and ultimately forced many writers and activists to think about and discuss the cultural imaginings of gay male masculinity.

Images appearing in gay periodicals also highlighted how visual content, unique or otherwise, established cues for gay male masculinity. These images helped frame (or stylize) the very content appearing in *TBP* and the importance of synthesizing erotic content with political messages. "Pin-up" culture could be found in British gay "lifestyle" magazine *Quorum* (1971–6), and Italian papers *Fuori!* (1971–82) and *Lambda* (1976–82). Indeed, most models in these papers wore very little clothing (underwear, if so) and would only don other attire, such as leather or a police outfit, to fit into a uniformed aesthetic.

The British paper *Quorum*, for instance, was conceived of as a homosexual publication that fostered gay literacy of world news, promoted political campaigning against homophobia, and provided readers with professional portfolios of photographic art. Created in Harrow (now part of London) in 1971 and run until 1976, the magazine used graphic photography to entice readers to purchase the magazine. Designed "for the adult male homosexual," *Quorum* was devoted to providing its readership with an array of nude male models, often thematic based, in a manner similar to *Playboy*.[26] In its first issue, editor-in-chief Roger Baker informed readers that, "We have approached many of the leading physique photographers and are compiling a portfolio of work which has not been seen before and which is of good quality."[27] The magazine actively promoted its use of male pin-ups despite acknowledging in the same issue that they threatened to "reduce real people to the level of sex objects ...[,] exploit sexism[,] ... support the myth that homosexual are only interested in luminous youth ...[, and] ... give those of us who are slightly less than Greek an inferiority complex."[28] *Quorum*'s emphasis on physique imagery from photographers such as Colin Clarke, who specialized in capturing the body in all its musculature, hair, and girth, arguably set the tone for how gay magazines *could* and *should* deliver sexualized content to their readers. Consulting individual photographers also meant that *Quorum*'s content to readers was unique to the magazine and would, by virtue, have boosted sales.

The white muscular men in Clarke's photographic scenes such as "What Can You Say About a Chap Like This?" and "The Changing Room" (Figure 1.3), both from 1974, as well as readers' demands for these men, demonstrates the predominance of white machismo as a popular gay male style within a flourishing gay culture.[29] In "The Changing Room," for instance, the masculinity of the male models on display is reaffirmed by the changing room's descriptive context. Emmanuel Cooper argues, "[s]hower rooms, swimming pools and bathtime have proved to be contexts in which naked men could legitimately be shown."[30] Despite the presentation of nude male models as passive objects for the reader to gaze upon, as Mulvey might argue, their placement within the "changing room" links their bodies with stereotypes of masculinity, ability, and sports.

According to sociologist R.W. Connell, "[t]he institutional organization of sport embeds definite social relations: competition and hierarchy among men, exclusion or domination of women. These social relations of gender are both realized and symbolized in the bodily performances."[31] In this case, the context of sports inscribes a heteronormative understanding of machismo onto the male models that is reinforced by their relaxed posture and disregard for their nudity. However, displaying their bodies unfettered by sports jerseys or equipment

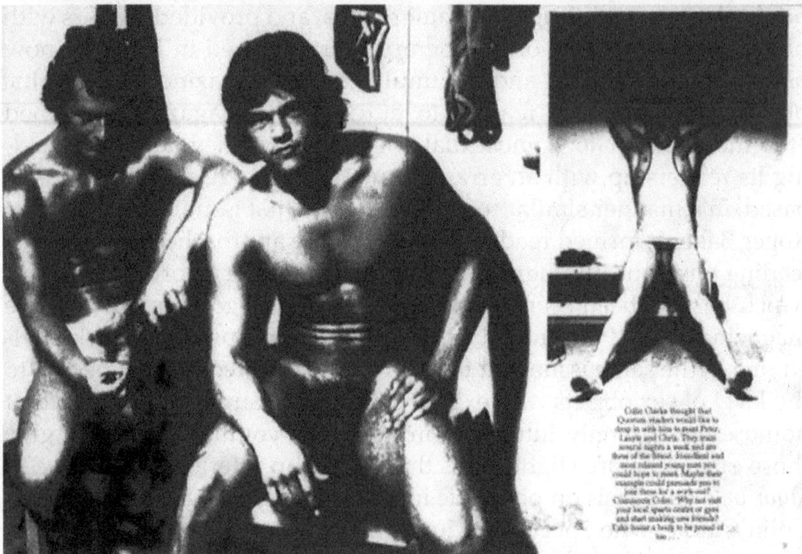

Figure 1.3 Image from "The Changing Room," *Quorum* 2, no. 12, 1974, 15. Photo Feature by Colin Clarke. The ArQuives, *Quorum* fonds.

produces a degree of homoeroticism and illustrates how particular settings shape performances of masculinity. This image highlights the inherent assumption that sports reinforce or define the "masculine heterosexual" body. At the same time, the changing room becomes a space where homosocial and even homosexual actions may take place.

Quorum's practices should not be taken out of context, however. The magazine appealed to a flourishing gay male culture that increasingly prized visibility and helped to foster an appreciation for the gay male body. These images acted as both a means of stylizing gay masculinity in a manner that spoke to heteronormative masculine endeavours and body types while also breaking from pre-existing stereotypes of gay men being inherently void of masculinity. However, the presence of white athletic men in other gay and lesbian European newspapers and magazines, such as Britain's *Gay News* and Italy's *Fuori!* and *Lambda*, suggest an increasingly uniform economy of sexuality in various gay male communities across Western Europe and North America.[32] Simply put, these images helped sell issues.

Some international periodicals, such as the Italian newspaper *Lambda*, used a mixture of photographs of naked male models and artwork in an attempt to make gay activism "sexier" and promote Italy's growing

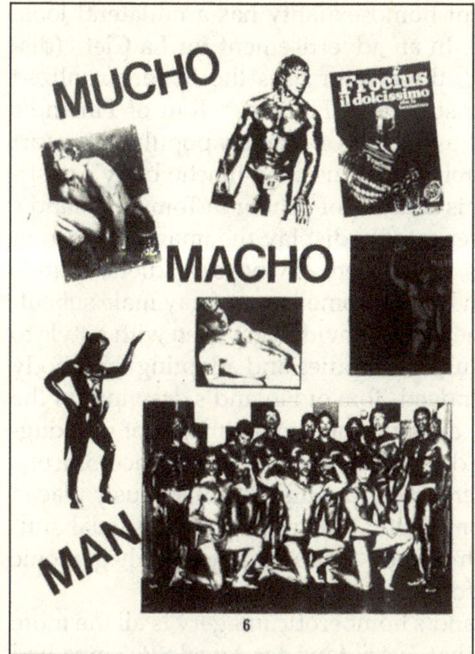

Figure 1.4 Images from "Mucho Macho Man," *Lambda* 23, September-October 1979, 6. The ArQuives, *Lambda* fonds.

gay nightlife. One photospread in 1979 included various macho men as part of a two-page special. As a celebration of the male body, *Lambda* featured an assortment of pictures featuring enabled, muscular white men entitled "Mucho Macho Man" (Figure 1.4). The images contained men who, by and large, represented a macho style of masculinity based on earlier bodybuilding magazines, such as *Physique Pictorial*. This photospread sought to present a homogenized vision of gay male masculinity while also deflecting homophobic assumptions of gay men as weak and effeminate. Indeed, the men are presented as both strong and sexual, owing much of that to the visual language of their semi-nude muscular bodies. The use of photography and artwork in this was a form of cultural resistance, allowing the gay community to assert its identity visibly but in a way that did not necessarily challenge the underlying gendered order of society.

Other Italian newspapers, such as *Fuori!*, only started portraying male nudity through artistic drawings by the mid- to late 1970s due to advertisers promoting their products or venues and writers addressing certain topics relevant to the male body. For example, Giuseppe Di Salvo's discussion of adolescent sexuality illustrated two semi-naked, muscular white men kissing and fondling each other.[33] The implication in this image is that adolescent homosexuality has a unilateral look: white, muscular, and enabled. In an advertisement for La Clef "(discogay)" discotheque in *Fuori!*, the creator uses the hypersexualized macho artwork of Finnish artist Tom of Finland.[34] Tom of Finland's macho, phallocentric style of drawing was extremely popular in gay art in the 1970s and 1980s, reinforcing the muscular, macho body's desirability. Martti Lahti argues in his analysis of gender in Tom of Finland's work that: "Tom's drawings repeatedly display the images of men in leather and uniforms – bikers, policemen, cowboys, soldiers, sailors, and lumberjacks – all of which have become icons of gay male subcultures. These images have for their part provided gay men with a style to follow, and a model for building their bodies and adapting their body languages and wardrobes."[35] Indeed, Tom of Finland's drawings of the 1960s inspired macho style by evoking traditional images of working-class masculinity, using men dressed as lumberjacks, police officers, tradesmen, and military soldiers. His drawings simultaneously placed these figures in seemingly homoerotic or explicitly homosexual situations, turning them into examples of "gay resistance" to hegemonic narratives of male gender performance.[36]

La Clef's use of Tom of Finland's homoerotic imagery is all the more significant when considering that *Fuori!* founder Angelo Pezanna had described gay establishments in Italy as being "not advertised at all" up until 1978. In an interview with *TBP*'s editorial collective in 1978, Pezanna stated that one of the reasons why *Fuori!* could produce homoerotic content without being censored was because the newspaper had a small circulation and did not "represent a danger for the establishment."[37] In addition, the small circulation of *Fuori!*, its relatively subdued content compared to *Lambda*, and its use of visual content that promoted macho men who did not transgress gender norms meant that the content of the paper presented little threat to public stability. As a result, *Fuori!* escaped more extreme forms of censorship largely because it operated within a state-sanctioned government party and under a moral code of endorsing gay bars and dance halls under the control of police or heterosexual owners. In the Canadian context, displacing connotations of homosexuality in visual content under the guise of bodybuilding or heterosexual plots was all the more important in a climate of censorship and suppression of homosexual content by the Canadian federal government.

Censorship and Obscenity

The Canadian federal government's efforts to censor gay and lesbian erotica stemmed from Cold War anxieties around sexual morality undermining middle-class notions of respectability. Efforts to restrict homosexual content were strengthened in 1959 when the Canadian Parliament passed legislation amending section 150(8) of the Criminal Code of Canada. As legal scholar Brenda Cossman argues, this amendment reflected efforts on the part of the state to "toughen up on Canada's obscenity laws" and reinforce the nuclear family and morality in society.[38] According to Cossman, Section 150(8) defined obscenity as: "'For the purposes of the Act, any publication a [*sic*] *dominant characteristic* of which is the *undue exploitation of sex*, or of sex and any one or more of the following subjects, namely, crime, horror, cruelty and violence shall be deemed to be obscene' (emphasis added)."[39] The Canadian federal government also aimed to censor pornography more specifically, stretching its meaning to fit a wide range of material. This allowed police to harass and incriminate men considered homosexual or "deviant" through measures deemed severe if carried out on heterosexuals.[40]

Censorship also contributed to the slower growth of lesbian and gay newspapers and magazines compared to the United States. The Royal Canadian Mounted Police (RCMP) frequently confiscated or interrupted the transportation, distribution, and sale of publications that advertised or endorsed homosexuality, were pornographic, or both. For instance, *Gay* magazine in Canada (1964–5) – renamed *Gay International* in 1965 – was published by the Gay Publishing Company in Toronto and was, according to librarian Donald W. McLeod, "one of the earliest periodicals to use the word 'gay' in its title." Not only did it include general articles on homosexuality, humour cartoons, fiction, and news from American gay and lesbian periodicals, but the magazine drew upon Roman-Greco aesthetics of male musculature, youth, and beauty. According to McLeod, however, *Gay* was discontinued after issue 15 (July 1965) because of an increasingly hostile environment to homosexual content and media in Canada in the 1960s.[41]

Furthermore, the distribution of obscene material was interpreted widely and even led to the arrest of individuals for possession of such content or showing it to the public. On 17 November 1973, Toronto police seized pornography from the home of Reg Hartt, the director of the Rochdale Cinema Archives. *TBP* reported that the police had charged Hartt with "possession of obscene material for distribution" for owning two gay sex films, *Boys in the Sand* and *Bijou*, after showing them to the public as part of the Rochdale cinema series that autumn.[42] *The Globe and Mail* only reported on the case once, on 16 November 1973, highlighting Hartt's defence that the Rochdale cinema was a film club rather than a public theatre – a challenge to the charge of distribution.[43] Meanwhile, the *Toronto Star* ignored it altogether, stressing the importance of *TBP*'s coverage of these acts of suppression and violence and serving as additional evidence that morality cases against homosexuals were not necessarily considered "newsworthy."

In 1978, concerns around the social effects of straight and gay pornography were raised by Member of Parliament Mark MacGuigan, who proposed expanding the definition of pornography. Presenting the Third Report of the Standing Committee of Justice and Legal Affairs in the House of Commons on Wednesday, 22 March 1978, MacGuigan called for the passing of Bill C-207 – a bill centred on redefining obscenity for greater "enforcement of the obscenity provisions of the Criminal Code."[44] The Committee proposed extending obscene material to include content where "a dominant characteristic of the matter or thing is the undue exploitation of crime, horror, cruelty, violence or the undue degradation of the human person."[45] By broadening the definition of obscenity, MacGuigan and the Committee were attempting to redraw a boundary between "nudity" as an art form and pornographic content, which implied degradation, immorality, violence, and crime.

MacGuigan built his case on the detrimental effects of pornography for women and society by calling upon anti-pornography feminists who believed that pornography was inherently misogynistic and objectifying of women. Debra Lewis of the Vancouver Status of Women gave her testimony on 1 March 1978, and Lorenne M.G. Clark, an associate professor in the Department of Philosophy and Centre of Criminology at the University of Toronto and an executive member of the National Action Committee on the Status of Women, addressed the Committee the following day. In Clark's statements to the Standing Committee on Justice and Legal Affairs, she argued that "[t]he typical way in which women are depicted in pornography certainly reflects a view of them as inferior to men, as inherently masochistic, and as primarily of value as instruments for the satisfaction of male sexual desire."[46] Lewis and Clark's position as anti-pornography feminists was invaluable to MacGuigan, since this form of feminism garnered significant support and viewed pornography as part of a broader struggle against patriarchy and women's objectification as sex objects for male pleasure. Canadian anti-pornography activist and author Susan G. Cole states that since 1978, Canadian groups such as the Canadian Coalition Against Media Pornography (CCAMP) and Women Against Violence Against Women (WAVAW) have raised numerous complaints about the reach of obscenity laws. The "decency contingent," the groups she refers to as buttressing traditional notions of morality, "complained that the law's teeth were not sharp enough." In contrast, CCAMP "complained that the teeth of obscenity dug too sharply into sexuality."[47]

While MacGuigan and the Standing Committee of Justice and Legal Affairs sought to further restrict sexualized material in Canada, their vision of a pornography-free country did not necessarily reflect Canadians' attitudes on the subject, especially those living in larger cities. A survey conducted by the *Toronto Star* in 1977 of 220 *Metro News* readers (Toronto residents) asked readers their thoughts on the availability and legalization of pornography for individuals over the age of eighteen. The newspaper results suggested that Canadians had become quite comfortable with pornography. Of those who responded, 74 per cent felt that pornographic material should be available for private consumption for individuals over the age of eighteen.[48] The extent to which these beliefs included homosexual pornography is unclear, but it was unlikely at best. As further evidence of the growing consumption of pornography, Mr. P. Maclellan, manager of public relations for publisher H.H. Marshall Ltd., informed MacGuigan and the Standing Committee that pornographic magazines comprised approximately 14–15 per cent of magazine sales, or in monetary terms, approximately 10 million dollars in Canada.[49] The large volume of pornography sales is a testament to the extent to which a sexualized visual culture developed, was fetishized, and consumed in the post-war period.

With gay and lesbian erotica at risk of being further criminalized, *TBP* and its collective were encouraged to present erotic content as part of sexual liberation. Any restriction on erotic content would undermine both the collective's political agenda as well as their ability to sell issues using those same sexual images. Since the primary goal of *TBP*'s editorial collective was to build up a strong readership, the threat of sexual suppression or negative connotations around pornography by the Canadian government in any capacity was deeply concerning. A collective decision was made in January 1974 that *TBP* would not censure nudity or refrain from publishing semi-naked or fully naked human men.[50] Again, in a 10 June 1978 meeting, it was noted that the "Collective has no position" on the controversial question of pornography and even acknowledged that "[t]here is no monolithic lesbian or feminist view on adult-child relationships."[51] With their political messaging reflecting the cultural and social changes of the sexual revolution, *TBP* positioned itself as a counterweight to the moral regulation of the Canadian state. Such a position, however, was not without consequence.

TBP was raided by the morality police on 30 December 1977. Gerald Hannon, Ed Jackson, and Ken Popert were charged under Sections 159 (using the mail to distribute obscene material) and 164 (possession of obscene material for purposes of distribution) of the Criminal Code.[52]

In response, *TBP* established a Free the Press Fund, which sought to alleviate the estimated $10,000–30,000 in legal costs.[53] Aside from the ongoing legal battles waged against *TBP* – which has also been well documented in both Thomas Warner's *Never Going Back* (2006) as well as McCaskell's *Queer Progress* (2016) – the editorial committee was cautious in the arguments about the importance of erotic content. For instance, Gerald Hannon argued that stifling erotica was too extreme and would restrict individual sexual expression, regardless of whether it exploited women or children:

> There should be no laws regulating erotic material merely for being erotic. And there are two good reasons to oppose such legislation, even if one agrees that yes, it does exploit women, and yes, it does abuse children. One. Pornography legislation has always been used, and will continue to be used, to harass and stifle erotica that is experimental. Or serves minority tastes. Or is dangerous to accepted 'truths' about the way people relate.... Two. It won't work. It never has. We have obscenity laws now and it is still possible to purchase what you want – if you have the money.[54]

For Hannon, the belief that pornography was a threat to society stemmed from the idea that it threatened the sexual status quo. Not only were attempts at controlling pornography ineffective, but Hannon believed that they threatened to destabilize "accepted truths" around human sexuality. Hannon went on to further condemn Lewis's and Clark's contributions to the Justice Committee because "[i]f they [the committee] can say that they have Canadian feminist [*sic*] behind them, so much the better [for them]."[55] MacGuigan's efforts to regulate and restrict pornography with the aid of some feminists reinforced the argument that sexualized material resulted from, and promoted, the systematic oppression of women. As a result, his case would appear less conservative with the support of anti-pornography feminists, but it nevertheless illuminated pornography as a major point of contention between some feminists and gay liberationists.

Anti-pornography feminism was one of two feminist positions on pornography, the other being pro-sex (sex-positive) feminism.[56] Differing feminist opinions on pornography established the feminist sex wars (also known as the porn wars) of the late 1970s and early 1980s. The sex wars saw many feminists divided on issues of prostitution, pornography, and erotica. Anti-pornography feminists, such as Andrea Dworkin, Catharine MacKinnon, and Susan Cole, perceived pornography as "possessing the power to have a profound and negative effect on the lives of real women."[57] In comparison to anti-pornography feminism, sex-positive feminism challenged censorship attempts by arguing that female sexuality expressed in specific contexts and venues was demonstrative of female agency. Feminists such as Lisa Duggan, Nan D. Hunter, Carol S. Vance, Ellen Willis, and Chris Bearchell suggested that female enjoyment of pornography was an example of women reclaiming an aspect of their sexuality, a form of rebellion against the sexual status quo.[58]

The sex wars were an equally important intellectual division that shaped how writers and editors of *TBP* wrestled with similar issues of objectification, legitimizing desire, and validating public expression of gay sexuality. For instance, the editorial collective published an adapted 1977 lecture from prominent anti-pornography feminist Dworkin entitled "Pornography: The New Terrorism?" in August 1978.[59] Meanwhile, collective member Chris Bearchell expressed concern over regulations on pornography or gay and lesbian content. Bearchell, who joined the collective in 1978, noted in *TBP* that gay and lesbian pornography would be most affected by legal frameworks and public morality.[60] Also a member of Lesbians Against the Right (LAR) and the Lesbian Organization of Toronto (LOOT), she stated in an interview with political scientist Miriam Smith that although some feminists "might have objected to images in pornography or the availability or the display of certain pornography in certain situations, they would not have recommended the use of the obscenity laws and the police as a way to respond to them."[61] Indeed, the primary concerns around sexualized content in *TBP* centred on state censorship of gay and lesbian material.

As a feminist scholar and occasional contributor to *TBP*, Mariana Valverde responded to Hannon's aforementioned article in a letter published in *TBP* in May 1978, whereby she refuted Hannon's belief that depictions of sexuality should be unregulated. Valverde offered a critical counter-perspective to Trow and Hannon's argument. She stated that "By upholding the 'right' of the porno industry to cater to 'minority tastes', *TBP* is implicitly supporting the view – so dear to the hearts of capitalists everywhere – that sexuality is a commodity, to be freely bought and sold on the open market." In addition, Valverde further problematized Hannon's subsequent critique of Lewis and Clark, describing it as an "indiscriminate condemnation of feminism." While acknowledging that sexuality should be expressed freely and that the government should not attack "all forms of eroticism," Valverde's concerns that feminism was under attack, especially by members of the editorial collective, was exacerbated by strife occurring within feminism around pornography at the time.[62]

Hannon and Valverde's discussion serves as a reminder that visual culture was understood to have an influential role in shaping the sexual tastes and the consumption of images that adhered to gendered ideals within *TBP*. The newspaper operated as a forum in which feminist ideology was both espoused and challenged by readers and writers alike when it came to representations of sexuality in gay and lesbian culture. Juan Carlos Mezo González notes, "From the late 1970s and throughout the 1980s, *TBP* consistently reported on the course of the 'sex wars,' allowing readers to actively participate in the debate."[63] The fervour around pornography and sexualized visual culture within anti-pornography feminism escalated to the point that there was swift backlash against *TBP* for publishing an advertisement for Red Hot Video, a chain of pornographic video stores in Vancouver, British Columbia, in June 1983. Anti-pornography feminists accused Red Hot Video of selling and renting "videotapes, some of which vividly depict scenes of heterosexual rape, sex with children, sex with unwilling virgins, and gang rape."[64] *TBP* informed readers below the Table of Contents in that issue that it had debated publishing the ad for months and ultimately decided to do so because the anti-pornography movement was both "bad politics" and played "into the hands of right-wing, moralizing elements in our society."[65] Historian David Churchill notes that many feminists were angry with this explanation, suggesting it undermined the complex feminist debates around pornography and further polarized the two broad positions.[66] In a much more dramatic fashion, three Hot Video chain stores in the Vancouver area were firebombed by the Wimmin's Fire Brigade in the early morning of 23 November 1982.[67] Clearly, pornography threatened not only to divide feminism but also gay liberationists as well.

TBP reader Stephen W. Forster from Dade County (Miami) wrote in 1979 that he felt feminism in gay periodicals frequently disparaged masculinity. He argued, "As I read through various gay journals, I am constantly informed that masculinity is a 'disease.'"[68] The sex wars, and pornography more broadly, not only raised concerns around societal misogyny but seemingly suggested to some readers that their masculinity was partly to blame. The perception that feminism, particularly anti-pornography feminism, was overly critical of masculinity nurtured some concern over the role of feminism in *TBP* at this time. In my interview with *TBP* writer David Rayside, he recalled the relationship between the editorial collective and feminism as such:

> Some people would take that core understanding and be significantly influenced by feminism. That would include me. Others would be very wary of too close an association with feminism, particularly because issues

> of sexual representations were becoming more contested and the whole liberationist idea was more inclined toward the rejection of any normative constraints on behavior rather than critiquing any particular expression of gender or masculinity in particular.[69]

Even famed gay rights activist turned academic Dennis Altman felt that gay men should tackle sexism in society, but not limit themselves to supporting the women's movement. In a 1974 interview with the collective (and before the feminist sex wars), Altman was already arguing that it was "strange to argue that gay men should not organise around their own experience of oppression, but around women's experience of oppression. This seems to me impossible; it is to deny the very real problems that gay men face in society."[70] The majority of the nearly all-male editorial collective aligned themselves with anti-sexist rhetoric early on and spent a great deal of effort examining the content of heterosexual pornographic magazines such as *Playboy*. Doing so not only deepened intellectual and political ties between gay liberationists and feminism but simultaneously allowed the collective to receive support from lesbians and women's rights activists.

From the mid-1970s onward, *TBP*'s male editorial collective were more attentive to questions of power, including class and race, and were particularly sympathetic to the objectification of women's bodies in mainstream pornographic magazines such as *Playboy*.[71] However, they did not apply such a framework to male pornography. An explanation for this is likely that doing so would discredit gay male pornography as a cultural artefact of homosexuality. Furthermore, it would not account for the different sources and outcomes of patriarchy that inherently render women's bodies as objects for men's sexual gaze. In 1975, *TBP* member Ed Jackson condemned the sexist exploitation of women's bodies in *Playboy* by focusing on women's vain attempts at achieving an impossible standard of beauty but failed to account for male pornography. Jackson argued that:

> The **Playboy** [*sic*] image of the buxom blond in a baby-doll negligee would almost be a joke, if women did not continue to measure themselves against this 'ideal.' Few people can conform to the rigorous standard, so most are coerced into spending vast amounts on cosmetics and clothing to make themselves into an approximation of what they can rarely be, or should not even want to be.[72]

His analysis implies that women are somehow more obsessed with their vanity and more likely to be tricked or coerced into conforming to societal expectations of gender than men. Furthermore, there was no discussion of gay men measuring themselves to a similar ideal of masculinity within heterosexual pornography, physique magazines, or, as *TBP* demonstrated early on, advertisements for bathhouses and clubs. This is likely because it was not quite clear what a prison these expectations could be for gay men.

With its visual content, *TBP* conceptualized gay male masculinity within a gay liberationist framework, meaning the editorial collective attempted to include images of gay male masculinity that challenged dominant discourses around heteronormative tropes of sexuality. However, the collective was forced to reconcile gay politics and community life with tenuous understandings of what it meant to be masculine in the 1970s and 1980s. By interweaving sexualized content with liberationist politics, *TBP* was an important vehicle by which the white, macho, muscular, enabled male would expand from a cultural image of sexual virility, desire, health, and masculinity to become a representation of the gay male community and gay liberation.

Visualizing the White Muscular Male Body in *TBP*

The editorial collective recognized early on the importance of controlling images and representations of sexuality. One of their first grievances was with the Canadian Broadcasting Corporation's (CBC) television special *Nothing to Hide*. Aired on 30 November 1971, the made-for-television documentary focused on providing mainstream audiences with insight into gay liberation. The collective published their undated letter sent to the CBC while simultaneously informing readers of the problems they found with the television special.[73] Members of the collective took issue with its dated nature, its overlooking of Canadian and US organizations such as The Mattachine Society, its focus on New York City's gay bars, steam baths, and the streets, and argued that the program excluded lesbians and "reinforce[d] strict conformity to sexual roles, denigrating so-called feminine qualities in men and applauding so-called feminine qualities in women." It was the emphasis on gender and sexual conformity that portrayed "the homosexual like an animal in a cage," the collective argued.[74]

By only emphasizing the sexualized qualities of gay culture, *Nothing to Hide* reduced gay culture to a life of "pornography, anonymous sexuality, 'sexual addiction and sadomasochism,'" according to the collective. They were particularly concerned over the visual portrayal of gay male life because "viewers retain far more of the visual impression than of the verbal content."[75] These criticisms around the visual portrayal of gay life compared to written accounts reverberate with critic and scholar Marshall McLuhan's argument in *The Medium Is the Message* (1978) that messages in the media change based on the delivered format. Looking at television specifically, McLuhan argues that "[t]elevision demands participation and involvement in depth of the whole being. It will not work as a background. It engages you."[76] The concerns of those reporting on *Nothing to Hide* emphasized the power of visual imagery in crafting an unfavourable image of gay community life among viewers. Thus, from its earliest issues, *TBP* featured cartoons and photographs depicting homosexual romance among men or nude male bodies.

On the back cover of its second issue, *TBP* featured a portrait of a nude young white male looking away from the camera. The image was taken by *TBP* founding member Jearld Moldenhauer. The young man, named "Rolf," lacked the muscle of the men often seen in homoerotic physique magazines or pornography of the period. However, his presence on the pages of *TBP* was important because it was an early step in visualizing gay male sensibilities.[77] In the words of historian David Churchill, "the control of images, representations, and identity [was] a core project of lesbian and gay liberation."[78] The decision to publish the portrait was rather contentious, according to Juan Carlos Mezo González, with the only two founding members, Jude and Aileen, rejecting the photograph's publication because it represented an objectification of the body and the pederastic desires of Moldenhauer.[79] Their rejection of the image on the grounds that nudity did not belong in *TBP* was also adopted by some male members, and the image foreshadowed other debates among feminists and gay liberationists about the purpose and cultural implications that male nudity might have in a radical activist newspaper.

Images of nudity did serve an important purpose, however. They allowed collective members and readers to legitimize their desires in an alternative manner to the models being presented in mainstream publications such as *Playboy* and *Playgirl*. In the fourth issue of *TBP*, the collective had published an artistic drawing depicting nude women and men alongside poetry and, in issue #5, nude men and women of all body sizes and shapes were featured in Gerald Hannon's article "Celebrate the Body! (Towards an Alternative Aesthetic)."[80] While no direct correlation between these images and the presentation of masculinity in gay male culture can be formed from these two examples alone, they did speak to the efforts of collective members in visualizing the gay male body.

Hannon's photospread, "Celebrate the Body!," exemplifies how *TBP* operated as a contested space for masculinity. Hannon not only sought to publish a range of photographs featuring nude men and women but also saved space for a textual critique of an increasingly commercialized gay male aesthetic:

> In the gay media it [aesthetics] has two main expressions: the Monstrous Phallus; where the body is reduced to 7 inches of detumescence, and the Artsy/Don't Leave a Blemish on My Body/Look Intense/Vaguely Like Rudolph Nureyev approach of glossies like After Dark. Both concentrate almost exclusively on men between the ages of seventeen and thirty – they have neglected women, they have neglected the young, they have neglected the old.[81]

Hannon saw an increasingly commercialized aesthetic of masculinity ignore those who were out of shape or old. The ubiquity of white gay men and the entrenched whiteness of gay male pornography was not addressed until the mid-1970s when readers began addressing white privilege in classified ads and editorials. Additionally, Hannon's comment of the "monstrous phallus" as a main expression of gay men suggested that gay media reduced gay men's identity to the size of their manhood – a continuation of mainstream anxieties around phallic girth and masculinity.

Hannon included images of older gay men and women, as well as young people with slim bodies that did not have much musculature, as a political statement against the macho clone's young and buff body. In the caption that followed these images, the collective stated: "In these photographs we present the body unashamedly as [an] object – a joyous, potent object."[82] While the editors presented alternative images of gay men and lesbians in early photospreads such as "Celebrate the Body!," gay male style was increasingly adopting a narrow aesthetic in subsequent issues, especially within advertisements. Advertisements drew upon white, muscular, enabled illustrations and images to promote their services, products, or venues. These images, along with their capitalistic purpose, seemed contradictory to the political and social message of *TBP*.

Since the formation of *TBP*, advertising had been extremely popular, especially since it provided much-needed revenue to the fledgling newspaper in its early years. In a "gaylup" poll conducted in 1972, Doug (last name unlisted) informed readers that "[m]ost readers (a surprising 88.5%) were quite in favour of advertisements" and that *TBP* had begun experimenting with "non-sexist" ads with that issue.[83] The definition of what constituted a sexist advertisement is unclear, but by the following issue, any attempt at diverting sexism in advertising had failed. Many ads appearing in issue #5 onward (1972–) validated the notion that looking and acting macho or butch was ideal for gay men. In attempting to naturalize macho masculinity as a performative style for gay men, advertisements alternatively demonstrate how highly manufactured macho style was and continues to be. Additionally, advertisements for lesbians were almost entirely non-existent, further reiterating *TBP*'s emphasis on building, critiquing, and reporting on gay male culture.

Advertisers cultivated (and capitalized on) a budding gay male culture that, for the first time, had become increasingly visible and commercialized in public spaces. Toronto's gay bathhouses or "steam houses" – the terms were used interchangeably – frequently advertised their venues as places synonymous with traditional styles of masculinity. Bathhouses were spaces in which gay men could socialize, carouse, be intimate, and relax with relative anonymity, away from the ever-watchful eyes of their friends, family, and community. They also advertised in *TBP* using cartoons or photographs of men who were white and muscular or lean as a "uniform" for gay masculinity.[84] Advertisements for The Roman (Sauna) Bath in Toronto featured an illustrative figure of a muscular man clad in neo-classical armour (1973). Toronto's The Library marketed itself using an illustration of a headless muscular figure (1973). Other bathhouses, such as The Club, would use stock photographs of white muscular men – helping to foster an appreciation for the clone aesthetic seen in chapter two.

The Club, for example, featured a shirtless, muscular, white male directly (and seductively) gazing at the viewer (Figure 1.5).[85] The young man in The Club's advertisement may not directly embody tropes of the muscular beefcake or bodybuilder, but his masculinity and sexuality were commoditized to sell memberships for a gay male bathhouse. His boyish youth, clean-cut appearance, and slender white body all serve as markings of what a "desirable" male body looks like. His seductive gaze mired by a youthful innocence posits him as a desirable sexual conquest: young, handsome, slender/almost muscular, and conventionally masculine. In many ways, this ad marks the beginning of a gradual proliferation of a particular style of masculinity by commercial interests hoping to attract customers. It also signified a growing relationship between the commercialization of gay male culture and the development of a desirable aesthetic of masculinity. Indeed, advertisements were – and remain – an important facet in the construction of gender and sexuality because they, according to historian Sharon Cook, exemplify "the modern intellectual and emotional landscape" of society.[86] In the context of *TBP*, advertisements reflected

Figure 1.5 Advertisement for Toronto's The Club bathhouse in *The Body Politic* 10, 1973, 22. The ArQuives, *The Body Politic* fonds.

particular ideologies around masculinity and encouraged readers to construct a visual identity with traditional signifiers of masculinity as a reference point.

In another ad, the gay bar Dudes and the Richmond Street Emporium equated hypersexuality, masculinity, and desirability in their advertisements as a means of drawing in customers with illusory sexual bait. Located on 10 Breadalbane Street in Toronto, Dudes announced their opening in a September 1977 ad by displaying two muscular white torsos. Dudes described its venue using a series of words alongside the two white figures: "faces, sounds, toys, dudes, friends, denim, mirrors, jocks, games, t-shirts, cruising, moustaches, fantasy, macho, and hunks."[87] These highly gendered key words constructed an image of masculinity that had physical characteristics and relied on clothing: denim and T-shirts. In one ad for the Richmond Street Health Emporium, a steam bath and gym on 260 Richmond Street East, six white athletic men are featured standing around with only towels covering their naked bodies with the caption "the busiest" displayed at the top.[88] In another of their ads, a very muscular white man with his right arm flexing and the tagline "Get into it" in March–April 1980.[89]

While bathhouse ads frequently drew upon the white, muscular body as a means of selling memberships or enticing patrons to visit, they were not the only ones. For instance, the all-male theatrical production of *Tubstrip* at the Global Village Theatre in Toronto was advertised in 1973 featuring an illustrative nude muscular male whose phallic girth was prominent. Promoting itself as "better than '*Boys in the Band*,'' *Tubstrip* was (and remains) a risqué comedy set at a gay bathhouse. Alongside that image, however, *Tubstrip* was selling more than its ability to make audiences laugh. It was marketing a "desirable" gay male body as part of its show. More broadly, however, these advertisements demonstrate that *TBP*'s editorial collective was forced to reconcile with increasingly traditional notions of gay male masculinity that came along with sorely needed advertising revenue.

Alongside this commercialized shift were cultural reviews of films and plays that seemingly addressed the importance of butch masculine style in gay and lesbian media. In 1973, editorial collective member Robert Trow reviewed Wakefield Poole's pornographic films *Boys in the Sand* and *Bijou*. Accompanying the review are two photographic stills. The first is that of a nude, muscular, white male sitting on a beach from *Boys in the Sand*. This figure is muscular and tan but angled in a way that his genitalia are hidden from view. However, Trow assures readers interested in the film that the "actors are slim, athletic, and (of course) well-hung with conventionally attractive though unmemorable faces."[90] His decision to describe the size of the actors' genitalia as well as their athletic builds (which is evident to readers with the photograph) suggests that the men found in *Boys in the Sand* – which upheld a white muscular masculinity – were not only desirable but the primary source of pleasure. The irony here is that Trow describes their faces as "conventionally attractive" – perhaps also meaning conventionally masculine looking – but "unmemorable," and yet laments that "pornography often limits itself by depersonalizing sexuality, rather than linking it with the whole personality." This perplexing argument suggests that muscular men and phallic girth in pornography are worth remembering as sources of sexual pleasure but the actors themselves are not.

The second image in Trow's review of *Bijou* was a photograph of two naked men next to each other. The first man on the left is rugged, muscular, and white. He has a dark beard and hairy chest and is seen looking down at the floor. Meanwhile, another bearded man is kneeling next to him, seemingly examining his buttocks. The premise of *Bijou*, according to Trow, is about "a young butch construction worker" who finds himself in a "darkened pleasure chamber where a flashing neon sign instructs him to undress" and where he subsequently has sex with another man.[91] Once finished, he leaves, and more men join to inevitably form an orgy. The construction worker's masculinity is made noteworthy, with Trow emphasizing his "butch" appearance and demeanour. The man's "butch" style serves as a positive point in an otherwise negative review of "the most uninspired orgy imaginable."[92] The emphasis placed on the butch style of masculinity found in these pornographic films simultaneously reinforces pornography as a legitimate medium of sexual pleasure and a particular body type and presentation of masculinity as the subject of that pleasure.

For *TBP* contributor and psychologist Greg Lehne, the aesthetics of gender were an important factor in shaping gay men's sexual desires. In 1973, Lehne sent out a questionnaire in *TBP* asking readers to describe the individuals, groups, erotic situations, feelings, specific sex acts, or types of relationships that they fantasized about.[93] He sought to understand how fantasies and the "types" of individuals in fantasies "may contribute to the development of sexual barriers."[94] Lehne asked readers to describe the sex, age, appearance, personality, and type(s) of person(s) in the fantasies, the frequency of the fantasies, the class background and job of the person(s), if there is a difference between their sexual type and the person they want to have a long-term relationship with, and whether or not their fantasy was similar or different from themselves. While Lehne was clear that he was interested in male and female sexual desires, his request for details such as "beard or moustache" while foregoing any female-oriented questions suggests that gay men's fantasies were foregrounded. Furthermore, his desire to know readers' "style of dress" indicates that clothing was a hypothetical determinant in shaping sexual barriers within the gay and lesbian community.

Lehne published the results from his questionnaire a year later, in August 1974. The results formed a collage of cartoon images of muscular men and the quoted responses of the fifty gay men who had responded.[95] The average age of the men was twenty-four, and their responses indicated that the aesthetic presentation of masculinity and the male body were fundamental aspects of gay male desire. Additionally, with no mention of any female respondents, it was clear that Lehne saw gay men's fantasies as *the* troubled site of sexuality worthy of exploration. Men's responses included: "Going out with very muscular men, but with a great deal of touching and caressing," "A beautiful boy who melts in my arms," and lastly, "I see myself being carried through the threshold of a door by a veritable Greek God of the utmost physical handsomeness and strength."[96] This is not to suggest that appearance was the sole desire for these men. Notably, "60% of gay men reported fantasies about a warm, loving relationship." However, the presentation of masculinity within these ideal male fantasies was almost entirely homogenous, except by one responder who stated,

"The guys I fantasize about aren't effeminate [and] neither are they super-masculine. They are quiet, self-assured in a down-played way, dressed in such a way [and] acting such that it is clear that they are not unhappy with their homosexuality or life in general."[97] Based on Lehne's findings, a macho style of masculinity was not just the aesthetic centrepiece of gay male desire, but it also shaped the process of coming out, love and lust, gay relationships, and even ageism in the gay male community.[98]

Finally, Lehne provided readers with a more thorough analysis of his findings in September 1974, including numerous statistics of the driving factors and outcomes of gay male sexual desire. Entitled "Gay Male Fantasies," the article immediately reported that 58 per cent of men reported "masculine" or "conventional" looking men as their desired counterpart, while it was "rare" that feminine men were part of any described fantasy.[99] These desires were further compounded by claims of promiscuity and the lack of social and emotional support for gay men. Lehne's findings not only corresponded with a realignment of sexual values towards monogamy among gay liberationists but also demonstrated a dominant aesthetic taking form: macho style.

Conclusion

The different sections of *TBP* reflected the importance of visual culture for selling issues, shaping early gay male sensibilities, and liberating sexuality from heteronormative mores. *TBP* included imagery that drew on a legacy of white macho masculinity in film and imagery across the twentieth century, culminating in Waugh's exploration of pornography as part of gay history. This historicization of gay male pornography, particularly as it unfolded in *TBP*, reflects the seriousness with which the editorial collective and readers alike approached images of sexuality and any attempts to regulate or curb sexual desires. As gay male culture flourished in the 1970s, magazines and newspapers such as *TBP* pursued the burgeoning market of sexualized visual culture by featuring rugged men donning little to no clothing. *TBP* reflected an international effort among gay periodicals to wrestle with the representation of desire. Ed Jackson's quote introducing the chapter represented a tension in *TBP* between navigating the politics of the male body and selling the body to attract readers. Indeed, Dennis Altman noted in a 1974 interview with *TBP* that "the sexual mores of the gay world are becoming the sexual mores of the straight world. Getting off with someone and not knowing their name until afterwards is [*sic*] increasingly as true of the straight world as of the gay world."[100] Visualizing gay male masculinity in *TBP* meant visualizing a reconciliation between gay liberationist politics and a surge of commercial and capitalist enterprises marketing themselves in the liberationist newspaper.

Throughout the 1970s, portrayals of gay male masculinity became increasingly homogenized into an aesthetic that resembled the muscular men and masculine performances of gender found in pornography. Gay and lesbian periodicals inscribed particular connotations of gender and sexuality onto the male body, which puts the male body at the forefront of readers' minds. Gay men's yearning for a muscular body was no less a response to other phenomena, such as bodybuilding culture, than it was to the spectacle of nude white muscular men scattered through gay-targeted periodicals. In a period that witnessed new displays of masculinity emerge, gay men continued to reinvent their masculinity in the 1970s to disrupt stereotypes of gay male effeminacy and weakness. However, such practices contributed to the growth of one of the most iconic gay male styles: macho masculinity.

The next chapter explores macho style in greater depth. The "macho clone," as he was frequently referred to in *TBP*, did not just represent an important aesthetic ritual for many gay men; he also symbolized both an embrace and rejection of the gendered status quo. Informed by Roman-Greco aesthetics, bodybuilding, and normalized performances of masculinity, macho style adorned the pages of the *TBP* and other lesbian and gay periodicals. Since macho style reflected patriarchal values of the male body, its continual presence in *TBP* and other gay periodicals in the 1970s relayed social values around masculinity that were already being prescribed by the government and mainstream culture. However, *TBP* editors like Joseph Interrante maintained a critical engagement with gay male masculinity into the 1980s, with Interrante claiming in 1980 that "You can still be macho and wash the dishes."[101]

Chapter Two

Pin the Macho on the Man

Our culture, as I see it, is anything but original. We have opted for heterosexual looks and actions. To be the slightest bit nelly is to be a gay leper. We have become prisoners of a stereotype: macho, which looks absolutely ridiculous on most.

– Noel Bari, "Prisoners of a Stereotype," *The Body Politic* 67, October 1980, 4

In the fall of 1980, Noel Bari ran into an old friend in Toronto. He was taken aback by this encounter. Not because it was a pleasant surprise, but because something had changed; his friend had changed. "The soft look that brought him so much attention had been replaced by what I call the clone look: moustache, plaid shirt, logger's boots, and ripped blue jeans," Bari recalled.[1] The "clone look" that Bari was describing was macho style. Bari was not just upset by his friend's change in dress, he went so far as to describe it as "drag." It was drag because it was based on a cliché image or stereotype of working-class butch masculinity. Bari's friend was gone, and in his place stood what he described as the "prisoner of a stereotype": the macho clone.

For Bari, this encounter was the tinder needed to spark his letter in *TBP*. Bari wrote to the paper to vent his frustrations about what he saw as a harmful way of acting and being in the gay male community. What some saw as a harmless style of clothing or mannerisms, Bari saw as an indication that gay male culture was becoming increasingly misogynistic and conducive to internalized homophobia. "Gay men are going to have to get it through their frightened little heads that every man, gay or straight, possesses feminine traits. You'll never get rid of them, and no matter how 'butch' some of these faggots look, they still haven't gotten rid of the femininity in them," he argued.[2] If macho style represented homophobia, then its increasingly visible presence in the gay male community was particularly worth lamenting.

Macho style emerged in the 1970s and lasted well into the 1980s. The term "macho" described a certain type of gay man who was seen as embodying traditionally masculine traits and behaviours. This can include physical appearance, mannerisms, and attitudes. By the time of Bari's article, macho style was the predominant aesthetic of gay male culture. Bari even noted that the "clone look" described "three quarters of the gay population."[3] The term "clone" was used by many in the community to describe the near-ubiquitous presence of this aesthetic in the gay community by the late 1970s and early 1980s. Whether three-quarters of gay men donned working-class attire, groomed their moustaches, or acted more butch is nearly impossible to discern. However, the prominence of macho style in gay male content, its early underpinnings, and its evolution are evident on the pages of *TBP*. Macho style proves particularly important in the study of gay male masculinity and the social and cultural politics of the period because, in the words of historian Alice Echols, "embedded in this macho turn were changes in gay men's identity and subjectivity."[4]

This chapter focuses on macho style as both an aesthetic style for gay men and a signifier for broader anxieties around gender and queer patriarchy. *TBP* reflected the efforts of many gay men to perform or convey a legible style of masculinity as a way of navigating the sexual and social dimensions of an increasingly visible gay male community. Macho style's rise and prominence as a cultural phenomenon reflected an important relationship between the aesthetics of gay male masculinity, questions about gender during gay liberation, and the commercialized politics of desire. Since macho style and the culture that came with it spurned the notion that gay men were womanly, deviant, or immoral, the aesthetic reveals a model of power in gay male culture that largely mirrors disdain for male effeminacy in heterosexual culture.[5] The understanding that macho style might embody gay male misogyny was particularly alarming to members of *TBP* because of their agenda to unite the community, both gay men and lesbians, self-identified feminists and otherwise.

Macho Style

Macho style was never a static aesthetic. It evolved throughout the 1970s and 1980s, but at its core included clothing associated with working-class labour: flannel shirts, jeans, fatigues, and boots in the early 1970s. For instance, Marlon Brando's character Terry Malloy, a dockworker in the 1954 film *On the Waterfront*, was an iconic reference point for macho style's early aesthetic. Brando donned tight denim and a white T-shirt to exemplify his muscles and slicked back his hair for the "bad-boy" look. The Levi's-and-denim culture of macho was not only an "exaggeration of gender codes by the 'right' sex," but represented a "hyperbolic masculinization of gay male bodies," according to Pamela Robertson.[6] Indeed, the "fit" of these clothes creates what Roland Barthes would describe as "an ethic of eroticism" that marks the body as a sexualized object.[7]

Theorists Adam Geczy and Vicki Karaminas explain that macho style emerged as "[s]igns of gay identity became more forthright, from earrings in the right ear (or two earrings; why hold back?) to back-pocket coloured scarves and bandannas."[8] Pocket hankies, in particular, provided gay men with a hidden code to communicate sexual availability and sexual interests. According to *TBP* writer John Forbes, macho men appropriated hanky codes from the effeminate legacy handkerchiefs once had in the 1960s, only to equate it with the "hip pockets of the New Butch" and the "Fifties theme of 'His & Hers' towels sets."[9] Meanwhile, Echols argues that, "Gay men's macho style first took off in the discos of New York and San Francisco, where it was most strenuously cultivated, but it spread even to European cities."[10] While discotheques were spaces in which gay men could display their machismo in flamboyant ways, *TBP* contains evidence of macho culture in early bathhouse advertisements and classified ads by gay men who did not necessarily partake in disco culture, demonstrating that macho style was the result of many cultural factors.

TBP writer Tony Metie argued that "macho" style represented gay men's idea of "straight" masculinity.[11] Even Bari critiqued macho style as a campy appropriation of the "heterosexual" aesthetic: "My God, you introduce yourself to someone and their voice goes down five octaves, the hands on the hips, the swagger when they walk. For Jesus' sake, you would think you were up north in an old miners' bar, an old heterosexual miners' bar, instead of a gay big-city disco."[12] There were clear correlations drawn between macho style and looking butch. However, the campiness of the entire performance of macho style was what led Bari to describe it as "drag." Indeed, macho style was campy and artificial in that it appropriated and played up traditional signifiers of "straight" masculinity that would have never been taken seriously in heterosexual communities.[13] It was simultaneously butch, camp, subversive, incomplete, ill-thought-out, and humorous in nature. Yet, it retained allure and power in the gay male community, enough so that it evoked myriad discussions around masculinity and desire.

Macho style always fell between "passing" as masculine or butch and a "campy" performance of masculinity. In his 1998 sociological study of the macho clone in New York's gay male community, Martin Levine argues, "[f]olkloric assumptions about macho masculinity lay at the heart of the manly presentational strategies. The term 'macho' implied overconformity to the traditional male gender role."[14] The overconformity of traditional male gender resonates with the underlying idea of queer patriarchy. By embodying traditional ideas of what masculinity looked and sounded like, men who embraced macho style were reinforcing traditional – and patriarchal – gender roles in a highly conspicuous fashion. Macho style thus simultaneously resonates with Gayatri Spivak's reading of the artistry of the faked female orgasm as "scrupulously fake."[15] It was fake because it embraced a campy *idea* of butch masculinity and, therefore, existed in a queer middle ground.[16] In a society that sociologist R.W. Connell argues "positions homosexual masculinities at the bottom of a gender hierarchy among men," macho style was not just a spectacle; it was an artistic performance to displace homophobic stereotypes of gay men as overly effeminate or weak.[17] Connell also notes that "[t]he number of men rigorously practising the hegemonic pattern in its entirety may be quite small. Yet the majority of men gain from its hegemony, since they benefit from the patriarchal dividend."[18] This "patriarchal dividend" was targeted early on by both the editorial collective and *TBP*'s readers, and macho style represented queer patriarchy.

The duality between passing and camp was satirized by Forbes in that, "To become a clone, you must have a mustache ('But, wear a mustache'); failing this, a T-shirt of Vic Tanny proportions. Clone chat is always minimal and revolves around these controversial excitements: 'hunks,' 'poppers,' 'barbells and workouts,' 'logging,' 'spinach salads' and 'interior decorating.' The persona of this pose is uneasily butch."[19] His definition provides insight into some of the cliché tropes around macho style at this time, notably the clone's interest in bodybuilding, and being sexually promiscuous by reference of "poppers" – a chemical that when inhaled provides a relaxing "high" that loosens muscles such as those in the anus. For Forbes, macho style and the clones who wore them as a "uniform" – the term was used often to refer to macho style – represented a vapid characterization of gay male life. Part of that uniform included muscles.

Macho style and "clones" proliferated with the greater extent of bodybuilding in gay male culture. In his 1979 article on gyms, cruising, and exercise, Michael Lynch acquiesced that, "The attractive body is no longer the exception it used to be." In an interview with the manager of the Imperial Health Club, the manager informed Lynch that gay men frequented the gym on Mondays, Wednesdays, and Fridays, but they embraced straight culture; in the manager's words, "there's not a toke of gay flavour in the place."[20] One regular patron of the Imperial was even reported praising the gym as "wonderful because it's so straight."[21] Bodybuilding was, therefore, understood by some as an activity that not only suppressed homosexuality but made gyms spaces where gay men were encouraged to perform queer patriarchal masculinity. Levine argues that within macho culture, the body itself was also manufactured to conform to the physique of a gym body: "tight buttocks, washboard stomachs, and 'pumped-up' biceps and pectorals."[22]

Along with muscles, macho style incorporated elements of BDSM (bondage, domination, and sadomasochism), notably leather and some bondage to varying degrees. Leather and denim have long been symbols of toughness and strength, and they are often associated with biker and outlaw cultures, as well as with working-class labour. The adoption of leather as part of macho style was famously documented by photographer Robert Mapplethorpe. His photographs of men in leather and denim both reflected gay stylistic practices of butch masculinity while simultaneously endorsing macho style as *the* sexy aesthetic.[23] Paul Martineau and Britt Salvesen argue that "[t]he wearing of leather is a symbol of ruggedness among the 'gay set' as well as the motorcycle gangs. This combination of style, fetishism, and 'rugged' masculinity not only informed Mapplethorpe's self-presentation but would become a chief concern of his creative work in the years to come [1970s onward]."[24] However, the use of leather in macho style should be understood as a fetishization of butch masculinity and queer patriarchy, not to be conflated with the fetishization of domination and submissiveness per se.

Additionally, macho style was almost exclusively presented as white. News articles, photographs, and advertisements in *TBP* perpetuated the myth that macho style was exclusive to white gay men. Historian David Churchill argues that "the whiteness of the 1970s gay 'clone' had a presumed status, not invisible but rather present, unacknowledged, a given. One would not, for example, describe someone as a 'white clone' because a clone was already assumed to be white."[25] Ruth Frankenberg argues that the privileged position of whiteness is the result of its "unmarkedness," meaning that it is not seen as being marked or fettered by racial politics.[26] Indeed, Rinaldo Walcott argues that the "unmarkedness" of hegemonic masculinity is deeply intertwined with the "unremarkable nature of whiteness."[27] While gay men of colour could, and did, see themselves as macho, their identity as macho clones was constantly in flux and questionable in the wider community. For example, in March 1981, John Yorke wrote into *TBP* sarcastically, stating that he was "unable to … bear the 'shame' of probably being the only Afro-Eurasian 'clone' on Howard Street."[28] His concerns suggest that some gay men of colour were not necessarily welcome to partake in macho culture or see themselves as "clones."

Representations of Macho Style in *TBP*

Macho style was more than an aesthetic style for gay men in the 1970s and 1980s. It represented the intersection of commercial interests, marketing a particular "type" or performance of masculinity and the cultural formation of gay male sensibilities. Moreover, the presence of macho style in *TBP*, an activist periodical, is evidence that gay liberationist efforts to dismantle gendered hierarchies and cis-heteronormative gender performances could be contradictory at times. Deeply enmeshed in the liberationist agenda of *TBP* were commercial and cultural politics that presented a queer patriarchal image of masculinity. These images of masculinity worked with (rather than against) messages of gay liberation to ultimately popularize an aesthetic of gay male masculinity that continues to pervade queer communities in North America.

On 9 December 1973, the Carriage House Hotel held a parade of macho men. That day, *TBP* editor Gerald Hannon reported on one of Toronto's first gay male pageant shows, the Mr. Club of Canada contest, in the newspaper. Fittingly, two of the judges for the contest were Jerry Batal, the American business manager of the Club Bath chain known for promoting white macho men in advertisements, and Derek Stenhouse, the gay owner of Manatee, Toronto's most popular "cooperative" dance club and one considered by *TBP* member Hugh Brewster to be "the most resolutely sexist of all the clubs, especially in its policy towards women – or lack of it." [29] In his article, Hannon noted that some in the audience thought that this parade of macho men was an example of the "sexist-objectifying-capitalist-exploitation" of the gay liberation movement.[30] This disparagement of capitalism, sexism, and objectification as mutually influencing forces of oppression reverberated with larger anti-capitalist sentiments among the collective. These comments are also a reminder that coverage of the contest – which was surely popular – had to be approached critically by Hannon because such media attention might serve to reinforce the macho body as *the* desirable body.

In the first round of the competition, contestants wore T-shirts and jeans for the look of tousled youth. This look was built on early ideas of working-class masculinity. Hannon did not spend much time covering this round but noted that many observers in the audience felt that their outfits were an important component in the pageant. This included one individual who called the parade of macho style "a gratuitous gift."[31] The adoption of a simple T-shirt and jeans look was an important aesthetic that marked a man as worthy of the Mr. Club title. During the second round, contestants were required to don their own choice of clothing, which ranged from "the panache of a professional model to a rather endearing ineptitude," according to Hannon.[32] Models were then asked a series of questions, including "What do you think of the new styles for men?" While the responses of the men were not directly quoted, the question does suggest that aesthetics and style were fundamental components for how gay men navigated their social environment.

Finally, the third round was a swimsuit competition where phallic girth was prized and the outline of genitals encouraged. Hannon paid the most attention to this segment of the competition. He thought the judging of phallic girth bordered on comical. Indeed, complementing the article on the page itself was a cartoon image of an old judge inspecting the exaggerated penis of a young, buff white man. This image (and the third segment more generally) resonates with Susan Bordo's argument that the penis is endowed with a "tumescent consciousness that is bold, unafraid, at the ready" – all characteristics of manliness.[33] Indeed, the assertive and bold nature of the penis was described as the "monstrous phallus" – a term used by Hannon to describe one of the predominant aesthetics of masculinity in gay media. His coverage of the contest highlighted the performative nature of masculinity by describing the contest as a "purely aesthetic act."[34] For the losers of the Mr. Club contest, C.J. Harrington, Master of Ceremonies, consoled them with the advice, "It's more important to be nice." As Hannon points out, however, by having Rod Polich, a white, physically fit, 5'7, 155-pound, 20-year-old man win this contest based on his looks alone, personality is relegated to a trait for friends, not for sexual partners.[35]

While some welcomed the objectification of these men as a celebration of the gay male body, it is evident that others, including Hannon, felt that it revealed deeper issues around masculinity and desire. As one patron was quoted as saying:

> To quote our M.C., this contest was a chance to represent the gay community as it is. Perhaps that was its failure: to have aspired to nothing, and to have succeeded. But let us go to washrooms [*sic*]. I feel the need of a faceless encounter. It is [the contest] such a purely aesthetic act.[36]

Rather than representing the gay community in all of its diversity, the Mr. Club contest was an award ceremony for white, muscular, enabled men who embodied the cultural ideals of physical and sexual desire. Some among the audience accused the contest of being a shameless advertisement for the specific type of man that frequents Batal's Club Bath chain of bathhouses. Representation was important for many gay men in the community, and the Mr. Club contest seemingly represented a narrow subset of men: white, butch, muscular, enabled, and willing to dress themselves in macho attire.

In a more subtle nod to macho style, *TBP* reported on gay engineer Trevor Mountford-Smith coming out in the national trade publication *Engineering* in 1975. Mountford-Smith was an engineer for Ontario Hydro when he disclosed his sexuality to *Engineering* after reading Connie Baillie's article "Why P. Engs Are Such Sterling Chaps." Baillie had stated in her piece that she had "never seen or heard of an engineer who is gay."[37] Believing this to imply that heterosexuality was one of the reasons why engineers were "sterling chaps," Mountford-Smith boldly declared: "I am a gay engineer, [*sic*] and am quite willing to acquaint her with this fact."[38] His coming out was newsworthy in *TBP* on account of his profession. Announcing his sexuality meant he was effectively challenging engineering as the "bastion of heterosexual jock values," in the words of the collective.[39] In reminding readers that many places of work were still largely homophobic, *TBP*'s coverage of Mountford-Smith implicitly emphasized the politics and desirability around passing for gay men while simultaneously calling for more action against discrimination.

Accompanying the news brief was a photograph of Mountford-Smith – a man who visibly embodied a macho style (Figure 2.1). Most news briefs up until then did not include photographs because they were bulletins meant to accentuate larger content pieces and articles on gay rights, politics, and world news. The included picture highlighted Mountford-Smith's rugged whiteness, his tight white dress shirt exemplified his muscular body, and his pose on a motorcycle reinforced the heterosexist aesthetics of macho style by disavowing any aspect of femininity. The emphasis on macho style in the photograph reinforced traditional ideas of masculinity, including physical strength and toughness. The editorial collective's decision to include this photograph in the news brief can be seen as a pushback against these traditional ideas of masculinity, challenging the notion that being gay automatically makes one less masculine.

The image also draws an explicit connection between macho masculinity and motorcycle culture (including denim in this picture).

Figure 2.1 Photograph of Trevor Mountford-Smith. Photographer: unknown. "Engineer Comes Out," *The Body Politic* 20, October 1975, 9. Image provided courtesy of Pink Triangle Press.

Mountford-Smith's denim jeans and pose on top of a motorcycle are seen as a way of performing and reinforcing this type of masculinity. Macho masculinity and motorcycle culture have often been associated with each other in gay popular culture. This association with toughness and rebellion contributed to their being incorporated into the visual language of macho masculinity. The photograph supported Mountford-Smith's assertion that being an engineer and gay were not incompatible and fit well with the *TBP*'s ideological assertion that the personal is political.

TBP featured more explicit content regarding macho style as the scope of the newspaper grew. Included among this growth was more attention paid to film, literature, and the fine arts. The editorial collective featured photospreads, for example, from artists to highlight the work being done around sexuality. This fit into the ethos of *TBP* nicely, for representing homosexuality and visualizing queer desire was an important aspect of gay liberation. Much of the imagery around macho style at this time reflected the adoption of leather and denim. Photographic spreads, commercial advertisements for bars, editorial columns, and classified ads in *TBP* reiterated the prominence of macho style in the gay male community, but they also reinforced tropes of *who* could be macho.

The importance of addressing macho style had an unusual catalyst in 1980, given that the topic of discussion was William Friedkin's 1980 film *Cruising*, a movie that did not come from the community but claimed to represent it. In February 1980, the film was released, and the editorial collective ran extensive coverage of it. Of concern was the film reinforcing tropes of gay male culture and gay male masculinity that were often hidden and misunderstood. The film stars Al Pacino as a heterosexual police officer, Steve Burns, and follows a series of murders in New York's gay S&M bar scene. *Cruising* was controversial upon its release due to its depiction of gay masculinity and its association with sadomasochism and violence. Gay masculinity in the film is depicted as hyper-masculine, aggressive, and deviant. The gay men in the film are shown engaging in various forms of BDSM and fetish activities, including donning leather and rubber gear.

For Scott Tucker, a reader from Philadelphia, "It [*Cruising*] … makes S&M mythologically dangerous and evil, the medium for the message that homosexuality and homicide go together like Peggy Lee's 'Love and Marriage.'"[40] Critics, like Tucker, argued that the film perpetuated the notion that gay men were dangerous and perverted and that the film's association of gay masculinity with sadomasochism and violence was harmful to the gay community. He believed the film reinforced a fear and misunderstanding of gay sexuality and that it contributed to the marginalization and discrimination of gay men. Some members of *TBP* also critiqued the emphasis placed on leather-clad macho men as representative of the gay community. However, others argued that the film was a more nuanced representation of gay masculinity. In doing so, it provided a glimpse into a subculture that was often hidden and misunderstood.

Those supportive of the film believed that it challenged traditional notions of masculinity and helped break down the barriers that separated gay men from mainstream society. Scholar and HIV/AIDS activist Vito Russo did not understand why many gay men were upset with the film. Hollywood had filmed "what Hollywood has always decided to film – the visible gay ghetto," in his words. His analysis of *Cruising* arguably stood as a precursor to his 1987 book *The Celluloid Closet*, in which he looked at the portrayal of lesbian, gay, bisexual, and transgender characters in Hollywood films. As Russo lamented in his letter, "What disturbed me greatly was the hostility of the 'respectable' gay community – not to the film or United Artists – but to other gays

Figure 2.2 Photographs by Norman Hatton presented in "Skinscapes." Photographs by Norman Hatton, *The Body Politic* 74, June 1981, 23. Courtesy of the ArQuives, *The Body Politic* fonds.

who had made the free choice to cooperate in their own oppression."[41] Rather than address macho style and S&M as possible examples of homosexual self-oppression and self-regulation, Russo focused on the anxieties within the community around Hollywood's portrayal of gay men in leather. Russo believed that macho style and S&M were *voluntary* forms of oppression in the gay community, keeping room for individual agency.

While Russo's analysis of the portrayal of gay men in Hollywood focused on the voluntary forms of oppression within the gay community, other artists and photographers were exploring the relationship between costume and masculinity in gay culture. One such artist was Norman Hatton, a prominent photographer in Toronto's gay community, whose work was featured on posters in various Toronto bathhouses and bars, and in several gay magazines, including *TBP*. Hatton's photographic collective "Skinscapes" was featured in *TBP*'s June 1981 issue and articulated the important relationship between costume and masculinity in gay male culture (Figure 2.2). He subtly used light and texture to accentuate and contrast the softness of flesh with "the hard look of leather, metal, and muscle," in the words of *TBP*'s editorial collective. This was noteworthy because his images evoked how leather and skin could be extensions of gay men's presentation of gender and sexuality.[42]

The individuals in Hatton's images are primarily white, muscular, in their underwear, and/or donning leather hats and harnesses. Some are smoking, often a shorthand for "sexy." The use of smoking as a shorthand for sexiness or glamour in images has a long history, dating back to the early twentieth century.[43] Additionally, a few of the models are lying on the ground exposed, while others are turned away from the camera – actively becoming objectified subjects for the viewer. These men are positioned and framed in a way that makes their bodies passively consumable for the pleasure of onlookers, but their musculature and clothing simultaneously classify them as butch and aggressive. Only one individual is staring into the camera with an aggressive stance and a domineering glare.[44] Hatton's images articulated to viewers that the macho body involved more than facial hair and muscle; it included accentuating the ideal physique with leather or jockstraps. This subtle tension between passive sexual object and active patriarchal presentation of masculinity is emblematic of macho style as a queer aesthetic. Men donning a macho style did so just as much for their own identity as they did for the attention and gaze of others.

Among Hatton's images was a single man of colour, arguably as a claim against the entrenched whiteness of macho style. Jennifer Evans argues that "images do not passively mirror historical change but actively constitute claims to representation."[45] However, there is an exotic theme playing out in the image of the Black man sitting and lying on the bed. He is sitting passively alongside objects such as a fern resembling a palm tree – theatrically displaying hints of orientalism. The Black man's positioning renders him as a docile object to be looked at rather than an active actor seen in the subsequent image of a white man exhaling smoke. In terms of masculinity, white men are defined primarily by their gender rather than race because white people are considered "nonracial or racially neutral," as Ruth Frankenberg contends. Therefore, white men become a standard to which racialized masculinities are compared.[46] In this instance, the passive Black body is adorned with hints of oriental objects, which displaces any perceived relationship or connection with the white bodies. As a result, Hatton's presentation of masculinity is shaped by racial ideas. This is particularly evident in the posing and framing of these men. White men are at the forefront, donning leather and an aggressive stance, while the men of colour are presented in more submissive or subdued poses.

Coverage of Hatton's "Skinscapes" in *TBP* signified that leather was becoming increasingly approved of as an erotic and non-oppressive manifestation of desire. In Hatton's words, "Leather is skin, too."[47] Gayle Rubin argues in her analysis of the leather community in post-war San Francisco that, "Leather jackets, jeans, boots, and Harley caps all became markers for butch gay men interested, sexually and socially, in other butch gay men."[48] The overt costuming of the male body to determine machismo, however, meant macho style's campiness was highly visible. While leather carried various meanings in the gay community – some associated it with BDSM, while others did not – it reshaped discourses around macho style and bodybuilding. Following the rise of the HIV/AIDS epidemic, it was stereotyped as inherently dangerous and, in the words of Rubin, became "assimilated into concerns over AIDS-related risks and hazards."[49] The absence of any serious critique of how Hatton used leather by the editorial collective raises the questions: When does art become art? And when does art become problematic advertising?

Advertising the Macho Body

TBP was at times a contradiction of politicized conversations around gender and macho style while featuring artwork, photographs, and advertisements from local businesses that arguably exploited macho style. If publications like *TBP* existed to create space for gay men and lesbians to liberate themselves from the gendered and sexual moorings of mainstream society, macho ads threatened to anchor gay men to queer patriarchal ideas of masculinity.

Commercial ads were, by and large, the greatest contributor to representations of macho style in *TBP*. The 1980s saw gay bars and bathhouses often depicting macho masculinity as a form of sexual fetish and fantasy. The ads frequently featured images of muscular, macho men in various states of undress, often in leather gear or fetish attire. These images were used to appeal to a specific subset of gay men who were attracted to a more hyper-masculine and sexually dominant ideal of masculinity. In the context of a political paper, however, these same ads also had the effect of equating such imagery with gay liberation more broadly. In some ways, the macho styles being presented in advertisements were a way for gay men to assert their masculinity and sexuality in a highly politicized climate. Indeed, some saw these representations as a way of subverting traditional norms of masculinity and reclaiming power, while others saw it as another form of self-oppression.

Ads presenting macho style as *the* desirable aesthetic often did so by relying on illustrative drawings. The use of illustrations may have been an opportunity to curtail any censorship, but often it was a marketing decision. Cartoons in advertising can be powerful tools, helping viewers see themselves in the lifestyle being presented.[50] By using caricatures or exaggerated imagery, bar and bathhouse advertisers create a sense of identification with the illustrative characters. They are also able to tap into the emotions of the audience through playfulness or humour, helping to create a positive association between the aesthetic of macho masculinity presented and the viewer's sexual desires. These figures were almost always white, always muscular, enabled, and donned denim, leather, or other signifiers of working-class or butch occupations. These ads reiterate the importance of fashion and clothing as extensions of the self and gay men's desire to be masculine. They also serve as a reminder that macho style was utilized by commercial interests to sell an illusory sexual bait. The frequency that macho style was represented in images exploded by the early 1980s. The following five ads for bars and bathhouses reveal the shifting aesthetic of macho style, from youthful muscular men to butch bodybuilders wearing leather and hardhats.

In the first example, The Barracks, a bathhouse located on 56 Widmer Street in Toronto, ran an ad in September–October 1974 featuring a white athletic man with no shirt on and his jeans unzipped (Figure 2.3).[51] The name of The Barracks itself is a queering of the military – a bastion of heterosexual masculinity. Furthermore, the ad communicates the notion that patrons are equally as masculine as heterosexual men in the military. It plays on the homosocial tension of the Canadian military and how there are no women to fulfill the heterosexual expectations for men. The figure is clean-shaven, white, with a defined muscular body, conforming to some elements of macho style. The figure's denim jeans and dog tags around his neck complemented the bar's advertisement that "cycle" (motorcycle) culture – a culture of rugged masculinity that relied on signifiers of denim and leather to display masculinity – was "spoken fluently" there.[52] While it is not entirely clear what it meant to speak "cycle" because the term was used very infrequently in *TBP*, it likely represented a system of codes, behaviours, and words associated with motorcycle culture.[53]

Those who frequented bathhouses and read this advertisement were sure to know the meaning of cycle, let alone appreciate that Toronto sex toyshop The Pleasure Chest endorsed their liberal sexual culture. Including reference to a sex toyshop affirmed toys, clothing, and accessories, such as harnesses, as important accoutrements for men to carry out their sexual fantasies. The Barracks marketed itself as different from other bathhouses by not only advertising gay macho men in its venue but also offering products that could enhance their sexual experience. The inclusion of The Pleasure Chest subliminally reinforced the

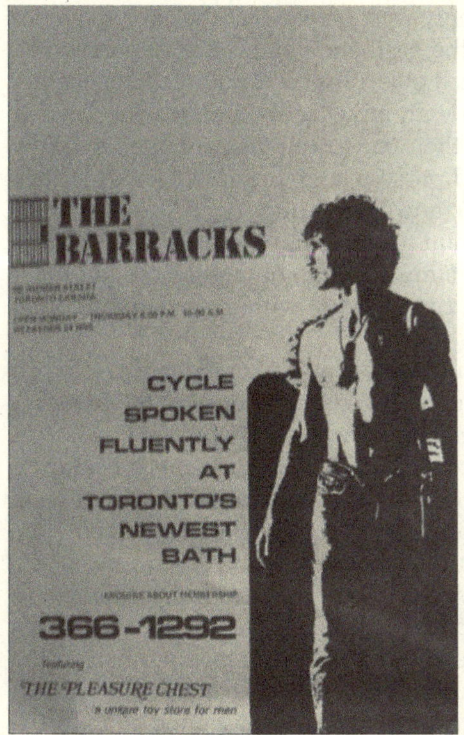

Figure 2.3 Advertisement for The Barracks bathhouse in *The Body Politic* 15, September–October 1974, 10. The ArQuives, *The Body Politic* fonds.

muscular figure's desirability by equating his chest with that of "pleasure." Hence, the muscular chest elicits pleasure or desirability.

In comparison, three bar ads from the early 1980s demonstrate the explosion of macho style as an aesthetic embodying leather and denim. The Toronto bar Boots featured an illustration of a shirtless muscle clone, wearing only denim jeans, a toolbelt, and a hard hat. He was styled with a moustache and evoked the traditional working-class attire that had long been evocative of macho style. He is, by definition, Levine's idea of the macho clone: "rippling with bulging muscles" and dressed in "blue-collar garb."[54] Meanwhile, the ad also featured the bar's name at the bottom but with two leather boots replacing the "o"s in Boots. This technique emphasized this space as a leather bar. These ads reflected a broader cultural shift towards a macho aesthetic while also demonstrating how this style was used to sell products and appeal to consumers who sought to embody the macho ideal. Similarly, the Toronto bar, Crowbar, featured an illustrated headshot of a white man with rugged facial features, square-jawed, wearing a hard hat and smoking a cigarette. Not only was the name of the bar a reference to working-class labour, but the aesthetic being portrayed revolved around this working-class butch masculinity.[55] Finally, Chaps leather bar featured two cartoon men with moustaches and donning leather chaps in an advertisement for their bar.[56] Both men are unequivocally butch in their presentation and possess large muscles. However, they are dressed entirely in leather and their buttocks are exposed. Not only do they not have any denim or other signifiers of working-class labour, but their image is very similar to that of motorcycle culture. It even draws from the aesthetic cues of S&M with the incorporation of police caps.

Fashion advertisements of macho style in *TBP* in the 1980s followed more subtle nods to advertising macho style fashions in *TBP*. In recognition that macho style was becoming increasingly prevalent, Leather Crafter Ltd. advertised its custom-made leather garments.[57] Featuring a white butch-looking man with a moustache and beard and wearing a Black leather jacket, they informed readers that patrons of their store fit in with the motorcycle culture aesthetic.[58]

Leather Crafter Ltd.'s advertisement portrayed masculinity as hyper-masculine, with an emphasis on physical strength, toughness, and a rugged appearance. The choice of a butch-looking man as the model for the advertisement further reinforced this image, as the butch identity has historically been associated with masculine characteristics and behaviours. The advertisement also played into the idea that leather garments were more than just clothing; they were a symbol of a subculture that celebrated masculine ideals. The use of symbols and codes to convey meaning is a common feature of subcultures, and the advertisement effectively allowed Leather Crafter Ltd. to position itself as a purveyor of authentic, custom-made leather garments that were associated with specific cultural styles of masculinity for gay men. While the advertisement may have been targeted towards a specific subculture within the gay community, it also reinforced the stereotype that all gay men were interested in hyper-masculine, butch styles of dress.

Meanwhile, It Store, a gay novelty store at 52 McCaul Street in Toronto, published an advertisement in *TBP* for their game "Pin the Macho on the Man." Complete with twenty-five "hilarious units" that resembled penises, the game featured a pin-up poster of a white, muscular man who had a target over his pelvic region. Players were to pin these units or "macho" on him – similar to pin the tail on the donkey.[59] Machismo, in this case, was not something that was automatically inscribed onto the illustrative figure, but rather acquired through proper placement of genitalia and, most importantly, through the eyes of the participant. By turning machismo into a party game with detachable penises, It Store effectively removed the power dynamic that is often associated with machismo. The game's objective was not to assert dominance or aggression, but rather to engage in a lighthearted and playful activity that centred around sexual anatomy. The fact that the machismo was not automatically inscribed onto the poster figure, but rather acquired through proper placement of genitalia, further reinforces the idea that machismo is a culturally manufactured image of gay male masculinity and sexual virility. The game, in a way, was a subversion of traditional notions of machismo, transforming it into something comical and even absurd. By doing so, It Store was challenging the dominant narratives around masculinity and sexuality and highlighting the agency and creativity of the gay community in shaping their own cultural identity.

Broadly put, advertisements were (and remain) important markers of cultural taste. Businesses sought to tap into the growing gay male culture and appeal to their desires and interests using macho style as a marketing ploy. Advertisements, such as those noted above, provided much-needed funding for *TBP*, allowing it to expand and grow its operations. However, for David Vereschagin, a newcomer to *TBP* in 1983, this reliance on advertising also had its downsides. Even though it brought in a significant amount of money, Vereschagin saw it as the primary factor contributing to what he referred to as the "cult of masculinity."[60] This term referred to the perception that the gay male community was increasingly fixated on a specific, macho image of masculinity, which was perpetuated by the constant stream of advertisements featuring this style. In Vereschagin's view, this "cult of masculinity" was harmful to the gay male community, as it reinforced harmful stereotypes and placed an unrealistic and unhealthy emphasis on physical appearance. He believed that the reliance on these ads to fund *TBP*'s operations came at a cost to the community and that a more balanced approach was needed to promote healthy and diverse representations of masculinity.

Almost immediately after joining the collective, Vereschagin put together a full-page article examining the consequential effects of macho style and advertising for gay men. Macho style had created unobtainable goals for gay men and articulated a patriarchal stereotyping of gay male masculinity. Inspired after seeing countless advertisements featuring macho clones in *TBP*, Vereschagin reflected:

> All these men informed me of that horrible truth: not only was I a faggot, I was a wimp. To be gay was forgiveable [*sic*], to be less than totally masculine

> was not. Luckily, ignoring them was easy. I simply closed the issue of The Body Politic that I was reading. No, I hadn't been in a bar, I'd been looking at ads. And while ignoring them may be easy, escaping from them is another matter.[61]

His statement suggests that he found the advertisements difficult to avoid or escape from. Indeed, ads increasingly populated the pages of *TBP*, reflecting the continued financial pressures that faced the newspaper. As a result, *TBP*'s editorial collective was forced to reconcile with, or at least ignore, the inherent contradictions that came with establishing a paper seeking to undermine the capitalist-hetero patriarchy, and publishing ads that seemingly reinforced it. Vereschagin was frustrated with the constant exposure to advertisements, particularly those that reinforce harmful stereotypes and unrealistic images. His perceived failure at being masculine was an insecurity created by these advertisements. Gender failure was ingrained in these images at the time of their creation because they borrowed, in his words, "from the straight culture around us."[62] By his logic, if macho style was a manifestation of straight imaginings of masculinity, then gay men emulating such an aesthetic were contributing to their self-oppression.

While some might chalk advertisements to not *actually* represent the gay male community at this time, Vereschagin argues that it "does reflect and effect [*sic*] a definite narrowness in the way many gay men choose to present themselves."[63] The representation and visibility of macho style had profound effects on how gay men styled themselves. If "personal" ads in the classified section of *TBP* are anything to go by, then gay men were increasingly attentive to their masculine image as more commercial advertisements appeared in *TBP*. Many ads included language that explicitly defined their masculinity or their "straight" appearance and would occasionally demand that those responding do so as well. While these ads may be clumsy attempts at defining one's sexual desire, they are evidence that "passing" as straight in a queer patriarchal world or donning particular styles of clothing were important markers of gay male masculinity. Indeed, "personal" classified ads reflected what Vereschagin had been arguing: "The blue jeans, t-shirts, western shirts, construction boots, cowboy boots, dark glasses and leather jackets affected by large numbers of gay men ... indicate that their thinking certainly moves in the macho direction."[64]

As Vereschagin argued, the prevalence of macho style in advertisements had an impact on how gay men presented themselves, and this trend was also evident in personal ads. While many ads clumsily attempted to define their masculinity or demanded that potential respondents be "straight-acting," the editorial collective scrutinized ads for racist or sexist language. The newspaper's attention to the ad section was consistent with their own social and political philosophy and was in keeping with the Canadian Criminal Code regarding discrimination. Moreover, the popularity of the classifieds helped contribute to the newspaper's financial success. The popularity of personal classified ads in *TBP*, however, reflected the narrowness of gay male presentation in the 1980s, one that simultaneously generated revenue for the newspaper.

The Politics of Desiring Macho Men

Since its creation in 1973, the classified ads section grew from being half of a single page to several pages by mid-decade – attesting to its popularity among readers. Personal ads required the client to submit a written ad for publication to *TBP* with a cheque or bring their ads and payment to the collective directly. This process did not change much throughout *TBP*'s lifespan; however, there was some consideration for ads to be submitted by telephone during the Canada Post strike in the summer of 1981.[65] The cost to run a personal ad in 1979 was approximately 20 cents per word, $4.00 dollars per run, and $2.00 for a mail drawer whereby mail would be forwarded to the advertiser.[66] In conjunction with the popularity of classified ads, *TBP* was well-positioned to make a small profit from connecting individuals, businesses, and organizations. Indeed, in 1981, it was noted in a collective meeting that "classifieds tend to generate their own growth" and revenue.[67] Furthermore, many ads refrained from racist or sexist language because *TBP* wanted to have its message match its political and social philosophy. The newspaper assured readers that each classified ad was scrutinized to adhere to the Canadian Criminal Code regarding discrimination.[68]

Some ads, such as a 1974 ad from a "Lonesome cowboy," stressed the importance of a particular subset of costume to indicate a butch masculinity. In this ad, the author described himself as "young and handsome, easy going, well educated, [and] white"; he informed readers that he had "good cowboy, police and leather outfits. Like high cut cowboy boots."[69] Ads demanding a specific costuming, such as police officers or cowboys, were few and far between in the early to mid-1970s. Their rarity in the earlier half of the decade suggests that any costumed aesthetic associated with machismo had not been entirely defined. However, the appropriation of traditionally heterosexual and extremely masculine occupations or aesthetics, such as police, construction worker, or cowboy, differed from the more generic image of white muscular masculinity presented in many commercial ads. It was a campy styling of the male body that both affirmed and challenged the assumed heterosexual masculinity found in these professions. The author's use of clothing reflected a subculture in gay male culture that resonates with Susan Sontag's theory of style as a codified language. Cowboy, police, and leather outfits were aesthetic adaptations that created an image or identity that was both individual and culturally meaningful.

Costuming gay male bodies with styles that drew upon traditional bastions of heterosexual performances of masculinity (i.e., the police officer, cowboy, or construction worker) added a campy theatricality to gay male sexuality that enhanced the "butch" role these men played. In the 1980s, a greater number of *TBP*'s classified ads contained increasingly specific requests for men donning styles tied to "butch" occupations. A classified ad written by a twenty-four-year-old man in September 1980 centred on his desire for an athletic police officer for sex and them to become "butch buddies."[70] Meanwhile, another classified ad in the same issue described the writer's desire for a "well-hung muscular male with apartment for occasional weekend encounters … [and] … guys who are into faded levis [*sic*], western wear, construction boots or leather," with similar ads following.[71] By appropriating traditionally masculine styles associated with occupation, gay men were subverting societal norms surrounding gender roles and sexual expression. Not only did gay men create a unique sense of identity from these aesthetics, but dress became an invaluable way of establishing a shared visual language for gay men to identify and connect.

Additionally, the increasing specificity of ads for men donning "butch" clothing or styles of dress reflects the growing visibility of macho style in the 1980s. These ads demonstrate the importance of physical appearance and style for defining and codifying gay male identities. The costuming of gay male bodies with traditional heterosexual markers of masculinity allows for the expression of sexuality in a way that was both subversive and socially acceptable. It created a unique visual language that facilitated community building and helped to define the parameters of a particular "type" of gay male identity that was deeply tied to specific styles of clothing and body types.

These ads also raise questions about the extent to which editors of *TBP* were able to scrutinize submissions. While the editorial collective informed readers since the inception of the classifieds section that they reserved the right to edit or refuse any ad, they did not direct readers on acceptable language until July 1978.[72] In their advertisement for their classifieds section, the collective encouraged readers to:

"[t]ell them about yourself and your interests – not about what you don't like. Specifying exclusions based on race or appearance (saying 'no fats or fems' for instance) is just plain rude."[73] The collective sought to address the practice of exclusion in ads, but attempts at policing classified ads were not always successful. Many ads found during *TBP*'s publication conveyed problematic messages around gender or race using subversive language.

Historian David Churchill argues that in addition to inherently discriminatory ads, "*TBP* members made attempts 'to educate readers to avoid inadvertent exclusions' such as GWM (gay white man) seek same,' by contacting individuals who placed such ads and asking them whether the ad copy reflected what they really wanted to say."[74] Ads engaging with the politics of "sameness" saw men describe themselves as white and masculine and demand the "same." Churchill's argument that the collective's attempts to negate exclusionary language rings true, but evidence such as the "houseboy ad," whereby a white man requested a Black "houseboy" in February 1985, demonstrates that these efforts were tenuous. Also overlooked is how the politics of "sameness" was utilized in *TBP*'s classified ads by men seeking to circumvent *TBP*'s restrictions.

An ad in 1973 read: "Male 5'8, 135 lbs, 29 yrs. Ath. bld. [athletic build] masc. [masculine]. vers. [sexually versatile]. Gd. bod. [good body]. Med. end. [medium endowment] Avg. lkg [average looking] Strt. app. [straight appearance] Would like to meet well end. [well-endowed] masc. [masculine]. 6 ft. to 190 lbs. for friendship fun. Do u fit?"[75] The difference between the writer's average looks and his "straight" appearance suggests that he affirmed his masculinity not just through physical traits or clothing but in the ability to pass as heterosexual. It is unclear what a "straight" appearance precisely meant, but it would have likely included clothing, accessories, and/or mannerisms considered butch and without indication of homosexuality. In another ad from 1974, a twenty-nine-year-old man named John, who described himself as "successful" and "good looking," demanded his partner be masculine when he wrote, "You must be slim to slim-medium build, average to good-looking, masculine (no femmes) age to 32."[76] The explicit desire for a masculine man could be chalked up to sexual preference, but the inclusion of "no femmes" was purposeful. It excluded gay men who failed to pass as heterosexual.

To avoid scrutiny or censorship, many men, particularly white men, explicitly described themselves as masculine or having a "straight appearance" and searching for the "same." For example, a twenty-seven-year-old white gay man submitted a classified ad in December

1975 describing himself as "masculine, mustache, non-smoker, light drinker, no drugs," in search of the "same, 26–35, tall, trim, muscular."[77] In this case, "same" applied to masculine, moustache, white, and the man's smoking, drinking, and drug use, since those were not adjectives used to explicitly describe his ideal partner. Another ad in the same issue featured a twenty-nine-year-old who did not disclose his race but stated he had a "straight appearance" and "wishes to meet the same" – articulating a desire for men with an equally straight appearance.[78] Finally, in September 1976, an ad appeared by a man describing himself as "fairly masculine" and "not bad looking" who sought the "same," or preferably "a policeman."[79] Using the word "same" opened up descriptors for race, gender, and ability without explicitly doing so. The word "same" could become particularly loaded with racialized ideas of masculinity that were the mainstay of the discourse in the classified section. The politics of sameness provided a space for racialized understandings of masculinity and ensured white privilege in *TBP*. Despite genuine attempts to address racism, ageism, and homophobia by members of *TBP*, the politics of "sameness" became a way in which some white gay men policed and regulated masculinity within a complex system of desire, a need for recognition, conformity, and fear of mainstream exclusion. More broadly, classified ads demonstrate that some gay men were asserting their right to express themselves and their individuality in a society that had long oppressed them. This process was not without its challenges, however.

The Clone Wars

Amid the coverage of macho style, many readers and writers for *TBP* expressed both celebration and ire for this narrowly defined aesthetic of gay male masculinity. For some readers writing to *TBP*, clones were emblematic of gay male misogyny. For others, it was a legitimate identity and expression of masculinity. The debates that follow highlight not just the importance of macho style as a pervasive point of contention within the gay community, but how the aesthetics of gay men became wrapped up in larger conversations around gay liberation. Indeed, macho style risked fragmenting or unravelling any unified image of the gay liberation movement that *TBP* and other groups had attempted to curate.

Hugh Brewster had been concerned about heterosexism and gay mimicry of straight conceptions of masculinity well before macho style even began to flourish. In his response to Tom Burke's December 1969 *Esquire* article "The New Homosexuality," Brewster pushed back against Burke's claim that mainstream society might finally be willing to "empathize with (if not quite approve of)" the stereotype of the homosexual.[80] Not only did Burke only look at gay men, he ignored the internalized homophobia that contributed to pressures on gay men to be butch. Brewster argued that while straight society might be ready to accept the homosexual stereotype, gay men were not.

Brewster attributed the contempt for the gay male effeminate stereotype to two cultural phenomena: the first being the desire of some gay men to circumvent any association with femininity by labelling themselves as "bisexual," and the second being a general discomfort towards female homosexuals.[81] Butch masculinity, not gayness or effeminacy, was seen as sexually desirable because it cloaked the body with pseudo-sexual "normalcy" that risked emulating patriarchal gender performances. Mary Louise Adams argues that during the post-war period, "the fear of being labelled delinquent [homosexual] was an effective form of self-regulation, a threat to those who might transgress sexual or moral standards."[82] This culture of fear around delinquency regulated gay men's gender performance, socializing gay men to perform their masculinity in traditional ways and desire those who did as well. Brewster noted that trends in gay culture, such as dress, manners, and behaviours, may have been loosened from the counter-culture movement of the 1960s, but asked: "Why must we continue to ape heterosexual life-styles?" To act butch was to don the "fixed and dogmatic" patterns of behaviour and dress that had, according to Brewster, become increasingly repressive within the community.[83] By his logic, macho masculinity was just as much about sexism and disenfranchisement for lesbians as it was for effeminate gay men.

Additionally, latent misogyny, the gendered split in the gay community, and broader heterosexist power structures around sexuality contributed to disdain for gay male effeminacy. In Brewster's words:

> "Dyke dislike" among gay men, (even young, "hip" gay men) is symptomatic of the great split in the gay community, or more precisely the ghetto non-community. The gay ghetto has for the most part functioned only as a kind of pseudo community, a marketplace based on sexual barter, and as such has not encouraged interaction between the sexes. This division results from our oppression and is then furthered by our own attitudes, when we see each other as nothing more than sex objects. Gay community can only be fostered by encouragement of the empathetic bond that exists between gay men and women.[84]

Brewster felt that patriarchal expectations of masculinity and the femmephobia that came with it were informing an emerging gay male culture. The existential threat of the "bisexual" man and the rejection of effeminacy caused some gay liberationists to view macho performances of masculinity with suspicion.

These concerns were echoed by *TBP* writer Michael Riordon, who described the repressive rhetoric coming out of Toronto's gay, macho leather/denim/motorcycle community. He claimed to overhear an executive of one of the local leather-and-denim groups at a leather garden party say, "We're only interested in people you could walk on the street with or introduce your mother to without anyone asking, 'Who was that faggot you were with?'"[85] According to Riordon, these men wanted to enjoy the privileges that gay liberationists fought for but never wanted to venture to the picket lines and protests themselves. Their butch understanding of masculinity and expectation for the same from others was symptomatic of a leather-lined closet. Sedgwick suggests that the act of hiding one's non-normative sexuality is not simply a private matter but has broader significant public and private significance.[86] In the case of the leather-clad gay men in Riordon's article, their demand for men to be butch is not only a rejection of queer effeminacy, becomes a possible crux, or simply collateral damage, for the cultural and political divides emerging in the community. While men adopting macho style were perceived to be open about their sexuality, their emulation of butch masculinity was seen by some as an alternative form of queer patriarchy and undermining liberationist efforts of challenging gender stereotypes.

Correlations between macho style and femmephobia seemed to become intertwined in both John Rechy's book *The Sexual Outlaw* (1977) and Herb Spiers's June 1977 review of it. In his book, Rechy argues that "[m]asculine homosexuals still heckle queens, who are true hero-heroines of our time, exhibiting more courage for walking one single block in drag than a straight-looking gay to 'come out' on a comfy campus."[87] *The Sexual Outlaw* provided chaptered accounts of Rechy's sexual experiences, dubbed "the promiscuous experience." These were separated by "voice overs" sections, where Rechy reflected on gay sexuality, gender, nightlife, relationships, and experiences with the straight world.[88] Spiers's review concentrated on the highlights of gay men re-enacting heterosexual masculinity in Rechy's book. Again, commentary on macho style from Rechy seemed to serve *TBP*'s efforts to dismantle artificial barriers around gender and sexuality and attempt to unite the community.

Spiers supported Rechy's assertions that macho style relied on "mistaken" understandings of masculinity. In his words, "He [Rechy] regrets too all the mistaken machismo, the red hankies and dangling keys which preclude even perfunctory sex communication. He regrets gay mimicking straight, and the false consciousness evident when gays try to appease straight condemnation."[89] By describing gay mimicry of straight masculinity as a "false consciousness," Spiers alluded to macho style as a form of self-oppression among gay men. Spiers's review thus became bigger than the book itself. It was an opportunity for Spiers to articulate his concerns around patriarchal influences going into macho style.

Behind the scenes of *TBP*'s review of *Sexual Outlaw* was a disagreement between Spiers and fellow *TBP* contributor Ian Young regarding S&M and macho style. Rechy had made the argument that S&M was another form of gay male homophobia and self-hatred, one "comparable only in destructiveness to the impact of repressive laws and persecution by cops."[90] Spiers endorsed Rechy's claims about S&M as a form of masochism, but also believed that S&M raised the "question of gay love versus gay hate: of loving ourselves and fighting our enemies, or of hating ourselves and acting out in our sex lives our heterosexually inflicted sorrows."[91] This sentiment, however, provoked *TBP* contributor Ian Young to respond in the subsequent issue.[92] Young, who participated in S&M culture, argued that Spiers's referral to S&M as "sexual suicide" stigmatized and marginalized gay men who found pleasure in it.[93] In response to Young, Spiers acknowledged that he was not immune to politics of masculinity and that his own "preoccupation with pyramidal pecs" was a manifestation of "unresolved machismo."[94] Rechy's book and Spiers's review of it, as well as their subsequent responses, demonstrate how different writing spaces in *TBP* interacted. Book reviews became gateways for broader conversations on masculinity and style, while the letters between Spiers and Young on S&M highlight the transparency of *TBP* as a platform for these discussions. Additionally, this debate around macho style in the *Sexual Outlaw* demonstrates how these reviews did not go unquestioned, especially by those of the editorial collective who felt that S&M was a legitimate expression of gay male sexuality.

Others, such as *TBP* writer Tim Guest, also struggled with macho style's place within the gay male community. As an active member of Gay Youth Toronto and the Revolutionary Workers League, he had witnessed firsthand the effects of masculine stereotypes and the ongoing identity crises young people were going through by trying to conform to them. In May 1978, he wrote a letter to *TBP*, stating, "We deal with our objectification in a natural way by expressing our alienation from it in our appearance – an appearance which tends to be a little extreme, almost a parody of itself – an image which, despite the alienation involved, allows us to exercise some control over our objectification."[95] He called for a more lenient understanding of the objectification of gay men and appearance as part of a complex and subtle form of "role-playing." In other words, Guest understood gay men to be active agents in their subordination or objectification with respect to style. Like other queer styles, macho style was an ideal that provided some men with agency while excluding and marginalizing others. Guest did not actively praise or idolize macho style but instead viewed it as another outlet of masculinity for gay men.

Readers such as Peter Bowen, an expat living in Xania, Crete, argued that "[b]eing discriminatory about a partner ... especially when it comes to sex, is the name of the game." He contended that ageism was an infallible part of gay cultural life: "Ageism (ugly word!) [*sic*] I'm a victim of myself, I guess, although I don't feel victimized, unless I read every ad that doesn't seem to want me as a personal, vindictive rejection of me."[96] Bowen's comments validated age discrimination as an indisputable aspect of sexual desire. He also raised the tenuous definition of masculinity in the gay male community by arguing that "'masculine' is, after all, a relative term, like 'tall' or 'attractive' – having highly subjective interpretations." His points of reference to make his argument, however, drew upon macho style: "It [masculinity] doesn't mean some chest-expanded macho who wants to drive his knee-length hobnail boots into my crotch nightly nor does it even mean being into denim and leather, although it *can* mean these things."[97] While he also admitted that he feels no less masculine for crocheting, Bowen's description of macho style and reference to leather and denim positioned it as a pervasive – and stereotypical – point of reference for gay male masculinity.

With macho style surging in popularity as *the* aesthetic of gay male masculinity in *TBP*, there was greater vocalization among the newspaper's readers regarding what they saw as reverse discrimination towards macho gay men. In November 1980, Jim Loveless, a self-identified clone from Topeka, Kansas, was tired of the gay community bashing clones and decided to defend what he saw as a legitimate form of gender expression. In his letter, he wrote: "No wonder gays have a difficult time making progress ... Again, we "clones" are taken to task for having professional positions and wearing our disgusting "uniforms."[98] Loveless's reference to "uniforms" was a nod to the generalization of macho style as unremarkable and ubiquitous. The word also implies that there was an expected aesthetic to macho style, such as denim, leather, T-shirts, sneakers, or work boots. Finally, uniform is often used when referring to clothing associated with employment. When placed next to his argument that clones have "professional positions," the term can imply that macho clones had bought into a capitalist that did not benefit all queers equally.

Loveless pit "professional" macho clones against liberationist "fairies" who pushed back against rigid gender norms because they were "disease-free from clonedom."[99] To surmise that clones were under siege because they were professionals and conformed to traditional gender roles demonstrates that some *TBP* readers felt that gay liberation was not irreconcilable with capitalism and traditional gender roles. Loveless's letter can be seen as one of the first inklings of homonationalist thought – whereby certain queers are embraced by the state because they uphold the status quo. The class dynamics of clone culture that Loveless nods to meant some who identified as clones did so, not because they necessarily enjoyed S&M, leather, or motorcycle culture, but because they saw pragmatic value in performing a butch masculinity. They were buying into a capitalist ethos based on neoliberal ideas of individuality and a mindset that was antithetical to that of *TBP*'s gay liberationist collective.

However, being a clone did not mean one's politics were in opposition to gay liberationist politics. Self-identified clone Dan Healey responded the following month to Loveless's attack on "fairies" and the assumption that clones were incompatible with the gay rights movement. Healey criticized Loveless's baseless claim that clones were under attack and believed that his judgment of "fairies" was unfair and reinforced harmful stereotypes that clones were wrought with internalized homophobia. He believed that Loveless contributed to the debate between the ideological differences between clones and radical fairies – implying that the gay community was becoming intellectually divided between gay men who embraced traditional gender norms and those who challenged them. Indeed, Healey noted that stereotypes of macho clones included "insanity, irresponsible 'disco' closetry, political indifference, reckless consumerism, rudeness in the street, and even hermaphroditism."[100] Such stereotypes were not the result of cis-heteronormative mainstream culture, nor did they stem from clone culture. Rather, these were judgments made by other gay men in the community, notably some at the forefront of liberation. If so, these sentiments indicate that gay liberation and the cohesive messaging of *TBP* risked being undone by the internal politics of desire and representation.

Conclusion

In August 1983, *TBP* writer John Allec reported that disco star and macho clone Paul Parker was coming out of "the modern gay ghetto, bringing its look and character with him."[101] That look was heavily butch. Next to Allec's column on Parker's discography and background was an image of Parker, sporting a moustache and an open leather vest revealing his hairy chest. By including Parker's image, Allec presented a specific aesthetic of what one might find in the modern gay ghetto: macho men. This image represented a popularization of clothing, notably leather, as an important accessory in how macho style straddled a campy performance of masculinity while still conforming to butch gender roles. The proliferation of disco, a musical genre known for ostentatious clothing and popular within gay-friendly establishments, played a role in promoting macho style. Indeed, in her analysis of disco culture, Echols argues that disco promoted the pageantry of the male body, "Worked-out pecs came to be called 'disco tits.'"[102]

As *TBP* broadened its focus to include the cultural happenings of Toronto and other major cities across Canada in the 1970s, discussions of macho style became increasingly apparent. This transition not only attracted old and new readers alike but ensured that *TBP* could remain relevant to shifting cultural and social developments in the gay male community. *TBP*'s coverage of contemporary events, such as the Mr. Club beauty contest or a letter from an engineer coming out in a trade publication, are examples in which the collective either intentionally or inadvertently discussed the politics of masculinity within the gay male community. Coverage of these events demonstrates that there were some among the collective who saw representations of gay male masculinity laden with social and cultural meaning at a time when gay male sexuality was becoming publicly visualized and discussed. Unlike the "naturalized" vision of masculinity seen in commercial advertisements, editorial coverage of macho style was more intellectually engaged, deconstructing how macho style might benefit or hinder the gay community. Editorials and commercial content in *TBP* suggest that gay men performed particularized and contextual styles of masculinity that incorporated manliness and homosexuality by which they constructed their very *being*.[103]

Throughout *TBP*'s publication, discussions of macho style continually changed to reflect how masculinity and passing equated with sexual desirability. The tensions that arose around macho style also highlight how the editorial collective negotiated macho style as an aesthetic to which many gay men, if able-bodied and white, were encouraged to adopt. Macho style was more than a stylistic expression of masculinity in the gay male community; it was the focal point of numerous articles, debates, and dialogue between readers and the editorial collective on gender and sexuality in *TBP*. With the collective feeling obligated to mediate representations of masculinity, *TBP* broadened from a political newspaper to a periodical discussing gay social and cultural developments across North America.

As *TBP* expanded in scope and content, it increasingly found itself as a space for community members to debate the cultural constructions of masculinity. The open dialogue between the editorial collective and readers gave the paper a unique foothold in the gay community. It provided intellectual conversations beyond the scope of lesbian and gay politics. In these discussions of macho style in *TBP*, the white, muscular gay male body came to represent broader tensions around gender, sexuality, desirability, and race within the gay male community. Furthermore, commercial advertisements and some classified ads demonstrate that macho style came to include more than the manufacturing of the gay male body but elements of S&M as well by the 1980s. In much of the latter editorial material on masculinity in *TBP*, macho style was not seen merely as a mask used by gay men to hide their sexuality, but rather a problematic negotiation between passing and camp.

By the early 1980s, macho culture had become synonymous with gay masculinity, and some gay men were seen as "insidiously" hiding themselves in society. Outside of the community, the presentation of gay male masculinity through macho style fuelled anxieties, especially around identifying homosexual men from their heterosexual counterparts. In 1985, Alan Stewart contended in *The Globe and Mail* that, "A middle-aged, balding man in an evening gown is not only immediately recognizable, but recognizable as a non-threat. A gay man is considered a threat to society, not when he wears a dress but when he does not, when he looks like everyone else. A gay man who can pass as a real woman might be a bit upsetting to some people, but a gay man who can pass as a 'real' man is even more so."[104] In other words, this was a dramatic shift away from Ron Poramro's argument in 1977 that men who conformed to heteronormative performances of masculinity in public were not a threat. Rather, the "threat" to society was that gay men were not transgressing gender and sexual boundaries enough to be identifiable. Indeed, by 1983, passing was portrayed in *TBP* as a precautionary measure taken by gay men to ensure that they did not face discrimination at work or in society.

The pages of *TBP* exemplify how the numerous and often competing mediations of gay male masculinity reflect an equally diverse cultural landscape in Toronto's, and arguably North America's, gay male communities. The editorial collective experienced a great deal of internal tension around the topic of masculinity, particularly as it related to gay liberation and oppression, as well as freedom of sexual expression. Yet, while macho style became increasingly defined along a single ever-changing aesthetic – adopting stylistic elements of leather and denim – the opinions among *TBP*'s editorial collective and readership on macho culture became more diverse.

Chapter Three

Stylizing Masculinity in Urban Spaces

Certain bars, certain parks, certain washrooms are allowed to be "ours" – most of the time – and we can be our disgusting selves there. If we leave, if we attempt to be ourselves on the job or in the schools or in the wrong park at the wrong time we are fair game. We can be attacked.

– Gerald Hannon, "Learning to Kill," *The Body Politic* 22, February 1976, 9

"Learning to Kill" is how Gerald Hannon described the need to protect oneself from violence. He suggested that just as Toronto provided spaces for gay men to engage in sexual acts, it also provided opportunities for them to fall victim to homophobia. Washrooms, parks, bars, and alleyways were constantly oscillating in meaning between sexual and/or social spaces and spaces of danger. Coverage of the brutal consequences faced by those who transgressed gender roles in public raised concerns about personal safety for gay men. Such incidents included the arrest of two men kissing on Bloor St. on 12 February 1976, or when twenty-two-year-old Bob Schissler observed a gang of teenagers threatening gay men in David Balfour Park in May 1976, and finally, the series of murders directed at gay men in Toronto between 1975 and 1978.[1]

The possibility of arrest for indecency or physical violence was a shadow to the pleasures that came with cruising for sex and participating in a flourishing gay male culture. Gay men performed their masculinity in ways that allowed them to circumvent police and RCMP efforts to regulate sexuality. Additionally, "codes" or language around sexuality and cruising, such as back-pocket hankies, developed in response to state-sanctioned regulatory efforts and allowed gay men to communicate their sexual desires and proclivities in subversive ways. Even "passing" as straight was noted by *TBP* as a purposeful tactic to avoid scrutiny. Unlike navigating public parks, washrooms, and the streets, however, masculine performances in bars centred on desirability rather than safety. Geographers Gill Valentine and Tracey Skelton argue that "Clubs and bars provide spaces where people can lose themselves and their troubles in music, dance and sex. They are expressive, performative spaces where people can enjoy themselves together in ways that can be empowering."[2]

This chapter examines the ways in which gay men restyled their masculinity in Toronto's urban environment. Gay men engaged in a range of stylistic practices to circumnavigate danger as they moved from their residences to bars and bathhouses for entertainment or to cruise, to parks and washrooms to engage in the thrill of public sex, or to gyms for bodybuilding. Gay male style was fundamental to how gay men navigated sexualized spaces and resisted police/state violence, while also serving as an opportunity for undercover police to entrap gay men or raid bathhouses while disguised in plainclothes. Stylistic developments of gay male masculinity, particularly the proliferation of the macho clone, reflected the spatial relationship gay men had with Toronto, as well as other major urban centres in Canada. In the words of Dick Hebdige, subcultures are "a coded response to changes affecting the entire community."[3] The city's ever-changing urban landscape included the formation of style-themed bars, a shift from bathhouses to gyms as sites of sexual pleasure, and the rise of self-defence classes to address violence towards gay men. Evolving aesthetics of gay male masculinity also reflected the potential dangers of entrapment, whereby plainclothes police adopted queer styles to entrap gay men on behalf of a heterosexually coded state to arrest gay men.

Drawing upon Leif Jerram's understanding that "space is material, location is relational and positional, place is meaningful," I argue that masculinity was stylized and re-stylized by gay men differently in gay bars, bathhouses, clubs, parks, alleyways, gyms, and public washrooms.[4] These spaces were constantly alternating in meaning as gay-friendly places or places of potential violence.[5] In their discussions of space and place, *TBP*'s editorial collective articulated to readers the excitement and risks of cruising in public, as well as the consequences of being caught in the many gay bars and bathhouse raids throughout the 1970s and 1980s. More broadly, the editorial collective turned *TBP* into a resource for navigating the physical and social spaces of Toronto. They did so by mapping out the city for readers and by discussing the gendered and sexual politics of parks, bars, bathhouses, and gyms. These efforts helped the editorial collective triangulate the relationship between space, gender, and sexuality in Toronto. Being openly gay may have allowed men to avoid dangerous situations and have a support system in the community, but for those who were closeted, understanding which spaces were available, including anonymous public spaces, was paramount.

While the editorial collective helped establish a framework for navigating Toronto's gay and lesbian establishments, they did remain sceptical of the purpose of these same bars and bathhouses. According to historian Tom Warner, there existed an "anti-ghetto theme … in the pages of *The Body Politic*.[6] In the second issue of *TBP*, David Newcome and Paul Pearce called for the end to the "exploitation of gays by the club and bar owners." Meanwhile, they praised the Community Homophile Association of Toronto (CHAT) for establishing a gay recreation centre for "people who find the sexually aggressive nature of the now existing ghetto unpalatable." Many collective members also expressed concern over the straight ownership of gay bars. Newcome and Pearce argued that, "The majority of the businessmen who feed off the gay community show their complete lack of concern for the plight of the people they serve by refusing to take advantage of their position as prominent and influential members of the business community to in any way change societies attitudes towards gays."[7] The sentiment continued during *TBP*'s publication with Ken Popert arguing in 1978 that while commercialized gay culture (bars, discotheques, and baths) "summons a collectivity into being – it mobilizes people and brings them together for someone's profit."[8] These were unsurprising critiques from a collective who were deeply rooted in anti-capitalist and Marxist ideologies. Additionally, straight ownership of bars was scrutinized because it went against the maxim of the collective: "The liberation of homosexuals can only be the work of homosexuals themselves."[9]

The concerns among the editorial collective regarding the exploitation in bars and bathhouses continued throughout the 1970s and into the early 1980s. *TBP* member Michael Riordon argued in 1977 that the higher ratio of bathhouses to bars in Toronto suggested "a socially-repressed Gay male population."[10] In another critique of the ghetto in 1983, *TBP* writer David Townsend argued that despite being "an important tool in our socialization as gays," bars "encouraged the alcoholism of some; they've exacerbated the loneliness and alienation of those for whom they don't work."[11] Despite the collective's scepticism of the capitalist motivations of bar and bathhouse owners, they simultaneously raised funds from these same establishments to meet the financial demands of a grassroots newspaper.

Guides to bars and bathhouses were necessary since that is where many gay men went. In my interview with *TBP* editor Tim McCaskell, he recalled:

> [t]here was always this feeling that this is where most people go and people need to know this stuff. It hadn't been developed theoretically. Popert did later in the early '80s when he talked about the bars and the baths being to the community what factories were to the working class. The place where we are actually constituted. There was always a sense that we have to provide this information to the community. That [it] would be crazy not to.[12]

The importance of gay bars was stressed by editor Ken Popert in 1982, who seemingly contradicted his previous message around capitalist exploitation. He wrote, "[b]ars and baths are to the gay movement what factories are to the labour movement: the context in which masses of people acquire a shared sense of identity and the ability to act together for the common good."[13] Popert's sentiments towards gay bars demonstrate the importance of these spaces in the creation and evolution of gay sensibilities and the need to have physical spaces in Toronto. His comments also reflect the influence of working-class neo-Marxism on lesbian and gay activist thinking in the early 1980s. The ideological importance placed on class and space in the gay community has informed gay and lesbian social histories, such as *Boots of Leather, Slippers of Gold*, whereby Elizabeth Kennedy and Madeline Davis argue that working-class bars not only contributed to the homophile movement but "were the central institution of resistance."[14] The editorial collective recognized that despite being a forum of gay liberation, they could also provide gay men with a tangible sense of community by compiling a comprehensive list of places in Toronto. Yet, the ultimate conundrum remained: *TBP* sought to inform and educate gay men and women on police tactics of violence and entrapment while knowing that the newspaper was read by those same police services.

To prevent gay men from being arrested or accosted by plainclothes police officers, the editorial collective dedicated a significant amount of energy and time discussing entrapment strategies used by police. At the same time, Gary Kinsman and Patrizia Gentile have extensively documented police efforts to read lesbian and gay literature in *The Canadian War on Queers*. They note that the Royal Canadian Mounted Police (RCMP) regularly "conducted surveillance of and collected announcements of gay dances and meetings."[15] In addition, RCMP "O" division files demonstrate surveillance and collection of material from gay organizations, such as the University of Toronto Homophile

Association, where they documented newsletters, meetings, and the approximate number of dance attendees.[16] The collective understood that police were using plainclothes officers and monitoring liberationist meetings. This meant staying ahead of police information and educating members of the community on how to evade police harassment and observation, as well as safer practices when cruising for sex.

Finally, *TBP*'s role as a community builder is all the more impressive and important given that Toronto's gay "village" was only beginning to take shape in the 1970s and early 1980s. Toronto's "Pride Week" first began in 1971 as a picnic on Toronto Island, eventually moving to Queen St. in 1974, and finally taking place around the Church St. and Wellesley St. intersection in 1981 following the largest set of police-led bathhouse raids in Toronto's history, referred to as Operation Soap.[17] The gay village – centred around Church St. and Wellesley St. – reflected the complicated relationship between sexual identities, gender performances, and space. Geographer Catherine Jean Nash argues that "The historical evolution of Toronto's gay village has to do with complex and unpredictable power relations ordering and reordering association between contested identities and places."[18] For example, the increasing number of gym advertisements appearing in the *TBP* by the late 1970s was not just a reflection of gyms catering to gay men and gay male financial resources but also represented the growth of macho style. Bodybuilding was part of an effort to stylize the gay male body as macho and, in some cases, counter notions that the gay male body was either weak or, in the early 1980s, debilitated by HIV/AIDS. In my interview with Ken Popert, he recalled, "I think a lot of guys built their bodies because it's the only thing they can do to make themselves stronger in the world."[19] Editorial content and commercial advertisements for gyms and bodybuilding emphasized the relationship between the muscular, athletic body and gym culture for gay male readers of *TBP*.

Toronto's Gay Spots

The urban centre of Toronto offered a variety of spaces that were conducive to gay sexual pleasure. *TBP* writer Amerigo Marras contended that the vibrancy of gay and lesbian culture was the result of the anonymity, support, and sheer number of lesbian and gay men found in urban centres, such as Toronto. The urban cores of cities were also a direct contrast to the spread-out suburban developments rapidly cropping up at this time. Marras viewed suburbs as sexually restrictive because they represented state control of social interaction: "It is part of the game to believe in a static society and so, for the slave to remain a slave; in this case of suburban living, it is part of the game to train people to maintain the state of things, denying both personal individuality and need for socio-sexual interactions among human beings."[20] Similarly, historian George Chauncey stresses the significance of the urban environment in developing gay male identities with his argument that "Only large cities had the social and spatial complexity necessary for the development of an extensive and partially commercialized gay subculture."[21] By their very nature, cities were designed to be the birthplace of a modern gay identity.

TBP's editorial collective recognized early on that newcomers to the city of Toronto might need help on where to go and where to meet other members of the queer community. *TBP* writers David Newcome and Paul Pearce even considered back alleys, bathhouses, nightclubs, gyms, and sex shops as parts of the "gay ghetto." Writing in *TBP*'s second issue (1972), they argued that "[t]he gay ghetto doesn't just include the bars, clubs, and baths. The ghetto is the whole so-called scene in Toronto. People go to some dark corner in a park, or go to some washroom, or walk down a certain part of a street, these are all part of the ghetto as well."[22] For the collective, Toronto's urban core was essential to the formation of gay culture, offering gay men opportunities and spaces to socialize, engage in sexual activity, and establish a community.

The editorial collective helped gay men and, less frequently, lesbians navigate the city by providing gay guides to major Canadian cities or by fielding calls from curious newcomers to the city.[23] For instance, in 1973, John Scythes wrote "Toronto's Gay Spots" (Figure 3.1), offering to help gay men locate spaces in the downtown area (bars, bathhouses, parks, and washrooms) that were conducive for sexual engagement. From bars, bathhouses, and restaurants to clubs and parks, "gay spots" included private and public spaces – many of which were commercial enterprises advertising in *TBP*. However, these spaces could not necessarily be classified as "safe," nor were they all strictly sexual. For example, the University of Toronto Homophile Association (#13), Glad Day Bookshop (#16), and the Community Homophile Association of Toronto (#18) provided, more or less, safe spaces for gay men, while not necessarily being sexual. In contrast, Scythes noted Yonge Street around Dundas and Bloor (#7) and the front of the YMCA on College (#9) as being particularly sexual spaces by explicitly referencing "cruising."[24]

The list of commercial venues in Scythes' map and their subsequent advertisements in later *TBP* issues were new sources of revenue for the

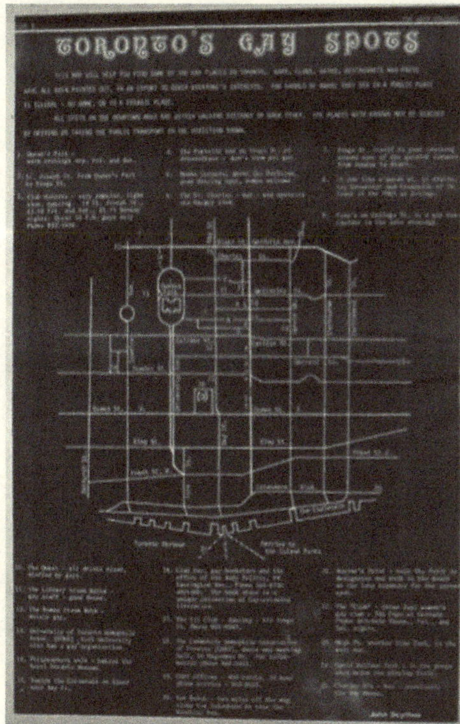

Figure 3.1 Map detailing all gay and gay-friendly spaces in the city. Illustrator: unknown. John Scythes, "Toronto's Gay Spots," *The Body Politic* 7, Winter 1973, 6. Image provided courtesy of Pink Triangle Press.

collective. Initially, only Glad Day Bookshop on 4 Kensington Avenue published an advertisement in the same issue as Scythes' map. Recall that many bars and bathhouses listed did not advertise in *TBP* during its formative years because of the collective's anti-capitalist standpoint and questions by establishment owners of the newspaper's readership size. However, this changed once *TBP* proved to be a sustainable publication with a sizeable reader base by the mid-1970s.

As a testament to the importance of spatially mapping parts of urban Canada, the editorial collective included maps of Montreal in late 1973, Toronto in 1974, and Halifax in 1978.[25] Unlike Scythes' Toronto map, the Montreal and Halifax maps categorized and differentiated public spaces from commercial establishments. The map of Halifax also supplemented a larger guide of gay establishments and cruising spots in Atlantic Canada. It featured two detailed editorials describing meeting spaces and cruising spots for men who were attending the sixth annual National Gay Conference held in 1978. The Halifax guide's editorials demonstrated a greater effort by the collective to strike a balance between political news and cultural information, such as effective cruising practices in different Canadian cities. However, *TBP* remained focused on Toronto during its publication. This emphasis was notably conveyed with the creation of the Out in the City section in 1978 – a forum dedicated to the arts and nightlife in Toronto – and evidence that Toronto readers were the primary focus and audience of *TBP*.

The Aesthetics of Desire and Exclusion in Gay Bars and Bathhouses

As the Mr. Club of Canada contest of 1973 at the Carriage House Hotel, and its winner, Rod Polich, signified: gay bars were spaces where the male body, particularly the macho body, was shown off in homoerotic and campy ways. Bathhouses similarly put masculinity on display for consumption. For instance, Club Baths at 231 Mutual Street in Toronto contained spaced-out rooms that allowed patrons to cruise and lounge, but they were forced to the basement to meet in the steam room or sauna (Figure 3.2). Men navigated these spaces in unique ways, using the various passageways of the bathhouse for sexual proclivities. The exhibitionist display of a bathhouse patron's masculinity is remarkably detailed in the excerpts of a series of letters to Herb Spiers by an unnamed young man visiting Toronto from southern Ontario in 1974.

After attending dances, bars, and a drag show, the young man's weekend trip culminated in a trip to an unnamed bathhouse. Spiers had given him a tour of the place, which his companion expressed gratitude for, "because omitting it would be like omitting the gay scene," in his words. Initially, he wrote of being "shocked at first by the small rooms where guys lay exposed with the door open, and others strolled down the halls examining them like a product they were pondering upon whether to buy."[26] Yet, the young man paid careful attention to the etiquette of the bathhouse, including how men motioned others in the hallway to come into their rooms. While the men put themselves on display for others, it was also noted that certain rooms were darker, allowing for greater anonymity. The importance of anonymity in bathhouse culture should not be understated. While many men enjoyed the exhibitionism of the open rooms, others preferred a more private and discreet encounter – the young man included. The darker rooms provided a level of privacy that was not available in the more open areas of the bathhouse and allowed men to explore their sexuality in more comfortable ways. Indeed, the young man noted in his final letter that

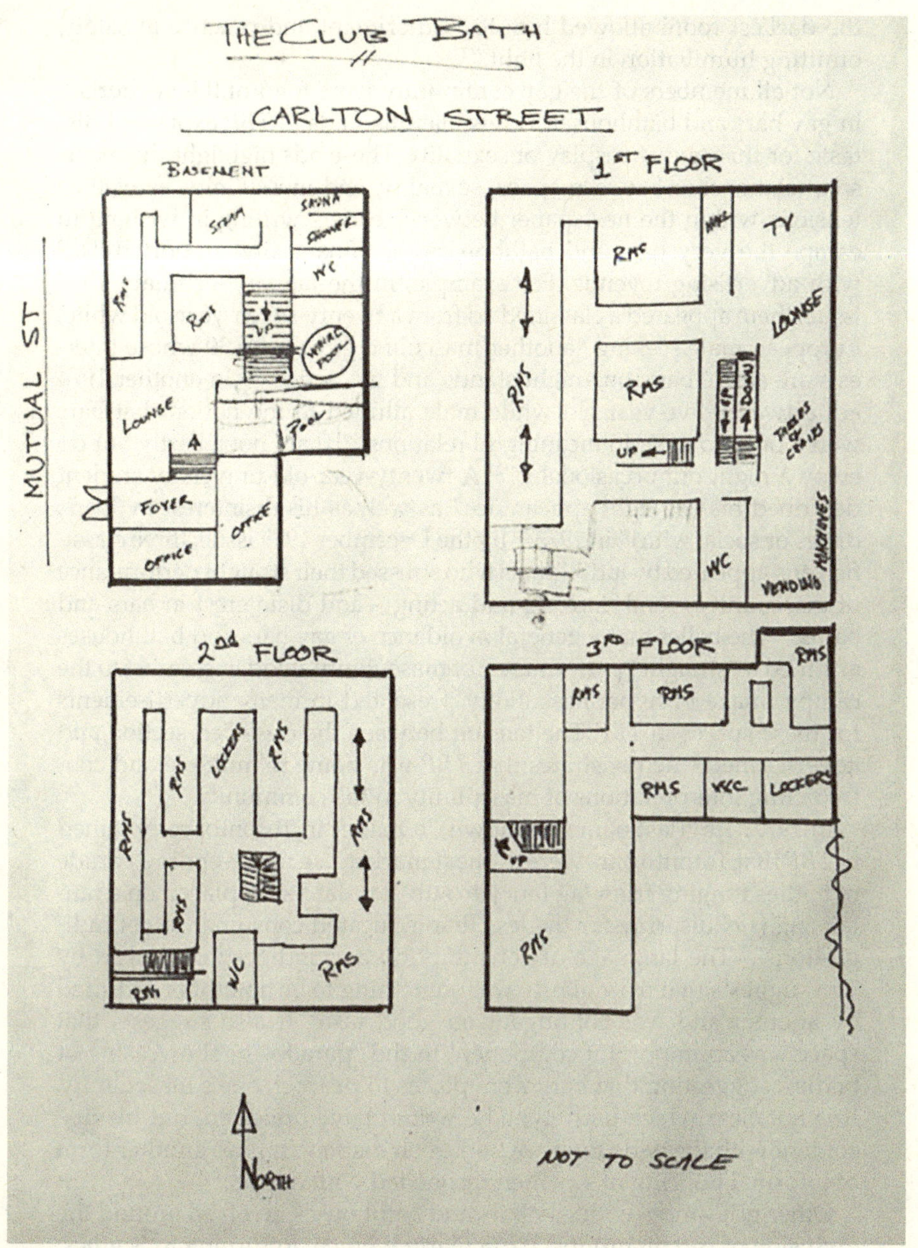

Figure 3.2 Drawing of Club Baths, undated. Illustrator: unknown. Courtesy of the ArQuives, Club Baths of Toronto vertical file.

the darkest room allowed him to "experiment and practise in safety, omitting humiliation in the light."[27]

Not all members of the gay community were fond of the voyeurism in gay bars and bathhouses. A few classified ads in *TBP* expressed distaste for this campy display of sexuality. These ads highlight the recursive relationship between space, sexuality, and masculinity, as well as tensions within the newspaper between readers writing in wishing to escape the very bars and bathhouses that financially supported *TBP* with advertising revenue. For example, in the January–February 1974 issue, there appeared a classified ad from a twenty-seven-year-old white, European male seeking "another masculine guy under 30 whose interests are above bars, one-night stands and gay scene."[28] In another 1974 ad, a twenty-five-year-old white male alluded to the notion that bars were not conducive to meaningful relations: "[I] am not a barfly but do enjoy a night out occasionally."[29] A twenty-year-old university student described his "straight appearance" as well as his disinterest in "bars, drugs or social whirl" in 1975.[30] By the December 1975 issue, three classified ads appeared by individuals who stressed their straight performance of masculinity – both looking and acting – and disinterest in bars and baths.[31] The belief that a general avoidance of gay bars and bathhouses affirmed a "straight" performance of masculinity stood in contrast to the campy image of hypermasculinity presented in many advertisements for these spaces in *TBP*. The tension between the classified section and advertisements demonstrates that *TBP* was home to multiple and contradicting interpretations of masculinity in the community.

In 1977, Tim (last name unknown), a reader in Toronto, complained to *TBP* that Toronto bars were a "meat market ... a never-ending parade of bodies ranging from fag fancy to sub-standard slut, placed on a tantalising [*sic*] disarray for the less than educated consumer to get indigestion."[32] The language of consumption and indigestion evoked by Tim suggests that masculinity was something to be bought or acquired by another and was contingent on good taste. It also suggests that space was an important component in the "parade" or showcasing of bodies, suggesting that bars were places to peacock one's masculinity. It is not clear which body type he would have preferred, but his discontent with the wide range of bodies on display implies another form of informal policing of gay men reconciled with desire.

Other grievances with gay bars and bathhouses revolved around the exclusion of certain groups, particularly women. Returning to Scythes' 1973 map, he described some venues as "guys only," such as Club Manatee on 14 St. Joseph Street, or the Parkside Tavern on Yonge Street at Breadalbane, which had a "men's room all gay."[33] These spaces were not only advertised as gay friendly but also partially or exclusively male-friendly. For instance, Jo-Jo's, a discotheque in Toronto, had at one point in the early 1970s excluded lesbians based on their appearance and dress – the evidence being that the editorial collective noted in August 1976 that the bar was no longer banning lesbians from wearing jeans.[34] Meanwhile, there were no dress restrictions on men. The rationale for the ban, according to the manager, was that lesbians who wore jeans were stereotypically "butches" and known to start fights in the gay bars.[35] Concerns around butch women, as gender theorist Jack Halberstam argues, is a result of "cultural anxiety about the potential effects of femaleness and masculinity."[36] This means that females are expected to act out scripted notions of female docility. Identifying and excluding women based on an aesthetic (jeans) – and assuming that to mean aggressiveness – suggests that categories of lesbians, such as "butches," was partly based on stereotypes of butch-femme clothing. Furthermore, Jo-Jo's dress policy is evidence that an individual's aesthetic presentation could result in people's exclusion from particular queer spaces.

Despite John Allec and Edna Barker writing in their 1982 guide of Toronto bars that "screening at the door is rare," they did admit that "[m]ost gay men's bars in Toronto tend to attract particular segments of the community."[37] Styles of gay male masculinity were addressed in Allec and Barker's description of costumed gay male bars in Toronto. They described The Barn, located on 83 Granby Street, as a "leather and western, casual stand-up bar and disco."[38] For gay men looking for dinner and a hotel with their leather and denim bar, 18 East (renamed The Tool Box in 1983), named after its location on 18 Eastern Avenue, was advertised as the place to be.[39] Finally, The Outpost on 319 Jarvis Street was described as popular for "any gay man even faintly interested in denim and leather." The popularity of leather and denim bars by the summer of 1982 speaks to the development of gay bars based on the proliferation of macho style. Leather and denim were one way that macho style could be re-envisioned by gay men seeking to define masculinity on their terms while also reinforcing a group identity within the gay male community.

Efforts to establish themed bars that catered to a specific subculture of the gay community were not without their consequences, however. Toronto-based activist Danny Cockerline found out in 1984 that the Toronto gay bar Cornelius, located at 579 Yonge Street, did not take kindly to transgressions of gender. Cockerline complained to readers of *TBP* that he was evicted from Cornelius for wearing eye makeup. "Guys aren't supposed to wear makeup, only girls are," said the macho "muscle-bound he-man" who asked him to leave. Despite being dressed in "men's overalls, running shoes and a military haircut,"

Cockerline's eye makeup was a transgression of gender, something that was becoming increasingly unacceptable at Cornelius and many other bars in the city. Following the lead of Chaps (leather bar) and their campaign against "new wavers" – those who experimented with gender – in the summer of 1983, gay bar Boots required "men in men's clothing and women in women's clothing." Meanwhile, Club 101 began refusing women who looked like "working-class dykes," according to Cockerline. He attributed exclusionary practices in bars to patriarchal and capitalist expectations of gender *within* the community. Cornelius, like so many other gay establishments, profited off a particular image of masculinity through advertising and catering to a macho clone clientele. If exclusionary practices around gender were informed by financial profit, then gay capitalism was a fundamental component in the maintenance and proliferation of queer patriarchal ideas of masculinity at this time. In Cockerline's words, these types of practices would "sanitize the image of gay people."[40]

Feeling disillusioned by the presence of ads for these establishments in *TBP*, Cockerline resigned from the paper in late 1983. He wrote in his resignation letter, "I do not like to have my sexuality and my maleness defined for me by gay capitalism any more than by straight ones."[41] Exposing these policies also contributed to the editorial collective's ideological stance that conformity to mainstream expectations – particularly gender – mired the vibrancy of the gay and lesbian community. Cockerline would continue, "The strategy of 'good' gays policing 'bad' gays must be seen for what it is: a recipe for self-oppression that offers all of us – the 'respectable' and the 'dirty and perverse' alike – the quickest route back to the closet."[42] Concern that gays were policing one another, particularly within gay establishments, was not only alarming but reiterated the consequences of appropriating conventional understandings of gender in the community. Not only was macho style readily apparent in the community at this point, but its aesthetic meant those who did not conform to butch presentations of masculinity risked being alienated altogether.

Indeed, Cockerline equated the exclusion of anyone who was gender non-conforming to the marginalization of drag culture. Transgressions of gender performance were only acceptable if "confined to the stage or the video monitor," in his words.[43] The restrictions on drag reverberate with Viviane Namaste's contemporary examination of trans people in the queer community. In her book *Invisible Lives* (2000), Namaste argues, "If drag queens are forced to remain within a space clearly designated for performance, transsexuals experience a similar staging within lesbian and gay male communities."[44] The actions of bar owners were particularly alarming for Cockerline, because bars were

Hot Spots: Toronto's Summer of '82

What to do on those hot summer days and nights in Toronto? If you're a tourist, it's a little hard to get a handle on what's going on, so we've drawn up some highlights you might not want to miss.

Any sunny day will find many gay people heading to **Hanlan's Point**, the gay beach at the far end of Toronto Island. Grab the ferry at the foot of Bay Street (bring a bike if you can). On the "mainland" is **Kew Beach**, reached by a very pleasant walk south from the Queen St East streetcar line (see Beaches). When you're bored with baking in the sun, take a walk east along the boardwalk. If you're hungry and want more than hotdogs, stroll up to Queen St to sample some of its casual eating spots — **The Beach Café, The Beehive, The Palm**.

You can spend a fun afternoon watching the gay **baseball teams** on sunny Saturdays and Sundays from 11 am to 6:30 pm, on the diamond to the north on the east side of Riverdale Park. There are usually a few women participating.

Another way to spend Saturday afternoon is strolling up and down Yonge Street from Bloor to College Sts — chances are you'll see some familiar faces from the night before. Drop into **Return to Sender** (628 Yonge) for the latest in postcards, and look through **Glad Day Bookshop** for lesbian and gay magazines, books and records (648 Yonge, 2nd floor). Then get a sidewalk table at the **Café New Orleans** (Yonge & St Joseph) — the food's dreadful but the sidewalk traffic is always entertaining.

Unfortunately, fun spots for lesbians are few and far between, but of particular interest are **Together** (437 Church St) with a mostly younger crowd, and **The Cameo Club** (Friday and Saturday nights, $4 cover) at 95 Trinity St, for a casual evening of dancing and pool. **The Mainstage** (251 King St E) is apparently beginning to attract women as well. One recommended and handy place for women-watching is at the south end of **The Eaton Centre**, on the benches under the Michael Snow geese sculptures.

The Toronto Women's Bookstore (85A Harbord St) is a must for any visitor. With a good selection of feminist and lesbian reading material, it also serves as a kind of women's community meeting place. Check out the bulletin board or ask one of the helpful women working there about upcoming events. If you need an afternoon refresher break after that, drop into one of the nearby cafés on Harbord St — **Harbord St Café, Major Roberts** or **Boulevard Café. Free Times Café** (320 College St near Spadina) is another place popular with lesbians.

Most gay men's bars in Toronto tend to attract particular segments of the community, but screening at the door is rare (or at least unofficial), so feel free to roam.

Boots (592 Sherbourne St) always manages to fill up its huge lounge area with a broad variety of men. **The Parkside** (530 Yonge St) is fun for a few early evening drafts and a Saturday stopover is almost a Toronto institution. **The Outpost** (379 Jarvis St) has been the hit of the last few months for any man even faintly interested in denim and leather, but its lack of outdoor space may be a serious drawback in the summer. **Buddy's** (370 Church St) consistently draws large crowds of collegiate and post-collegiate types, and you really should drop into **Les Cavaliers** (418 Church St) next door for a more relaxed atmosphere — join in the chorus of "I'm Gonna Wash That Man Right Outta My Hair" around the piano.

Sunday afternoons, peaking about 4:30 pm, will find all sorts of men heading south to King Street East to do the seven block shuffle between the outdoor patios of **18 East** (official home of the leather clubs) and the **Albany Tavern** (base for the baseball teams). Be prepared for a bit of *déjà vu*. Cheap hamburgers are available at both. Later on, until 11 pm (last call on Sundays), the crowds drift uptown to the small dance floor at the **Barn** at 83 Granby St (no cover charge — great music).

Dudes (10 Breadalbane St) is the place to go every night after the other bars have closed down. It's unanimously condemned as an "attitude bar," but it's usually full, nonetheless. Discos generally get off the ground near midnight, except for **The Manatee** at 11A St Joseph St ($4 cover, men only), not licensed for liquor, which draws the under-18 set early on. **Charly's**, above the St Charles ($3 Friday, $4 Saturday, men only), and **Stages**, above the Parkside ($6, mixed), can usually guarantee good music and lighting. A devoted following flocks to Stages at midnight every Sunday to greet the beginning of the week. Friday promises to be a hot night as well.

The Rivoli (334 Queen St W) has a wide variety of events which appeal to the New Wave and art crowds around Queen Street West, including lots of gay people at the Pan-Am dances every Tuesday night, 11 pm to 4 am. **Twilight Zone** (185 Adelaide St W) and **The Voodoo Club** (5 St Joseph St) draw similar crowds. **The Quest** and **Katrina's**, both mixed, attract younger crowds eager to show off the latest fashions. The Quest is also popular with Asian men.

Up-to-date information on coming events can be gotten from the 923-GAYS recorded message line, or by calling the TAG information line, 964-6600. Women can also phone the Lesbian Phoneline, 960-3249.

Enjoy the summer!

John Allec and Edna Barker

Figure 3.3 Cartoon complementing John Allec and Edna Barker, "Hot Spots: Toronto's Summer of 82," *The Body Politic* 85, July–August 1982, 22. Illustrator: Paul Aboud. Image provided courtesy of Pink Triangle Press.

some of the few spaces in which many gay men could be openly gay. By restricting the image of gay culture to "masculine 'normal-looking' men and excluding the queer-looking ones," bars were spaces that regulated gender performances and styles in the gay community.[45] The presence of Cockerline's article in *TBP* also indicates efforts by the collective to illuminate these discriminatory practices as a testament to deeper heteronormative influences informing gay culture. His experience exemplified the collective's belief that macho style and desire for the macho clone was bringing with it a new form of queer patriarchy.

Restrictions on gender performance and the exclusion of non-conforming individuals from gay spaces were particularly alarming because bars and bathhouses were some of the few venues where gay men could be open about their sexuality. Bars and clubs were seen as safe havens where gay men could be themselves and socialize with others who shared their experiences. By imposing rigid gender norms and excluding those who did not conform, these spaces became more exclusive and further marginalized some gay men who did not fit the mould of what a man should look or act like. For some men, however, being seen at a gay bar or bathhouse was an immediate indication of their homosexuality, and they engaged in more subvert strategies to meet men, such as cruising in public. Cruising did not come with the same risks of exclusion that Cockerline faced, but it did present challenges. One such challenge was the constant risk of rejection, which could leave one's ego bruised and battered. Another was the danger of being entrapped by the police, arrested, or subjected to violence. Gay men were compelled to be vigilant and cautious while cruising, taking care not to draw too much attention to themselves or make any missteps that would lead to disaster.

Cruising to Win

Cruising was a part of the quintessential gay male experience for many men in the 1970s and 1980s. Activist, artist, and writer John Grube described cruising in *TBP* in 1983 as "a fundamental social skill required by all gay men. It's as basic to a functional gay life as calculus is to engineers or drawing is to artists."[46] Historian Steven Maynard argues that homosexual identities were spatially contingent and cities conducive to what he describes as the "journey to sex" long before *TBP* and gay liberation.[47] In Maynard's words, the journey to sex helped forge "what has been described as the most 'ubiquitous form' of the homosexual subculture, one revolving around 'public' sex in parks, laneways, and lavatories" at the turn of the twentieth century.[48] However, as historian George Chauncey notes in his 1994 monograph *Gay New York* – a germinal work in queer urban history – cruising historically "referred to a streetwalker's search for partners before it referred to a gay man's."[49] According to Chauncey, the appropriation of cruising as a gay male activity involved a set of stylistic codes and practices of gender and sexuality to indicate sexual availability and viability as a partner. As a result, cruising became inextricably linked to individual self-presentation and the identities of those who cruised. Cruising was not simply about seeking out sexual encounters; it was also a way for gay men to signal their presence and desire to others in a world that shunned them. Through cruising, gay men asserted their right to exist and acquire recognition from one another in a society that sought to deny them the pleasure of sex.

Cruising was not limited to the bars, bathhouses, alleyways, parks, and washrooms of urban Canada. In 1972, Hugh Brewster described the similarities between visiting a discreet gay bar in his hometown (unknown) in Ontario and his life back in Toronto. The two tables that made up this small makeshift gay bar in the "Ladies and escorts" room of a small hotel in his hometown held the same codes, behaviours, and conversations that mirrored similar conduct found in Toronto's bars and bathhouses. Brewster recalled "the same conversation, the same jargon, 'tricks, butch, queen, etc.,['] and the same desperation" in the back room of the bar. Simultaneously, the "secret side glances at attractive young men were carefully veiled, as they knew from experiences that the response was usually a punch in the mouth," in his words.[50] The risk of transgressing moral boundaries arguably appealed to many gay men's desire to engage in cruising and possibly a public sexual encounter.

In his analysis of gay life in early twentieth-century London, historian Matt Houlbrook notes that men would cruise using a series of codes and practices that "remained hidden from casual observers, so they [queer men] were thus also invisible to official surveillance."[51] Cruising in this context echoed the class component of men's identities found in Steven Maynard's analysis of Toronto, emphasizing class as a category which separated men who cruised. Houlbrook notes that "[t]his movement [cruising] was often represented by discarding middle-class styles of dress … and disrupting the visual cues of class."[52] Returning to *TBP* and the 1970s, visual cues to cruising developed alongside the stylistic appropriation of working-class culture in the gay community.

During the 1970s, there were a few articles in *TBP* that focused on the clothing of cruising, and they were either humorous, satirical, or both. For example, John Forbes described the use of clothing when cruising in his 1978 satirical article "Hanky Panky." Forbes listed the numerous colours of handkerchiefs and their position in either the left or right back pocket as an indication of what type of sexual "kink" a man was into and whether he preferred to perform said act or have it done to him. The colour black, for example, indicated an interest in S&M culture. On the left side meant that the wearer was a "Heavy S&M, Top" – penetrator – while the right side indicated he was a "Heavy S&M, Bottom" – the penetrated.[53] Even as a satire, Forbes's article demonstrates that there was a system of codes tied to gay men's accessories. These accoutrements facilitated cruising habits for gay men and helped them ostentatiously display their masculinity and sexual habits.

Following Forbes's article, *TBP* reader Amy Groves wrote into the newspaper a few months later arguing that handkerchiefs were essential to promoting sexuality and gender. In her words:

> Gay men have been sporting them for years, without any apparent disasters – but not with the intention of defining their total sexuality. A piece

> of cloth hanging out of someone's back pocket won't do that any more than an ad in *TBP* will tell readers everything there is to know about a given restaurant. The point of a handkerchief is not to analyze, but to advertise.[54]

The use of colour-coded handkerchiefs was also adopted by lesbians, with Mariana Valverde describing the system as offering the opportunity to liberate "women from romantic monogamy, from dependence on one and only one romantic lover or one and only one sexual position; it liberates women from the girl-meets-girl approach to lesbian happiness."[55] Not only did the handkerchief code extend beyond gay men, but it also demonstrated that this system provided a means of communication and expression for members of the queer community. Indeed, Forbes and Valverde described handkerchiefs as a common component in displaying one's sexuality and sexual habits for gay men and women. Despite their popularity, though, the use of handkerchiefs did not receive much coverage or recognition by *TBP* and the editorial collective. Arguably, a lack of coverage of the handkerchief code may have emphasized its discretionary nature, but this would contradict the collective's efforts to help readers navigate gay and lesbian community life. More likely, however, was that the handkerchief code was not discussed widely or acknowledged outside the queer community, and dedicating significant space to the code would have been unproductive.

TBP emphasized the importance of style and clothing when cruising in their review of Lenny Giteck's book *Cruise to Win: A Guide for Gay Men* (1982). This review represented the editorial collective's decision to participate in discussions around the spatial, stylistic, and even racial elements of cruising. Reviewed by Gerry Oxford in his 1983 article "Men Looking at Men Looking at Men," Giteck's book focuses on interviews with fifty gay men about cruising, successful matches, best practices, how to dress, and challenges to the practice. In one interview, an individual named Jeff noted that displaying machismo was done in stylistic ways, where "they'll [men] stand under spotlights, and they'll be wearing tight T-shirts, or tank tops, or they'll have no shirt on at all, and they'll just stand there and flex."[56] Here, clothing is arguably just as important in stylizing the body as flexing is. Highlighting musculature either through tight clothing or by flexing the undressed body was, according to Jeff, fundamental to self-presentation in the gay bar. In addition, Giteck asked psychologist Alan Sable about body stance and cruising, to which Sable responded that there was a sexy stance based on "[t]he conventional image of the sexy man – the Marlboro man – [he] has a closed mouth, narrowed eyes, set jaw, and an aggressive kind of body language. It says the man is strong, powerful, independent, a loner, not emotionally vulnerable."[57] Giteck's emphasis on the posture of the body as part of a man's image harkened to Erving Goffman's concept of body language as an example of a sign-vehicle to indicate one's social presence.[58]

In attempting to discern if Giteck's book was an effective guide, Oxford asked six of *TBP*'s readers to describe their own experiences cruising after reading it. Beginning with his own review, Oxford admitted that the book had its flaws but was a helpful start for gay men because "[w]hat, after all, can be more self-defeating than standing around in a bar trying to meet a man whom you have chosen on the basis of how well he fits his T-shirt, his jeans, or your fantasies?"[59] A theme that resonated with Oxford was the objectification of gay men and the presentation of the gay male body in Giteck's book. The book seemed to reinforce a culture in which men are judged based on their physical appearance and sexual desirability, rather than character or personality. Oxford inferred that the objectification could lead to harmful stereotypes against those who may not fit the idealized gay male image. To address these concerns, the editorial collective believed that cruising codes and practices should be debated and tempered in ways that Giteck failed to do in his book.

Reader Brian Hickey argued that *Cruise to Win* was a guide to flirting not cruising since the myriad forms of cruising described in the book, included "smiling and nodding/winking/waving, appreciative glances at tits, baskets [groins], key-rings and hankies."[60] The importance of how one styled their body and presented themselves when cruising was part of a "*fantasy image*," according to reader Michael Caplan. He acknowledged, however, that he was surprisingly aroused by the touch of "someone whose appearance didn't excite me."[61] Caplan wrote that he was attracted to the individual because the touch formed a visceral connection that allowed him to project his sexual desires and fantasy image onto the person, marking the importance of individual/personal space in both cruising and the shaping of desirability. Finally, Ken Chaplin of St. Catharines admitted that standards for appearance and style dwindle as cruising stretches out over the course of the night: "I watch the clock and lower my standards in terms of looks and brains as the minutes tick towards last call." When considering whether *Cruise to Win* reflected his own experience cruising, Chaplin agreed with Giteck's argument that being rejected desensitized oneself to it over time. However, he acquiesced, "I'm not sure my rubbery ego could stand it!"[62]

The editorial collective's decision to publish six reader responses that far outsized Oxford's own review of *Cruise to Win* is evidence that *TBP* was centred on community conversations relating to a budding gay male culture. This was also a response to accusations that the collective had become too "high-brow." In August 1980, Scott Tucker wrote into *TBP* criticizing Ken Popert's concern in April that year that intellectualism had fallen behind activism in the gay community. Tucker had responded, "The philosophers have only *interpreted* the world, in various ways; the point is to *change* it [emphasis in original]."[63] Meanwhile, the collective had previously reconciled in a meeting in March 1977 that some ex-subscribers felt *TBP* was "too sexual" or "too political (too left)."[64] It was a tough juggling act, to say the least, but reaching out to readers for their thoughts on *Cruise to Win* helped to distance the collective and *TBP* from criticisms of high-brow intellectualism or being out of touch with its readers. It also served the secondary purpose of maintaining the paper as a voice of the community, albeit from a white, largely male perspective.

Finally, it should be noted that most accounts of cruising in Giteck's book ignored the topic of race altogether. The book centred white men as the de facto object of desire. Quan Minh, a Vietnamese reader of *TBP* from Montreal, critiqued the privileged position of white men cruising and argued that cruising was a practice that revolved around "fancy housing and other luxurious things" that only certain men could afford.[65] Another writer, George Xuereb, highlighted how whiteness was contextually defined and relied on continually renegotiated cultural frameworks. Xuereb was picked up at an American disco while on vacation in Puerto Vallarta, Mexico. He described his experience in Mexico as one where he became "more of a Canadian, shedding a lot of my original Mediterranean characteristics" because he had been picked up rather than having to do the cruising. For Xuereb, the exotic space of a disco in Mexico reshaped traditional boundaries of gender and race, whereby he felt "whiter." The connection he makes between feeling more Canadian and "made to feel attractive without having to make the first move" suggests that his race was defined differently in Mexico than in his home of Winnipeg, and that being seen as white or associated with a "white" country in the Global North brought with it a sense of desirability.[66] Moreover, Xuereb's experience demonstrates how race and whiteness played a crucial role in shaping the dynamics of cruising culture and the ways in which desire and attractions were constructed.

The intersection of race and cruising brings to light the contextual nature of cruising as a practice. Minh and Xuereb both offered critiques of the privileged position of white men in cruising, but that did alleviate the risks that came with cruising in public back in Canada. With cruising taking place primarily in public spaces, its pleasures rivalled the dangers posed by police entrapment and homophobic violence. Some of the risks of cruising came from the involvement of "heterosexual" married men. The editorial collective noted in October 1976 that public sex included: "married men [who] came to the parks, older men who saw an orgasm in the park or a washroom as representative of the totality of gay life, young men wracked by guilt for what they feel driven to do, who have not heard of The Body Politic [*sic*]."[67] The occurrence of "straight" men engaging in homosexual acts in washrooms arguably opened a space where police could insert themselves for purposes of entrapment.

Dangers and Disguises

Of all the dangers that public cruising involved, the editorial collective focused the greatest on entrapment and police harassment. Entrapment involved police prosecuting individuals by setting up a situation or environment to induce someone to commit a crime they may have otherwise not committed. Historians have documented police efforts to entrap gay men by luring them with the possibility of sexual pleasure.[68] However, the ways in which style was used by police to entrap gay men remain unexplored. Police posed as gay men or as sexually curious by engaging in flirtatious behaviour and even gesturing towards sexual acts with other men to create a false sense of safety and intimacy. This would often lead to further sexual advances and ultimately an arrest for indecent exposure, gross indecency, or other related offences. The editorial collective paid significant attention to how heterosexual police officers dressed the part of civilians and engaged with a queer style conducive to ensnaring gay men for public sexual acts and subsequently arrest them for gross indecency.[69] The use of style underscores how power and privilege were exercised through cultural practices and symbolic codes – clothing and other stylistic cues that would attract the attention of gay men or at least avoid scrutiny. By appropriating elements of queer style, police officers were able to infiltrate public or queer establishments and use these cultural codes against the community.

Since 1971, *TBP* had reported on instances of plainclothes officers arresting gay men. Dave Scott of the *Toronto Daily Star* reported on police entrapment of gay men in High Park and the police spying on people in the park's washrooms by "peering through a baseboard grate."[70] The police in this situation closed off a stall in the washroom and placed a fake ventilation grill to allow them to observe and effectively control gay men's activity in the cubicle next to it.[71] These efforts facilitated gay sex only to subsequently punish it. Indeed, *TBP* reported that Toronto Police were using a glory hole at the Greenwin Square shopping mall and apartment complex near Bloor and Sherbourne between April and June 1979 to entrap gay men.[72] Plainclothes officers from Toronto's 51 Division had been reportedly "arresting gay men on an almost daily basis" at this location.[73] However, the Toronto Police dismantled the spy post in the Greenwin Square washroom after significant pressure from the gay community and city politicians.[74]

In June 1972, then president of the Community Homophile Association of Toronto (CHAT) and occasional writer for *TBP,* George Hislop advised readers thinking of cruising: "Don't grope strangers (introduce yourself first)."[75] Reports on entrapment by plainclothes police officers highlighted the potential consequences of desiring traditional performances of masculinity, particularly from those who passed for heterosexual. The desire to conform to queer patriarchal standards could make individuals more vulnerable to being targeted by plainclothes police officers, who would pose as gay men to lure and arrest them. Indeed, on 5 March 1973, Hislop informed readers of *The Globe and Mail* that "They [police] represent themselves as being interested in homosexual activity, and when approached they arrest the person."[76] According to Robin Hardy of *TBP*, touching a plainclothes officer in this context was referred to as "assault."[77] *TBP* continued to post warnings of entrapment in local news, with some messages as simple as: "Gays cruising in Toronto park areas should take precautions against being entrapped."[78] However, the collective framed cruising as an individual issue, one that required vigilance and self-awareness of the potential risks associated with public sex.

In the context of police entrapment, "passing" referred to two distinct kinds of performances. First, police had to pass as ordinary citizens to observe and take photographs of gay men and lesbians at rallies, washrooms, bars, bathhouses, and various other social functions. They had to blend in and appear non-threatening to avoid arousing suspicion among those they were observing. This kind of passing relied on the officers' ability to blend in with the crowd and appear unremarkable. The second kind of passing involved plainclothes police officers who entrapped gay men or infiltrated and raided bars and bathhouses. To enter these venues without raising suspicion, they had to pass as homosexual or at least sexually fluid. This involved adopting certain mannerisms, language, and dress that would allow them to avoid detection. These plainclothes police officers blurred the line between performing homoerotic acts on behalf of a heterosexual state and being read as homosexual or having their sexuality questioned by gay men.[79]

During the entrapment process, plainclothes officers appropriated a form of queer style that embodied components of macho style. Police co-opted macho style as "paraphernalia of state power," in the words of Anne McClintock. While McClintock examines S&M (sadism and masochism) and fetishism in the late Victorian era, her understanding of S&M and its use of uniforms as a visible reversal of social power and staging of hierarchy lends itself to how police turned macho style into a threat to the very community in which it emerged from – transforming public pleasure into public punishment.[80] The theatrical performance of plainclothes officers enticing gay men in public washroom facilities was not homosexual, however, because these officers were enforcing heterosexual norms prescribed by the state.[81]

In *TBP*'s very first issue, writer Rombus Hube reported that the Toronto Police's morality squad was "cleverly disguised as greasers" while patrolling Philosopher's Walk, a pedestrian pathway between Queen's Park and Bloor Street known for its gay cruising.[82] The appropriation of greaser style (a rock and roll aesthetic popular in the 1950s) provided the Toronto Police with the opportunity to disguise their officers for reconnaissance and potentially appeal to gay men. Police were enticing homosexuals by acting as "agents provocateurs," a term that became a common reference for officers engaged in tactics of entrapment.[83]

The theatrics of entrapment had become so pronounced that they even permeated the cultural fabric of gay life in the form of the musical *In Gay Company* at Toronto's Teller's Cage in 1975. While the show offered an understanding of which washrooms of the Toronto Subway were dangerous for cruising, Hannon charged the musical with trivializing gay experiences by failing "to give any hint of whatsoever [that] is the human misery attending the many arrests which occur in washrooms like the one in the Bloor-Yonge subway station." Hannon continued, "[e]ach verse provides a surprisingly comprehensive guide to the washrooms in Toronto that *are* worth cruising, and ends with the big-eyed/big smiles injuction [*sic*] to avoid the TTC. With a warning like that, the worst you'd expect in the transit toilets is a long wait."[84] He believed that cruising in the play catered to a straight and gay audience who needed to be reassured that the gay urban lifestyle was in no way superior to the suburbs. Hannon was critical of the play, defining gay male sexuality as promiscuous and dangerous. According to Hannon, *In Gay Company* did not cover the profound impact that cruising-related arrests had on an individual's life, but it did shed light on how police officers utilized queer aesthetics as a means of controlling sexual behaviour. The play's use of washrooms reflected the desirability of risqué sexual encounters in public and the unease about the safety of bars and bathhouses following ongoing police raids throughout the 1970s.

By 1975, there were widespread cases of undercover police officers entrapping gay men in public washrooms, parks, bathhouses, and bars across Canada. That year, Hannon referred to the increasing number of arrests and entrapments as the "war on sin."[85] The arrest of a young man attempting to pick up an undercover police officer in Allan Gardens park, as well as reports of entrapment in the washroom of the St. Charles Tavern on Yonge St. and the park along Philosopher's Walk, signalled that the Toronto police and their morality squad were escalating their harassment.[86] In the July–August 1975 issue, *TBP* reported that Montreal undercover police had already arrested "40 ... in the washroom of Place Ville Marie" as part of an effort to crack down on deviance before the 1976 Montreal Olympics. With the imminence of the world at its doorstep, the Montreal Urban Community Police raided gay bathhouses, including Aquarius on 4 February 1975. They charged thirty-five men with being "found-ins in a bawdy house."[87] John Blacklock and Paul Trollope of *TBP* noted that the Montreal Police used undercover officers "in the guise of ordinary bath patrons."[88] In another instance, Vancouver plainclothes police had arrested approximately "100 gays on morals charges primarily in the English Bay area" between January and May of 1977.[89] These reports in *TBP* served as both a reminder of the disguised dangers that lurked within parks, bars, and bathhouses, as well as the secondary consequences of these raids: discouraging patrons from ever coming back.[90]

The increase in arrests of gay men by undercover police in 1975 led John Towndrow – a pseudonym – to publish an important reflection in *TBP* of his own experience with entrapment at the second-floor men's washroom at the Canadian National Exhibition in Toronto approximately five years prior. Towndrow recalled being lured by a police officer disguised as a "fairly handsome, mid-twenties, husky truck-driver type" who had "made some simulated jack-off movements." While the officer's clothing was not remarkably campy or "queer," the combination of his clothing and actions were part of a style of masculinity performed by police to entrap gay men. Towndrow's description of the officer suggests that he was deliberately performing a certain type of masculinity that would be attractive to gay men. Following the undercover officer engaging in homoerotic actions and successfully luring Towndrow, his uniformed partner arrested Towndrow and charged him with both counselling to commit gross indecency and attempting to procure someone to commit an act of gross indecency. The fact that the police officer was able to successfully lure Towndrow into a trap is evidence of the power of style in policing sexuality. The officer's performance was so convincing that Towndrow was unable to detect any insincerity or duplicity. This underscores the importance of how clothing and behaviour were fundamental to strategies of regulation against the queer community. Towndrow's warning was simple: "don't get caught. That good-looking truck driver may turn out to be a good-looking but repressed, frustrated and not so friendly cop."[91] The rampant homophobia of the Toronto police – evident in their brutality towards the gay and lesbian community – seemingly played into their butch performances of masculinity. This was particularly true for officers who chose to remain in the closet.

When several gay police officers had phoned or written into *TBP* about being gay and on the other side of the law, Michael Riordon responded with an article on the duality between being gay and working for an institution that enforced sexual "normalcy." In the 1978 article "Remember When 'Mounties' Meant the Musical Ride?," police officers who spoke with Riordon seemed to be distressed about punishing gay men for actions they could or would engage in themselves. According to Riordon, they rationalized their actions on the grounds that they worked within a "rigid authoritarian sexually-repressed gruesomely macho situation."[92] Such actions taken by closeted police officers also would have had the benefit of allowing their own sexuality to remain unquestioned and free from reprisal. However, any sympathy for gay police officers struggling with their duties was tempered by the harsh realities of police brutality – a point of contention that continues to reverberate with contemporary concerns around police presence at pride parades and marches.

Riordon used this opportunity to describe how police uniforms grant police officers, who are just citizens, authority and power. He wrote, "Take a constable out of Police Drag and you have a plainclothes policeman. Or, as in a baths raid, a policeman in a towel. Trying desperately to conceal a hard-on with his notebook."[93] His reference to police uniforms as "Police Drag," insinuated that the police uniform was an example of the theatrical display of power and authority granted by clothing – the stylization of power. In addition, Riordon suggested that police officers, even those mildly interested in other men, must subvert their homosexuality or same-sex desire by hiding their "hard-on" while carrying out their duties. Susan Faludi argues that in the postwar period, a "quasi-militarized peacetime economy and a national security state" had ushered in a standard of manhood that reflected the United States – and arguably Canada – as masculine nations.[94] While uniformed police officers embodied the relationship between the state and the policing of sexuality, plainclothes officers could not rely on their uniform to visibly validate their masculinity or heterosexuality.

Police entrapment continued throughout the 1970s and 1980s to include even the most minor of infractions. In June 1982, *TBP* reported that a man was arrested in Toronto's David Balfour Park at night for peeing in a bush. Not only was the man alone, but he had made every attempt to remain hidden. However, two undercover officers had found him and, under suspicion that he was cruising, charged him with "indecent exposure."[95] After reading about this incident, an anonymous reader from San Francisco suggested that *TBP* start a photographic repository of undercover cops. In their letter to the collective, they suggested: "once you have a file of photos of undercover cops, either TBP or an anonymous individual could publish that info – place photos in the usual cruising areas."[96] Such tactics never materialized, but they do demonstrate an active effort by some to address such blatant abuse of power by undercover police.

Other ways in which entrapment was carried out included using *TBP* for purposes of harassment and persecution. While the aforementioned guides to city life published by *TBP* were intended to make navigating urban cities like Toronto easier, they also aided police to more easily access gay and lesbian spaces. Kinsman and Gentile note that the Toronto Municipal Police and the RCMP read lesbian and gay newsletters, newspapers, pamphlets, and posters to acquire the location and time of gay activities.[97] Scythes' map, for example, could help police patrol gay spaces of pleasure and gather intelligence on the gay community. More insidiously, however, there is evidence of police using *TBP*'s classified ads to entrap gay men.

One such example of this form of entrapment was the arrest of Toronto teacher "Bob" – a pseudonym used by the collective – in June 1979 by an undercover police officer. On an undisclosed evening in June, Bob had received a phone call from an unbeknownst police officer named Wally after he had seen Bob's classified ad in *TBP*. After chatting briefly, Bob invited Wally over to his house and proceeded to show him "his little 'dungeon' – a chamber off his bedroom where he kept his toys – leather masks and restraints, whips, chains, [and] pictures of men in leather," according to Hannon.[98] Wally, who was described by Bob as being "in his early thirties, good-looking, tough, maybe a little reticent but certainly not nervous or uneasy," produced his badge and informed Bob that he was under arrest for "keeping a common bawdy house." Hannon's coverage of Bob's house being labelled a bawdy house highlighted the tenuous definition of sexual spaces for gay men at this time.[99] Wally was arrested for an antiquated law despite the two sharing no intimate contact, it being a private residence, and no commercial or financial transaction taking place. Bawdy-house legislation fell under the Criminal Code of Canada and was designed to shut down enterprises involving female sex work, namely, brothels. However, in 1917, it was broadened to "include places habitually resorted to for acts of indecency," which later included gay sexual activity.[100] These laws could be used against gays engaging in consensual sex and were one of the primary means for the state to regulate sexuality and morality in Canada.

In addition to the precariousness of bawdy-house designation, coverage of Bob's arrest reiterated the apparent dangers of police adopting a queer style. It was Bob's desire for "tough" Wally, along with his collection of bondage and sadomasochism (BDSM) paraphernalia and photographs of men in leather, that led to his arrest. Up until this point in time, there had been no reports of personal residences being cited as bawdy houses due to a resident's sexual proclivities. Following Bob's arrest, however, the editorial collective lamented that: "It is not a big step ... to judging any act of lesbian or gay sex indecent, any home where such acts take place a 'bawdy house' – and each one of us a potential 'keeper.'"[101] If places of pleasure such as bathhouses and personal residences could be designated as places of danger, then discussions of the sexual politics of space in Toronto became even more necessary for the livelihoods of gay men. As such, the collective's coverage of Bob's arrest stressed the possibilities of entrapment beyond the scope of alleyways, public washroom facilities, and parks to include private domiciles.

The dangers that underscored cruising in parks, bars, and bathhouses included a series of violent attacks of gays and lesbians outside bars in the mid-to-late 1970s, bathhouse raids, and even murder. In one instance, *TBP* reported a violent attack on two gay men leaving Jo-Jo's discotheque on 12 September 1976.[102] The circumstances of the attack outside Jo-Jo's were never fully delved into by the collective, but it was that charges were never pressed against the assailants once police arrived. While it was noted that the two victims had agreed to forget the incident, less than a year later *The Globe and Mail* published an article suggesting that violence against gay men and lesbians was no longer an issue, particularly for those who performed their appropriate gender roles.[103] According to *TBP*, Jo-Jo's remained a fraught space, with lesbians frequently being escorted out of the bar, sometimes even by the police. Despite reports of arrests and entrapment at bars, bathhouses, and in public washrooms, the continued patronage of these spaces demonstrates how danger can become eroticized in these spaces. Historian Matt Houlbrook contends that "[c]ruising – like public sex – was erotic and exciting because it generated the electric thrill of social and spatial transgression."[104] Yet, *TBP*'s continued coverage around violence and cruising illustrates the changing discussions of space, particularly personal space, with respect to sexuality, gender, safety, and the body.

For *TBP* writer Robin Hardy, it was the murders of fourteen gay men in Toronto between 1975 and 1978 that affirmed the need for gay men to be conscious of the dangers that came with the urban environment. These murders were not committed by one man, nor were the victims linked. Six of the fourteen murders had resulted in arrests or convictions, with those "solved" involving "robbery, fights over payment for sex, and violent assault resulting, unintentionally, in death."[105] While Hardy's summation of the murders was that death was "unpredictable," if anything, these murders were an example of the dangers of societal homophobia in the urban environment.[106] The known victims included: Brian Latocki, Arthur Harold Walkley, Fred Fontaine, James Kennedy, Alexander (Sandy) LeBlanc, William Duncan Robinson, James Taylor, Donald Rochester, and Colin Nicholson. Coverage of these murders and police efforts to find the killer(s) raised questions and commentary in *TBP* about the need for self-defence and the tenuous relationship between space and masculinity for many gay men. However, they also generated discussions around macho style, sexual desirability, safety, and how masculinity is stylized after a particular age. How did these men find themselves in these dangerous positions to begin with?

Titled "Overkill,"[107] Hardy's article began by informing readers of the murder of twenty-four-year-old William Duncan Robinson a few months prior. Last seen on 26 November 1978, Robinson had been heading home from the St. Charles Tavern with a man described as "lanky" with "dark brown greasy hair, sloppy shoulders, large dirty hands and feet, and an offensive body odour." Hardy's description of Robinson's companion was made from various unnamed sources rather than any personal account. His bewilderment that Robinson would go home with such an unappealing man was readily apparent: "Robinson's companion walked clumsily and was scruffy in appearance. It's hard to imagine why anyone would take him home."[108] A neighbour had reported to the police that they had heard a "peculiar hollow noise" from Robinson's apartment in the early hours of 27 November. There had been no indication of anything amiss from the outside of the apartment, but Robinson had not been seen since.

The following day, Robinson was discovered stabbed to death in his apartment.[109]

Hardy's description of the suspect in Robinson's murder was informed by questions of taste and physical attraction. The man heading home with Robinson was described as unappealing; thus, Hardy was baffled as to why Robinson would leave with him in the first place. The suspect's unattractiveness was a point of emphasis for Hardy, suggesting that he may have believed that Robinson's decision to leave with the man was of poor judgment or desperation. This attitude reveals a cultural bias against those who are not conventionally attractive or fit a particular mould. Hardy's comment infers that it would have been much more reasonable or understandable if Robinson had put himself in danger by taking an attractive stranger home. Robinson's murder was part of a larger string of murders towards primarily older gay men in Toronto during the mid-decade, all of which seemed to be entangled with the aesthetics of gay male style to some extent.

On 18 February 1975, Arthur Harold Walkley's roommate discovered him nude and stabbed several times in his back and chest. The killer of the fifty-one-year-old history teacher had even stolen his credit cards.[110] According to John Allan Lee, a sociologist and author of *Getting Sex* (1978), Walkley was an example of why older men were likely victims. As a friend of Walkley, Lee described the victim as someone desperate for attention: "[f]or some time before his murder he would take anyone home. He was getting older, losing his looks and was lonely. He had difficulty finding lovers he could be compatible with. By the time closing hour came around at a bar he would settle for anything."[111] Lee argued that victims like Robinson and Walkley were similar in appearance and likely faced similar obstacles while cruising. Not only did Lee propagate the ageist myth that older men were undesirable and unhappy, but that with age came danger.

A year following Walkley's death, forty-one-year-old painter James Taylor was found beaten to death with a baseball bat on 1 February 1976. He had been referred to as a "recluse" by neighbours. Six months following that, a caretaker finds James Kennedy (49) dead in his apartment. Kennedy, like some of the other victims, was last seen at the St. Charles Tavern the night before. The presumption was that these men were undesirable because of their age or appearance and therefore put themselves at greater risk due to sexual desperation. These victims were either incapable of cruising – they were shy and did not know how to interact with people – or they were "desperate, unattractive and usually older men," according to Lee. Hardy acquiesced that "[t]here are older men who grew up long before the renaissance of gay liberation, men who internalized the vicious myths of the aging, unhappy, friendless gay man."[112]

Not all the victims were older men, however. Brian Latocki was twenty-four years old when he was found in his bedroom beaten to death on 25 January 1977. Like Walkley and Robinson, he had last been seen heading home from the St. Charles Tavern. All three men also shared a timid and quiet nature. Friends of Latocki described him as "shy and new on the gay scene."[113] Hardy argued that they all faced a familiar contradiction: "uncomfortable in the gay world because they were not 'out,'; not 'out' because they were uncomfortable with the gay world."[114] It was argued that the straight world was to blame for isolating these men and placing them in danger, but part of the rationale given by police and expert sociologists was that these men put themselves in danger because they were undesirable in either appearance or personality. Such a rationale, however, did not sit well with some among the editorial collective.

TBP editor Paul Trollope accused Lee of perpetuating stereotypes about age, desirability, and violence in the gay male community. In April 1979, he penned a letter countering Lee's argument that the murders were linked through the victims' appearance: "Lee has completely internalized the sexist, ageist and objectifying myths which constitute one of heterosexist society's most powerful weapons against gays," he argued. He went on to state that "there is the problem that as gay people we have been brainwashed by the hegemony of straight society's criteria for defining and severely constraining the idea of 'physical attractiveness.'"[115] Trollope's critique exemplified the collective's ongoing concern with the politics of desire, masculine presentation, and safety in the gay community. The collective recognized that these issues were being used to rationalize the violence experienced by gay men whose appearance or bodies did not fit socially prescribed ideals. The legacy of these murders was, therefore, not only the human casualties but also a re-evaluation of "safe" cruising practices by the collective.

It is unlikely that the murders brought about any significant change when it came to gay male cruising practices. They did, however, indicate that gay men in the community were associating violence with gender non-conformity. Hardy recommended that gay men rethink their cruising practices in response to this growing epidemic of violence. In his words, "There are techniques for screening people which should be a part of every man's cruising."[116] These included getting to know someone before taking them home, pretending to have a roommate, or restricting sex to a bathhouse where others would be around to (ideally) prevent an assault. Recommendations such as these demonstrate a considerable overlap between gender performance and personal safety. As a result, the desire for gender conformity (or over-conformity in the case of macho style) could have simultaneously been a response to the pressures of violence on gay men.

Discussions such as these centred around safety, risk, masculinity, and sexuality in *TBP* and reflected the spatial developments around sexuality over the course of the newspaper's publication run. A map published by the collective in August 1984 illustrates that gyms, bars, and discotheques proliferated at the cost of bathhouses.[117] Continual police raids had affected both the financial health of gay establishments and patrons' sense of security in these spaces. Maps in *TBP* also indicate a greater number of gay bars, bathhouses, services, and accommodations along Yonge Street south of Bloor Street and north of Gerrard Street, near Church and Wellesley – considered the contemporary gay "village." The development of gay urban life and the gay village reverberated with the stylistic changes of gender in the gay community. Additionally, the number of gyms in the community almost seemed to fall in step with the ever-greater number of articles and letters from readers on safety, police raids, the gym, and bodybuilding in *TBP*.

Staying Safe: Self-Defence and Style

Protection from personal violation was entangled in tropes of masculinity. In February 1976, Gerald Hannon was taking self-defence classes at the YMCA after being physically assaulted by numerous individuals on Yonge Street, north of St. Clair. It was the fear of violence that encouraged Hannon to begin bodybuilding four times a week. In his words, "I am in danger. That is why I am at the Y four times a week trying to undo the effects of some years of a very sedentary lifestyle, why I spend at least one night a week learning the rudiments of self-defence. Why I have ostensibly joined the ranks of those men who are trying to become Real Men."[118] Hannon's sarcasm about becoming a "real man" is not lost in this message. However, the implication remained that it was through violence and "learning to kill," as he described it, that he was becoming a "real man." This statement conveyed the notion that donning a style of masculinity that was aggressive and even violent – performing masculinity in a quintessentially patriarchal fashion – was a form of protection for gay men. Hannon's statement illustrates how the fear of potential violence shaped the bodies of some gay men. The need for protection in public spaces such as bars and alleyways led some gay men to adopt a style of masculinity that was hypermasculine to deter potential attackers and assert their dominance.

To assuage any insinuation that self-defence required a great deal of muscle, the editorial collective assured readers for years that "[t]he idea of having the perfectly toned body before enrolling in such a course is the wrong one."[119] The collective recognized that self-defence skills were not dependent on physical appearance or a specific style of masculinity but on training and technique. The entanglement of personal violation and masculinity underscores the need for a more nuanced understanding of how style and identity intersect. While adopting an aggressive style of masculinity offered some men a sense of security, it could also perpetuate a queer patriarchal masculinity along with oppressive patriarchal power dynamics.

The formation of groups such as the Gay Liberation Union (GLU), which began conducting self-defence classes in 1979, and the Gay Street Patrol in 1981 by Toronto's Right to Privacy Committee, reflected a renewed interest in bodybuilding and self-defence. In May 1980, *TBP* writer Michael Riordon described how feet, knees, elbows, and hands could be weapons, meaning gay men could protect themselves by working on their bodies. Bodybuilding is a visible display of one's ability to protect oneself. Historian Shaun Cole contends that "[t]he queen protects herself by dressing in women's clothes, and the bodybuilder protects himself in muscles – so-called 'men's clothes.'"[120] In addition to moulding one's body into a weapon, Riordon noted that self-defence included "attitude," which involved learning how to scream in a lower voice by roaring from the belly. This manner of self-defence was understood as a performative act, one that countered notions that gay men were weak or vulnerable. The correlation Hannon and Riordon made between bodybuilding, aggression, and self-defence reinforced the notion that an aggressive display of masculinity afforded a degree of protection. Donning muscle as a style of protection can thus be seen as one explanation for the simultaneous increase in gym advertisements in *TBP*, the resistance towards homophobic violence by gay men, and the increased presence of macho masculinity.

Under the guise of bodybuilding, gay men could also subvert police observation by using gyms as spaces for cruising and the showers for sexual contact. However, the closure of the Richmond Street Health Emporium reminded the community that gay "gyms" or gyms located in bathhouses needed to operate as dedicated bodybuilding facilities rather than as complementary to spas to avoid surveillance or raids. Gyms, such as the YMCA, were not targets of the February raids because they were never "gay gyms," but rather gyms where gay men frequented. This understanding of space resonates with Leif Jerram's idea of space in which spaces like gyms can become gay places, but the relationship between space and place may constantly shift. Unlike gay bars brimming with sexuality, gyms were spaces that oscillated between the heterosocial and homosocial. They were spaces where gay men could work out, but also potentially engage in sexual acts. The sexual coding of gyms provided a limited and perhaps false sense of security for gay men. The ambiguity of gyms meant that police raids were not necessarily an issue, unlike that of gay bathhouses and bars.[121] Apart from staying safe, gyms became synonymous with different subcultures in the gay male community, attesting to both the significance of style as an outlet for identities and the demarcation of masculinities along spatial lines.

Advertisements for gyms and bodybuilding facilities in *TBP* demonstrate how sexual innuendos served to communicate gay male masculinity as anything other than frail while presenting the muscular body as sexually desirable. Unlike Richmond Street Health Emporium, which advertised its venue using sexualized imagery, Backdoor Gym placed an ad in September 1980 only containing the words "gym & sauna" alongside the image of a keyhole.[122] The keyhole symbolized a door and, by extension, the exclusivity of Backdoor. It also served as a euphemism for anal sex, whereby the keyhole represented the anus and a source of pleasure. Finally, the keyhole could have also referenced the action of peeping through or peeking at that which is behind the door, hinting at the space as one where voyeurism was encouraged but sexual activity was not. Indeed, the minimalist nature of the ad, in contrast to the campy imagery of other gym and bathhouse advertisements, also suggested that the Backdoor Gym was a place of discretion. By focusing on the gym aspect rather than the sexualized nature of the space, the ad attempted to position the Backdoor Gym as a legitimate business rather than a seedy underground establishment. This advertising tactic may have been an attempt to assure gay men that the Backdoor Gym was primarily a gym and, therefore, safe from homophobic violence or police raids.

TBP's Out in the City section frequently discussed gyms as "safe" spaces for cruising and working out.[123] Established in 1978, Out in the City came about when the editorial collective realized that the budding sexualized culture of the community in Toronto warranted critical commentary. What began as a one-page guide to Yonge Street's nightlife grew to include guides, critiques, and exposés on theatre, cinema, music, bars, dancehalls, bathhouses, gyms, art galleries, and community resources that catered to a lesbian and gay clientele.[124] In many ways, Out in the City was a reaction to the growing synthesis of politics and cultural nightlife occurring in the 1970s. By offering readers a brief insight into these various spaces, *TBP* mapped Toronto's spatial and sexual subculture, and indirectly demarcated "safe" and "unsafe" spaces for sexual activity. Yet, there was an awareness among the collective that police would read *TBP* to track gay men's and lesbians' social and sexual activity. This raised concerns among some, such as Mariana Valverde, that police would abuse this information or become suspicious if it were to suddenly stop being published by the collective.[125]

In 1979, Michael Lynch published an article covering the relationship between bodybuilding spaces, sexuality, masculinity, and cruising at five different gyms across Toronto. It was humorously titled: "Young (and Old and Middle-Aged Too) Men's Cruising Association." Lynch described the exercise facilities at the University of Toronto's Hart House in a way that virtually promised sexual gratification. Lynch wrote that, "[e]rections are not rare in the showers, and hard cruises of the sort you find at the baths aren't either. But for a site, the guys either head for one of the many busy cans in the university domain or meet on the outside steps and head homeward."[126] By informing gay men where they could combine the activities of bodybuilding and sexual gratification, *TBP* proved to be an invaluable source of information for gay men seeking to navigate the spatial politics of gyms in Toronto.

The College Street YMCA was a space with exceptional tension between the "body-building homophobia" of the weight room and the sexual liberation that came with gay male cruising in the showers. In Lynch's words, "Before and after classes the locker room comes to life with a gay sensibility: a looseness, a quiet, a tasseled fringe of camp."[127] The showers were seen as enjoyable because they housed an entire system of sexual codes that confirmed others' gayness; however, the exception was "the weight room, which retains corners ... of straight body-building homophobia," according to Lynch.[128] Popert recalled in our interview that, "[w]hat would happen is that you would progress to the gym floor from the locker room where, you know, body language and eye contact would determine/confirm if there was interest or not, and if there was an opportunity you went into the steam room to have sexual relations."[129] The result was that the weight room became a space of tension between gay and straight, unlike the sexual tension of the showers. While the showers liberated sexuality, the weight room suppressed it.

The College Street YMCA in Toronto was frequented by gay men despite the broader organization's reputation as an early opponent of gay rights.[130] In 1977 and 1978, there were several reports of gay sexual activity occurring at the YCMAs across Toronto. Ian Young reminded readers of *TBP* that the YMCA had an extensive history of homosexual encounters by reminding them of Walter Jenkins, an aide to US President Lyndon B. Johnson. Jenkins got caught in a YMCA lavatory doing "unchristian things with another gent" in 1959.[131] It was no coincidence that in 1978, *TBP* contributor James Wilson reported that music group The Village People was creating a new album dealing with "among other things, life at the YMCA" – a move that would later make the YMCA symbolically synonymous with gay culture.[132] Perhaps as a result of a lack of fitness venues for gay men in the early 1970s, the YMCA on College was considered *the* gym for gay men to work on their bodies. Ken Popert states in his recollection of working out at the "Y" that, "I think it [bodybuilding] came into gay culture [because] obviously, gay men are concerned, especially in their young years, they are very concerned with making themselves attractive to other people, and it's also a way to meet people in a quasi-bathhouse context because I have never yet been to a gym where there wasn't sexual activity – casual sexual activity – going on between men."[133] Lynch described the YMCA as a relatively safe and sexual space to work out: "if you want to be fit and comfortably gay, take your bod to the YMCA. Even the showers are fun."[134]

The popularity of the YMCA had just as much to do with the opportunity for sex as it did with the safety it afforded. Indeed, it remained a cruising scene for many gay men throughout the 1970s and into the 1980s. Unlike bathhouses, which also offered lacklustre gyms, the YMCA was a full-fledged gym. It was also a Christian organization which provided a degree of protection from police incursion. These attributes meant it was never raided by police, and gay men were therefore free to engage in sexual acts without necessarily risking arrest.

The necessity for personal safety when cruising or working out (or both) was crystallized when the bathhouse Richmond Street Health Emporium was raided and shut down in 1981. On 5 February, the Richmond Street Health Emporium, The Barracks, The Club, and The Roman Spa were targeted by this undercover sting referred to as Operation Soap.[135] In the *Toronto Star*, Brent Hawkes and George Hislop referred to this night as the "gay equivalent of 'Crystal Night in Nazi Germany – when the Jews found out where they were really at.'"[136] Tom Hooper has extensively documented the lead up to, and repercussions of, these raids, noting that "Operation Soap was a six-month investigation, culminating in a mass raid on February 5, 1981. It involved hundreds of hours of undercover investigations." The raids led to the arrest of approximately three hundred gay men and the subsequent protests involving 3,000 gay men and lesbians.[137] The

Right to Privacy Committee, which had formed in 1978 as a response to state and police raids of gay establishments and private homes, was in "shambles" following the raids.[138] The Right to Privacy Committee, according to Tom Hooper, "was a complex organization that faced an onslaught of controversial interactions with the police. Some of these attacks were viewed as political opportunities for action, but this shaped how the group developed their program for change."[139] Catherine Nash argues that in defence of the bathhouses, "the RTPC developed arguments that conceptualized the importance of gay commercial spaces to gay identity, politics, and social life."[140] The financial and personal consequences of the raids were widely felt. Closeted individuals expressed fear that they might be "outed" by police, while bar owners were uncertain of how they would ever recoup from the destruction of property or the damage to their reputation in the community. The following month, Gerald Hannon noted that the financial strain from damage, fines, and slow business meant gay bars and bathhouses were no longer "as safe" to frequent, deterring gay men, especially closeted gay men.[141]

As bathhouses were being targeted by police raids, it implored gay men to seek out alternative spaces to mix bodybuilding with other sexual activities, much to the dismay of some. *TBP* reader Paul Agius vividly described the consequences of the Richmond Street Health Emporium's closure in a letter to *TBP* in April 1981. Agius lamented the loss of the "Richmond Street" because it had provided three characteristics that heterosexual gyms lacked: it allowed for voyeurism, it had a nightclub-like atmosphere, and it was a place for cruising. In his words, "Because it was gay, none of the guys would take offence if I stared for a while as he lifted weights or did sit-ups. In this atmosphere I could overcome my fear of really looking at and appreciating the beauty of the male body." Agius noted that the gym increased his success at having sexual encounters and meeting lovers – the latter involving some emotional depth – because it was a space that "seemed to free me from acting or faking my needs and desires."[142] Despite the nuances of those needs and desires remaining unclear, it is evident that gyms provided multiple functions for Agius: the manufacturing of "beautiful" male bodies, providing a space for him to gaze unapologetically at other men, and supplying him with potential sexual opportunities.

Agius's letter suggests that some gay men saw the gym as a place where more "authentic" interactions or connections could take place in comparison to bars because performances of masculinity in gyms were perceived as less theatrical or artificial. Tying a muscular or butch performance of masculinity to bodybuilding naturalizes working out and the muscular body as a part of what it means to be a man. His comments also suggest that masculinity is somehow less artificial than femininity because it involves less theatricality. However, the manufacturing of desirable bodies is a performance in and of itself. Bodybuilding is culturally defined as an individual effort that allows one to exert direct control over the shape and presentation of one's body. Susan Bordo describes this process as "plasticity" in her book *Unbearable Weight*. She further argues that "the body's materiality is played out *concretely* in our postmodern imagination of the body as malleable plastic, to be shaped to the meanings we choose."[143] Bodybuilding can be read as an attempt at moulding the body to accommodate cultural expectations of gender or compensate for a void or absence of identity that arguably "manifests itself inversely" as a crisis of masculinity.[144]

For example, the Edmonton bathhouse Pisces Spa re-opened as The Biltmore, a "private athletic club" for gay men on 1 August 1981. The manager, Rick Boviak, stressed to Hannon that gay men having difficulty being masculine would not be allowed to enter. As The Biltmore, the club's focus was on bodybuilding: "We don't allow hustlers and we don't allow people who have trouble with their masculinity."[145] To mitigate sexual relations at the club, members were asked to sign a statement acknowledging that the club was "not to be used for sexual purposes."[146] While The Biltmore was originally a bathhouse that catered to its patrons' unbridled sexuality, its new existence as a place of bodybuilding meant performances of sexuality and masculinity within it were narrowed or even restricted. In doing so, the redevelopment of the club from a bathhouse to a gym seemingly reiterates the important relationship between performances of masculinity and space or place.

Gyms were spaces where gay men could carry out bodybuilding, cruise, or engage in sexual activity without much risk from police. *TBP*'s collective published articles on gyms, bodybuilding, and self-defence to inform members of the community on how to best protect themselves from threats of violence. Their articles seemed to add new depth to macho style as a performance of masculinity, one that was manufactured in the heterosexually coded weight room. *TBP* collective member Phil Shaw succinctly wrote in October 1984 that "[w]ith the swelling of gay pride and the need for self-defence, gay men had headed back into the gym even before the hets [heterosexuals] did."[147] Shaw's experience returning to the gym and rediscovering the relationship between his body, gender, and sexuality highlighted his "maturation as a man," as he called it, but most importantly, "his self-definition as a *gay* man."[148] His identity was linked to a space for building a particular macho body that separated him from his former "skinny, weak" self. Classified ads reflect the extent to which bodybuilding and gym culture had shaped the desires of some men by the early 1980s. While only a minority of classifieds in the 1970s used the words "bodybuilding" or "bodybuilder," it became increasingly prevalent by the turn of the decade. In January 1982, one man described himself as "Masculine W/M [white male], 38, 160, 5'10" and was in search of a "passive muscular guy to 40. Prefer athlete or bodybuilder."[149] Months later, in July 1982, another man's ad was published with the description, "White masculine, muscular, well-educated male, late 20s, into bodybuilding."[150] Finally, in September 1982, an ad by a "GWM [gay white male], 23, 158 lbs, 5'11, athletic bodybuilder" appeared.[151] By the March 1983 issue, several ads had mentioned bodybuilding. Working out had become ingrained into gay male community life because it was presented as conducive for sexual opportunities, protection from violence, and, by 1982, seen as a means of combatting the debilitating effects of HIV/AIDS.

Conclusion

TBP played an important role in describing how different aesthetics of masculinity flourished within the purview of particular spaces. In addition to restaurants, health and social services, as well as sports and fitness facilities, the collective noted nineteen bars, three bathhouses, and five discotheques in Toronto as of 1984.[152] Maps in *TBP* played a critical role in helping gay men cruise Toronto using (stylistic) codes or frequenting spaces that were aesthetically in line with their interests. Additionally, the spatial dimension of gay male masculinity was just as evident in the numerous discussions of gyms, which oscillated between being sexualized spaces and spaces dedicated to bodybuilding. These same maps, however, were read by law enforcement.

The police inserted themselves into gay and lesbian spaces in order to disrupt same-sex encounters by going undercover in plainclothes. Such encounters were contingent on police performing a type of queer style that would appeal to gay male sensibilities. This was evident from the greaser aesthetic of police patrolling Philosopher's Walk to the "husky truck-driver type" that led Towndrow to be arrested on charges of gross indecency. Towndrow's story of entrapment was not just a cautionary tale of police donning a type of queer aesthetic; it was a reminder that the aesthetics and presentation of the gay male body were important components in the act of cruising. This manner of state disruption was not exclusive to bars, bathhouses, and other public spaces, however. The arrest of Toronto teacher "Bob" for running a bawdy house suggests that even private dwellings could be redefined to curtail same-sex acts.

Providing cruising guides risked alienating some who felt that navigating state violence was a temporary fix to the much larger issue of state-sanctioned homophobia. For instance, *TBP* reader Billy Schoefl wrote in October 1976 that stories like Towndrow's were not real solutions. Schoefl remarked:

> People like 'John Towndrow' – pathetic tearoom travelling closet cases – always seem to be asking for what they get. Granted, entrapment is downright awful – but I'm sure that most of you at **BP** [*sic*] are well aware that the real answer to ending entrapment is to completely obliterate the conception of homosexual behavior as criminal. Men like Towndrow don't help in the slightest.[153]

By referring to Towndrow as a "pathetic tearoom travelling closet case," Schoefl shamed those who engage in public sex by assuming they are closeted while also critiquing how "closeted" men perform their gender and sexuality. His remarks demonstrate a tension between *TBP*'s editorial collective, who addressed the reality of how masculinity was performed by gay men and police alike in the act of cruising, and some of the more engaged readers who thought any assistance in helping gay men "pass" as straight to avoid detection detracted from the collective's main objective of eradicating homophobia and disrupting ideas of sexual "normalcy." The notion of closeted men who compartmentalize their sexuality as selfish echoed *TBP* editor Michael Riordon's critique only months prior that closeted men were "people who want to have their cake and eat it," and were arguably obstacles to gay liberation.[154]

Additionally, maps published in *TBP* illustrate the greater materialization of gay bars, bathhouses, services, and accommodations along Yonge Street south of Bloor Street and North of Gerrard Street, near Church and Wellesley – considered the contemporary gay "village." This was a slow evolution, not else because the concept of a gay "village" implied a capitalist underpinning to gay liberation whereby shops, bars, and bathhouses could profit off (and arguably exploit) gays and lesbians. While *TBP* portrayed the gay ghetto as nearly ubiquitously white, it often described the plight of gays and lesbians in racialized terms. This comparison was notably addressed by Popert in 1980 when he argued that the gay community could be viewed as any other minority community because gays tend to ghettoize themselves, like "Toronto's Chinese or Greeks or Italians." In his words, "the minority community picture of gays directs attention away from those aspects of gay life which straights find so offensive and alien; things like washroom sex, steambaths, one-night stands."[155] Viewing the gay community as a ghetto allowed Popert to highlight the importance of space in defining sexuality in the gay community. However, these same discussions of the ghetto also reproduced Western (mis)conceptions of race, sexuality, and masculinity. Whether this was an accurate reflection of the racial demographic of Toronto's gay community is uncertain, but racialized gay men did appear in the newspaper, and they *did* participate in gay community life. Nevertheless, *TBP* arguably upheld the notion that white urban communities were central to the formation of queer identities.

Chapter Four

"The Cowboy Hat Will Never Fit Quite Right": Intersections of Race and Masculinity

Sure, we can puff up our tits, buy Lacoste and wear Levis, but the eyes will always be Asian, the skin will always be Black, and the cowboy hat will never fit quite right.

– Lim, "GWM," *The Body Politic* 78, November 1981, 4–5

In his letter published by the editorial collective, Lim (last name withheld), a public relations officer for Gay Asians of Toronto (GAT) and contributor to *TBP*, actively decried racism on the grounds of style and appearance in the gay community. His quote introducing this chapter suggests that styles of masculinity in the gay community and the dressing of the gay male body were enmeshed in the politics of race. Moreover, the ubiquity of ads and content featuring macho style in *TBP* consistently reminded him of the entrenched politics of whiteness in Toronto's gay male community. As an act of resistance, however, Lim used the paper as a platform to challenge racialized constructions of masculinity that stemmed from colonial notions of gender. These were stereotypes grounded in specific colonial understandings of race, such as Asian docility, Black hypersexuality, and Latino sexual insatiability. Lim's writings, along with other men of colour, including *TBP* regulars Fo Niemi and Richard Fung, demonstrate that *TBP* was utilized by men of colour seeking to disrupt racial stereotypes around gender and sexuality.

This chapter analyses the overlapping politics around race and sexuality in *TBP* to demonstrate that the racialized dynamics of sexuality disrupted any cohesive or unified image of gay liberation. At the crux of these intersectional politics lay gay male style and the aesthetics of desire, particularly the white imaginings of masculinity and sexuality. While gay liberationists sought to balance their manifesto of individual sexual freedoms with the racial politics in the community, the newspaper's political message of sexual libertarianism reflected and reinforced the privileges afforded to white gay men in the community. Not only did this alienate gay men of colour, but it also served to reinforce stereotypes and expectations of them. The editorial collective's responses to concerns of racism in the community were often reactive, not active. Instead, readers such as Fo Niemi played an important role in mediating race in *TBP*. The dialogue between editors and readers served as an opportunity for those in the community to push back against racist depictions or essentialist understandings of sexuality, transforming the newspaper into an early platform for deconstructing intersections of gender, sexuality, and race. Whether it be reviews of film, artwork, and literature, classified ads, or articles on racialized machismo, *TBP* contained numerous different forums whereby readers and the collective alike wrestled with the social and sexual dimensions of race, inclusion, and whiteness.

Many of these discussions of race in *TBP* can be approached using Edward Said's concept of "Orientalism" – a discourse of binary essentialism whereby the Global South or "East" is sensual and feminine, while the Western world is rational and masculine.[1] The Orient is not a fixed location, but a theatrical stage on which "appear figures whose role it is to represent the larger whole from which they emanate."[2] Orientalism captures how so often people and cultures are overlooked and misunderstood not only through stereotyping but as part of a broader set of power relations. Orientalism is not about ignorance or a lack of knowledge, but rather a particular set of knowledge or "truths" that is used to reinforce beliefs and values of non-Western people. *TBP* demonstrated that assumptions around race, sexuality, and gender were more than ill-thought-out assertions, but rather "exotic" desires that reflected a deeper fetishization of gay men of colour that attempted to confine them to the periphery of gay desire.

Finally, concerning terminology, I recognize the use of African Canadian, Afro-Canadian, and Black Canadian in scholarship. However, in this book, I refer to people of African descent in Canada as Black Canadians. My choice to use Black Canadians is inspired by the work of David Sealy, whose work highlights the tenuous relationship between Blackness, Canadianness, and modernity. He asserts that "it's impossible to be both Black and Canadian at the same time, since Canada is imagined either as a place without Black people, or where the few Blacks there are well-behaved, even apolitical. … The very calling of oneself as Black … are reappropriations of a term of ultimate degradation to empower African diasporic peoples."[3] Additionally, I use the term Indigenous when referring to First Nations and Indigenous people, despite the historical uses of "Indian" to refer to both Indigenous people and South-East Asians. This is to better nuance categories of race found in classified ads and articles in *TBP* and as an extension of reconciliation towards Indigenous peoples in Canada.

Background of Race

Initially included as a means of comparing and understanding the deep-seated nature of gay oppression, race became a singular topic of discussion in *TBP* by the late 1970s. The collective and many of *TBP*'s readers took issue with the whitewashing of gay culture, with most of the dialogue centred around the politics of sexual desire. The ever-changing composition of *TBP*'s editorial collective had much to do with shifts in thinking about intersections of race and sex. At the time of Lim's writing, the paper was predominantly male and white but was supported by the heavy anti-racist work of contributors and readers. By 1983, however, Lloyd Wong had joined the paper, working in the office on subscriptions and distribution, while David Chang was working in layout and design. Meanwhile, Richard Fung was involved in the paper to varying degrees, often contributing his writing and occasionally aiding in the paper's daily workings. When their voices were present, gay men of colour used *TBP* to rebuke racialized understandings of masculinity and sexuality. However, determining the tenure and involvement of many of these individuals remains elusive, since the paper tended to have a revolving list of names in any given issue. One can only speculate that commitments beyond *TBP* and changes in one's economic and social situation contributed to this fluctuation of involvement.

In my interview with David Rayside, he reflected on the initial unease members of *TBP* had with the topic of race: "I think there was broadly an awareness of that [race] and an unsettlement about that but more acute for some members of the collective than others, and Tim McCaskell was one of those who was especially conscious of the way masculinity was constructed in relation to minorities."[4] McCaskell, a white editor for *TBP*, was highly conscious of race in the gay community and one of the most vocal critics of racial preference as a legitimate sexual preference. He attempted to mediate the fetishized desires for gay men of colour as an extension of larger processes of white privilege and racism. However, McCaskell wrote from the perspective of a white gay man – a recurring critique *TBP* would receive from readers and fellow collective members.

Efforts to address racism in the gay community (and in *TBP*) were catalysed by the formation of gay and lesbian groups by people of colour, such as GAT in 1980 and Zami in 1984.[5] As one of a few gay and lesbian organizations of colour to form during *TBP*'s existence, GAT inspired more resistance by readers and contributors to address racism disguised as sexual preference. GAT was particularly vocal in *TBP* because it was co-founded by *TBP*'s Gerald Chan, Richard Fung, Tony Souza, and Nitto Marquez.[6] As one of the first major gay Asian organizations to form during TBP's existence, GAT connected the Asian and gay communities and published their magazine, *CelebrAsian*, in the 1980s and 1990s. According to Thomas Warner, GAT not only sought to unite and support gay Asians but also advocated for issues pertinent to its members and promoted culturally sensitive social and support services.[7] Similarly, Zami provided members with social and support services, "including peer-counselling and discussion groups."[8] Zami was less vocal in *TBP* than GAT, but its members were nevertheless dedicated to building dialogue between new groups of gays and lesbians of colour (Canadian-born and those of other national origins) and the gay community.[9]

One such example of the editorial collective's attempt at attempting to be more racially inclusive was in an advertisement for *TBP*'s subscription plan on the back cover of the ninety-fifth issue. Featuring an Asian man working out (Figure 4.1), the ad communicated to readers that they could expect an intellectual workout from reading the newspaper: "To get results, you have to work out regularly with us, once a month."[10] Rather than use a white macho body to sell subscriptions to *TBP*, the collective's purposeful inclusion of an Asian man positioned the paper as a mediator of masculinity, race, and desire in the gay community. The individual in this ad is stretching while maintaining a direct stare at the viewer. His gaze, muscular body, and active stance are a direct contrast to racist assumptions of Asian men as fragile, docile, or submissive. His body is also one that is manufactured in the gym and could be read as an attempt to be butch. Whether the decision was affirmative action towards inclusion or a means of responding to a changing racial readership is unknown. However, the editorial collective capitalized on the sexual appeal of the model, serving as a reminder that visual imagery was an important component in securing resources for the politics of gay liberation.

The White-Washed Politics of Race in *The Body Politic*

Writing in 1982 from Montreal, activist Fo Niemi asked readers of *TBP*: "Has this gay culture become so monolithic and 'white-washed' that it

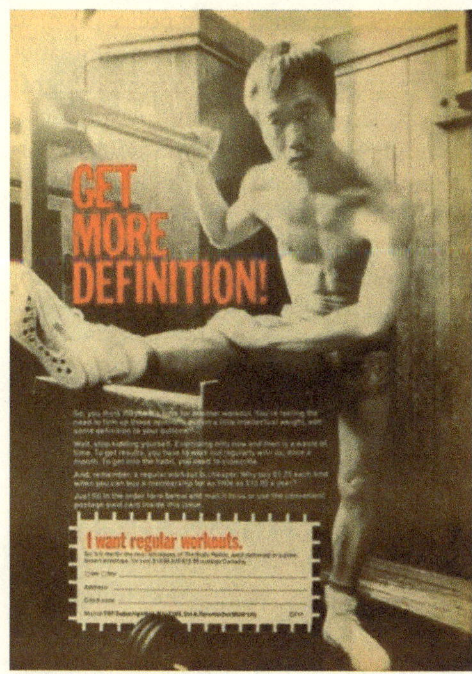

Figure 4.1 Back cover of *The Body Politic*. Photographer: unknown. "Get More Definition," *The Body Politic* 95, July–August 1983. Image provided courtesy of Pink Triangle Press.

turns homosexuality into a strictly North American phenomenon which subtly compels Black, Asian, Latin, Native and East Indian gays to relinquish their backgrounds and to pass as gay 'coconuts'?"[11] Niemi's question is a reminder of the broader privileges and politic of whiteness in gay communities across North America. Gay liberation brought with it a culture *for* and *by* white queers. For a newspaper aspiring to disrupt the way gay men understood themselves and the world around them, *TBP*'s editorial collective was not entirely cognizant of the experience of gay men of colour. By no means was the editorial collective ignorant of racism in the gay community, nor did they *consciously* perpetuate existing tropes around racial masculinity unless attempting to make a strong statement about race and sexual desire. In comparison to sexuality and gender, however, race received relatively little critical attention from the collective until racist, pornographic magazines and classified ads began to appear in the paper. Momentum for these discussions increased as *TBP* shifted away from a white framework of liberation by the late 1970s when gay people of colour acquired a greater foothold in the paper.

The earliest discussions of race in *TBP* were as a point of reference for understanding gay oppression. David Newcome and Paul Pearce, writers for *TBP*, argued in 1972 that the "Metro Toronto police do their best to confine us to the ghetto. The Jews, Blacks and other minorities have suffered under this same police oppression."[12] Framing gay rights as another example of minority oppression, especially civil rights, was a long-standing tactic common in the 1960s for social movements to garner broader support. For instance, historian Sean Mills highlights how Montreal Black Power advocates in the 1960s, "reached out to Native Canadians in their first attempt to build solidarities across different movements."[13] On 29 September 1969, Edmund Michael, a writer for the Montreal Black community paper *UHURU*, compared the oppression of Black Canadians with that of the Indigenous by using the language of postcolonial theorist Frantz Fanon.[14] The shared oppression of seemingly disparate social movements created the image of a more unified resistance to the social, political, and economic status quo.

To highlight the overlap of racial civil rights and sexual civil rights, the editorial collective published author and social critic Paul Goodman's "The Politics of Being Queer" (1969) in May 1979.[15] In this specific essay, Goodman bluntly states, "my homosexual needs have made me a n*****."[16] Goodman chose the N-word to describe the similar brutality faced by gays and lesbians as that of Black men and women.[17] His approach to gay discrimination and inequality through a racial framework did not, however, work through the intersectional dimensions of race and sexuality. Nor was it informed by the experiences of Black, Indigenous, Asian, or other gays of colour. Rather, he drew on previous experiences in which he had faced discrimination, including being fired from various jobs because of his sexuality and being excluded from both the publishing world and certain gay organizations because his message was too radical.[18] By appropriating the derogatory racial term and applying it to both homosexuals and himself, Goodman attempted to redefine homophobia and position sexual oppression as equivalent to that of racism. Yet, his adoption of the N-word whitewashed the brutal history of slavery and ongoing anti-Black racism and, again, reflected the centricity of whiteness among many visible gay and lesbian communities in North America.

Historian and writer Jeffery Escoffier notes that gay men and lesbians of colour received very little attention within the formative years of gay liberation because it was "primarily white gay men and lesbians who have settled in gay neighborhoods and owned businesses serving the community."[19] Instead, gay men and women of colour, especially those newly immigrated, often remained within their ethnic neighbourhoods because they were afraid to alienate their ethnic communities or risk their chance at obtaining Canadian citizenship.

McCaskell noted in April 1984 that "gay community leaders were worrying that immigrants caught up in the raids, many of them people of colour, might face deportation if they were found guilty of bawdy-house charges."[20] Amendments to the Immigration Act in 1952 barred "homosexuals" from entering Canada or applying as immigrants or permanent residents.[21] Historians Patrizia Gentile and Gary Kinsman argue that "Citizenship is defined not only by place of birth but also by loyalty to the state. If you are not loyal to the state and are deemed a risk to national security, you lose your citizenship rights, becoming subject to surveillance and interrogation."[22] Fears of losing or being ineligible for citizenship were exacerbated by Cold War rhetoric that equated homosexuality with communism, threats to national security, and the dismantling of the Canadian nuclear family. As a result, immigrants were consistently informed of proper ways to conform to the Canadian way of life in newspapers and magazines, none of which included acceptance of, let alone education on, homosexuality or gay culture.[23]

An article in the September 1980 issue of *TBP*, "A Minority Within a Minority," spoke of why Chinese gay men chose to remain on the periphery of gay cultural life because they feared upsetting their Chinese friends and family. The anonymous author argued that "[v]isibility as gays in a homophobic and hostile 'ethnic' community is not safe, but an Asian in the gay community has no choice in his/her visibility as an Asian."[24] Historian Jeffrey Escoffier contends that "[g]ay people of color must commute to the gay community districts in order to participate in the gay community – and they often encounter discrimination."[25] Accordingly, some gays and lesbians of colour wrestled with a multitude of cultural and sexual identity politics that limited their participation in early gay and lesbian organizing. This meant that organizations such as the Community Homophile Association of Toronto, the Toronto Gay Community Council, and *TBP* itself were consistently shaped by white viewpoints.

Most critiques on the whitewashing of gay culture were extensions of broader concerns of colonialism and sex tourism in the Global South. Writings on sex tourism frequently stripped racialized men of agency, construing them as passive objects of white consumption. In Richard Fung's coverage of the National Third World Gay Conference held in Washington, DC, in 1979, he noted that gay cultural life revolved around middle-class white men, while individuals from other racial backgrounds were relegated to the margins. Asians, Latin Americans, and Blacks existed on the periphery as "oysters," in his words, while Indigenous peoples were not even recognized.[26] Fung then used the language of food as a way of highlighting the fetishization of gay men of colour as a form of racism: "I feel like a fortune cookie in a tray of cheese Danishes. ... I can't grow a moustache. I'm stuck with the costume I was born with. It's a costume because I have been to Asia only on holidays and I don't speak any Asian language. Yet someone can tell me seriously that he 'really gets off on orientals.'"[27] This metaphor was also taken up by Gerald Chan in November 1981 in a response to a two-part short fiction written by Robin Hardy, whereby white gay men had disappeared from the world. Chan sarcastically lamented the "horrible situation wherein the Homos (a special breed of inverts who are whiter than white ...) had disappeared" and suggested "no more than a few fortune-cookie messages to help sensitize a person with Mr. Hardy's intelligence to the problem of racial prejudices within the larger society as well as in the gay community."[28] Fung and Chan (both co-founders of GAT) viewed racially essentialist understandings of sexuality in North American gay and lesbian communities as extensions of deeply rooted colonial constructions of orientalism and white supremacy.

In his trip to Calcutta, India, on New Year's Eve in 1981, an Australian writer wrote to *TBP* of the privilege and power afforded to white gay men in the Global South.[29] Jackson had noticed the abundance of male sex workers who actively sought his attention. And yet, he informed the collective that he had hesitated to pay for sex from the young men because he believed it was exploitative. In his words, "To pay a boy for sex, I felt, would have been ... obtaining pleasure from somebody else's misery, degrading us both in the process – me because I exploited, the boy because his smooth, lithe body was his sole commodity."[30] The negotiation for sex with young homosexual men in foreign countries was, for Jackson, a form of colonial conquest carried out on the bodies of these young gay men. His experience served as an example of systemic exploitation of gay men of colour in the non-Western world. By framing sex tourism through the lens of race, Jackson's article exposed different power relationships developing in a more global context of desire, sexuality, and the commodification of the body.

Despite his trepidations around engaging in sex with the local population, Jackson insinuated in his article that he had sex with a twenty-five-year-old Indian man named Ashok who worked for his father's tea exporting company. While Jackson was walking down Sudder Street in Calcutta – the centre of Calcutta's red-light district – Ashok pursued Jackson in his car. "I sat silently wondering at how geography (a street) and technology (a car and a streetlamp) can determine aspects of gay behaviour across cultural boundaries," he wrote.[31] Jackson saw this interaction as evidence of cruising as a near-universal phenomenon that was seemingly ubiquitous in the Western world. Still living at home and careful not to be seen on Sudder Street, Ashok took Jackson to the Whooley River wharfs where it was insinuated that they were intimate with one another. Jackson believed that this sexual connection was not exploitative because Ashok was financially secure, indicating a class element to negotiating sex in Calcutta. The message to readers of *TBP* was that those who engaged in any financial transaction with destitute young men in the non-Western world – unlike Ashok, who did not need the money – were exploitative and exerted white capitalist privilege. His argument complicates the narrative of white exploitation of young men in the non-Western world by suggesting that men of colour could be agents in sex, but only if their class allowed for it. The relationship between oppression and class becomes foregrounded while simultaneously subverting intersections with race.

In response to Jackson's article, Winnipeg resident Jeff O'Malley submitted his thoughts on "misconceptions which may have arisen from the commentary of man/boy love in Sri Lanka" to *TBP*.[32] In 1980, at the age of eighteen, O'Malley travelled to Sri Lanka through the Canada World Youth exchange program, where he was assigned a Sri Lankan guide whose name was not disclosed. Having discussed the topic of homosexuality with this young man, O'Malley recalled being told of the public shaming, denouncement, and humiliation that his guide had experienced when caught engaging in same-sex acts by one of the boys' fathers. Many of these young men were sexually exploited because they had to separate their sexuality from their social world while having little, if any, resources or social support. According to O'Malley, homosexuality in the Third World was different from "gayness" – the emotional love shared between two same-sex partners as foreigners understood it – because it was an economic mode of survival and occurred mostly within an "emotional vacuum."[33] While admittedly not all young men saw their sexuality strictly in economic terms, the economic transaction associated with the procurement of sex in the Third World illustrates the intricate relationship between whiteness, sexuality, and Western capitalism. By describing white foreigners as the purchasers of sex, Jackson and O'Malley centred white men as the dominant actors in homosexual relationships, consequently relegating Asian men as docile and the objects of consumption and never fully granting them agency.

Individuals like Jackson and O'Malley were exposing the systemic exploitation of racialized men and the power relationships that were developing in a more global context of desire, sexuality, and the commodification of the body. When it comes to sex tourism, the demand for sexual experience with men of colour is often driven by the belief that they are exotic and sexually submissive, perpetuating stereotypes of non-Western men as being hypersexual and primitive. Dana Collins notes that these spaces are "complex, constituting what Joan Nagel describes as contact zones or 'ethnosexual frontiers,' which shows the hybridization of identity, culture, and socioeconomic practice."[34] As such, the encounter between gay men from the Global North and men from the Global South becomes deeply entangled in power relationships around access to bodies for sexual purposes. The assumption that white gay men have a privileged access to gay men of colour in the Global South not only asserts a white queer patriarchy in the Global South, but that domination returns with these white gay men when they return home.

Tension between white privilege and colonialism is further evidenced when John D. Stamford, the editor of gay travel guide *Spartacus*, had previously spoken out against the exploitation of "third-world boys." In a series of *Spartacus* editorials in 1980 called "The Rape of the Third World," Stamford argued that some gay tourists "go with loads of money, hand it out like confetti, and, in doing so, destroy the pride and satisfaction of native life-styles – and then we complain bitterly of the results."[35] However, *Spartacus* stated in profiles to countries such as Sri Lanka that "[a]ge of consent has so far not been a problem either (providing, of course, all parties are willing) and most boys from slightly before puberty onward are sexually active."[36] According to *TBP*, Stamford defended tourists' relationships with youths in a proceeding editorial, arguing that those in the Philippines, Sri Lanka, and Thailand "who became sexual companions of adults, even foreign adults, did rather well, [and] lived happily."[37] *TBP*'s news article appeared to insinuate that youth in the Global South benefitted from sex tourism while neglecting the subordinate position, sexual and otherwise, of these Sri Lankan and Indian boys to the white men who were having sex with them.[38] Again, these men were described as passive sex objects, while white male tourists were the sole actors in these deeper power relationships stemming from colonialism.[39] The inability to discern a concrete argument either in favour of or in opposition to sex tourism in the Global South is evidence that the politics of sexuality undermined more noble arguments against colonialism, exploitation, and white privilege. As discussions of the Global South illustrate, the subversive process of "othering" gay men of colour by white gay men reproduced a legacy of orientalism within the gay male community.

A Racial Battleground in the Classified Ads

As *TBP* demonstrates, racism and racial desire in gay male communities were not limited to practices of sexual or cultural exclusion. Racism was also evoked through the language of desire and, as a result, continued to marginalize gay men of colour as subjects to be fetishized. Classified ads in *TBP* could, at times, reproduce racial stereotypes – but they could also challenge those very same stereotypes. In an interview between Joseph, a Chinese man from Hong Kong, and Tim McCaskell, the former stated, "[a] lot of people go to bed with Asians or Black men for very, very racist reasons." Joseph's comments had to do with how white gay men fetishized gay men of colour based on racist stereotypes. McCaskell agreed, noting that "[t]he Black man who finds himself expected to be 'more sexual and well-hung,' the Asian who finds himself expected to be 'passive,' the Chinese who finds himself expected to be 'interested in older men,' may find that situation as objectionable as being rejected."[40] Classified ads are particularly important given that broader debates around race and sexual desire were mobilized by racist classified ads and how white men fetishized gay men of colour. It is important to note that not all classified ads contained racist or racially pointed language. More ads emphasized a traditional notion of masculinity than any proclamation of racial preference. However, the ads that evoked extremely racist or exclusionary language initiated a maelstrom of debates around racial desires, racism, racialized masculinity, and censorship.

Classified ads were popular among readers of *TBP* because they allowed for a degree of anonymity and connected men for companionship and/or intimacy. While most ads did not perpetuate racial stereotypes, including those where race was explicitly referenced, some ads proved to be particularly contentious when their writers espoused racist desires or explicitly stated their distaste or disinterest in people of colour. This led to debates on issues of racism, desire, and white privilege among and between *TBP*'s editorial collective and the readers of the newspaper. Compounding concerns of racism in *TBP* were anxieties that sexual expression might be regulated or censored. Attempts to regulate content alienated some readers who believed it was detrimental to the community because censorship was a tactic for homosexual suppression by the Canadian government. The discussions and debates that follow illustrate the vitriol and complex range of responses to issues of race. For instance, racial terminology used in classified ads reflected ever-shifting "orientalist" understandings of racial categories in a predominantly white queer patriarchal culture. Black men, Asian men, and Latino men experienced equations of racism differently, and their masculinity was brought into focus in differing ways. Their masculinity was racialized by the white observer in different ways, and I contextualize these debates and ads carefully to address the specific colonial underpinnings that inform specific stereotypes. Nevertheless, orientalist language in classified ads served to both reinforce equations of gay culture with whiteness as well as relegate gay men of colour to the sexual whims of white men.

For instance, classified ads reflect the varied and tenuous understandings of masculinity or machismo in South America and how it was entangled with whiteness, reiterating the racial hierarchies ingrained in many South American cultures because of colonialism. José B. Torres, V. Scott H. Solberg, and Aaron H. Carlstrom argue that "[v]ariations of what is generally perceived as machismo and conventional conceptions of masculinity popularized in the White/European American society are predominantly associated with Latinx in general and with Mexicans and Mexican Americans in particular."[41] Among Latino writers of classified ads, many used "White" as an adjective in addition to "masculine" and "straight-acting" to nuance or subjugate their ethnic identity. One such ad in November 1981 read, "Attractive white Latino, 25, masculine, beard, not sophisticated, straight-acting, seeks buddies. Looking for same (same-35)."[42] Another man from an unnamed small town in Ontario described himself in June 1985 as "white, masculine Latino man, 28, hairy, bearded, 5'7" 142 lbs, attractive" and sought a man who was "masculine, tough and tender and down to earth."[43] These ads are examples of how whiteness was understood to hold a privileged position among white Latin Americans who idealized their Spanish-European heritage.[44] They demonstrate the unstable definition of "white" and who constitutes being "white." While not all self-described Latino men used such language to stylize or white-wash their bodies, those who did so capitalized upon the politics of whiteness in the construction of gay sensibilities. By using these terms in *TBP*'s classified ads, some South American men sought to nuance or subjugate their ethnic identity, which was often associated with conventional conceptions of masculinity popularized in White/European American society.

Moreover, the use of terms like "masculine" and "straight acting" among South American men was an extension of this tenuous relationship between machismo and whiteness. These intersections occur at the site of the body and are reinforced by the racial hierarchies ingrained in many Latin American cultures because of colonialism. During the colonial era, Spanish and Portuguese conquerors introduced a hierarchical racial system that placed Europeans at the top, followed by mixed-race people, and then Indigenous and African peoples at the bottom. This system perpetuated the idea that whiteness equated to superiority, which in turn was linked to masculinity.[45] In many societies, this dynamic has had a lasting impact on South American culture, where ideals of machismo and masculinity are often associated with white European ancestry.

These ads were complemented by articles such as Michael Riordon's July–August 1981 article "A Space for Ourselves," which explored masculinity as a style in many South American cultures. Riordon interviewed Lucho Carrillo and Aquiles Molina, men who "grew up gay in societies where machismo is a sort of second religion," according to Riordon.[46] Both men noted that sexuality was expressed through clothing and physical behaviour, but it was not intrinsic to one's identity. Molina was quoted as saying, "In Santiago I was a straight man by day and then gay at night. My clothing and manner changed completely when I went into a gay space."[47] Meanwhile, Carillo noted that, "In Peru, the conception of gay men is that they're primarily effeminate; of lesbians that they're primarily masculine. I had sex with men in Latin America, but I didn't define myself as homosexual."[48] Rather, it is inferred that many gay Latino men may have felt a disconnection between their identity and actions.[49] They could engage in same-sex acts without identifying as homosexual. Instead, their masculinity remained a crucial aspect of how they came to terms with their sexuality and their sense of self, taking it with them beyond their places of origin.

Yet, classified ads could also reflect the racist and fetishistic desires of many white readers of *TBP*. In a letter submitted to *TBP* in September 1976, Susan Henderson and Peter Prizer from Portland, Maine, complained that the classified ads were harmful, racist, and homophobic. "Phrases such as G/WM [gay/white male], 'young chickens,' 'very masculine appearing,' and others are offensive to persons struggling to free themselves from a culture which, for openers, is racist, classist, sexist, and ageist," they argued.[50] The collective responded by assuring readers that "we edit out phrases like 'no blacks' 'no orientals,' 'no fats or fems,' etc … [w]e do allow ads which are directed to generally oppressed groups: 'Gay male seeks black friend,' would be acceptable, 'Gay male seeks white friend,' would not."[51] Given this policy, ad writers could still express fetishistic desires for gay men of colour grounded in culturally determined, essentialist notions of Asian passivity or Black hypersexuality. The racialized language in classified ads reflected white orientalist notions of racialized sexuality, with some ads even including the word "Oriental" itself.

The term "Oriental" in classified ads was not only imprecise but varied from writer to writer. A "very masculine" white male in Toronto wrote into *TBP* in June 1983 looking for "hot and creative times with good-looking Orientals and Latinos" in 1978.[52] In December 1984, a gay Black male sought "uncut [l]atinos, [o]rientals."[53] The imprecision of the term "Oriental" was also evident in an ad from a twenty-five-year-old male from Toronto who sought responses from "Orientals and Asians."[54] The use of "Oriental" can be traced back to the history of colonialism, whereby a particular Western thought and system of representation constructed the East as the exotic and inferior "other" to that of Western Europe. The European colonial project relied on the belief of Europeans' cultural and racial superiority to justify the subjugation of non-Western people, denigrating them as Oriental to reinforce such differences.

Additionally, the terms "Native" and "Indian" were used interchangeably in classified ads. This makes it difficult to know if some people requesting an "Indian" were specifically referencing Indigenous men, East Indians from Asia, or West Indians from the Caribbean. Some classified ads, such as one submitted in 1982 by a white man requesting an East Indian man, were particularly specific in what they meant by the term "Indian."[55] On the other hand, some Indigenous men were quite specific in defining themselves, with one particular ad from a thirty-year-old "Native Indian" in Toronto who was looking for a "tall, hairy gay or bi male [and] into active/passive French and active greek [*sic*]."[56] Seemingly, the little discussion of Indigenous or Métis peoples and issues perpetuated their exclusion from conversations on race, and thus their invisibility in the community. The lack of nuance afforded to Indigenous issues in the gay community reinforced language that conflated Indigenous people with East and West Indians under the banner of "Indian." Notable exceptions include a February 1979 article on the development of Saskatoon's new Gay Community Centre for gay Métis and Indigenous people.[57] Historian Scott Morgensen notes that Nichiwakan was one such group in Winnipeg that came about in the 1980s, while Vancouver had "already hosted the Native Cultural Society, which brought Native people together in an annual drag ball and other activities."[58] In Toronto, other groups such as Gays and Lesbians of the First Nations of Toronto (2-Spirited People of the First Nations in 1991 and later 2-Spirits) formed after *TBP* had ceased publication in 1987.[59]

The inconsistency of racial terms demonstrates the arbitrary nature of racial categories constructed by Orientalism. Diverse ethnic groups are lumped together into a homogenized "other" that serves to reinforce the superiority of the West or white men. Daniel Gawthrop refers to this "othering" in his 2005 memoir of his time working in Asia, where he notes that this attraction to Asian men was/is based on certain stereotypes and fetishes, thus rendering him the offensive label of "Rice Queen." Drawing on Richard Fung's ground-breaking 1991 essay "Looking for My Penis," Gawthrop argues that the complexity of desire renders "usual discourses of power" around sex and ethnicity to be reductive or limiting.[60] Most notably, sexual attraction in the "West" is deeply invested in power dynamics that are not only culturally created but contribute to the fetishization and objectification of people of colour.

When the collective responded to Henderson's and Prizer's concerns, this was one of – if not *the* – first time that the editorial collective directly addressed censorship in the newspaper. Any attempts to regulate content alienated some readers of *TBP*, such as George Peterson, who believed that any attempt at stifling white men's sexual expressions or desires was a detriment to the community. Peterson wrote into *TBP* in October 1976 expressing concern about the process by which white classified ads were scrutinized for racism. He argued that "to arbitrarily single out some races against which your advertisers may discriminate (while you protect other races) is to commit an act of bigotry and hypocrisy."[61] Published alongside Peterson's letter, the editorial collective responded with the statement: "In Canadian society, we are not preventing anyone from meeting a white person by not allowing phrases like 'white only.' It would be difficult not to meet white people at every turn in Canada. The only possible purpose for saying 'white only' is to exclude and, intentionally or not, insult members of other races."[62] The exchange between George Peterson and the editorial collective is demonstrative of broader tensions around censorship and the assumption that sexual liberation meant unfettered sexual expression. Not only did threats of censorship risk alienating some gay men who saw it as antithetical to the movement at large, but inaction on the part of the collective would have undermined the more radical members' attempts at multi-issue organizing with racial civil rights.

Peterson's comments also reiterate the assumption that gay culture was largely created for white gay men. To navigate this quandary, some classified ad writers reiterated the whiteness of gay male culture by noting that gay men of colour were welcome to respond. For instance, a September 1979 ad from a "Scottish Canadian Male" in Toronto seeking "lasting friendship" noted at the bottom: "Would also like to hear from Asians or Blacks."[63] The ad implies that men of colour are passive and require the explicit invitation of white men to engage in sexual encounters. Similarly, a white male from Toronto wrote in 1980, "Sexy Black dudes, Asians, write too."[64] Ads such as these conveyed the idea that white men were still the primary demographic of interest, while gay men of colour were an afterthought. Additionally, it reinforces the assumption that white gay men were the active agents in seeking out sex. This is a direct extension of the orientalist idea that "configures the Asian American man as contemptible: 'womanly, effeminate, devoid of all the traditionally masculine qualities of originality, daring, physical courage, creativity,'" according to David Eng.[65] Indeed, this type of language also serves as evidence that gay men of colour were still on the margins of a white patriarchal gay culture.

Even among some Asian men writing into *TBP*, evidence of their negotiation of these racial politics is evident in ads. In October 1979, a self-described twenty-four-year-old Canadian "Oriental gay male" wished to "explore the fascinating and vibrant styles of the white Caucasian homosexual world."[66] For a Canadian-born "Oriental" gay man to perceive gay culture as both "Caucasian" and based on "styles" reiterates the centrality of white (macho) styles of homosexuality in gay culture. His desire for a white man to help him navigate gay culture may have been an attempt to access greater social and cultural capital within the gay community. The desire for cultural assimilation is not necessarily uncommon among minority groups who may have felt marginalized and excluded on the grounds of race. In the case of this individual, he may have seen embracing the styles and cultural norms of the white gay community as a way to explore his sexuality, as well as gain acceptance and legitimacy within the community. However, his desire to explore "the white Caucasian homosexual world" reiterates that the dominant culture within the gay community has been defined and shaped by white gay men, with little regard for the experience and perspectives of gay men of colour. In another ad, a twenty-one-year-old Asian sought "masters under 35" for "B&D [bondage and domination], pain, humiliations, etc." in March 1983.[67] BDSM is emphasized because the writer wants to be the submissive partner in this relationship. Indeed, he is actively partaking in a sexual subculture of the gay male community that has largely been imagined as white. The author is simultaneously seeking sexual domination while resisting racial domination.

Responding to assumptions of whiteness in classified ads, Fo Niemi argued in the September 1981 issue of *TBP* that racism and the sexualized nature of gay culture were synonymous. "One can repeatedly accuse others of having discriminatory behaviour, yet such dehumanizing beliefs are so institutionalized that it is virtually impossible to get rid of them," he contended.[68] Niemi asked the following questions: "Do those gays who include in their ads 'WM wants same' or 'Orientals and Blacks welcome' realize the tiny difference between racial favouritism and racist prejudice? And do gay interracial relationships reinforce white supremacy on an intimate level, allowing the white partner to dominate his 'coloured' mate like a straight man and his subjugated wife?"[69] The nuances of racial desire did not escape Niemi, but it appears that his writings did not lead to any changes in the editorial collective's scrutiny of classified ads that used "exotic" language to describe gay men of colour.

In July 1979, a white male in Toronto submitted an ad wanting Black men because "Black men are the best lovers," he argued.[70] In two other classified ads, the writers propagated myths around Black endowment, with ads requesting a "well-endowed Black man up to 35 years"[71] or a "well-hung Black guy under 35."[72] The myth of Black endowment in these ads resonates with Neal A. Lester and Maureen Daly Goggin's argument that "[B]lack men have been constructed as hypersexual – their sexuality and power located in their genitals (i.e., their body)."[73] These ads perpetuated Black men as hypersexual beings and reinforced the idea that their worth was based on their sexual performance. The language of these ads reduces Black men to sexual objects for the pleasure of white men. Historically, Black individuals were objectified and exploited for the pleasure of white colonizers. They were emasculated and their sexuality, in the words of Shawn Taylor, was "turned into a poison."[74] The sexualization of their bodies was used to justify the brutal treatment of Black individuals and reinforce the idea of white superiority.

However, resistance to racial stereotypes such as these speaks to the shifting racial makeup of *TBP*'s editorial collective, as well as gay men themselves, who were frustrated with white imaginings of gay sexuality. Some classified ad writers challenged racial stereotypes around Black sexuality or reclaimed these stereotypes for their benefit. A twenty-five-year-old Black man in Montreal described himself as "passive and lonely," searching for "affection, gentleness, love, warmth, sophistication."[75] Another Black man sought a "rugged masculine dominant male up to 22."[76] Finally, in February 1984, an ad appeared from an "attractive Black male" in search of the macho aesthetic, including "Black, Italian or Greek bodybuilders."[77] This latter ad indicates that while macho style was assumed to be white style, there was a desire for men of colour to conform to the aesthetic. These examples of resistance through classified ads illustrate the complex ways in which individuals negotiated and challenged racial stereotypes around sexuality.

They also show that while some individuals attempted to subvert or reclaim these stereotypes, others may have still desired to conform to them, even if they were not part of the dominant racial group associated with a particular aesthetic style.

John Yorke, the Afro-Eurasian reader who had described his experience as the only macho "clone" on Howard Street in the March 1981 issue of *TBP*, submitted another letter critiquing the racism prevalent in the classified ads of *TBP*. Reading ads from the February 1981 issue of *TBP*, Yorke argued that fifteen of the forty-one ads from Toronto were racist in some fashion. Meanwhile, sixteen of the ads were ageist, and another sixteen came from "closet queens," stressing that racism in the gay community was entangled with other forms of discrimination.[78] As he described it, "[t]hey ranged from 'We are: white, 21–35, moustache, no beards, 5'8, well-built, good-looking. You are 'same' to the insidious liberal '(blacks welcome).'"[79] Racism could be communicated through the use of the word "same," which was used prominently by white men who described themselves as straight-acting or straight-looking. In this context, however, "same" frequently meant *white*. The prevalence of such ads in *TBP* contradicts Churchill's claim that the magazine's editorial team scrutinized the classifieds section for any "inadvertent racism."[80] While Churchill acknowledges *TBP*'s attempts to stymie racism in classified ads, Yorke's findings are evidence that some ad writers used the word "same" to circumvent the editorial collective's efforts.

In light of Yorke's conclusion, reader Peter Bowen responded in a letter defending white men's racial preferences in classified ads. "If we prefer WASPs … , then we're racists; if we like or are attracted to or want to get to know non-whites, then we're something called 'insidious liberals,'" he argued.[81] Apart from demonstrating white privilege, his letter sparked a response from *TBP* contributor Lim, who argued that combatting racism was the responsibility of the entire gay community. Using Bowen's own words as an example, Lim contended that, "When you are white, whether you are hairy or hairless, muscular or slim, well-endowed or not, you are still white. However [*sic*] the ethnic division of sexual preferences places Asians, Blacks and latinos [*sic*] in a subordinate position."[82] For Lim, white men were capable of donning various styles of masculinity, while gay men of colour were relegated to racial stereotypes. Lim heeded that gay male aesthetics were made to be a *white* style, and any attempts to participate in white gay male culture, even aesthetically, were entangled in deeper racial politics.

Resistance to racial stereotypes arose from frustration with the way that white people historically imagined gay sexuality and perpetuated harmful stereotypes about people of colour. In March 1983, Niemi responded to a white man from Toronto searching for "Black Men/ other 'exotic' races/ nationalities."[83] The original ad by a man named Andy began with his desire for an "exotic" racialized man. The use of the word "exotic" reiterates a broad fetishization of gay men of colour rather than a perpetuation of specific racial stereotypes of Black, Asian, Latino, or Indigenous men.[84] The use of the term to describe Black people and other gay men of colour was offensive to Niemi, who argued that "it implies the notion of white supremacy and colonialism left from the 'White Man's Burden' days."[85] In referring to the White Man's Burden, Niemi demonstrated how such contemporary comments that prize whiteness as desirable and everything else as "exotic" were not only rooted in the xenophobic and racist mentality of colonialism, but also perpetuated the belief in racial uplift.

This sentiment was shared by reader Quan Minh, who argued that "[i]nterracial interaction … is often a symbol of upward mobility and acquired prestige for a lot of non-whites."[86] He believed that cruising was a "sexual game" that treated men like sexual objects rather than people. Minh noted that the white standards of desirability to which he (and other gay men of colour) was expected to strive meant a subjugation of his racial identity. Minh suggested that conforming to the white ideal of beauty and desiring white gay men risked turning him into "a gay Uncle Tom who only goes for GWMs [gay white males], who silently accepts the gay politics of racial exclusion or who tries to appear physically as 'white' as possible."[87] According to Minh, the entrenched whiteness of gay male culture impeded interracial cruising, "except in cases where a white man is either into 'exotic' people or is so indiscriminate in selecting sexual partners as to notice and respond to non-white cruisers' 'signals.'"[88] Minh's observations of cruising highlight the historical legacy of racial exclusion and marginalization of racialized groups and how that legacy manifested itself within gay sexual practices. If cruising encouraged gay men to treat other men as sexual objects rather than as individuals, then racialized understandings of sexuality encouraged white gay men to subjugate racialized individuals to white standards of beauty and desirability as an extension of queer white patriarchal privilege.

Addressing Racism and "Exotic" Styles of Gay Masculinity

The discussion around crude racial stereotypes within *TBP* served to highlight its position as one of the most influential and intellectual platforms for the gay and lesbian community at this time. Dialogue between gay men of colour and a largely white readership and editorial collective reveals a largely ignored tension between *TBP*'s collective, who sought to temper assumptions around race and readers who pushed against any type of censorship. The heated debates and differing opinions presented within the pages of *TBP* reflect the ideological differences that existed within the larger gay community, particularly around issues of race, power, and sexual liberation. The assumption that sexual liberation should allow for the autonomy of white gay men to choose their sexual partners was challenged by those who recognized the inherent racial prejudices that existed within Canadian society and the gay community itself.

The exoticization of gay men of colour in many classified ads triggered a response from *TBP* on why racism was a gay issue and how the politics of sexuality, desirability, and masculinity were bound up in the politics of race and white privilege. According to McCaskell, the foundation of white masculinity in the gay community was laid by sexology at the turn of the century.[89] He argued that early twentieth-century science was partly to blame for racism in society. Sexology perpetuated racist notions of intelligence and sexuality and upheld ideas of white dominance and privilege, which became enshrined in Canada. As a result, white men represented a benchmark for masculinity in the gay community because white machismo was emphasized in gay literature, pornography, and commercial advertisements.

The racist discourses found on the pages of *TBP* reflected racialized understandings of sexuality perpetuated in gay pornography and a burgeoning queer visual culture at large. On this topic, McCaskell stated:

> The gay community did not invent racism, but we have our own special ways of reinforcing the message that we are, or should be, all white here. Take our porn, for example: the images that we consume and produce are largely of white people. Our standards of beauty, of who is hot, or even who is gay, are produced and reproduced along specific genetic lines. Those images are obviously only a small part of what determines our standards of attractiveness. But they do convey the message that a [B]lack or Asian person is definitely a specialty item for a subgroup with exotic tastes. Normal taste, normal gay, is white, and not only for whites. Gay men of colour who find themselves attracted only to whites are not an uncommon phenomenon in our white-dominated society.[90]

While pornography was but one source for reinforcing fetishized depictions of gay men of colour, McCaskell's statement speaks to gay male

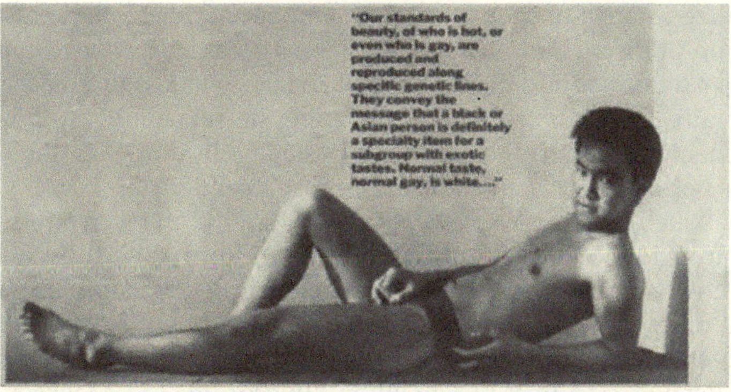

Figure 4.2 Picture of a model posing in underwear. Photographer: unknown. Tim McCaskell, "You've Got a Nice Body for an Oriental," *The Body Politic* 102, April 1984, 35. Image provided courtesy of Pink Triangle Press.

style as it has been associated with whiteness and Eurocentric beauty standards. The ideals being perpetuated around masculinity, consumption, and desirability are shaped by a visual culture dominated by white models. *TBP* was no exception to this assumed whiteness of gay male style. In addition to ads for bars and bathhouses, editorials in the newspaper drew on white gay male style, evidenced by the prominence of macho style. Even McCaskell noted that "the vast majority of advertising images are of whites."[91] To combat this trend, however, McCaskell included an image of an Asian man on both the cover of the article as well as the bottom of the second page (Figure 4.2).

Positioned in a seductive pose and wearing only underwear, the model is lean and looking directly at the camera, capturing the gaze of the reader. The model makes direct eye contact with the camera, one that becomes shared with the reader. It is anything but passive. He is being assertive in his sexuality as well as welcoming the viewer to look upon his body. Being "served" to the reader in an almost passive and objectified pose, yet maintaining a direct gaze at the camera, this model highlights the quiet tension that photograph models share as both object/subject for the viewer and as an active participant in the modelling process. He willingly has his body, sexuality, and identity captured on camera but must also relinquish control of the final product that may be used to sell a product, promote an issue, or simply arouse the reader. Indeed, the model appears next to McCaskell's argument regarding standards of beauty, changing the inherently sexualized image of the man into an equally political one. This combination of visual and written language forces the reader to consider their sexual tastes and perceptions of Asian sexuality and masculinity while also being forced to acknowledge the sexuality of the model, albeit tempered by tropes of Asian passivity. In doing so, the model serves both a political and sexual purpose for *TBP*.

McCaskell's article was well received among many readers, with Toronto reader Scott Lee describing it as "informative" and mindful that most white gay men were, in Lee's words, "xenophobic (afraid of the unknown and unfamiliar) rather than racist."[92] Some readers, however, such as Richard Maddocks, felt that it was hypocritical for the collective to address racism when, "[a]ccording to Ed Jackson, only six Asians, total, have participated [in *TBP*], and only two do now. If Asians are not getting fair and adequate gay media coverage, part of the blame can be laid directly on *TBP*'s doorstep."[93] Maddocks argued that since McCaskell did not advise on which bars to boycott for racism, that must have meant it did not occur in Toronto. He also felt that McCaskell's Asian lover, Richard Fung, had influenced McCaskell's opinion and understanding of racism. While acknowledging that racism is present in society, Maddocks cautioned McCaskell to "not dump on the gay community just because it was once primarily white and male."[94] Evidently, any challenge to racism (systemic or on an individual level) did not resonate well with some readers who felt that *TBP*'s efforts were misguided, threatened the privilege white men were afforded, or – worse – made gay men of colour sound like "whining, powerless whimps [*sic*]."[95]

Published alongside Maddocks's letter was McCaskell's response in which he accused Maddocks of utilizing "a series of classic manoeuvres used by people trying to avoid recognizing any responsibility for discrimination against minorities – manoeuvres used against gay people as well as against people talking about racism."[96] Seven manoeuvres, ranging from bringing up examples of reverse racism to blaming the victim, could be used to dismiss or upend thoughtful conversations around race. These strategies reinforced a "racist system" that discounted the different meaning of loss racial minorities experience when coming out as gay or lesbian and "the risks … greater," in the words of McCaskell. His reference to a "racist system" – one that shaped by social and economic modes of privilege and oppression – suggests that some writers for *TBP* were committed to racial equity. *TBP*'s collective struggled with tempering sexual libertarianism but also appeasing readers such as Maddocks, who felt entitled to express their sexual desires even at the expense of others. According to Emily

K. Hobson, this inconsistency of parallel commitments for gay rights and civil rights reflects the split between separatism and liberalism among some members of the gay community and more radical members "in favour of multi-issue alliances and left movement building."[97]

One of the most critical discussions of whiteness in gay male culture came in 1983 when the editorial collective largely decided against running an advertisement for the white-centric pornographic magazine *White Ass Super Pricks*. Editorial member Ken Popert disagreed with the decision, demonstrating that not all members of the collective agreed with suppressing what they saw as sexual expression despite concerns of racism. Popert's article "Race, Moustaches, and Sexual Prejudices" reveals his struggles with navigating sexual liberation and the racial politics of desire, arguing that the struggle to overcome racism was a "noble sentiment," but racial desires were symptomatic of growing up in a white society. He continued, "If my sexuality is racially tinged, it is not because I am a racist, but because I have grown up in a society which attaches great importance to race."[98] In no way condoning racism, Popert believed rather that racial shadings of desire – and the desire for white men – was beyond any individual's ability to challenge. However, he asked readers, "[s]hould we push ourselves into sex with individuals we're not attracted to as a way of breaking down the barriers?"[99] His answer was clear: "[t]hat strikes me as truly repulsive."[100] In this sense, an individual's inability to change their sexual desires or proclivities was equivalent to being unable to change one's sexual object choice from men to women. Popert compared racial desire to his desire for men with moustaches (whom he termed moustachosexuals) and a lack of desire for "many (most?) Asian and native men;" all of which were expressions of a mysteriously moulded sexuality.[101] The example of moustaches emphasized the significance of sporting facial hair as a symbol of masculinity.[102] Comparing the sexualization of men of colour to the sexualization of those with moustaches, it becomes clear that gay men of colour were subject to the fickle and precarious nature of sexualization and desexualization within a white, queer patriarchy. Moreover, Popert failed to recognize that his desire for moustaches, which were considered a symbol of machismo within the gay community, was being shaped by this emerging queer patriarchy.

The lack of analysis of whiteness in *TBP*, particularly by the editorial collective, is because being white is often understood to be translucent or unfettered by racial politics. English scholar Rebecca Aanerud contends that whiteness is constructed "as 'unraced,' or racially 'neutral.'"[103] Thus, white individuals are not perceived to be subjected to the same intersectional processes that affect racialized notions of gender, neither of which is accurate. Richard Dyer contends that, "[t]he uncertainties of whiteness as a hue, a colour and yet not a colour, make it possible to see the bearers of white skin as nonspecific, ordinary and mere, and, it just so happens, the only people whose colour permits this perception."[104] However, whiteness *is* just as politicized as Black, Asian, Latino, and Indigenous identities, to name a few, albeit invested in a privileged exercise of power rather than subjugation and violence.

Popert's article sparked a fervour, to put it mildly. *TBP* subsequently published six letters from readers on the topic of racism in the gay community. In this series of letters, entitled "Racism and Action," readers pushed back against Popert's argument that "[r]acism will go out of our sexuality when racism goes out of society, and not before."[105] Reader Eng K. Ching of Toronto was not convinced by Popert's belief that racism and the desire for white men in pornography was an inevitable consequence of the dominant white makeup of gay communities in North America. He argued that "[b]y refusing to struggle against the racism in our homosexuality, we let straight society define our sexuality and also block the further advances of gay liberation."[106] Ching also acknowledged the relationship between the body and sexuality when he noted that white pornography and literature "invalidate my existence, my experiences and my body."[107] This quote reiterates the important role of visual culture in "validating" acceptable styles of gay masculinity. The lack of Asian men in "GWM [Gay White Male] porn," as Ching called it, prevented readers from breaking free of preconceived notions of racialized masculinity and sexuality.

Other readers, such as Mair Morton, Holly Cole, and Joyce Harley, wrote to the newspaper accusing Popert of white privilege and "defining the reality of the oppressed group."[108] Self-identified lesbians often wrote in to *TBP* challenging misogyny or the lack of female-oriented content, but interventions in racism were not as common. As a merger of these two forms of oppression, this group of women compared heterosexism and racism by arguing, "If we expect heterosexual people to be responsible for their homophobia … then how can we justify or ignore our own racism by using the same excuse?"[109] Their comparison highlights the grievances many lesbians had for the innocuous influences of heterosexism and covert racism disguised as sexual preferences. It also demonstrates that lesbians were critical of an inherent white privilege and queer patriarchal message coming from some within the editorial collective. Not only were lesbians vocal in their anti-racist messaging, but they were at the forefront of many anti-racist organizing during the 1970s and 1980s.[110] Sadly, however, their bold messages did not always come through in *TBP*.

One reader, John Clifton of Guelph, Ontario, wrote the longest and most scathing critique of Popert's article. Clifton disagreed with Popert's laissez-faire approach to sexual desire and argued that "We are responsible for the content of our desires to the extent that we are responsible for the nature of our ideas and attitudes. If we harbour racist beliefs, then these are bound to influence our sexuality."[111] Clifton believed that if individuals harboured racist beliefs, these beliefs were bound to influence their sexuality. Therefore, individuals needed to examine their own attitudes and beliefs about race to eliminate prejudices in society. People could not claim to be progressive or anti-racist if they still harboured racist beliefs built on white conceptions of race and sexual desire. Clifford's sentiments suggest that not all gay men saw racialized desires as an outcome of living in a predominantly white country, and any excuse along those lines was a rationalization that separated individual moral culpability from the cultural stereotypes of a white society.

Richard Fung agreed with Popert that "racism cannot be effectively combatted at an exclusively personal level, that his [racism] is an institution of our society that must be fought in the context of larger social change."[112] However, he encouraged gay men and women to make an effort to challenge racism. In his words, "just as I'm not going to wait for the revolution to grant me my gay rights, I'm not going to wait for the revolution to start fighting against racism."[113] Fung's call for action destabilized the progressive narrative of gay liberation and also stressed that combatting racism did not mean limiting sexuality. On the contrary, confronting racism meant broadening the availability of sexual opportunities for gay men. Fung's rationale resonated with Tony Souza, a Toronto reader, who believed that Popert's perspective on this matter denied "the need to *act*" and was the equivalent of allowing heterosexism to continue in the gay community.[114] After all, "[r]acism is about power," Souza argued, and the editorial collective's analyses of the issue did not provide a comprehensive understanding of how race intersected with sexuality.[115]

Months later, the editorial collective attempted to address concerns of racism. In a letter to Gays of Ottawa, they wrote: "We have urged our readers to support struggles against racism."[116] Yet, their inaction reaffirmed to readers that whiteness remained at the heart of gay cultural life and that cultural outlets such as pornography were integral to its maintenance. McCaskell best summed up the importance of visual culture in shaping desires when he stated, "we have our own special ways of reinforcing the message that we are, or should be, all white here. Take our porn, for example: the images that we consume and produce are largely for white people."[117] Critiquing the ubiquity of white men in gay media and in *TBP*, McCaskell demonstrates that internal debates around *TBP*'s role in changing the white image of gay culture were still very much alive.

Popert's article was an "important antecedent," in the words of Churchill, for the "houseboy ad" controversy, one of the most thought-provoking moments around race and sexuality in *TBP*'s history. The vitriol that the houseboy ad produced was the culmination of years of build-up between sexual libertarians and anti-racist activists in the gay community. The 1980s were marked by this tension between white readers and editors who accepted any form of sexual expression and desire as valid, since authenticity was central to gay liberation, and their racialized counterparts who challenged the processes which informed these desires.[118] David Rayside recalled that in the wake of the ad, "there was an extremely intense discussion about what liberation meant in relation to people's sexual desires and whether sexually desiring and exoticizing a person of colour or not desiring people of colour was for some people thought to be part of the nature of sexual desire. And it was not *TBP*'s job to cast judgment on that and other people disagreed."[119] Undoubtedly a critical moment for discussions of race in *TBP*, the houseboy ad represented long-standing divisiveness in the gay community around the politics of desire. Long-time collective member Popert felt that the "houseboy ad" resulted in a lot of "misplaced anger," but that it effectively "facilitated some sort of discussion [on race]."[120] While the ad remains an important moment in *TBP*'s history, it also serves as an example of how the newspaper played a critical role in mediating and exposing racialized understandings of sexuality within the gay community at the time.

When the ad was received in January 1985, it immediately caused concern among some volunteers at *TBP*. The ad was written by a white man searching for a "young, well built BM [Black man] for houseboy."[121] The term "houseboy" was not new to the Classified section – it first appeared in a Calgary classified ad in 1976 by a business executive searching for a "young lover houseboy."[122] Yet, the mid-1980s were marked by an increasing intolerance for racism, even guised as sexual preference. According to the collective, their existing classified ad policy was vague in this regard, and it was undecided if the ads could be considered racist. And so, they published the ad and hoped for the best.

Just as the February issue was hitting stands, Zami was contacted by one of the volunteers who was upset with the ad. Zami was asked they be present at *TBP*'s 21 January meeting, three days after the February issue had made it to the newsstands.[123] When no consensus between Zami and the collective could be reached at the meeting, another meeting was set up on 5 February to discuss how to move forward with members of GAT, Lesbians of Colour, and Zami.[124] That meeting lasted for hours and, if anything, only further fractured the collective's relationship with members of these racialized organizations. Alan Li of GAT recalled that "the duration of the meeting was almost three hours, at the conclusion of which those of us representing non-white minorities felt that the proceedings of the meeting and the attitudes of certain collective members were far more offensive and dangerous than the ad itself."[125] He noted that Popert had argued that "'the inviolability of sexual desire' was the ultimate goal of gay liberation." Such a stance positioned gay libertarians against anti-racist advocates within the community. Others, such as Gerald Hannon, were not convinced that the ad was racist and would not give in to "pressure from other people's emotional reactions."[126] Churchill notes that the division within the collective around the ad was primarily generational: older members who defended racial preferences as an inescapable consequence of growing up in a predominantly white society and younger members who felt that conscientious action was needed to tackle racism in the gay community.[127] Gerald Hannon, Ken Popert, and Rick Bébout were the most vocal members of the collective in support of sexual liberation and in favour of publishing the ad because it adhered to the libertarian nature of *TBP* and reflected the libertarian views of the editorial collective.[128]

The collective, realizing that the damage had already been done, attempted to explain their rationale for publishing the ad. "31 Words," as the article was named, was the cost of irreparably damaging *TBP*'s credibility and any semblance of unity among gay liberationists. The article began with a joint statement whereby the collective described their struggle to publish the ad, noting that they were "seriously divided" on its publication.[129] To afford readers transparency around the decision-making process, the collective published internal memos alongside "31 Words." Just as Churchill argues, Popert and Hannon reiterated a sexual libertarian view that should not be undermined at any cost. In his 24 January memo, Popert wrote, "When people start censoring classified ads for political reasons, I feel a draft. And when my own sexual desires and practices are prejudicially characterized as belonging only to a privileged minority, I definitely start to shiver."[130] Meanwhile, Hannon saw the ad as evidence of the cultural, economic, political, and personal desires of a largely white society, which were problematic in their own right but integral to sexual libertarianism.[131]

Accompanying these memos were a host of letters from activists and gay men of colour angry about the collective's decision to prioritize sexual freedom over racist desire. Richard Fung argued that publication of the ad meant *TBP* was a platform for, at best, maintaining white dominance in gay culture and, at worst, racism.[132] "I am sorry if people see this as repressive, but I cannot justify one person's pleasure at someone else's expense and oppression, especially when it's mine," he contended. Fung was unsurprised by the volatile reactions surrounding the "houseboy" fantasy and the collective's decision to publish the ad, considering the collective's previous efforts to temper charges of racism with the right of sexual expression. He argued that "by advocating sexual libertarianism as its main priority over community organizing, the paper maintains the colour, class and, up til [*sic*] recently, gender of the people who work there."[133] Fung's comments reveal a deep-rooted issue with *TBP*'s prioritization of sexual libertarianism over community organizing, leading to the alienation of members who did not adhere to white sexual liberation. Equally unhappy, Lim argued that the collective's decision to publish the ad demonstrated that *white* sexual libertarianism was the real goal of the collective, even if it further marginalized gay men of colour: "If the philosophy of the BP collective is sexual libertarianism at any cost, then please do not call yourself a gay liberation journal, 'cos [*sic*] I'm part of the gay liberation, and when your liberation oppresses my life, it ain't no liberation." Some readers, such as Brian Mossop, maintained that the anti-racist rhetoric of the *TBP*'s editorial collective was reason enough for racial minorities to continue to support the newspaper. In his words, "[g]ay Blacks and Asians should in my view continue to support *TBP* as long as it opposes racially motivated bashings, racist admission policies at bars and the like."[134] For Mossop, any anti-racist rhetoric by the collective was enough to be considered inclusive.

Rhetoric alone, however, did not sway Siong-huat Chua, founder of Boston Asian Gay Men and Lesbians, from publishing an article a few months later in *TBP* stressing that white gay sexual libertarians were flexing their privilege and power. In his editorial "Beyond Racism," Chua complicated the relationship between men of colour, white "anti-racists," and the experiences of gay men in the Global South. He was sceptical of "anti-racist" white men and women's intentions, believing them to "always be at the centre of all social processes, always the motivators, always the initiators of all human activity." He suggested that the appropriate response to the white makeup of gay liberation was continual input from racial minorities and people of the "Third World." In his words, "[w]hile people of the Third World have always contributed to the advance of capitalism from passive positions as subjugated and economically exploited groups, it is important that we do not now take a back seat in the modern liberation struggles engendered by the progress of capitalist development."[135] So while *TBP*'s efforts were commendable, the newspaper and its predominantly white editorial collective reflected these global hierarchies of power and race stemming from colonialism.

Appearing near the end of *TBP*'s publication run, Chua's article and the houseboy ad demonstrate that the issues of racism and racialized stereotypes of gender and sexuality were still unresolved by the time the newspaper ceased publication. As a result, the very nature of gay liberation and the meanings of inclusivity remained tenuous at best. For Chua, racial inclusion was contingent upon racial identities becoming an "organic part of the community."[136] Yet, the numerous discussions around the houseboy reveal the ongoing struggle in the gay community to overcome racism and the racial politics of desire. Some among the editorial collective sought to deconstruct racial sexual preferences (or the lack thereof) to illuminate deeper orientalist ideas of race in the gay male community. However, such complications of sexual desire in the gay community sparked ire from some readers and those within the collective itself who felt that individual sexual expression outweighed racialized politics. As a result, *TBP* played a fundamental role in providing a platform for both men of colour to articulate their intersectional experiences in the community and their white counterparts who sought to deflect, and in some instances uphold, the entrenched whiteness in gay liberationist circles.

Conclusion

TBP was undoubtedly torn between challenging the privileged position of white gay men, a large percentage of their readers, and not attacking white masculinity. The writings of Fo Niemi or Peter Jackson were reminders to readers of *TBP* that race was a deeply divisive issue for the gay community, despite activists such as Paul Goodman framing homosexual oppression as equivalent to that of racism for African Americans. The sexuality and gender performance of gay men of colour appeared to be contingent upon racialized and "orientalist" understandings of their bodies. From the stylization of their bodies in photographs to their portrayal in books and articles, these men experienced varying degrees of fetishization and exoticization. By no means were all men of colour treated equally, nor did they have their masculinity brought into question in similar ways. Rather, the various historical stereotypes and narratives around Asian, Black, Latino, and Indigenous men that had stemmed from colonial understandings of race served to inform different styles of masculinity. Classified ads demonstrate, for instance, how men of colour were expected by some gay men to embody *expectations* of racialized performances rather than strictly gender performances. At the same time, these same ads could also reflect how the politics of exclusion and marginalization extended far beyond the category of race and included those who had long been invisible in both gay and straight culture alike, including disability.

Classified ads are just one example among many provided in this chapter of the complicated and rich history between race, whiteness, and gay liberationist politics. A turning point by the end of the 1970s saw considerations of whiteness, the experiences of gay men of colour, and the racialized aesthetics of gay male style in the gay male community take place in *TBP* and the community at large. The fraught politics around race at this time brought with it important discussions around white privilege and processes of racialization that continue to be had in many queer communities today. Much of this important work, however, was done by gay men and women of colour – again, reinforcing the white-centric expectation that people of colour must be the ones to carry the burden of racial justice. Any cohesive or unified image of gay liberation was dismantled with the propagation of neocolonial understandings of race, largely through an orientalist lens. Not only were these assumptions of race, gender, and sexuality alienating for the very minorities who sought to be included within the community, but they revealed the deep-seated orientalist understandings of gender and sexuality disguised as sexual libertarianism. As some of the letters mentioned in this chapter suggest, the threat of censorship or addressing racial desire sparked ire among some readers of *TBP*, demonstrating that some activists or community members were not ready to relinquish the privileges afforded to white gay men in the community. Yet, the dialogue between editors and readers in *TBP* is evidence that gay men of colour did not sit idly by as orientalist and queer patriarchal understandings of gender were propagated; they actively engaged with these tropes and made their voices heard. In doing so, gay men of colour transformed *TBP* into an important forum for activists of the 1970s and 1980s to address oppressive forces that carried over from a white cis-heterosexual mainstream society.

For many activists of the late 1970s and 1980s, the turn to intersectional politics was a much-needed effort to address what some saw as an adoption of the racial, gendered, and enabled status quo. An anonymous article published in March 1984 examined how people with disabilities, racial minorities, homosexuals, women, and people with criminal records are lumped together as "socially handicapped."[137] The politics of differentiation are highlighted in this article, with the author arguing, "[t]he disabled don't want to be associated with criminals and homosexuals ... [r]acial minorities don't want to be considered among people about whom something is wrong, rejecting the implication that there is anything wrong with not being white ... [and] [h]omosexuals are leary of any suggestion that they might be either sick or criminal."[138] Yet the author also argued that "[n]one of us should have trouble identifying with the physically, mentally disabled, coloured, gay, criminal, female population. We are victims of nothing but a social brutality we can change."[139] This article emphasized the similarities in prejudice that affect men and women of colour while also considering the implications of being able-bodied. In the early 1980s, discussions of disability became more prominent, especially as rhetoric around HIV/AIDS spilled over from mainstream media.

The notion that those infected by HIV/AIDS were debilitated by the disease was a precursor for the stylization of gay male sexuality in the 1980s and lasted well into the 1990s. The repercussions of gay male bodies being inherently unfit or polluted are still reflected in regulations banning men who have sex with men from donating blood to the Red Cross. Gay men with disabilities, and, for a brief time, victims of HIV/AIDS, were stylized in a way that rendered their bodies and ailments invisible during the 1980s. The stylization of masculinities in the gay community was contingent on able-bodiedness, as well as perceptions of sexual virility and health. While racialized masculinity was often affirmed by white gay men and relegated to specific sexual proclivities, disabled gay men and men suffering from HIV/AIDS were put in a precarious position in which their bodies did not *perform* masculinity in a conventional understanding of gender.

Chapter Five

Stylizing Disease and Disability[1]

As gay individuals, we must come to see death and dying not as opposed to life, but rather as a part of living. In short, we must make dying gay – *in our own terms*. Morbid? Not at all. The only morbidity lies in turning our back on our ill or dying friends, or abandoning them to die straight deaths within alien families or institutions.

– Michael Lynch, "Living with Kaposi's," *The Body Politic* 88, November 1982, 33

In November 1982, Michael Lynch described his friend Fred's long battle with Kaposi's sarcoma (KS), an AIDS (acquired immunodeficiency syndrome)-related cancer. When in hospital for treatment, Fred's mother, Selma, noted that her son "persisted in calling his illness 'Kaposi's,' which to her was his way of saying to everyone he was gay."[2] KS was not only a highly visible skin disease – forming lesions on its victims' skin – but it became synonymous with gay men and gay promiscuity when it was discovered to be a common secondary disease of AIDS.[3] While Fred had acquired a small support group led by his lover, Bruce, following his diagnosis, he was dismayed when many of his good friends "stopped seeing us, even stopped bothering to call."[4] Lynch described Fred's resentment for feeling invisible or even feared by those caught up in the hysteria of contagion. The emphasis placed on Fred's sense of invisibility in Lynch's article turned what could have been a story of AIDS into one of the earliest cultural commentaries on gay male culture and the invisibility of people whose bodies were deemed to be "failing." On 20 November 1982, the same day that the December issue of *TBP* was on Toronto newsstands, Fred was receiving visitors in his apartment in New York City. He died the next morning.[5]

Stories such as Fred's are heart-wrenching, and they should not be read as merely case studies for tracing the development of gay male masculinity or responses around disease within the community. The emotions in these stories – compassion, anger, sadness, trauma, and love – illustrate the significance that HIV (human immunodeficiency virus) and AIDS (referred to hereafter as HIV/AIDS) had in shaping gay communities across North America. The disease brought people together as well as tore them apart. Within these narratives, however, are discussions around gay male masculinity and the presentation of the gay male body. For Fred, the lesions on his skin were a corporeal reminder that health and gay male sexuality were being reimagined in the 1980s. The muscular, enabled male body was no longer just a sex symbol; it was an icon of health, well-being, and a sexuality presumably unencumbered by HIV/AIDS. According to David Buchbinder, "Although the early appalling media images of emaciated patients with AIDS led briefly to a foregrounding of the *overweight* male body as demonstrably HIV-free, the muscular male form rapidly reasserted itself, now not only reclaiming its position as *the* object of male homosexual desire but also proclaiming its status as healthy – indeed, even as 'unnaturally healthy.'"[6] HIV/AIDS sparked new questions and debates among readers around individual sexual choices, responsibility for personal well-being, and how gay men might restylize themselves to combat media portrayals of their bodies as frail, infected, "polluted," or "disabled." At the same time that the muscular male body was celebrated for being "healthy," those weakened and debilitated by AIDS became increasingly secluded from gay culture.

Coverage of the social consequences of HIV/AIDS brought with it renewed attempts to pathologize gay men's bodies. In particular, discourses around HIV/AIDS drew from the medicalization of disability. The disease threatened to obstruct or debilitate gay male sexuality as it had been socially imagined, just as disability had done before it. As a result, two seemingly separate issues of disability and disease were woven together, establishing a dichotomy between the unhealthy and healthy, afflicted and non-afflicted, disabled and enabled. This chapter examines how the gay male body served as a figurative and literal site of collision between disability and disease in *TBP*. Discussions of gay male aesthetics and sexuality in *TBP* during the early HIV/AIDS epidemic wove together issues of frailty, disease, and death with narratives around physical disability. In a gay ableist culture deeply informed by queer patriarchy, HIV/AIDS placed gay male sexuality, social practices, and the body under greater medical scrutiny. Indeed, controversial medical and media reports on the transmission and cause of HIV/AIDS reshaped certain sexual practices which had once seemed ubiquitous in gay male culture, such as cruising. Referring to the July 1982 issue of the New York City publication *The Gay Men's Health Crisis Newsletter, TBP* writer Robert Trow stated that "gay men are abandoning drugs and casual sex in droves, convinced that 'life in the gay fast lane kills.'"[7] The disease raised broader questions in the gay male community around sexual desire, safe sex, the aesthetics of the male body, and what it meant to be healthy or enabled. Despite the work of groups such as the AIDS Committee of Toronto (ACT), which called for greater support for AIDS victims as early as 1983, those perceived as sick with HIV/AIDS were frequently reduced to their disease, made invisible, or construed as being void of sexuality.

Historians are quick to point out that HIV/AIDS has long been used to tell the history of the gay male community. There is an almost inexhaustible list of scholarship describing the political and social fallout of the disease for white gay men.[8] More recently, however, scholars such as Dan Royles have explored the social and cultural reverberations of the HIV/AIDS epidemic for gay men and lesbians of colour.[9] While the racial and cultural dimensions of HIV/AIDS have been subject to greater inquiry, the intersection of this disease with disability remains tenuous and understudied. This gap not only hinders a comprehensive understanding of the diverse experiences within communities affected by HIV/AIDS but also underscores the importance of inclusive scholarship that addresses the intricate interplay between health, identity, and societal structures.

This chapter is divided between HIV/AIDS and disability to highlight the body as an important cultural site that entangles discourses of disease and disability.[10] If the stylization of the body was fundamental to the politics of sexual liberation and the formulation of visible gay male communities (which it was), then narratives around disease and disability in *TBP* demonstrate how perceptions of bodily "failure" transferred from the disabled body onto the diseased body during the HIV/AIDS epidemic. Imagery and text in *TBP* reflect the shifting expectations for how people with HIV/AIDS or with a disability ought to act upon their sexuality during the early epidemic. Numerous reports and articles from 1982 onward described the "debilitating" and "disabling" effects of HIV/AIDS; language that had social and cultural consequences. The use of such language perpetuated the perception that the HIV/AIDS-affected body transformed into something comparable to the physically disabled body, unable to meet expectations of how bodies should function and operate on a sexual level in a neoliberal, capitalist, and ableist society. While I focus on disability and disease differently, I am always keeping the relationship between the two in mind. Additionally, disability was discussed almost exclusively in terms of physical mobility or characteristics because invisible disabilities were – and largely remain – stigmatized and unrecognizable. This remains a major point of contention that continues to mobilize debates in queer communities around the politics of desire and inclusion.

During the HIV/AIDS epidemic, gay men's bodies became a battleground between the conservative segments of society, the medical profession, and gay community politics. This was dubbed "AIDS panic" by Ed Jackson in March 1983.[11] Some men reportedly felt themselves become "lepers," disabled, or pariahs following their diagnosis. These individuals noted that their diagnosis resulted in their isolation from the gay male community. This binary was marked by tension and, at times, hostility. Termed "horizontal hostility"[12] by writer and activist Eli Clare, he argues that "[m]arginalized people from many communities create their own internal tensions and hostilities, and disabled people are no exception."[13] For those who acquired HIV/AIDS, they could be relegated to the periphery of gay cultural life, just as many persons with disabilities had been before them. This was especially true for those with visible "conditions." Disability theorist Robert McRuer describes the process by which more stigmatized members of a community are distanced from those desiring to be "normal," or at least seen as normal, as "stigmaphobic distancing." Evidence of stigmaphobic distancing is readily apparent in the narratives and experiences of gay men who "failed" to uphold queer patriarchal ideas of healthy "able-bodiedness."[14]

Rosemarie Garland-Thomson argues that "disability is a representation, a cultural interpretation of physical transformation or configuration, and a comparison of bodies that structures social relations and institutions."[15] HIV/AIDS threatened to obstruct or debilitate the gay male body as it had been celebrated in the 1970s. Overlapping representations of disability and HIV/AIDS reinforce scholar Lennard Davis's argument that with "disease-generated disabilities – AIDS, tuberculosis, multiple sclerosis, arthritis, chronic illnesses – the instability of the category 'disabled' begins to appear."[16] Historically, the meaning given to disability and the disabled body has been culturally manufactured and stems from a cultural panic around the body, hygiene, morality, decency, respectability, and beauty in nineteenth- and early twentieth-century America.[17] Additionally, capitalism and the need to support oneself contributed to the marginalization and emasculation of men with disabilities before the post-war shift to neoliberal economics.[18]

Disability scholar Dan Goodley contends that "[m]any of us fail to meet the demands of neoliberal ideals. And debility is to be found at that moment when disability collides."[19]

Disability in *TBP*

The early 1980s saw a greater shift in *TBP*'s recognition of disability rights and needs. In June 1981, Fo Niemi – the same outspoken activist against racism – called for "[a] clearly visible and well-organized handicapped gay group [that] will help promote the needs and goals of disabled gays and facilitate the members' reintegration in the mainstream of society."[20] Advertisements for disability seminars began appearing in the Classifieds section of *TBP* around the same time. Wilf Race and Chris (last name withheld) advertised their "[f]our-session seminars for physically disabled gay men" in May 1981.[21] Two months later, the Fredericton Lesbian and Gays organization advertised their upcoming 4th Atlantic Community Conference of Lesbians and Gay Men, noting their commitment to childcare and "accommodation for the disabled, the hearing impaired and the sight-impaired."[22] While these programs and conferences addressed important accessibility needs, they did not aim to address systemic ableism or prejudice which equally contributed to the isolation felt by gays and lesbians with a disability.

The first in-depth cultural examination of disability in *TBP* was Gerald Hannon's 1980 article "No Sorrow, No Pity." In it, he claimed that "at the back of our own closets we have built another one, and into it we have shoved our gay deaf and our gay blind and our gay wheelchair cases, and we've gone on with the already difficult enough problems of living as gay people." Hannon believed that the lack of visibility for gay people with disabilities in the community or *TBP* stemmed from the same oppression faced by gay men and women in mainstream society. Using the metaphor of the closet, he took disability out of the realm of medicine and institutionalization and challenged readers to consider how they have enacted their own forms of oppression. Hannon acknowledged that while race, class, sexuality, and gender were important registers of identity in gay culture, disability had perhaps been forgotten because of "our dogged insistence on our essential health as gay people, on our persistent view of ourselves in our own media as whole, active, healthy, bright and beautiful."[23] To add an empathetic (and humanizing) relatability to his article, Hannon began with the personal anecdotes of Richard (last name withheld) and Scott McArthur, two gay men with disabilities living in Toronto.

Richard had been born blind, while McArthur was diagnosed with cerebral palsy after oxygen to his brain was cut off during birth. Both men described the difficulties of being gay while under the supervision of parents and medical professionals at institutions for the disabled. According to them, two of the biggest obstacles facing gay men with disabilities were the lack of privacy and the contradiction that their disability construed them as asexual despite identifying as homosexual. For Richard, his constant supervision by the staff at the Canadian National Institute for the Blind led him to describe the place as "The Zoo." It was a "zoo" because people would always be coming through to observe, in his words, "the poor blind kids." Having little opportunity to explore his sexuality as a result, Richard noted that this constant observation perpetuated the perception that "Blind people don't fuck."[24] Similarly, McArthur was constantly under observation, telling Hannon how he had been caught engaging in sex acts with other men while institutionalized. People with disabilities and those who are institutionalized lack privacy because they are inundated by medical observation and an invasion of their personal space. However, Richard was able to perform acts of oral sex on his roommate after the chaperoned dances held every second Friday. In doing so, he acted upon his sexuality as a gay man in an ableist culture and within an environment that regulated disabled bodies.

Disability rights activist James Charlton argues that assumptions around disabled asexuality stem from both a medicalization of disabled bodies and an inherent paternalism that consigns those perceived to be disabled as children.[25] The perception of asexuality was a dramatic shift from early twentieth-century narratives of those with cognitive disabilities as "social menaces and sexual predators," according to Michelle Jarman.[26] This consequently meant that some people with disabilities were unafforded the education and knowledge of their sexuality. This was the case with Scott. When Scott spoke to the staff psychologist about his developing sexuality, he was subsequently discharged and thrust upon his parents. He told Hannon, "I didn't call myself gay – I didn't know what it meant. But I knew I wanted men."[27] Disability Studies scholar Tobin Siebers maintains that "[o]ne of the chief stereotypes oppressing disabled people is the myth that they do not experience sexual feelings or that they do not have or want to have sex."[28] Evidently, those whose minds did not function in ways understood to be "normal" were excluded from participating in society, homosexuality being no exception. Moreover, the notion of homosexuality itself shares a long history with disability.[29]

Meanwhile, Richard's blindness and lack of access to written material on gay culture also meant that he had "developed some very peculiar ideas about what gay people were like," in the words of Hannon. Richard discerned gayness by "the stereotyped lisping, mannered male voice." Evaluating sexuality by the tone of voice meant that Richard's aesthetic of gayness and masculinity – or in this case, effeminacy – was auditory rather than visual. The use of sound was a break from conventional methods of assessing sexual attractiveness in a visual society. Hannon wrote that Richard "knew that he and those 'queenly' voices were after the same things, and somehow it was all wrapped up in a man who would be taller than he, and have a deep, resonant voice and a furry, muscular arm – something he could get to check ... since it happens to be perfectly okay for a blind man to take another man's arm when walking."[30] Richard's emphasis on the lisp in a man's voice is evidence that queer style encapsulated much more than musculature or clothing. Masculinity included the ability to enunciate clearly and with a deep tone of voice. The absence of such traits could be read as a failed performance of masculinity and indicative of effeminacy or homosexuality. Additionally, Richard's assessment of a man's masculinity (be it a "deep" voice or "muscular arm") suggests that gay men, regardless of ability, participated in the maintenance, and even reinforcement, of a queer patriarchal idea of masculinity.

As a way of encouraging readers to actively see the people "behind" the category of disability, Hannon included photographs of McArthur and Richard. The former, McArthur, is (presumably) pictured in a wheelchair and smiling directly at the camera (Figure 5.1). Meanwhile, a headshot of another man, presumably Richard, is featured on the following page. Both are fully clothed and appear happy. These photographs provided a visual language of disability, one distinct from the enabled men presented in commercial advertisements or photographic spreads. The pictures of Richard and McArthur also refute the social invisibility of different types of impairment and, in doing so, disrupt the presence of normate bodies in *TBP* and the community. They force the reader to think about the centrality of their own body concerning sexuality and desire and see "disability in terms of a socially uneven geography," in the words of Benjamin Fraser.[31]

In an attempt to rethink what it meant to be disabled, Hannon argued that infancy and old age brought with them some of the same effects of having a disability. He argued that while limitations from age are "not the same as spending your life blind, or deaf or in a wheelchair ... it does indicate that we are talking about a spectrum here, not discrete

Body Politic

We say gay people are everywhere.
They are. But there some closets that
most of us would rather not look into.

NO SORROW, NO PITY

A report on the gay disabled
by Gerald Hannon

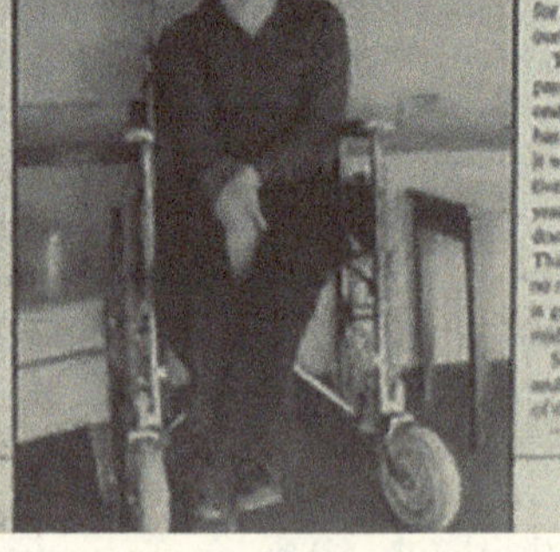

FEBRUARY 1980 THE BODY POLITIC/19

Figure 5.1. The first page of the article "No Sorrow, No Pity," including a photograph of Scott McArthur smiling. Photographer: Gerald Hannon. Gerald Hannon, "No Sorrow, No Pity," *The Body Politic* 60, February 1980, 19. Image provided courtesy of Pink Triangle Press.

and mutually exclusive groups."[32] Hannon broadened the scope of disability to bring the experience of having a disability that much closer to readers. Hannon challenged the static nature of ableism and highlighted the inevitability of impairment, a move that would later be taken up by scholars in the late 1990s.[33] He did not, however, address cultural stereotypes of disabled men as being void of sexuality.

Concluding "No Sorrow, No Pity," Hannon interviewed gay activist and scholar Tom Warner, who spoke of a time when he was picked up by a man with a physical disability. Warner proceeded to go to bed with him, only to find it did not work out because "his legs were so cold. I flinched every time they touched me and of course he sensed it."[34] Warner's experience stresses a reactionary discomfort with how the man's body failed to perform. It also demonstrates that even those who were conscious of how disability intersected with sexuality struggled to navigate their desires for men whose bodies deviated from the "normative" standard.

Hannon's examination of the discrimination faced by those with a disability appears to have been sparked, at least partially, by an interview he had conducted with disability activist John Kellerman in 1980. Kellerman had previously requested $2,000 from the Ontario provincial government in 1974 to fund a conference on sex and sexuality for people with disabilities.[35] He was also actively involved in organizing the International Year of the Disabled taking place in 1981. This was compounded by the Canadian federal government's consideration of independent living resource centres to allow those with a disability to overcome structural, financial, and social barriers – the outcome of which was the federal government's *Obstacles Report* (Special Committee on the Disabled) in 1981.[36]

Kellerman described to Hannon how he was refused entry into gay baths in Winnipeg for being disabled. The ostracism he faced as a man with cerebral palsy discouraged him from socializing and being present in gay male spaces: "I want to develop a relationship with someone, but nothing much has happened with either men or women. I've often wanted to go to the baths, but I'm afraid to because I'm afraid they wouldn't let me in."[37] *TBP* reported that both the St. Charles and Parkside Taverns had refused service to people with cerebral palsy in wheelchairs.[38] Richard noted being belittled by other gay men who were particularly surprised that he intended to attract someone. "One man came up and asked if I knew what kind of bar this was. I said, sure, it's a gay bar. He said you mean you go home with people? And I said no, I simply stand around all night like a statue," he told Hannon.[39] These types of social discrimination, including a lack of service, undoubtedly discouraged people with disabilities from participating in gay cultural life, reinforcing their invisibility in an ableist subculture. In a survey among business owners and managers of local gay bars, bathhouses, and discos about accessibility and attitudes towards gay men and women with disabilities, the collective found that "most establishments would rather admit to clubbing baby seals to a pulp than to closing their doors to the disabled."[40] Evidently, there had been no real attempt at including gays and lesbians with a disability into the social fabric of the community.

For nineteen-year-old Warren Camp of Mississauga, Ontario, the societal prejudice towards people with a disability was the source of his frustration with the gay male community. Writing into *TBP* in November 1983, Camp began his letter by challenging the use of the term "disabled." He argued that "it has done as much to reinforce stereotypes today as the archaic 'crippled' did in years past."[41] He did not offer an alternative term but noted how various physical or mental disabilities are often generalized together, reducing people to the same experiences of oppression. Instead of focusing on his physical disability, Camp saw the opportunities that his prosthetic legs provided. Not in need of a wheelchair, Camp admitted that his ability to get past the physical barriers and socialize in bars made his coming out easier. Yet, he still struggled with the popular sentiment that people with disabilities are not sexual beings. This had everything to do with how gay male masculinity has been styled around the body. In his words, "With so much emphasis placed on physical appearance, they [disabled people] represent an unsightly fringe element. They're better off just not coming out!"[42] His point reiterated Hannon's aforementioned argument that the gay community had built a closet within itself. Evidently, the International Year of the Disabled and Hannon's coverage of disability in 1981 had done little to change the politics around desirability and disability.

During Camp's many conversations with men at the bars, he engaged in some degree of consciousness-raising work. He challenged those who felt his disability was an impediment to sexual engagement by attempting to demonstrate that disability is a fraction of a person's identity. He argued that "[w]hen all the clothes are shed and we are stripped down to raw reality, we find warts on everyone, making that a fact of life to be reckoned with, and *not ignored* [emphasis in original]."[43] This statement was a critique of masculinity as a style that involved the covering up of the flawed elements of the body. By comparing disabilities to "warts" found on everyone, Camp positioned disability within the realm of aesthetics, suggesting that what constituted disability was a matter of perspective since nobody epitomized the ideal body or was always enabled.

Physical barriers also proved to be quite challenging for gay men with physical disabilities. The Richmond Street Health Emporium informed *TBP* that people with disabilities were welcome but cautioned that "there are a lot of stairs, and the washrooms are not designed to accommodate wheelchairs."[44] Even the collective noted that "Most gay watering holes in this town do seem to have a lot of stairs, and none have washrooms adapted to wheelchairs, so a willingness to be friendly certainly doesn't solve all problems."[45] Despite these issues, there was no mention of accessibility practices at gay bars and bathhouses in *TBP*'s city guides. For instance, John Allec and Edna Barker's "Hot Spots" guide to Toronto in July–August 1982 made no mention of disability or accessibility, instead assuming that readers of the newspaper were enabled. The absence of any meaningful discussion of accessibility following Hannon's article raises questions about *TBP*'s role in creating meaningful change for gays and lesbians with a disability.[46]

Despite these social and physical barriers, some gays and lesbians with disabilities co-opted spaces for their own needs. For example, the York Rainbow Society of the Deaf regularly met at the Parkside Tavern after they formed in 1977. Founder Raymond Barton wanted to replicate the consciousness-raising efforts he had witnessed in San Francisco earlier that year. He told *TBP* in an interview that he wanted to "duplicate in Toronto what he'd found in SF [San Francisco] – gay deaf meeting gay deaf in places other than the bars."[47] Hannon observed the group at the Parkside Tavern in 1980, noting that they enjoyed themselves but "seemed impenetrable as a social group."[48] His inability to "penetrate" these informal deaf meetings because he did not understand sign language not only reflects enabled privilege, but it simultaneously inverts the notion of disability. Hannon is the one unable to "penetrate" this social group as a gay man with hearing, positioning Hannon as the outsider to a social situation that was not conceptualized with him in mind. While the Parkside Tavern was not necessarily a space for cruising or overtly sexual in nature, Hannon's use of the word "impenetrable" prompts one to consider how the lack of social access extends to the lack of sexual access. Additionally, the presence of the York Rainbow Society of the Deaf at the Parkside is further evidence that gays and lesbians with disabilities were not absent from queer spaces. This is a particularly important point because the history of the Parkside has been almost entirely focused on the experiences of enabled gay men and lesbians.

Other gay men with disabilities contested erasure through education and awareness using *TBP*'s classified ads. This allowed those unable to overcome social and physical barriers to participate in a budding sexual culture. In May 1982, *TBP* published a classified ad from Scott, a thirty-year-old gay white man living in Toronto. It is unclear if this is the same Scott from Hannon's article, but he described himself as "wheelchair-bound with cerebral palsy," and assured readers that "[e]xperience with disabled was unnecessary, will teach."[49] He also informed readers that he lived in a private apartment.[50] Scott's explicit mentioning of his private apartment first speaks to a preconceived assumption that those with disabilities could not, or did not, live alone. This is particularly important because the disabled body was made to be invisible or, at best, isolated from the rest of the queer community, particularly as a result of paternalistic practices by the state, such as institutionalization. Second, his willingness to teach enabled gay men how to be intimate with a disabled body demonstrates that education became a tool through which some gay men with disabilities entered and participated in a sexualized gay male culture. However, there remained an ableist politics of accommodation in this ad. By placing the onus on those with a disability to educate or make enabled persons aware of their sexuality, these ads reaffirmed sexuality as assumedly able-bodied.

The following month, Richard, the same man from Hannon's interview, submitted an ad stating that he was aroused by "taller, hairier huskily-built types. Late 20s to early 30s preferred, but young at heart matters most."[51] Not only did Richard refer readers to his description in Hannon's article, but he also requested a picture at the end of the ad. In his interview with Hannon, Richard mentioned how he determined "gayness" by the sound of someone's voice rather than on visual markers.[52] Requesting a photograph seems to defy the stereotype that blind gay men were unable to read, let alone appreciate, the visual elements of queer style. Indeed, disability operates on a spectrum, and Richard may have very well been able to appreciate a photograph up close. It is unknown if Richard examined the photograph himself or had it described to him, but Richard's ad demonstrates that gay men with disabilities were also active participants in the policing of queer styles.

For some gay men, the desire to be with someone with a disability required justification – reiterating ableist cultural expectations around masculinity, sexuality, and desirability. Evidenced by the few classified ads explicitly involving the language of disability, a submission by a man in Toronto in search of men with disabilities stressed the "sincere" intentions of his ad. His October 1980 ad went: "gay male, 23, 6'1," 170 lbs" in search of "amputee or disabled under 25 for sincere relationship."[53] Another ad from December 1984 requested "people who use leg braces, wheelchairs, and especially amputees. Nothing kinky, just an honest friendship/relationship wanted. Ages 21ish to 32ish."[54] It is unknown if the writer of this ad, Alan, identified as disabled, but his request for a disabled partner suggests that disability was not necessarily seen as a barrier to sexual desirability. Additionally, Alan's ad suggests that his desire for traits we associate with the disabled body could be (mis)interpreted as a fetish or kink. By explicitly stating that his desire for someone disabled is "[n]othing kinky," he speaks to an awareness that people with a disability are stereotyped as lacking a sexuality of their own and therefore become sexualized through the "kinky" proclivities of enabled others.[55] This may also explain why the former classified ad writer sought a "sincere relationship" because it spoke to a wider belief that such desires would be viewed with suspicion. Such stereotypes are grounded in expectations of how bodies "should" function in a neoliberal, ableist society. With disability described in no uncertain terms as being an outlier to the normate desires of many men, this same language would be appropriated in discussions of disease.

Just as disability had been stylized in myriad ways, the HIV/AIDS body had been framed using similar language of debility or frailty in *TBP*. This articulation of disease was shaped by the same neoliberalism and ardent individualism of the post-war era that witnessed the baby boomer (1946–64) generation experience historically unprecedented socio-economic mobility. Bodies were (and continue to be) expected to function in ways that facilitate and mobilize industrial capitalism. Yet, those who are disabled or diseased are often viewed as incapable of doing so despite some recent academic efforts to provide alternative valuations of disabled bodies in society.[56] The resulting stigma around disability and disease was exacerbated in a cultural hysteria around HIV/AIDS, where transmission and life expectancy were unknown in the very early years of the 1980s. The fear-mongering that accompanied HIV/AIDS threatened to re-pathologize gay men, their sexuality, and their bodies, not just from those outside the gay community but from those within as well. What follows is both a history of how HIV/AIDS was described as "debilitating" for the gay male body and the social and cultural repercussions such descriptors had for those affected by the disease.

TBP and the "Gay Cancer"

"Gay cancer" was a term many readers of *TBP* came across in September 1981. It was reported that Kaposi's sarcoma (KS), a rare form of cancer, had been found among forty-one gay men, mostly in New York City and San Francisco.[57] The findings emerged on 3 July 1981, when Lawrence Altman published an article entitled "Rare Cancer Seen in 41 Homosexuals" in the *New York Times*.[58] This news piece was subsequently reprinted in hundreds of North American newspapers, with much of the coverage framing this rare form of skin cancer as a "gay disease." Initial medical discourse implied a link between KS and homosexuality as a result of either genetics or lifestyle choice.[59] *TBP* writer Robert Trow argued that "the medical world has pointed to the gay male syndrome of numerous sexual contacts, repeated infection with sexually-transmitted diseases, heavy antibiotic treatments over periods, and overuse of recreational drugs."[60] Yet, in the context of rising moral conservatism in the United States, *TBP*'s editorial collective thought that the article was an attempt at sensationalizing gay culture.

Collective members immediately critiqued the *New York Times* article for misrepresenting linkages between gay men and KS. They noted that there were numerous errors in Altman's approach to the unpublished work of Dr. Alvin Friedman-Kien, which initially linked KS with gay men.[61] Michael Lynch was perhaps the most prolific writer on the subject of what would be called HIV/AIDS in *TBP*, at least during the early epidemic. He and others at the newspaper were sceptical of these findings, because there was a long history of medical pathologies around homosexuality, as well as contemporary religious efforts in the 1980s to demonize gay men and women. He dubbed this combination the "moral-medical right" for its crude and oppressive definitions of gay people that frequently linked homosexuality with mental or physical illness.[62] Moreover, Lynch criticized the medical profession for treating "homosexuals as objects, alien creatures to be studied and classified and labelled."[63] He felt that those in the gay community, as well as those writing for *TBP*, should be critical of medical "expertise" on gay men's sexuality, bodies, and health, especially as some within the medical establishment understood HIV/AIDS as a "gay disease."

Even some medical professionals shared Lynch's scepticism towards Dr. Friedman-Kien's findings. Drs. Bill Lewis and Randy Coates understood KS to commonly manifest itself in men over fifty years of age and to grow at a relatively slow pace. In their *TBP* article "Moral Lessons; Fatal Cancer," Lewis and Coates both noted that the coverage of KS among young gay men appeared to be part of a more insidious message from mainstream media that gay men should re-examine their lifestyles.[64] Perhaps they sought to quell further distrust of medical practitioners among gay readers. Regardless, mainstream media's messaging was already working. Toronto physician Dr. Donna Keystone, who had a sizable gay clientele, informed *TBP* that "gay men have been coming to her with suspicious skin lesions after reading a recent report on KS in the Globe and Mail [*sic*]."[65] She reassured those at *TBP* that no evidence of KS had presented itself, but such reassurances did little to alleviate the anxiety many men felt. Despite the initial scepticism around rising cases of KS, even from medical practitioners writing into *TBP*, it would soon be clear that this new disease was neither a fallacy nor a fib.

Concrete evidence of HIV/AIDS began to emerge by 1982. Initially known by various names such as acquired community immunodeficiency syndrome (ACIDS) and gay-related immune deficiency (GRID), it became increasingly evident that HIV/AIDS was not a conspiracy theory. It was Lynch's trip to New York City in the summer of 1982 where he realized that HIV/AIDS was not some fictitious epidemic whose creators wanted to strike fear and panic into Americans' minds; it was an all-too-real struggle for survival. In our interview, David Rayside points to Lynch's visit with Fred as a major shift in the editorial collective's approach to HIV/AIDS: "We thought it was just a hoax and another way of demonizing homosexuals, and finally it was Michael Lynch that [*sic*] really told me [that] something serious is going on and we need to address this [pandemic]."[66] This realization included the disease's effects on gay community life, gay male masculinity, and the gay male body. As an increasing flurry of information around this new disease hit headlines across North America, *TBP*'s editorial collective had to think about how they could protect sexual liberationist values while navigating this new epidemic.

By August of 1982, *TBP* reported that "[o]f the 300 cases reported across the United States, 242 are homosexual or bisexual men."[67] The newspaper consistently provided HIV/AIDS statistics since the disease's discovery in 1981, noting in September 1982 that five cases of the disease had been reported in Canada.[68] Slowly, the disease multiplied in Toronto, though the city was spared the worst of the epidemic compared to New York City or San Francisco. In February 1984, Ed Jackson had reported eleven cases of AIDS in Toronto, all among gay men aged between their mid-twenties to early forties.[69] This number increased to thirty-nine cases in the metropolitan Toronto area alone by December of the same year.[70] The Laboratory Centre for Disease Control in Ottawa recorded a total of 165 cases of AIDS in Canada as of 8

January 1985.[71] This was notably fewer compared to the United States, where AIDS casualties surged from 1,400 in 1983 to 15,000 by 1985.[72] It was also at this time that scientists had reportedly discovered evidence linking AIDS to a virus that affected the immune system.[73] Despite disproportionate infection rates, the rapid spread of HIV/AIDS in the United States and Canada pushed the editorial collective to wrestle with the politics of safety, identity, and sexuality in a changing social landscape for gay men.

It is crucial to recognize that *TBP*'s coverage of HIV/AIDS primarily focused on the experiences of white gay men, inadvertently overlooking the devastating effects of the disease for gay men of colour. Historian Martin Duberman notes that the *New York Times* published "only three articles between 1981 and 1993 that focused primarily on black gay men with AIDS."[74] This emphasis on white male experiences was partly rooted in the entrenched whiteness of gay liberationist politics. In the words of Harry Britt, a gay member of San Francisco's Board of Supervisors, AIDS was seen as a "white gay man's disease."[75] Britt's comments came in response to the United States' Centers for Disease Control (CDC) October 1983 report revealing "57.9% of AIDS patients were white, 21.1% were non-Haitian blacks and 14.1% were of Latin American origin. Asians and native Americans each made up less than 1% of the total cases. Of the total, 4.7% were Haitian."[76] However, these statistics were contested by many, including Britt, who argued that they were inaccurate and reflected a whitewashing of gay culture. "'Gay' triggers into the American consciousness a certain image – a white image," Britt argued.[77] Roger Bakeman, a reader of *TBP* in Atlanta, Georgia, shared concerns that white men with HIV/AIDS were overrepresented in the media. He pointed out that this skewed representation led some people to incorrectly perceive HIV/AIDS as "just a white boy's disease."[78]

Canadian cases among gay men of colour were not available for *TBP*'s editorial collective because the race of victims was not tracked (or at least made publicly available until 1998).[79] Without such statistics, the effects of the disease on Canadian communities of colour, particularly Indigenous communities, remained largely invisible. As a result, *TBP*'s scant coverage of gay men of colour's experiences with HIV/AIDS was primarily from the United States. Even when these stories were reprinted in *TBP*, they focused on issues such as financial exploitation and sexual morality rather than the narratives of isolation, emaciation, and hair loss that shaped their white counterparts.

In the United States, artists like Joseph Beam and Essex Hemphill challenged the silence surrounding African Americans with HIV/AIDS.

Their work addressed the intersections of racism, capitalism, and homophobia, as well as the loneliness of African Americans affected by the disease.[80] Referring to Hemphill's 1993 poem "Vital Signs," Darius Bost argues that the legacy of slavery and "antiblackness ... marked black people as 'socially dead,' thereby rendering their suffering as normative and unremarkable."[81] As a continuation of this legacy of Black gay men from HIV/AIDS was suppressed by more prominent narratives of the disease's effects on white gay men. While mainstream and gay and lesbian publications tended to ignore the impact of HIV/AIDS on African Americans, another kind of silence about HIV/AIDS was fuelled by a distrust found in many Black communities. Instances of Anti-Black medical violence, such as the Tuskegee Syphilis Study, and the long history of racial segregation that limited Black people's access to medical services, created a backdrop where, according to James H. Jones, many Black gay men saw HIV/AIDS as the latest manifestation of "racial genocide."[82]

Re-evaluating Gay Male Sexual Culture

TBP's editorial collective was undoubtedly burdened with having to evaluate information, misinformation, and mere opinion around HIV/AIDS that flooded into every issue. Amid the rising cases of infection, *TBP* included the advice and opinions of medical experts, even if such opinions seemed antithetical to the newspaper's broader ethos of sexual liberation. In early 1983, three doctors – Dr. Daniel William, Dr. Lawrence Mass, and Dr. Brian Willoughby – wrote to *TBP*'s editorial. Their letters expressed concern that the epidemic was not being taken seriously by community members, but they were also laden with a moralistic tone that *TBP*'s editorial collective had previously warned about. Perhaps the collective published these letters as evidence that gay men risked becoming re-pathologized subjects within medicine. More likely, however, publishing these letters saved the collective from having to be the ones to suggest that gay men's sexual habits would have to inevitably change with the uncertainty of contagion.

All three doctors forged new links between HIV/AIDS and morality as they paternalistically discussed gay men's sexual habits. Dr. William, a physician in New York City, addressed Lynch's saddening story of Fred, contending that, "had he known the relative risks of different behaviour long before he became ill, he would have changed that small portion of his total gay life style that so drastically shortened his life."[83] Meanwhile Dr. Lawrence Mass, a gay man himself and doctor in New York City, argued that *TBP* and the collective fuelled the gay community's aversion from healthy (heteronormative) sexual habits. His response was blunt: "I would suggest that *TBP*'s coverage of this epidemic that has killed approximately two hundred gay men, that threatens to kill many hundreds more, and that includes a growing number of cases in Canada, parallels *TBP*'s coverage of fistfucking."[84] Mass was critical of *TBP*'s sexual liberationist politics and suggested that a restrictive approach to sexuality would benefit the gay community. Yet, it was Vancouver doctor Brian Willoughby's attack on Lynch's credentials that was the most inflammatory. He scathingly wrote: "Might I simply suggest that we would all be best served by supporting Mr. Lynch in his dancing career and disregarding [*sic*] his writing."[85] Willoughby believed that Lynch was blindly critical of any genuine attempts on the part of the medical profession to understand this health crisis. By dismissing Lynch's efforts to help gay men navigate their unease, Willoughby espoused the very elitism that wrought ire from within the gay and lesbian community.

The presence of medical opinions in *TBP* demonstrates the delicate balance that was required at the time between sexual liberation and the health and welfare of the gay community. Despite having his credentials and authority on the matter of gay health challenged, Lynch still felt that the presence of medical expertise in *TBP* demonstrated that some within the medical profession were willing to have a conversation about gay men's health in an open forum. In his rebuttal to Dr. William and Dr. Mass, Lynch wrote: "These two letters, in failing to address my main argument concerning medical control over our lives, assure me that continued iffiness [*sic*] is still our wisest policy. But the two letters are encouraging signs."[86] For the editorial collective, the suppression of sexuality or reimagining gay male sexuality along a heteronormative framework of monogamy was antithetical to gay liberation.[87] He argued that the medicalization of the gay male body threatened the sexual freedoms afforded by gay liberation, particularly promiscuity, which had become "the foundation of our identity."[88] Indeed, more room for medical reports on HIV/AIDS in *TBP* could potentially curtail gay male promiscuity among its readers. However, doing so risked changing the very message of *TBP* from sexual liberation to one of sexual conformity. Thus, *TBP* served to facilitate gay sexual engagement and the very medical discussions of HIV/AIDS which sought to curb sexual practices and posed a threat to *TBP*'s model of sexual liberation. For Lynch, an increase in coverage of the medical discourses in *TBP* could add legitimacy to medical pathologies of gay men's bodies and sexuality, effectively returning power to the medical community, which so often used "dehumanizing" language.[89] Such rhetoric could, as Lynch continued, "rip apart the very promiscuous fabric that knits the gay male community together."[90]

Disagreements around the politics of sexual liberation and promiscuity in the gay community became fissures in the early 1980s. Many could not seem to agree on whether sexual liberation, promiscuity, and the ethos of sexual libertarianism were worth it anymore. Michael L. Callen, a gay man living with AIDS in New York City, wrote to *TBP* in April 1983 criticizing Lynch's and Lewis's dismissals of early medical opinions. Callen viewed Lynch's and Lewis's responses to medical professionals in *TBP* as a minimization of approximately four hundred gay men who had been diagnosed with AIDS by that point. In his words, "As a gay man with AIDS, I am disgusted by Lewis's and Lynch's willingness to belittle the very real possibility of my own death, and by Lewis's willingness to sacrifice my life because of his selfish and short-sighted fear that 'lesbians and sexually active gay men are going to have their rights denied and infringed upon – all because four hundred cases of a disease have appeared among twenty million of us.'"[91] Callen's rejection of *TBP*'s ethos of sexual liberation suggests that the newspaper risked alienating the very people it sought to liberate.

Many readers were actively engaged in discussions of HIV/AIDS in *TBP* – some supporting the newspaper's coverage for its "humanity" and others condemning it for its "shrieky" and "bathetic" tones.[92] The mixed reactions surrounding discussions of HIV/AIDS highlight the sensitive nature of the disease, particularly as it risked reshaping (or eliminating altogether) activities and behaviours that had become synonymous with gay men's masculinity, such as cruising. These varied responses to *TBP*'s coverage of AIDS were also a result of the convoluted information around AIDS transmission in the 1980s. Dr. Roger Enlow, Director of the New York City Department of Health's Gay and Lesbian Health Concerns, noted that a panic ensued soon after the term "body fluids" was used in association with HIV/AIDS. Enlow stated, "people started asking things like 'What about sweat contaminating pools and equipment in gyms?'"[93] In October 1985, Canadian magazine *Maclean's* informed readers that "researchers discovered that heterosexuals could catch the disease through sex contact – or even from a victim's saliva," according to *TBP* writer Rick Bébout.[94] While anal sex was known to be a high-risk mode of transmission for the disease by this point, the misguided notion that sweat could be a mode of transmission heightened pre-existing fears around the ease to which HIV could be acquired, and ultimately catalysed how some men viewed health, sexuality, and gay male culture.

Classified ads in *TBP* highlight the extent to which HIV/AIDS was at the forefront of many men's minds. Writers described themselves and/or their ideal partner using terms such as "healthy," "health-conscious," and, to the dismay of some, "clean" to articulate sexual viability. Before the discovery of HIV/AIDS, "healthy" only appeared alongside other adjectives such as "muscular" and "fit," while "clean" was associated with personal hygiene or venereal disease.[95] During the HIV/AIDS epidemic, however, these words took on new implicit meaning with "clean" becoming a coded language for HIV-negative. This not only resulted in the implication that HIV-positive individuals were "dirty," but re-established and reframed a Victorian morality that linked "deviant" sexuality with bodily disease and pollution – a pejorative stereotype that continues to this day.[96] A man from Edmonton wrote in March 1983 that those responding to his ad should be "clean and responsible."[97] The narrative of disease and individual responsibility is again evoked in this ad, accompanying debates around individual changes in sexual behaviour and the neoliberal quality of personal well-being.[98] In February 1984, a thirty-five-year-old white man described himself as "[c]lean and discreet."[99] The use of "clean" and "discreet" as complementing adjectives in this instance indicates that some readers felt that discrete performances of sexuality, a lack of promiscuity (despite being an ad to engage in sex), and the successful passing of one's gender were conducive to being healthy or HIV-negative.

Reader Michael Young criticized the "high-profile emphasis given [to] promiscuity." He believed that endorsing promiscuity reinforced an image of gay life that restricted gay men to notions of hypersexuality. Not only did promiscuity affect gay men's health by subjecting them to sexually transmitted diseases, but it took an emotional toll by "reducing sex to the level of a mundane, meaningless experience that lessens the individual's feelings of self-worth," in his words.[100] Following Young's critique, David Palmer, another reader from Toronto, also pushed for monogamous relationships over promiscuity as a response to *TBP*'s coverage of cruising. He felt that "[a]fter countless men, styles of clothing, drugs galore, nights of partying and a handful of lovers, I look closely and discover that it has given me practically nothing."[101] It was the threat of AIDS that made Palmer reconsider his participation in the bars and baths central to gay male culture. The divisive issue of promiscuity led both Young and Palmer to expose the same rhetoric around sexual promiscuity and self-worth, health, and security that was being conveyed by social conservatives at the time.

Another reader, Harvey Hamburg, felt that AIDS warranted a curbing of some sexual acts, but in a manner that still validated gay men's sexuality. Wondering why *TBP* did not promote less risky sexual practices, he acknowledged the fears of a "self-oppressive gay response to AIDS." He concluded, however, that gay men's sexual practices would inevitably change as the number of infected increased.[102] Similarly, James Johnstone wrote to the newspaper in 1984, arguing that monogamous relationships were increasingly attractive as the threat of AIDS persisted. The myth of gay male promiscuity, in Johnstone's words, "is going to decimate and eventually destroy us, not AIDS."[103] Both readers were not only re-evaluating their own sex lives but raising fundamental questions around the responsibility of *TBP* to act as a moral compass for the gay male community. HIV/AIDS disrupted the sexual libertarian agenda of many among the editorial collective.

Heeding these concerns, writers for *TBP* re-evaluated promiscuity and cruising in gay culture. They began to question how gay men might express their sexuality and, indirectly, their masculinity in the climate of HIV/AIDS. Collective member Rick Bébout included a section on the social ramifications of HIV/AIDS near the end of his December 1983 article "Is There Safe Sex?" Following a questionnaire conducted at Toronto's Hassle Free Clinic in September 1983, Bébout reported that of the "90 responses, 58 percent said their sex lives had changed in the past year, and cited concern about AIDS as one reason." While respondents stated that they had more sex in the recent past, "[a]bout a quarter said they had less anal sex, active or passive – though 15 percent were fucking *more* often. Seventeen percent said they'd started using condoms; 21 percent reported an increase in mutual masturbation."[104] In the same article, it was reported that a similar survey of 105 gay men found that "More than half of the men ... said their sex lives had not been affected by AIDS. Three-fifths of these were monogamous."[105] These varied results indicated that some gay men had adopted condom use, changed sexual practices, or entered monogamous relationships in response to early reports of HIV/AIDS.

A catalyst for changing attitudes around changing sexual practices was the advertising campaign of the AIDS Committee of Toronto (ACT). In May 1985, ACT produced an advertisement in *TBP* captioned "Anal Sex," encouraging men to wear condoms when engaging in sexual intercourse. The ad featured two men engaging in anal sex, both of whom were slender and their faces either faced away from the camera or explicitly blurred – allowing the reader to see themselves in the sex act.[106] As a result, the advertisement became more about the sex act itself rather than the individuals having sex. The image not

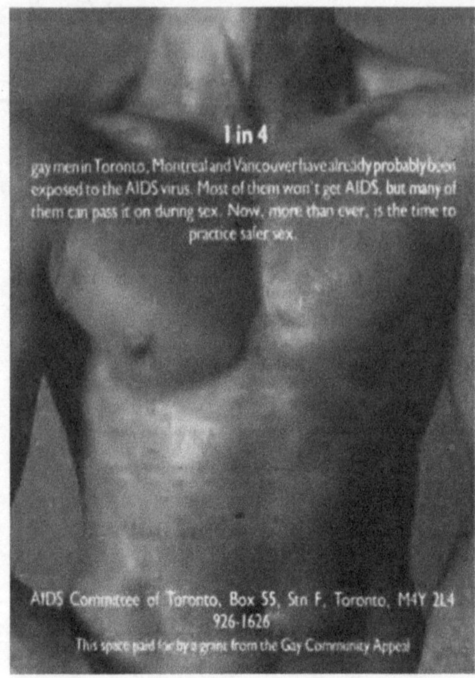

Figure 5.2 Advertisement from AIDS Committee of Toronto. Photographer: unknown. "1 in 4," *The Body Politic* 119, October 1985, 27. Image courtesy of AIDS Committee of Toronto (ACT).

only warned of the risks of unprotected anal sex but encouraged men to either use a condom or "don't do it."[107] This message would have been unfathomable years prior, highlighting both the gravity of the epidemic as well as the extent to which HIV/AIDS had redefined the relationship between promiscuity and sexual liberation.

A subsequent ad by ACT (Figure 5.2) informed readers that "1 in 4 gay men in Toronto, Montreal and Vancouver have already probably been exposed to the AIDS virus."[108] This advertisement not only communicated a statistic about the prevalence of the virus but also employed visual elements that conveyed specific stereotypes and assumptions about the demographics at risk. The claim that one in four gay men in major urban Canadian cities had likely been exposed to the virus served to heighten the sense of urgency and personal risk among readers. However, the accompanying image of a muscular, male torso introduced a layer of complexity to the message. At a superficial level, the image could be interpreted as a visual representation of the general population at risk: muscular (conventionally attractive) gay men. The absence of a head in the image depersonalized the individual. This dehumanization technique was likely deliberate, aiming to create a universal representation that anyone could become a victim of the disease. And to encourage readers of *TBP* to practice safer sex, ACT employed similar marketing techniques to those of commercial interests to make "safe sex" appealing.[109] In doing so, however, their advertisement adopts a queer patriarchal assumption that muscular men are more sexually active and, by extension, more susceptible to the HIV/AIDS virus. Thus, the ad subtly emphasizes the connection between physical fitness and sexual prowess.

More broadly, *TBP*'s editorial content reflected how HIV/AIDS brought with it a new form of regulatory gaze in the gay male community, one similar to the medicalization and observation of disabled bodies. For instance, Gerald Hannon informed readers that gay men in New York City had established the JOE (Jerk Off Enthusiasts) Club in 1985 as a way of acting on their sexual urges during the HIV/AIDS epidemic.[110] The JOE Club was a space for gay men to masturbate together, but no bodily fluids were to be exchanged. As Hannon walked into the bar, he was handed the rules of the JOE Club on a piece of paper – each patron received one upon admittance. The number one rule of the JOE Club was that "Activity is strictly J/O. No oral or anal sex will be tolerated." Additionally, the entire space had been redesigned to guard against HIV/AIDS transmission. Hannon noted that "everywhere, on benches, on shelves, were stacks of paper napkins."[111] These hygienic offerings created an environment that innocuously sent the message that bodily fluids were to be discarded and not shared. If that did not work, two men aptly named the "Fluid Patrol" policed ejaculation in this space. They were, by all intents and purposes, evidence that HIV/AIDS brought with it a renewed regulatory gaze *within* the community.

Donning blue shirts with realistic police badges, the Fluid Patrol was a light-hearted mockery of police, state surveillance, and power (recall Michael Riordon's analysis of police drag in 1978). In this space, however, their outfits were rewoven with the same authority to scrutinize and control sexuality as that of the actual police.[112] Hannon informed readers that he questioned whether the Fluid Patrol would hand out tickets or escort violators from the premises. Similar to how police patrolled parks and alleyways, the Fluid Patrol "strolled together slowly from room to room, looking altogether too benign."[113] While no infraction was noticed by Hannon during his visit, the presence of the Fluid Patrol reflected the conundrum bar and bathhouse owners found themselves in. Some felt obligated to invert the regulatory gaze of society: becoming sites of internal "police" surveillance while also affording patrons the ability to avoid society's moral-medical gaze. Yet, the JOE Club demonstrated that HIV/AIDS may have changed gay male sexual practices, but it did not diminish them. Rather, the disease refashioned the social, political, and even aesthetic dimensions of gay male sexuality in response to personal and community responsibility. Consternation around sex, the body, and health led to new forms of self-regulation among gay men.

Other evidence of the sexual regulation of those affected by HIV/AIDS can be found in *TBP* writer Rob Joyce's article on social isolation as a form of sexual regulation in the gay community. In his article, he interviewed three HIV-positive men: Warren Jensen, Kevin Brown, and Lawrence Fisher, all of whom described how HIV/AIDS changed their sexual lives. Brown noted that AIDS turned the gay male body from a source of pleasure into a source of fear. He told Joyce, "For awhile [*sic*] you go through a real feeling that you're some kind of Typhoid Mary or something; or that you're a walking death even if someone touches you. It's a real stopper. You're in a bar and you see someone nice and then you say, 'By the way, you know, I have AIDS,' and you pick them up off the floor." For others, the fear of HIV/AIDS had the potential to turn into anger. Fisher recalled being berated by the same man after he had learned that Fisher had AIDS. Expletives aside, the man told Fisher that he "would never have had sex with him in the first place if he had known he had AIDS."[114] These episodes illuminated the prejudices against those with HIV/AIDS within the gay community. Ableist assumptions around sexuality were extended to broader equations of well-being overlapping with bodily function. HIV/AIDS did not just deteriorate one's health but threatened one's social standing in the gay community – a marginalization not unlike the social isolation facing those with a disability.

TBP's collective felt it necessary to dismiss perceptions that HIV/AIDS meant the end of intimacy in the gay community. As Joyce put it, "unlike some gay men who disavow their sexual orientation after diagnosis, all three wear it with a shine."[115] Yet, all three men demonstrated that HIV/AIDS was either shrouded under the self-oppression of one's sexuality or "worn" – perhaps not physically, but mentally – in a way that encouraged visibility of the disease. Despite their positive attitudes, it was clear that this disease wrought new regulatory measures and practices within the gay male community. A separate report in that same issue of *TBP* noted some gay men had "[g]iven up sex altogether (still not a popular option, and vows of celibacy have a way of dissolving in desperate moments) or, more likely, given up trying to make it safe every time."[116] It was one thing to have the state oppress and limit gay male sexuality under the guise of morality and national security; it was an entirely new phenomenon to have such regulatory practices occur within the gay community.

Among those who considered the idea of regulation from within the community was journalist Douglas Janoff. He referred to some gay men with HIV/AIDS as "demons among us," in an unpublished article submitted to *TBP*. Janoff shed light on this would-be article in a letter that was published by *TBP* in the December 1985 issue. According to Janoff, the article had centred on his interview with an unnamed gay man living with primary lateral sclerosis (PLS) and AIDS in Montreal.[117] Janoff noted in his letter that the individual had bragged about how he had unprotected sex with men while knowing his HIV/AIDS status. "Horrified" with this revelation, Janoff concluded that "not all people with AIDS are suffering stoicly [*sic*]. There are also people with AIDS who are irresponsible, selfish and psychotic."[118] In his thinking about public health, Janoff imposed his perception of morality onto already stigmatized men, expecting those infected to conform to separate standards of sexual activity. Janoff posited in his letter that his complaint might "open the floor to a full-scale debate ... on the ethics of identifying sexually-irresponsible people with AIDS and ARC – maybe even to the proportions of the '[B]lack houseboy' debate!"[119] Janoff suggested that curtailing HIV/AIDS exposure entailed the sexual regulation of people with AIDS, beginning with identification. It is unclear whether Janoff believed that the policing of people with HIV/AIDS should involve the state or remain within the gay community, but his recommendation concerned *TBP*'s editorial collective, especially at a time when provincial and federal governments had begun to consider similar ideas.

For collective member Ken Popert, any form of identification for gay men with HIV/AIDS was unacceptable. Popert had witnessed, like so many others, how identification could be weaponized against gay men and lesbians and used as blackmail – the "purge" campaigns of queer individuals from the RCMP, federal civil service, and military are particularly poignant examples.[120] He also felt that Janoff's article risked further marginalizing gay men with HIV/AIDS. Janoff's description of gay men with HIV/AIDS who knowingly spread the disease as "demons" stigmatized gay men with the disease, even those who had sex with other men with condoms.[121] In Popert's words, Janoff "arouses the reader's fears and then heartlessly proposes the man with PLS as a defenceless scapegoat." Additionally, Popert noted that other details surrounding the unnamed individual's life had been left out of the article, including his PLS diagnosis, lack of sufficient food, depression, paralysis of one hand, and distrust of the AIDS groups working with Janoff.[122] For Popert, as well as others on *TBP*'s editorial collective, it was important for *TBP* to express support and make those with

HIV/AIDS visible in the community; however, any formal regulation and identification of these individuals was considered *too* visible, especially if it involved the state.[123]

In 1983, Ontario passed the Health Protection and Promotion Act, which allowed public health officials to request and receive positive findings of reportable diseases. Collective member Ed Jackson expressed dismay over the passage of the Act, worried that the ambiguously worded Act might also be used by public health officials to detain healthy gay men. More insidiously, those working for the state could also gain support by conjuring up the notion of the "'loose cannon' – the active prostitute or promiscuous homosexual who refuses to stop having unsafe sex with unwitting strangers," in Jackson's words. Just as Janoff suggested regulating gay men with HIV/AIDS, this piece of legislation meant that gay men afflicted with the disease would be required to have regular check-ups, while new infections could potentially be linked back to them. In the words of Jackson, "Screening people as opposed to screening blood, keeping the records, and the use to which those records might be put to use are the real issues."[124] The efforts of the Ontario government to identify – even for statistical purposes – and potentially regulate the sex lives of people with HIV/AIDS differentiated them from the rest of the gay community as an "other."

The politics of visibility for those with HIV/AIDS was further captured in *TBP* when it cabled a news report from San Francisco's *Bay Area Reporter* that the US Public Broadcasting Service (PBS) was filming a documentary special on Fabian Bridges, an impoverished Black gay man with AIDS venturing from Cleveland to Houston between July 1984 and May 1985.[125] Featured in the PBS special *AIDS, a National Enquiry* (1986), Bridges was a symbolic representation to the American public of life with HIV/AIDS; and the portrayal of Bridges was not a sympathetic one either. Many activists noted that PBS seemed to cast Bridges as sexually irresponsible and a "prostitute who knowingly spread AIDS to his clients." The insinuation that Bridges engaged in irresponsible sex drew on a legacy of racialized men and women being seen as "morally suspect," in the words of Christina Simmons.[126] John Barnich, an individual who helped Hill care for Bridges in Houston, believed that Bridges told reporters he was a sex worker out of denial of his affliction with HIV/AIDS. According to Barnich, "What more appropriate form of denial (that he has AIDS) than to say he is still having sex and getting paid for it." His comment suggests that people with AIDS were expected to be abstinent.[127] For readers of *TBP*, the messaging of the PBS documentary was clear: gay men could not be sexual beings the same way healthy men could be. The scrutiny of Bridges' sexual practices, as well as how he navigated his sexuality amid failing health, triggered the same regulatory gaze and language that had been historically aimed at people with disabilities. Gay men with HIV/AIDS were evidently expected to act upon their sexuality differently (or not at all) from uninfected men.

Overlapping Narratives of Disability and Disease

References to the debilitating effects of HIV/AIDS in *TBP* simultaneously established the healthy and sexually desirable body as "normal" and the unhealthy and sexually undesirable body as "abnormal" within the gay community. Sociologists Kathy Charmaz and Dana Rosenfeld argue that the visible cues of disabilities transform the *disappearing* body (one we are unaware of in everyday life) into the *dysappearing* one, whereby the person is lost behind the disability and the disabled body becomes a place of confusion, anxiety, and anger.[128] In the case of gay men with HIV/AIDS, coverage of their experiences frequently touched upon their inability to perform or function in sexually expected ways. As a result, gay men with the disease attempted to subvert stigmatized notions of their masculinity and sexuality by stylizing their bodies in ways to subvert the heteronormative/ableist and medical gazes on their "abnormal bodies." They sought to resist labels of pollution and dread from both within and outside the gay community.

In the August 1985 issue of *TBP*, Gerald Hannon wrote of his "disgust" that his friend, Jim Black, lay in a hospital bed while "[d]eath seemed to be inside him clawing its way out and the not very pretty marks of that struggle were everywhere on his thin and wasted frame."[129] This visceral recapturing of death "clawing" out of Black was a traumatic illustration of HIV/AIDS that gave the disease a life of its own. The description of his "thin and wasted frame" provided a corporeal image of the AIDS-affected male body. It was described as if it were a frame with no painting, a hollow shell of what was once filled out with muscle, vibrancy, and desirable masculinity. Historian Heather Murray argues that "[t]he physicality of AIDS went far beyond connotations and hints of contamination. … Those with full-blown AIDS became shockingly disfigured."[130] Black served as both an example of the horrific realities of HIV/AIDS and communicated to readers of *TBP* that the disease was reshaping gay men's bodies.

HIV/AIDS threatened to cloak gay male sexuality and the body under discourses of disease. When Michael Lynch recalled the withering effects AIDS had on Fred's body in the March 1983 issue of *TBP*, he wrote: "Fred now was utterly weak, a skin-and-bones echo of the vibrant thirty-three-year-old redhead Bruce had met sixteen months before." During his time with Fred, Lynch recalled Fred's partner Bruce straightening "the illness-thinned body on the bed." This vivid detail established an image of emaciation that has long been synonymous with disease.[131] Indeed, the reference to Fred as "skin-and-bones" evoked an aesthetic of the male body far removed from the idealized muscular body. In their monograph *Looking Queer*, John De Cecco and Dawn Atkins quote gay activist Victor D'Lugin, saying, "For a long time, outside and inside the community, the face of AIDS was the emaciated body."[132] The loss of muscle and undesirable thinness symbolized a loss of masculinity because emaciation was embedded in tropes of frailty and vulnerability, the opposite of muscularity and strength.

As more narratives of HIV/AIDS began to appear in *TBP*, the newspaper was put in a difficult position. The collective was compelled to highlight the experiences of gay men with HIV/AIDS to raise awareness of the disease, but doing so risked sensationalizing the epidemic as well as the social and physical repercussions of having HIV/AIDS. For instance, during one of Lynch's visits to see Fred in hospital, he noted that Fred "had lost half of his hair because of the chemo, and his skin was all broken out." By way of coping, Lynch and Bruce used humour to soften the impact the disease had on his appearance. After Fred returned home, Lynch quipped, "I don't think of Fred as having cancer anymore. I don't remember what he looks like with hair!"[133] Yet, Fred associated his masculinity with his facial hair. After finishing his first round of chemotherapy, Lynch informed readers that Fred had "grown back his hair and, a source of great pride, his moustache."[134] To regain his moustache was to regain a sense of machismo, virility, and a connection with gay male macho culture. Just as white macho culture was a queer patriarchal appropriation of clothing associated with the working class, including tight jeans, white shirts, and a macho demeanour, it also frequently included moustaches as part of this masculine aesthetic. When those who developed AIDS began to see their bodies waste away from the disease or a related illness, it was reported that their ability to communicate strength, vitality, and masculinity through their body also seemingly disappeared.

For Gary, a reader in Kitchener, Ontario, Lynch's time with Fred provided a relatable experience as he, too, cared for a partner who had recently been diagnosed with cancer. Gary noted the lack of support from friends within the gay community, perhaps because of a fear that all cancers might be indicative of HIV/AIDS. He argued that illness and dying were not part of gay life.[135] Similarly, Vancouver social worker Bryan Teixeira wrote into *TBP* in September 1983 concerned that AIDS risked ostracizing its victims in the gay community because "AIDS indicates some small degree of contamination."[136] Inspired by Susan Sontag's reference to the leper as a social text for corruption in her book *Illness as Metaphor* (1978), Teixeira argued that as long as HIV/AIDS was labelled a "gay disease," gay men were at risk of denying themselves the pleasures of gay sex and, in the process, condemning those with AIDS "not as brothers to be supported," but as "lepers to be denied."[137] His sentiments around bodily pollution and AIDS would be reiterated by Sontag herself in her 1989 monograph, *AIDS and Its Metaphors*.[138] For those *visibly* affected with AIDS, such as Fred or Black, the disease became an example of the health and social risks associated with gay sex.

Becoming a pariah seemed to be the social consequence of the disease for twenty-eight-year-old Peter Evans. He described the social stigma he faced as a person with AIDS to Ed Jackson in an interview for *TBP* in October 1983. After being diagnosed with AIDS in December 1982 while living in London, England, Evans's symptoms included Crohn's disease and bouts of psoriasis. The latter, and notably more visible symptom, led him to quit his job because people had begun to refuse his service as a waiter. Evans described the social repercussions he felt from having AIDS as the "leper approach."[139] After returning home to Ottawa between late 1982 and early 1983, Evans felt isolated from friends and family, society, as well as the other patients with AIDS during his time in hospital.[140] He told Jackson:

> My brother also went very strange for a while. I realized one day that he just wasn't seeing me. He was going out of his way to avoid me, saying he was busy. That was due partly to an irresponsible family doctor. He knew that both of us were gay and that I had AIDS. He saw my brother several times and tried to do a real psychological number on him. He started by saying, "You're going to have to stop being gay. You'll have to be straight. Don't sleep with a man again or you'll get AIDS and die." A real homophobic number![141]

Even Evans's dentist turned him away, stating, "I don't feel I can treat you and I'd rather not have you here."[142] This blend of social and medical ostracization played into HIV/AIDS hysteria and socially punished those with the disease, isolating them from the very professionals meant to help them.

Ed Jackson referred to Evans as "Canada's national person with AIDS" because he was one of the most outspoken advocates for HIV/AIDS research.[143] According to journalist Ann Silversides, Evans "put a face on AIDS. He appeared at press conferences in Winnipeg, Toronto, and Ottawa, gave scores of media interviews, and spoke at many public forums."[144] His interview with Jackson served as a personal account, albeit a politically driven one, by *TBP* to undermine the invisibility of those affected by HIV/AIDS. Jackson's article was not just a commentary on mainstream society, but that of the gay community itself, serving as a reminder that a new closet in the gay community formed when people with HIV/AIDS became hidden in hospital rooms or private residences. Six months after going public, Evans succumbed to the disease on 7 January 1984. His obituary in *TBP* by the AIDS Committee of Toronto (ACT) read: "Beyond grief … we are proud to have known Peter. He demonstrated to all Canadians that a person with AIDS has much to teach his friends, the general public, and those who have or live in fear of this syndrome."[145] Even in death, Evans was framed as an example that HIV/AIDS could cloak its hosts with stigma and fear.

Stigma was, in part, the consequence of the effects of HIV/AIDS on the face. The face is an important part of the body in the context of HIV/AIDS because secondary diseases, such as KS, were difficult to cover from the gaze of onlookers. Heather Murray argues that "[t]he faces of those suffering with AIDS … could be ravaged by the purple-brown lesions of Kaposi's sarcoma, as though gay men with AIDS carried the visual lacerations and markings of a perceived non-ascetic life."[146] The realities of the disease on the face were captured by *TBP*'s editorial collective in June 1986, when writer Phil Shaw reviewed Arthur Bressan Jr.'s 1985 film *Buddies*.[147]

The film follows a New York City gay man, David, who takes care of Robert, another gay man dying of AIDS in the mid-1980s. Friendships blossom as David acts as a "buddy" to Robert in his final days. One scene in particular – and that which was highlighted in *TBP* – contains a healthy-looking young man in the background (presumably David) and Robert dying from AIDS in the foreground. The power of the chosen image lies in its ability to convey the stark reality of AIDS, particularly focusing on the face as a poignant symbol of the disease's impact. Robert, the man portrayed in the still, gazes into the distance, his darkened eyes and visible lesion under the lip serving as visceral reminders of the toll exacted by AIDS. The dishevelled, sullen appearance and the hospital gown further contribute to a visual narrative that encapsulates the medicalization and institutionalization of the gay community's struggle with AIDS. By featuring such a striking image, *TBP*'s editorial collective takes a bold step in confronting the uncomfortable visual aspects of the epidemic, fostering a dialogue that

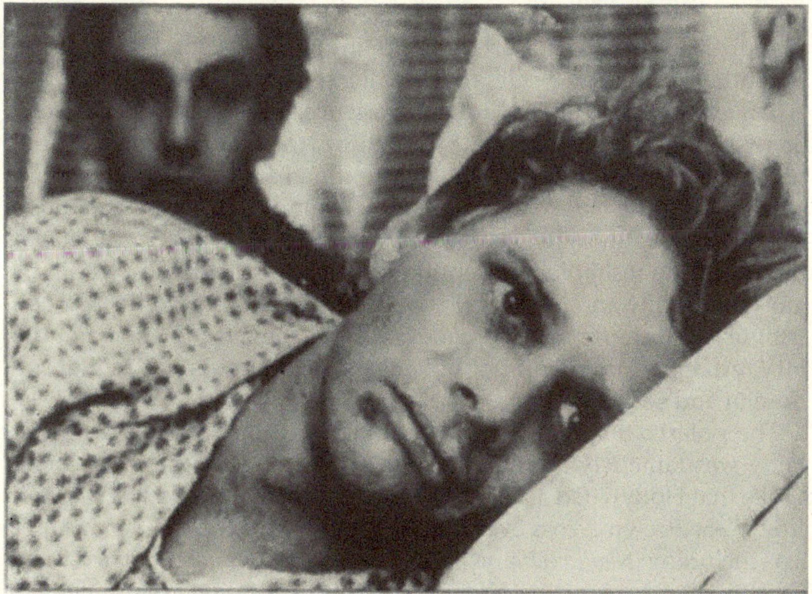

Figure 5.3 Film still from Arthur Bressan Jr.'s *Buddies* (1985). Phil Shaw, "A Celluloid Valentine to the Gay Community," *The Body Politic* 127, June 1986, 32.

extends beyond the emotional toll to encompass the broader societal implications.

While the film created this image, Phil Shaw's purposeful inclusion of this film still speaks to the role of *TBP* in balancing stereotypes around the "look" of HIV/AIDS with the desire to highlight the emotional toll of HIV/AIDS. His deliberate inclusion of a still from *Buddies* in *TBP* demonstrates a nuanced and purposeful effort to contribute to the ongoing discourse surrounding HIV/AIDS during the mid-1980s. The film itself, centred around the care of a gay man dying from AIDS, is a poignant representation of the devastating physical consequences of the disease. Shaw's choice to feature an image from this film in the newspaper underscores the publication's commitment to addressing the multifaceted dimensions of the HIV/AIDS epidemic, moving beyond mere stereotypical depictions.

Shaw's editorial decision becomes even more significant when considering the juxtaposition within the image itself. The inclusion of a healthy-looking young man in the background serves as a powerful counterpoint to the foreground narrative of illness. This juxtaposition is not merely aesthetic; it is a deliberate commentary on the varied experiences within the gay community during the HIV/AIDS crisis. The presence of the supportive figure in the background suggests the potential for love and solidarity, challenging the stereotype of HIV/AIDS as a solitary and isolating experience. In essence, *TBP*, through Shaw's strategic use of visual storytelling, transcends mere reporting of facts; it engages in a critical dialogue aimed at dispelling stereotypes surrounding the "look" of HIV/AIDS. By emphasizing the emotional toll of the epidemic alongside its physical manifestations, *TBP* plays a crucial role in reshaping perceptions and fostering empathy within the gay community and beyond. Shaw's editorial choices within *TBP* contribute significantly to the broader cultural conversation surrounding HIV/AIDS, portraying it not only as a medical crisis but as a deeply human and social one.

The polarization of healthy muscularity against the AIDS-afflicted body was famously brought into the public consciousness after news broke that Hollywood actor Rock Hudson was diagnosed with AIDS in July 1985. Strewn across every tabloid and newspaper in North America, including *Newsweek* and the *National Enquirer*, Hudson's health condition and, more insidiously, his homosexuality exemplified the morbid portrayals of HIV/AIDS on the body. Before-and-after photos of the Hollywood actor established a "chronology," in the words of film scholar Richard Dyer, whereby a "healthy, strong, gorgeous" Hudson is transformed into a diseased man whose masculinity and virility were compromised due to his homosexuality. Writing for *TBP* in December 1985, Dyer argued:

> Such a juxtaposition of beauty and decay is part of a long-standing rhetoric of gayness. It is a way of constructing gay identity as a devotion to an exquisite surface (queens are so good-looking, so fastidious, so stylish, so amusing) masking a depraved reality (unnatural, promiscuous and repulsive sex acts). The rhetoric allows the effects of an illness gotten through sex to be read as a metaphor for that sex itself.[148]

Images of Hudson insinuated that gay men were frail, weak, and a source of disease and that gay sex could lead to the destruction of the body. Revelation of Hudson's homosexuality further challenged any preconceived notion that physical traits such as muscularity or a "square jaw" were signifiers of heterosexuality as a stable construct. According to Dyer, Hudson's homosexuality challenged "US men's style of antiseptic machismo."[149] The cover of *Time* highlighted a critical aspect of gay male style during the HIV/AIDS epidemic: the healthy male body is representative of heterosexuality, while the frail male body becomes emblematic of homosexuality. This duality suggests that "gayness" – as a performance of sexuality and gender – potentially masks that which is undesirable. Writing at the time of the AIDS epidemic, scholar Jeffrey Weeks noted: "AIDS is a disease of the body, it wrecks and destroys what was once glorified."[150] That which was glorified, however, was the muscular, white, enabled body.

Conclusion

While *TBP* stressed to readers the very real stigma that those with HIV/AIDS might expect to encounter, other parts of the paper, such as articles, film reviews, letters from readers, and even classified ads, served to reinforce or remind readers that the disease also brought with it social consequences. *TBP* frequently contained descriptions or analyses of HIV/AIDS that evoked the language of disability. Writers and readers of *TBP* alike described and debated the ways in which HIV/AIDS threatened gay men and the gay male body. Stories of gay men left alone in their apartments or placed under medical observation in hospital wards overlapped narratives of people with disabilities reconciling with the sexual politics, as well as social and physical barriers, of the gay community. In doing so, the trauma and shame experienced by individuals who acquired HIV or AIDS became construed with the similar trauma experienced by people with disabilities in a culture defined by enabled men.[151]

With the fear and panic that HIV/AIDS had incited, ideas of gay male masculinity were re-envisioned as the disease permeated gay cultural life. *TBP* just so happened to serve as a vehicle for both information on HIV/AIDS and shifting ideas around sexuality and the embodiment of healthy masculinity amid the epidemic. In the formative years of the HIV/AIDS crisis, namely 1981 and 1982, there were discussions that gay men's homosexuality or promiscuity was the cause of the various illnesses that gay men seemed to be suddenly experiencing. As debates around gay male promiscuity raged on, the white, muscular, macho male had taken on the mantle of health and virility. The consequence of this was a polarization of macho style as the embodiment of health and sexual virility against the diseased, frail, and sickly aesthetic of AIDS.

Within *TBP*, depictions of people with HIV/AIDS and those perceived to be disabled visually and imaginatively entrenched an "abnormal" body in the gay community that simultaneously buttressed macho style as normal. *TBP* reflects how and why the privileged position of white, muscular, enabled masculinity remained unfettered even as fears and misinformation around HIV/AIDS slowly diminished with research and treatment. The gay male body became a battleground for competing interests and ideas of identification and the stigmatization of those visibly ill, as well as overlapping discourses of disability to describe the effects of the disease. In a world with HIV/AIDS, stereotypes of asexuality and emasculation that had surrounded men with disabilities had extended to able-bodied gay men in this new climate. Such similarities demonstrate that bodies perceived to no longer "function" as expected became restylized or, rather, cloaked under similar discourses of health, de/sexuality, and disability.

Even nearing the end of *TBP*'s publication in 1987, readers and the editorial collective alike raised questions around the freedom of gay men's sexual and gender expression. Throughout the 1980s, the newspaper described the rapid development of anxieties both from outside and within the community around the regulation of sexuality and the gay male body. In a climate of social intolerance and fear around gay men's health from outside the community, some gay men felt compelled to restylize themselves and their sexual lifestyles to something akin to heterosexual monogamy; some men did not. Nevertheless, performances of gay male masculinity became increasingly narrowed under a banner of healthy heterosexual "normalcy." Similar to other sexually transmitted infections, HIV/AIDS brought with it significant discussions about the aesthetics of disease. But unlike those diseases discovered before it, HIV/AIDS centred on the gay male body and sparked apprehension around disability – resonating with Weeks's powerful quote that AIDS wrecks what was once glorified.[152]

Conclusion: Reflecting on *The Body Politic*

In *TBP*'s final issue, Gerald Hannon reflected on the collective's decision to cease publishing the paper: "And though I wept the night we did it, and though I woke trembling from an agonizing nightmare that same night, I would be lying if I said I didn't feel a sense of relief as well. It was like putting down something heavy that I'd been carrying for years."[1] The editorial collective did not take the newspaper's demise as evidence that lesbians and gays had achieved equality. Rather, *TBP* shuttered because sales of the newspaper had been gradually decreasing, classified and advertisement revenue was down, and letters from readers were steadily declining.[2] Adding to these financial woes was competition from more radical liberationist writings appearing elsewhere in the mid-1980s. *Rites*, for instance, formed in 1984 and sought to address some of the perceived shortcomings of *TBP*, namely by exploring the interconnections between gay and lesbian liberation, the women's movement, anti-racist activism, the peace movement, labour unionization, dis/ability activism, and the fight against apartheid in South Africa. And so, on 16 December 1986, the editorial collective decided that the gay community might be better served through other means, one of which was *TBP*'s successor, *Xtra!*, a magazine that spoke to a new generation of gay men and women, and one printed every two weeks for Toronto residents.[3] The public would read the last issue of *TBP* in February 1987.

For Hannon, the decision to fold *TBP* offered an opportunity to reflect on his experiences at the newspaper. His involvement lasted over sixteen years and included innumerable memories. As he began to write his final article for *TBP*, Hannon went through hundreds, if not thousands, of images and memories. Three photographs stood out the most: a picture of him with his then lover Chris Lea on Christmas Eve, 1982; one of a kicked-in door, a smashed-in wall, and a cot from the 5 February 1981 police raids; and, finally, a photograph of several collective members in front of the Ontario legislature in 1974. In his words, "One leads me through a very particular person to the whole network of interlocking faces (and sometimes bodies) that were this place. Another plunges me into the community turmoils that created and polished gay life in this city. And one takes me through the day-to-day civil rights plodding that climaxed in this province on December 16, 1986."[4] From the early emphasis placed on unapologetically loving someone of the same sex to the sexualized politics of space and place, Hannon's images represent the varying aspects of gay cultural life in Toronto and *TBP*'s role in capturing it. These photographs remind us that *TBP* was much more than its political accomplishments. It provided readers and writers the opportunity to wade into debates around sexual expression, desire, gender, race, dis/ability, and health.

Over five chapters, this book establishes a chronology that is both unique to *TBP* while also reflective of the aesthetic developments around masculinity, race, dis/ability, and sexuality during the decades of gay liberation in English Canada. I argue that the editorial collective examined, critiqued, and commented on gay male aesthetics as politicized statements charged with deeper social, cultural, and political meanings. By using a critical discourse analysis of the various components of *TBP* and being ever mindful of queer patriarchy and queer style, I broaden *TBP*'s legacy to include the mediation of a burgeoning gay culture rife with tensions and anxieties around gender, race, sexuality, and the body. In doing so, this book disrupts the long-standing narrative that *TBP* was solely an engine of gay and lesbian political activism.

While true that *TBP* has been remembered for its role in confronting homophobic violence, heralding calls of unrest and protest, and fostering a budding gay community in Toronto, the editorial collective also paid close attention to constructions of gender, sexuality, race, and dis/ability in a flourishing and highly visible gay culture. The opinions and arguments presented on the pages of *TBP* transformed an otherwise political newspaper into an important vehicle for understanding the gendered politics of gay liberation, particularly amid the formation of a modern gay male identity. *TBP* exemplified the entanglement of visual culture, queer patriarchy, masculinity, and larger questions of what gay liberation meant during the period. The newspaper was a key resource that helped shape a burgeoning gay and lesbian culture by legitimizing same-sex desires and providing material to fulfil those desires. However, there existed a tension between the Marxist and libertarian gay liberationist who aimed to disrupt heteronormative and capitalist aspects of sexuality and the very capitalists who marketed their goods, services, and venues using a narrow aesthetic of gay male masculinity.

The ubiquity of white, muscular, enabled men was driven in part by paying advertisers who provided much-needed financial support for a fledgling activist newspaper. These ads brought with them questions as to how the paper was to accommodate a growing gay male consumer class who enjoyed the content and messages of gay liberation that called for the dismantling of the gendered status quo. Indeed, the varying depictions and subsequent discussions of gay male masculinity in *TBP* reflect a widening chasm between gay liberationist goals of representing and visualizing a variety of sexualities and genders, and a gay male culture being curated by the commercialization of sexuality and images of ideal masculinity. This tension reflects a larger issue within the gay community of the time: the struggle between embracing sexuality as an important part of liberation and recognizing the ways in which sexuality can reinforce existing social hierarchies, including patriarchy, sexism, racism, and ableism. It also highlights the importance of visual culture and the media in shaping attitudes around gender and sexuality.

Recalling Masculinity in *The Body Politic*

Reading *TBP* as an archive reveals how narratives around gender, sexuality, race, and dis/ability sit in tension with the memories of former members of the editorial collective. Former members of *TBP* are interviewed frequently regarding the history of gay liberation in Canada because of their status and role as "early" activists in the community. They have even produced their own histories of events as they unfolded, notably Tim McCaskell's history of Canadian queer activism from 1974 to 2014 entitled *Queer Progress: From Homophobia to Homonationalism* (2016).[5] With oral history proving to be a useful methodology in the writing of queer history since the mid-1980s, I thought it imperative that I speak with former collective members when writing a book centred on *TBP*.[6]

My interviews with Gerald Hannon, Ken Popert, David Rayside, and Tim McCaskell in 2015 suggest a progressive narrative of *TBP* as a publication which continually strove towards greater inclusivity and visibility for the lesbian and gay community. Additionally, they felt that masculinity was primarily discussed when broader questions of race, health, or HIV/AIDS were brought up. When I asked Hannon about *TBP*'s role in shaping or mediating masculinity, his answer was concise yet equally complex: "I don't think we addressed it directly very much from my memory of what I wrote."[7] Indeed, all interviewees felt that gay male masculinity was a tenuous topic. Rayside believed that despite gender being integral to *TBP*, "there was a variety of views, or sometimes just an ambivalence about how to think about various expressions of masculinity."[8] Perhaps this was the result of having a largely white male collective edit, write for, and publish *TBP*, making the political and volatile moments around race in *TBP*'s history all the more memorable while leaving conversations around gender behind. Or maybe it was because the theoretical tools to dismantle gender, notably examining gender as "a primary way of signifying relationships of power," in the words of Joan Scott, did not emerge until the mid-1980s.[9] Ken Popert suggested in his interview that, "We might not have had the right vocabulary for talking about it or an extensive enough analysis, but certainly that [gender] was *the* subject right away, one of the subjects."[10] Indeed, discussions of masculinity permeated the themes of politics, nightlife, travel, health, and art; they were woven into the very fabric of *TBP*.

The notion that *TBP* had little influence in reinforcing or challenging styles of masculinity arguably stems from a belief among some collective members that American cultural forces played a greater role in shaping Canadian sexualized content. When asked how *TBP* approached masculinity, McCaskell stated that "the hegemonic notions of masculinity probably came up from the States rather than were generated here in Toronto."[11] Placing such importance on American content in the construction of gender and sexuality in Canadian gay and lesbian communities signifies how interconnected gay cultural life was across North America, yet it does not consider how *TBP* allowed for Canadian voices to actively engage in these conversations. In its book and film reviews, letters, editorials, and news reports, *TBP* was an important vehicle for allowing Canadians to address Western European and North American ideals around the male body, whiteness, gender, sexuality, and health. Indeed, there was no Canadian publication that was as far-reaching in scope and volume as *TBP*.

These interviews also raise numerous questions about how we think about and recall performances of gender. Reflecting on the words of Judith Butler that gender is assumed to be an "internal essence" and is naturalized through "a sustained set of acts, posited through the gendered stylization of the body," I question if recollections of gender are equally naturalized or "performed."[12] Greg Dening's argument that retelling the past is a performance, involving "the whole person, all the senses, all the emotions, memory, a sense of presence, co-ordination of mind and body," is particularly useful in approaching how the largely white cisgender male collective have come to shape narratives of *TBP* and Canadian queer history.[13] Some of those interviewed did not necessarily see gender as a focal point of discussion in *TBP* because feminist critiques of gender were naturalized throughout it – after all, the collective was very much informed and polarized by feminist interpretations of gender at the time.

In his interview, David Rayside, a collective member deeply involved in *TBP*'s fundraising efforts, claimed that during the publication of *TBP* "[t]here was certainly a sense that there was a contestation in the community, or not contestation necessarily – there was a strong sense, because these are smart and observant people, that there were versions of masculinity played out in the larger community."[14] Readers and writers alike approached questions around masculinity with apprehension and uncertainty. The differing viewpoints on masculinity in *TBP* either challenged or buttressed racial, sexual, and gendered stereotypes that hindered or limited gay men's sexual desires and expressions. For example, in the May–June 1975 issue of *TBP*, reader John Kyper decried the near-ubiquitous whiteness of sex and masculinity in gay culture after reading Rand Holmes's comic *Harold Hed*. The comic was of two white men engaging in sex after discussing psychiatry and supposed "cures" for homosexuality. For Kyper, it suggested that gay sexuality and gay life centred around white men. He demanded that the community better reflect its diversity: "We need to see more Blacks, Orientals, Indians."[15] Kyper's call for greater racial inclusion reflected a growing dissatisfaction with white gay activism among some readers. More discussions and letters from readers addressing race and racism followed in the latter half of the 1970s. These responses to race are not explicitly remembered, however.

McCaskell's memory of the fight for racial diversity in *TBP* is heightened because of his extensive writings on the subject. Joining the collective as a volunteer in 1974 and subsequently taking a brief hiatus between 1976 and 1977 before returning, McCaskell noted that the collective's difficulty in understanding the influence of race on gender and sexual desirability was a reflection of their hesitation to address the changing racial makeup of the gay community: "By the '80s, we're [Toronto] approaching almost a quarter of racialized people. So the fights around race that happened in *TBP* happened around the absolute incomprehension of this white collective of anything that wasn't white. They just did not get it."[16] Furthermore, it demonstrates that many within the collective had difficulty understanding the intersectional experiences and viewpoints being expressed by readers and contributors in letters – reinforcing the argument that *TBP*'s overall ability to challenge and mediate constructions of masculinity relied in great part on the readers of the paper.

Altogether, the interviews suggest that the contentious moments in *TBP*'s history, such as the houseboy ad, played a central role in how categories of identity or identity politics are remembered and/or forgotten. What does the emphasis on the houseboy ad reveal about the banality of white masculinity in gay periodicals at the time? Furthermore, how does it usurp and erase the numerous discussions around race, desire, and sexuality that occurred *before* the houseboy ad ever appeared? In his interview with me, Hannon assumed that the collective had taken a more proactive approach to racism in the gay community. This assumption suggests that contemporary politics around racism in the gay and lesbian community shift our understanding of past political and social practices as arguably more inclusive than they were. My understanding of these interviews as performances of contemporary queer politics is informed by Irial Glynn and J. Olaf Kleist's monograph *History, Memory and Migration*, where they note that politics inform the very consciousness of how we perceive the past. In their words, "the politics of memory are historical and respond to general developments and changes in society, both by adjusting the perception of the past to shifts in social constellations and because actors can utilise memories to meet new challenges."[17] Those interviewed emphasized *TBP*'s political accomplishments and, apart from McCaskell, stressed the inclusivity of the newspaper in a manner that spoke to contemporary concerns around misogyny and racism in the gay community.

Oral historian Alessandro Portelli argues that "memory is not an instantaneous act of recall ... but rather a process and a generator of meaning."[18] Portelli's book, *The Death of Luigi Trastulli and Other Stories*, is an intervention in the making of history by engaging with storytelling and oral history to show how the past is accessed in ways that are meaningful to the present. In Paula Hamilton's reflection of Portelli's work, she contends that "[t]o struggle with the past is also to pose questions of the present – what the past means in the present."[19] Comments from former collective members stand in stark contrast to the discussions and content appearing in the newspaper. I do not dismiss these oral accounts for any "misrememberings" or exaggerations as many traditional critics of oral history, such as Eric Hobsbawm, have done.[20] Rather, I see these discrepancies as a political act of remembering.

The ways in which masculinity is recollected and/or forgotten in the interviews exemplifies how gender is reconstructed in the very retellings of *TBP*'s history. I do not suggest that my analysis of *TBP* is either somehow closer to the "truth" or more "accurate." Indeed, David Rayside cautioned me in his interview that a poststructuralist reading of *TBP* could slip into misrepresenting the newspaper's focus or the agenda of the editorial collective.[21] Heeding his words, I use my interviews with former collective members as opportunities to substantiate my analysis or contextualize masculinity in *TBP*. Yet, I am also cognizant that recollections of *TBP* tend to forgo the more mundane conversations and moments around categories such as race, dis/ability, or health. If they are not viewed with importance, it reinforces white, enabled hegemony in gay culture. Assumption of gay activism as inherently white naturalizes correlations between queerness and whiteness, which reduces the experience of gay life in the 1970s and 1980s to that of white gay men – a problem this book seeks to address.

The interviews reinforce my own misgivings about how *TBP* has been remembered and how it is accessed as an archive in and of itself – a concern informed by Jin Haritaworn, Ghaida Moussa, and Syrus Marcus Ware in *Marvellous Grounds* (2018). I am aware of the contemporary challenges to *TBP* as a source of white narratives of activism and encourage historians to approach gay and lesbian periodicals from an understanding of implicit whiteness. Marginalized groups and their contributions are frequently relegated to the periphery of historical narratives of heroic activism because they raise questions around the unity and cohesiveness of the movement. More work needs to be done around the inherent challenges of memory-making in Canadian queer history. The limited formal role given to queers of colour or people with disabilities in early activist organizations and publications are illuminated by the very interstices present in histories of queer activism. In an effort to remedy this, I pay careful attention to the ways in which whiteness and ability was upheld within *TBP*, and how it had been challenged by other editorial collective members and readers long before contemporary efforts to address racism and ableism within queer activist circles.

As I have demonstrated throughout this book, the voices of men of colour, dis/abled men, or men living with HIV/AIDS do appear in *TBP*. They do so in the Classified section, letters to the collective from readers, or in editorials on these subjects. Reading *TBP* for these voices not only reveals the sought-after visibility that so many desired but suggests the newspaper can be more than an archive of white gay activism in the 1970s and 1980s. There are further stories to be told about the relationship between *TBP* and femininity, dis/ability, and other queer experiences. Future research in dis/ability studies may consider the relationship, or lack thereof, between dis/ability groups that emerged in the late 1970s and more mainstream gay and lesbian activism, such as that associated with *TBP*. Doing so would historicize the processes that have sustained contemporary queer stigma around people's bodies labelled as dis/abled. The newspaper is also a useful source to explore how gender "transgressions" by drag performers as well as trans, gender fluid, or queer persons were policed within the queer community.[22]

Mediating Gay Male Masculinity and a Modern Gay Identity

This book is a history of Canadian gay liberation activities as it is told through styles of gay male masculinity presented, consumed, and challenged in *TBP*. While *TBP* was a liberationist newspaper bent on fighting for sexual freedom and equality, it was also a periodical that was, in various ways, restricted by queer patriarchal expectations around the stylization and performance of men. We can acquire a better understanding of this complicated and rich relationship shared between representations of gay male masculinity (and gender more broadly) and the patriarchal and gendered socio-cultural politics of gay liberation by looking more closely at the newspaper. The ubiquitous presence of white macho "clones" up until the newspaper's folding demonstrates that white, cis, enabled "styles" of masculinity continued to inform the imaginations of gay men. These styles of masculinity were most common in advertisements, articles, and photographic campaigns found in *TBP*. Meanwhile, Asian men were viewed with an orientalist lens by some who considered them effeminate. Black men were often stereotyped as sexually virile and hypermasculine, and Latino men were met with (and occasionally reproduced) mixed assumptions of whiteness embedded in colonial discourses around race in many South American cultures. Additionally, the sexuality of dis/abled men and men living with HIV/AIDS were compelled to legitimate their presence in the gay community – declaring themselves sexual beings in an ableist culture. Each issue of *TBP* speaks to these competing representations amid an increasingly commercialized gay culture that aided the pragmatic demands of an activist newspaper.

While *TBP*'s editorial collective may not have purposefully reinforced any single dominant aesthetic of gay male desire, their newspaper reflects an institutionalization of whiteness as the benchmark on a spectrum of masculinities and how macho culture became an almost exclusively white ableist subculture that remains enshrined within the gay male community. As white macho culture became deeply entrenched in the gay male community, it seemingly alienated men of colour as well as those who failed to or refused to live up to its aesthetic expectation or demand. Macho style was an aesthetic ideal, one to be emulated but never fully replicated. Yet, this emulation has had ripple effects into the present. The continued presence of macho culture in the contemporary gay community helps to reinforce gay activism, the gay community, and gay public spaces as privileged spaces for white, enabled gay macho men, leaving those who do not conform feeling voiceless and invisible.

Apprehensions around gay male masculinity and the constitution of a modern gay male identity did not disappear with the folding of *TBP*, nor have gay men since acquired any unilateral understanding of what it means to be "masculine." Gay male masculinity remains fraught around butchness or "masculine" performances of gender. There remains a subconscious effort on the part of queer media to fit into a patriarchal society whereby male effeminacy is shunned. One need only look at popular social media websites or applications to see damaging expectations that gay men should not be effeminate or that they should maintain statuesque bodies. Statements such as "Masc [masculine] for Masc" in dating profiles, for instance, are not hyperbolic statements disconnected from culture. Rather, they are an attempt at policing and regulating performances and styles of masculinity among gay men. The misconception, however, is that this is a relatively recent phenomenon within the gay community.

This book demonstrates that the policing, regulation, and mediation of gay male masculinity from *within* the community has been an ongoing issue since gay liberationists began carving out their own spaces. Classified ads, bar advertisements, and photospreads on the body in *TBP* simply evolved into advertisements, articles, and commentary on Facebook, Instagram, Grindr, and Tinder, among others. The platforms may have changed, but the message around gender has not. While not dedicated to consciousness-raising per se, these new platforms are cultural vectors of a modern gay consciousness and identity, one arguably still centred on white, muscular, enabled men.

On 26 June 2015, writer Brian Fleming wrote an article for *Fashion* magazine entitled "All About That Pride Body: A Painstakingly Detailed Guide to What It Takes to Look Your Best." In the article, he described the onerous process of exercise, religious dieting, tanning, and buying in-season luxury goods, such as Tom Ford sandals, as part of gay men's preparation for Toronto's Pride Week.[23] The article carefully elaborated on how an individual's perceived success at having sexual encounters or merely enjoying Pride activities involved a very specific cultivation and presentation of their body. For Fleming and those interviewed for the article, queer style was fundamental to how they saw themselves in the queer community. And while Fleming and his article faced backlash by many in the community for presenting a narrow archetype as desirable, it inadvertently contributed to the "Body Pride" movement – a movement that encourages people to love their bodies the way they are. Nevertheless, the body and style remain integral to navigating the social and sexual channels of an ongoing patriarchal gay male community. In many ways, this is a history of these sexual politics.

Notes

Introduction

1 Emphasis in original. Ed Jackson, "Nudity and Sexism," *The Body Politic* 21, December 1975, 12.
2 Emphasis in original. Jackson, "Nudity," 25.
3 Jackson, "Nudity," 13.
4 Heidi J. Nast, "Queer Patriarchies, Queer Racisms, International," *Antipode 34*, no. 5 (November 2002): 881.
5 Robert Trow, "Diamonds in the Buff," *The Body Politic* 10, 1973, 11.
6 See Gary Kinsman and Patrizia Gentile, *The Canadian War on Queers: National Security as Sexual Regulation* (Vancouver: University of British Columbia Press, 2010); Ann Silversides, *AIDS Activist: Michael Lynch and the Politics of Community* (Toronto: Between the Lines, 2003); and Thomas Waugh, *Romance of Transgression in Canada: Queer Sexualities, Nations, Cinemas* (Montreal and Kingston: McGill-Queen's University Press, 2006).
7 Nast, "Queer Patriarchies," 881.
8 "Post-Partum Issue #64," 16 June 1980, Box 1, F0002–01–028, *TBP* fonds.
9 See Stuart Hall, "Encoding, Decoding." *The Cultural Studies Reader*, 2nd ed., ed. Simon During (New York: Routledge, 1999 [1973]), 507–17; Jon Wagner, "Constructing Credible Images: Documentary Studies, Social Research, and Visual studies," *American Behavioral Scientist* 47, no. 12 (2004): 1477–506; Glen Creeber, "The Joy of Text?: Television and Textual Analysis," *Critical Studies in Television* 1, no. 1 (2006): 81–8; David Machin and Andrea Mayr, *How to Do Critical Discourse Analysis: A Multimodal Introduction* (New York: Sage Publications, 2012); Stuart Hall, Jessica Evans, and Sean Nixon, eds. *Representation*, 2nd ed. (New York: Sage Publications, 2013); and Norman Fairclough, *Critical Discourse Analysis: The Critical Study of Language*, 2nd ed. (New York: Routledge, 2013).
10 Elspeth Brown, *Work! A Queer History of Modeling* (Durham, NC: Duke University Press, 2019), 5.

11 Tom Warner, *Never Going Back: A History of Queer Activism in Canada* (Toronto: University of Toronto Press, 2002), 46.
12 Kinsman and Gentile, *Canadian War on Queers*, 287.
13 Tom Hooper, "Queering '69: The Recriminalization of Homosexuality in Canada," *Canadian Historical Review* 100, no. 2 (2019): 258.
14 Jaime Bradburn, "Historicist: I Sing *The Body Politic*," Torontoist, 14 February 2015. https://torontoist.com/2015/02/historicist-i-sing-the-body-politic/
15 *The Body Politic* 3, March–April 1972, 2.
16 Much more on *TBP*'s history from the perspective of editor Tim McCaskell can be found in McCaskell's book, *Queer Progress: From Homophobia to Homonationalism* (Toronto: Between the Lines, 2016).
17 The constitution is a handwritten document stored in the ArQuives. "Constitution," undated, Box 1, F0002–01–002, *The Body Politic* fonds.
18 David Churchill, "Personal Ad Politics: Race, Sexuality and Power at *The Body Politic*," *Left History* 8, no. 2 (2003): 115.
19 Warner describes counterpublics as not only related to a subculture (he gives the example of gay men and lesbian sexual culture), but "enables a horizon of opinion and exchange; its exchanges remain distinct from authority and can have a critical relation to power; its extent is in principle indefinite, because it is not based on precise demography but mediated by print, theater, diffuse networks of talk, commerce, and the like." Warner, *Publics and Counterpublics*, 57.
20 In addition to being a relation among strangers, Warner further described public as a group that is addressed by the same speaker, writer, advertisement; a social space where people participate or are reflexive in this space; as having temporality in ongoing discourse; and, as "world making" whereby people belonging to a public engage in a performative act with specific expressions, vocabulary, and gestures that create discourse which shapes the public itself. Warner, *Publics and Counterpublics*, 75.
21 Warner, *Publics and Counterpublics*, 199.
22 Catherine Jean Nash, "Toronto's Gay Village (1969–1982): Plotting the Politics of Gay Identity," *Canadian Geographer* 50, no. 1 (Spring 2006): 3.
23 Rick Bébout, "Planning for 1983," 6 January 1983, Box 2, F0002–01–034, *TBP* fonds, The ArQuives, Toronto, Canada [hereafter *TBP* fonds].
24 "I Just Want to Thank You," *The Body Politic* 30, February 1977, back cover.
25 "Where to Buy the Body Politic," *The Body Politic* 4, May–June 1972, 15.
26 Chris Bearchell, "Everyfaggot's Dyke – Everydyke's Faggot," *The Body Politic* 44, June–July 1978, 10.
27 See Liz Millward, *Making a Scene: Lesbians and Community Across Canada, 1964–84* (Vancouver: University of British Columbia Press, 2015); Cameron Duder, *Awfully Devoted Women: Lesbian Lives in Canada, 1900–65*

(Vancouver: University of British Columbia Press, 2011); Elise Chenier, *Strangers in Our Midst: Sexual Deviancy in Postwar Ontario* (Toronto: University of Toronto Press, 2008); Becki Ross, *The House That Jill Built: A Lesbian Nation in Formation* (Toronto: University of Toronto Press, 1995); Joan Nestle, *A Restricted Country* (Ithaca, NY: Firebrand Books, 1987); and Mariana Valverde, *Sex, Power, and Pleasure* (Toronto: Women's Press, 1985).

28 Rick Bébout, "What Happened?" *The Body Politic* 135, February 1987, 4.

29 Bébout, "What Happened?," 4.

30 Roland Barthes, *Image – Music – Text*, trans. Stephen Heath (New York: Hill and Wang, 1977), 153–4.

31 Tim McCaskell (editor for *The Body Politic*), interview by Nicholas Hrynyk, 20 March 2015, interview 1, transcript.

32 Nast, "Queer Patriarchies" 881.

33 Nast, "Queer Patriarchies" 881.

34 Adrienne Rich describes compulsory heterosexuality as "a manmade institution … as if, despite profound emotional impulses and complementarities drawing women toward women, there is a mystical/biological heterosexual inclination, a 'preference' or 'choice' that draws women toward men. Adrienne Rich, "Compulsory Heterosexuality and Lesbian Existence," *Signs* 5, no. 4 (Summer 1980): 637.

35 In addition to being the "deportment, the dress and accoutrements" that are related to the word "queer," queer style is "the unstable, bizarre other to heterosexual normativity." Adam Geczy and Vicki Karaminas, *Queer Style* (London: Bloomsbury Press, 2013), 4.

36 See Cathy Cohen, "Punks, Bulldaggers, and Welfare Queens: The Radical Potential of Queer Politics," in *Sexual Identity, Queer Politics*, ed. Mark Blasius (Princeton, NJ: Princeton University Press, 2021).

37 For more information, see Elspeth Brown, *Work! A Queer History of Modeling* (Durham, NC: Duke University Press, 2019); and Charlotte Charteris, *The Queer Cultures of 1930s Prose: Language, Identity and Performance in Interwar Britain* (London: Palgrave Macmillan, 2019).

38 In doing so, I am building the approach of a few historians, notably Kathy Peiss, who have been willing to see historical subjects as gendered beings concerned with physical appearance. See Kathy Peiss, *Hope in a Jar: The Making of America's Beauty Culture* (Philadelphia: University of Pennsylvania Press, 2011).

39 Susan Sontag, *Against Interpretation: And Other Essays* (New York: Farrar, Straus and Giroux, 1966), 36.

40 Maurice Merleau-Ponty, *Phenomenology of Perception* (New York: Routledge, 2002), 174.

41 Kelby Harrison, *Sexual Deceit: The Ethics of Passing* (Lanham, MD: Lexington Books, 2013), 115.

42 Judith Butler, *Gender Trouble: Feminism and the Subversion of Identity* (New York: Routledge Press, 1999 [1990]), xv.
43 Butler, *Gender Trouble*, 140.
44 The term "passing" is imbedded in sociology and was prominently used by historians studying race and how racialized subjects subverted hegemonic categories of "other" by concealing their racial identity to be perceived as a member of a social group other than their own.
45 Allyson Hobbs, *A Chosen Exile: A History of Racial Passing in American Life* (Cambridge, MA: Harvard University Press, 2014), 8.
46 Eve Kosofsky Sedgwick, *Epistemology of the Closet: Updated with New Preface* (Berkeley: University of California Press, 2008), 3.
47 Shaun Cole, *'Don We Now Our Gay Apparel': Gay Men's Dress in the Twentieth Century* (Oxford: Berg Press, 2000), 95.
48 Fabio Cleto, "Introduction: Queering the Camp," in *Camp: Queer Aesthetics and the Performing Subject: A Reader*, ed. Fabio Cleto (Ann Arbor: University of Michigan Press, 1999), 2.
49 Susan Sontag, "Notes on 'Camp,'" in *Camp: Queer Aesthetic and the Performing Subject*, ed. Fabio Cleto (Ann Arbor: University of Michigan Press, 1999), 53. First published in Sontag, *Against Interpretation*.
50 Richard Dyer, "It's Being so Camp as Keeps Us Going," *The Body Politic* 36, September 1977, 13.
51 Joseph Bristow's article considers how sexual identities are a play of constraint and opportunity, necessity and freedom, and power and pleasure. See Joseph Bristow, "Being Gay: Politics, Identity, Pleasure," *New Formations* 9 (Winter 1989): 70.
52 The hidden system of verbal and written codes resonates with James C. Scott's concept of the "hidden transcript." A hidden transcript represents the relationships between discourse and power. Utilized by both elite and marginalized, hidden transcripts are "typically expressed openly – albeit in disguised form." James C. Scott, *Domination and the Arts of Resistance: Hidden Transcripts* (New Haven, CT: Yale University Press, 1990 [2008]), xiii. See Steven Maynard, "Through a Hole in the Lavatory Wall: Homosexual Subcultures, Police Surveillance, and the Dialectics of Discovery, Toronto, 1890–1930." *Journal of the History of Sexuality* 5, no. 2 (October 1994): 207–42.
53 Maynard, "Through a Hole," 209.
54 Matt Houlbrook, *Queer London: Perils and Pleasures in the Sexual Metropolis, 1918–1957* (Chicago: University of Chicago Press, 2005), 46.
55 See Becki Ross, *Burlesque West: Showgirls, Sex, and Sin in Postwar Vancouver* (Toronto: University of Toronto Press, 2009).
56 See Brown, *Work!*
57 Jennifer V. Evans, "Seeing Subjectivity: Erotic Photography and the Optics of Desire," *American Historical Review* 118, no. 2 (April 2013): 432.

58 Peter Geller, *Northern Exposures: Photographing and Filming the Canadian North, 1920–1945* (Vancouver: University of British Columbia, 2004), 35.

59 See David Johnson, *Buying Gay: How Physique Entrepreneurs Sparked a Movement* (New York: Columbia University Press, 2019); and David Johnson, "Physique Pioneers: The Politics of 1960s Gay Consumer Culture," *Journal of Social History* 43, no. 4 (2010): 867–92.

60 Colin Gordon, afterword to Michel Foucault, *Power/Knowledge: Selected Interviews and Other Writings, 1972–1977*, trans. Colin Gordon, Leo Marshall, Joh Mepham, and Kate Soper; ed. Colin Gordon (New York: Pantheon Books, 1980), 242.

61 Chris Dummitt, *The Manly Modern: Masculinity in Postwar Canada* (Vancouver: University of British Columbia Press, 2007), 11.

62 David Ciarlo, *Advertising Empire: Race and Visual Culture in Imperial Germany* (Cambridge, MA: Harvard University Press, 2011), 15–16.

63 Since Marchand's pioneering study, histories of beauty culture, gender, and race, as seen through the lens of visual culture, have proliferated. Roland Marchand examines race, gender, class, and nationalism as registers that have become inextricably linked with modernity through advertising in interwar America in his 1985 book *Advertising the American Dream*. See Roland Marchand, *Advertising the American Dream: Making Way for Modernity, 1920–1940* (Berkeley: University of California Press, 1985), 238.

64 Peiss, *Hope in a Jar*, 46.

65 Peiss, *Hope in a Jar*, 48.

66 Sharon Cook, *Sex, Lies, and Cigarettes: Canadian Women, Smoking, and Visual Culture, 1880–2000* (Montreal and Kingston: McGill-Queen's University Press, 2012), 11.

67 Cook, *Sex, Lies, and Cigarettes*, 5.

68 See John D'Emilio, *Sexual Politics, Sexual Communities: The Making of a Homosexual Minority in the United States, 1940–1970* (Chicago: University of Chicago Press, 1983); John D'Emilio and Estelle Freedman, *Intimate Matters: A History of Sexuality in America* (New York: Harper & Row, 1988); and John D'Emilio, *Making Trouble: Essays on Gay History, Politics, and the University* (New York: Routledge, 1992).

69 These histories have emerged from the effort of scholars such as James T. Sears, who have deconstructed sexuality and race as part of an intersectional analysis. See James T. Sears's work *Growing Up Gay in the South: Race, Gender, and Journeys of the Spirit* (New York: Routledge, 1991). Discussions of class divisions within the gay and lesbian community are most pronounced in Elizabeth Kennedy and Madeline Davis's *Boots of Leather, Slippers of Gold: The History of a Lesbian Community* (New York: Routledge, 1993); and Maynard, "Through a Hole." Concerning race, Nan Alamilla Boyd and Elizabeth Armstrong argue that the gay community's

white foundation also made racism all the more prolific and subversive. See Nan Alamilla Boyd, *Wide-Open Town: A History of San Francisco to 1965* (Berkeley and Los Angeles: University of California Press, 2003); and Elizabeth A. Armstrong, *Forging Gay Identities: Organizing Sexuality in San Francisco, 1950–1994* (Chicago: University of Chicago Press, 2002). Also see Lillian Faderman, *Odd Girls and Twilight Lovers: A History of Lesbian Life in Twentieth-Century America* (New York: Penguin Books, 1992); and Jeffrey Escoffier, *American Homo: Community and Perversity* (Berkeley: University of California Press, 1998).

70 Also see Bryant Keith Alexander, *Performing Black Masculinity: Race, Culture, and Queer Identity* (Lanham, MD: AltaMira Press, 2006); and E. Patrick Johnson, *Sweet Tea: Black Gay Men of the South* (Chapel Hill: University of North Carolina Press, 2008).

71 Both scholars approach contemporary and historical gay and queer identities from an intersectional standpoint. In doing so, they challenge any sense of shared experience by gay men of different classes, racial backgrounds, and even gender expressions or identities as they grapple with multiple competing identities. See Elizabeth Jane Ward, *Respectably Queer: Diversity Culture in LGBT Activist Organizations* (Nashville: Vanderbilt University Press, 2008).

72 Mirrors are just one of many examples of heterotopias. Foucault and Miskowiec argue that "[i]n the mirror, I see myself there where I am not, in an unreal, virtual space that opens up behind the surface; I am over there, there where I am not, a sort of shadow that gives my own visibility to myself, that enables me to see myself there where I am absent." Michel Foucault and Jay Miskowiec, "Of Other Spaces," *Diacritics* 16, no. 1 (1986): 24.

73 In Adams's words, heterosexuality is "a discursively constituted social category that organizes relations not only between men and women, but also between those who fit definitions of heterosexuality and those who do not, and between adults and youth." Mary Louise Adams, *The Trouble with Normal: Postwar Youth and the Making of Heterosexuality* (Toronto: University of Toronto Press, 1997), 167.

74 Chenier, *Strangers*, 5.

75 Foucault suggests that structures of power (in this case, heteronormative gender and medical psychiatry) marginalize subjugated knowledges (queer sexuality and desire).

76 George Chauncey, *Gay New York: Gender, Urban Culture, and the Making of the Gay Male World, 1890–1940* (New York: Basic Books, 1994), 70.

77 The medical-psychological "inversion" model of homosexuality was dominant in North America during the early twentieth century and, as Nealon notes, was predicated on "the idea that homosexuals are people whose souls are trapped in the body of the 'other' sex." Christopher

Nealon, *Foundlings: Lesbian and Gay Historical Emotion Before Stonewall* (Durham, NC: Duke University Press, 2001), 2.

78 Nealon, *Foundlings*, 2.

79 Michel Foucault, *History of Sexuality: An Introduction* (New York: Random House, 2012), 95.

80 D'Emilio, *Sexual Politics*, 65.

81 Elise Chenier, "Liberating Marriage: Gay Liberation and Same-Sex Marriage in Early 1970s Canada," in *We Still Demand: Redefining Resistance in Sex and Gender Struggles*, eds. Patrizia Gentile, Gary Kinsman, and L. Pauline Rankin (Vancouver: University of British Columbia Press, 2017), 30.

82 Herb Spiers, "Creative Psyche and Homosexuality," *The Body Politic* 4, May–June 1972, 6.

83 The internalization and self-policing of appropriate gender performances in the gay male community require an engagement with Foucauldian theories of power, knowledge, and processes of normalization through discourse. Foucault argues, "[P]ower is everywhere; not because it embraces everything, but because it comes from everywhere. And 'Power,' insofar as it is permanent, repetitious, inert, and self-reproducing, is simply the over-all effect that emerges from all these mobilities." Foucault, *The History of Sexuality*, 93.

84 See Millward, *Making a Scene*; Duder, *Awfully Devoted Women*; Jack Halberstam, *Female Masculinity* (Durham, NC: Duke University Press, 1998); and Kennedy and Davis, *Boots of Leather*.

85 Chauncey, *Gay New York*, 115.

86 See Murray Healey, *Gay Skins: Class, Masculinity and Queer Appropriation* (London: Cassell, 1996); Peter Hennen, *Faeries, Nears, and Leathermen: Men in Community Queering the Masculine* (Chicago: University of Chicago Press, 2008); Johnson, *Sweet Tea*; Tim Edwards, *Erotics and Politics: Gay Male Sexuality, Masculinity and Feminism* (London: Routledge, 2012); David Johnson, *Buying Gay: How Physique Entrepreneurs Sparked a Movement* (New York: Columbia University Press, 2019); and Arturo J. Aldama and Frederick Luis Aldama, *Decolonizing Latinx Masculinities* (Tucson: University of Arizona Press, 2020).

87 R.W. Connell, *Masculinities*, 2nd ed. (Cambridge: Polity Press, 2005 [1995]), 40.

88 Bobby Noble, "Boy to the Power of Three: Toronto Drag Queens," in *Troubling Masculinities: Reimagining Urban Men*, ed. Ken Moffatt, 143–66 (Toronto: University of Toronto Press, 2011), 156.

89 Jin Haritaworn, Ghaida Moussa, and Syrus Marcus Ware, *Marvellous Grounds: Queer of Colour Histories of Toronto* (Toronto: Between the Lines, 2018), 11.

90 In addition to GAT and Zami, numerous other groups aimed at marginalized gays formed following *TBP*'s publication run. Salaam, a

group dedicated to providing support for gay Muslims, was founded in 1991 in Toronto by lawyer El-Farouk Khaki. According to Aisha Geissinger, Salaam was temporarily disbanded after Khaki received death threats from "several persons claiming to belong to Islamic Jihad cells" after writing an article about gay Muslims in a student paper at the University of Toronto. It resumed operations, however, in 1998 following news that gay Muslim group Al-Fatiha formed in the United States. Aisha Geissinger, "Islam and Discourses of Same-Sex Desire," in *Queer Religion: Homosexuality in Modern Religious History*, eds. Donald L. Boisvert and James Emerson Johnson (Santa Barbara, CA: Praeger, 2012), 82–3.

91 More recently, work has been done on the correlation between masculinity and whiteness. Michael Kimmel, a prominent sociologist on masculinity, has recently begun writing on the intersections of masculinity and whiteness. Birgit Brander Rasmussen, Eric Klinenberg, Irene Nexica, and Matt Wray also contend that racism only affects people of "color," thus conveying the need to problematize whiteness and calculate its wages. See Michael Kimmel, *Angry White Men: American Masculinity at the End of an Era* (New York: Nation Books, 2013); Michael Kimmel, *Manhood in America: A Cultural History* (Oxford: Oxford University Press, 2012); and, Birgit Ramussen et al., *The Making and the Unmaking of Whiteness* (Durham, NC: Duke University Press, 2001).

92 Jennifer C. Nash, "Re-Thinking Intersectionality," *Feminist Review* 89 (2008): 12.

93 Ruth Frankenberg argues that white people are defined primarily along their gender rather than race because white people are often considered "nonracial or racially neutral." Ruth Frankenberg, *White Women, Race Matters: The Social Construction of Whiteness* (Minneapolis: University of Minnesota Press, 1993), 1.

94 Frankenberg contends that "whiteness" refers to "a set of locations that are historically, socially, politically, and culturally produced and, moreover, are intrinsically linked to unfolding relations of domination." Frankenberg, *White Women*, 6.

95 Martin Levine, *Gay Macho: The Life and Death of the Homosexual Clone* (New York: New York University Press, 1998), 10–11.

96 Gordon Pon, "Queering Asian Masculinities and Transnationalism: Implications for Anti-Oppression and Consciousness-Raising," in *Troubled Masculinities: Reimagining Urban Men*, ed. Ken Moffatt (Toronto: University of Toronto Press, 2012), 97.

97 The notion of "othering" originates from post-colonialist Edward Said and his concept of the "other." Said describes Western Europeans studying the Orient as the "other" to define better Europe and its place in the world. In his words, the "Orient or Oriental or 'subject' which could be admitted, at the extreme limit, is the alienated being, philosophically, that is, other than

itself in relationship to itself, posed, understood, defined – and acted – by others." Edward Said, *Orientalism* (New York: Knopf Doubleday, 2014), 97.

98 Race and whiteness have been constructed in very different ways throughout space and time. See David Goldberg, ed., *Anatomy of Racism* (Minneapolis: University of Minnesota Press, 1990); Londa Schiebinger, *Nature's Body: Sexual Politics and the Making of Modern Science* (Hammersmith, UK: Pandora, 1993); Anne McClintock, *Imperial Leather: Race, Gender and Sexuality in the Colonial Context* (New York: Routledge, 1995); Ann Laura Stoler, "Making Empire Respectable: The Politics of Race and Sexual Morality in Twentieth-Century Colonial Cultures," in *Dangerous Liaisons: Gender, Nation, and Postcolonial Perspectives*, eds. Anne McClintock, Aamir Mufti, and Ella Shohat (Minneapolis: University of Minnesota Press, 1997), 344–73.

99 One of the most famous incidents of police brutality and raiding of gay bathhouses in Toronto was Operation Soap. Operation Soap was a raid by the Metropolitan Toronto police against four gay bathhouses on 5 February 1981 involving the arrest of more than three hundred men. The CLGA has extensive sources based on CHAT contributors, such as Pat Murphy, and vertical files from the Church-Wellesley Neighbourhood Police Advisory Committee: Toronto documenting this incident but also provide extensive coverage of instances of police harassment, brutality, and raiding in Toronto over the course of the 1970s and 1980s.

1. A Sexualized Culture to Gay Liberation

1 Alan Miller, "Beefcake with No Labels Attached," *The Body Politic* 90, January–February 1983, 33.

2 Miller, "Beefcake," 33.

3 David Johnson, "Physique Pioneers: The Politics of 1960s Gay Consumer Culture," *Journal of Social History* 43, no. 4 (2010): 884.

4 David Johnson, *Buying Gay: How Physique Entrepreneurs Sparked a Movement* (New York: Columbia University Press, 2019), 230.

5 Johnson, "Physique Pioneers," 873.

6 See Alexandra M. Lord, "Models of Masculinity: Sex Education, the United States Public Health Service, and the YMCA, 1919–1924," *Journal of the History of Medicine* 58, no. 2 (2003); Gail Bederman, *Manliness and Civilization: A Cultural History of Gender and Race in the United States, 1880–1917* (Chicago: University of Chicago Press, 1995): 123-152; and, John F. Kasson, *Houdini, Tarzan, and the Perfect Man: The White Male Body and the Challenge of Modernity in America* (New York: Hill and Wang, 2001).

7 While traditionally men are not the object of gazing, the display of musculature is naturalized because, as film theorist and *TBP* contributor

Richard Dyer contends, "Muscularity is the *sign* of power – natural, achieved, phallic." Richard Dyer, "Don't Look Now," *Screen* 23 nos. 3–4 (1982): 68.

8 Mulvey argues that fetishistic scopophilia "builds up the physical beauty of the object, transforming it into something satisfying in itself." Laura Mulvey, *Visual and Other Pleasures* (New York: Palgrave, 1989), 21.

9 "Meeting Minutes," 3 March 1980, Box 1, F0002–01–28, *TBP* fonds.

10 Thomas Waugh, "A Heritage of Pornography," *The Body Politic* 90, January–February 1983, 30.

11 Waugh, "Heritage," 33.

12 Waugh, "Heritage," 32.

13 Waugh, "Photography, Passion, and Power," *The Body Politic* 101, March 1984, 29.

14 Susan Sontag, "The Image-World," in *Visual Culture: The Reader*, eds. Jessica Evans and Stuart Hall (London: Sage Publications, 2004), 82.

15 Waugh, "Photography," 33.

16 Tim McCaskell (editor for *The Body Politic*), interview by Nicholas Hrynyk, 20 March 2015, interview 1, transcript.

17 Paul Frosh, *The Image Factory: Consumer Culture, Photography, and the Visual Content Industry* (Oxford: Berg Press, 2003), 107.

18 Frosh, *Image Factory*, 2.

19 Daniel Harris, *The Rise and Fall of Gay Culture* (New York: Hyperion, 1997), 65.

20 The national narcissism that Fain addressed was rooted in the shift in post-war definitions of bachelorhood and masculinity. The single bachelor's self-indulgent lifestyle represented a narcissistic contrast to the conservative notion of spending money and time on the family. Nathan Fain, "The Age of Narcissus: Here's Looking at Me, Kid!" *After Dark*, January 1979, 37.

21 David Armstrong, *A Trumpet to Arms: Alternative Media in America* (Boston: South End Press, 1981), 251.

22 See Douglas Kimmell, "Patterns of Aging Among Gay Men," *Christopher Street* 2, no. 5 (November 1977): 28–33; Seymour Kleinberg, "Where Have All the Sissies Gone?" *Christopher Street* 2, no. 9 (March 1978): 3–12; Johnny Greene, "The Male Southern Belle," *Christopher Street* 3, no. 5 (December 1978): 20–32; and Johnny Greene, "Gay Rites, Straight Style," *Christopher Street* 3, no. 6 (January 1979): 13–15.

23 See Victor Amador et al., "Butch: Gay Machismo, Illustrated," *Christopher Street* 2, no. 9 (March 1978): 13–18.

24 *Playgirl* functioned as a quasi-gay magazine since readers were either women or homosexual men. The magazine was marketed in a manner that suggested, according to Kenneth MacKinnon, "no 'real' – that is, self-categorizing heterosexual – male is expected to see a male object in erotic

terms." Kenneth MacKinnon, *Love, Tears, and the Male Spectator* (Madison, UK: Fairleigh Dickinson University Press, 2002), 110.

25 Emmanuel Cooper, *Fully Exposed: The Male Nude in Photography* (New York: Routledge, 1995), 94.

26 Roger Baker, "Editorial," *Quorum* 1, 1972, 3.

27 Baker, "Editorial," 4.

28 "Quorum's Sex Objects," *Quorum* 1, 1972, 23.

29 Roger Baker noted in Quorum's ninth issue that demand for fashion editorials and Clark's images was continually growing. Roger Baker, "Editorial," *Quorum* 9, May 1973, 3. Also see "What Can You Say About a Chap Like This?" *Quorum* 2, no. 6 (1974): 15–17; and "The Changing Room," *Quorum* 2, no. 12 (1974): 14–17. Photographs by Colin Clarke.

30 Cooper, *Fully Exposed*, 115.

31 R.W. Connell, *Masculinities* (Berkeley and Los Angeles: University of California Press, 1995), 54.

32 Both *Gay News*, one of the largest LGBT newspapers in the English-speaking world with a readership of approximately 50,000, and *Fuori!* (Fronte unitario omosessuale rivoluzionario italiano, "Italian United Homosexual Revolutionary Front") frequently contained images of men that followed a similar aesthetic. See "British Paper Struck by Financial Crisis," *The Body Politic* 90, January–February 1983, 19.

33 Giuseppe Di Salvo, "Per Farlo Meglio [To Do It Better]," *Fuori!* 21, March–June 1979, 35.

34 Advertisement, "La Clef (discogay)," *Fuori!* 24, February–March 1980, 9.

35 Martti Lahti, "Dressing Up in Power: Tom of Finland and Gay Male Body Politics," *Journal of Homosexuality* 35, nos. 3–4 (1998): 192.

36 Lahti, "Dressing Up," 193.

37 The newspaper's founding organization, a group with the same name, was also accepted as an official group within the Radical Party of Italy, with Pezanna serving as the first openly gay in the parliament in Italy. The Radical Party protected against state and religious efforts to shutter the newspaper. "Our Battle Is Against Moral Attitudes," *The Body Politic* 45, August 1978, 27.

38 Brenda Cossman, *Bad Attitude/s on Trial: Pornography, Feminism, and the Butler Decision* (Toronto: University of Toronto Press, 1997), 15. The relationship between moral puritanism and the censorship of pornography is reinforced by Tom Warner when he argues that "Following the Second World War … a new drive to counter the increasing availability of pornography was launched, as a renewed social purity movement took root." Tom Warner, *Never Going Back: A History of Queer Activism in Canada* (Toronto: University of Toronto Press, 2002), 22.

39 Emphasis added by Cossman. See Cossman, *Bad Attitude/s*, 16.

40 A significant degree of the literature on censorship and pornography approaches the topic from either a legal standpoint, considering how definitions of erotic material evolved over time, or the role of feminist groups in shaping efforts to restrict pornography in the late 1970s onward. See Allan C. Hutchinson and Klaus Petersen, *Interpreting Censorship in Canada* (Toronto: University of Toronto Press, 1999); Mark Cohen, *Censorship in Canadian Literature* (Montreal and Kingston: McGill-Queen's University Press, 2001); Cossman, *Bad Attitude/s*; and Susan G. Cole, *Pornography and the Sex Crisis* (Toronto: Second Story Press, 1992).

41 Donald W. McLeod, *Lesbian and Gay Liberation in Canada: A Selected Annotated Chronology, 1964–1975* (Toronto: ECW Press, 1996), 5.

42 "Toronto Police Confiscate Films," *The Body Politic* 11, January–February 1974, 6.

43 See "Police Seize Rochdale Porno Films," *The Globe and Mail*, 16 November 1973, 13.

44 The definition of obscenity could also be applied if "the matter or thing depicts or describes a 'child' engaged or participating in an act or simulated act of or simulated masturbation, sexual intercourse, gross indecency, buggery or bestiality" or "displaying any portion of its body in a sexually suggestive manner." A "child" was understood to be "a person who is or appears to be under the age of sixteen years." Canada, House of Commons, *Minutes of Proceedings and Evidence of the Standing Committee on Justice and Legal Affairs* 18 (22 March 1978): 8.

45 Canada, House of Commons, *Minutes* 18, 8.

46 Canada, House of Commons, *Minutes of Proceedings and Evidence of the Standing Committee on Justice and Legal Affairs* 15 (7 March 1978): 8.

47 Cole, *Pornography*, 76.

48 "For Over-18s: Poll Shows 74% Approve Selling Hard-Core Porn," *Toronto Star*, 28 December 1977, A3.

49 Canada, House of Commons, *Minutes of Proceedings and Evidence of the Standing Committee on Justice and Legal Affairs* 7 (14 February 1978): 14.

50 "Meeting Minutes," 27 January 1974, Box 1, F0002–01–024, *TBP* fonds.

51 "Meeting Minutes," 10 June 1978, Box 1, F0002–01–026, *TBP* fonds.

52 Gerald Hannon, "Statement from Gerald Hannon," 5 January 1978, Box 1, F0002–01–021, *TBP* fonds.

53 Gerald Hannon, "Raided and Charged Gay Paper to Publish This Week," 30 January 1978, Box 1, F0002–01–021, *TBP* fonds.

54 Gerald Hannon, "MP's Hit Hard at 'Porn,'" *The Body Politic* 42, April 1978, 5.

55 Hannon, "MP's hit hard," 5.

56 Helen Hester, *Beyond Explicit: Pornography and the Displacement of Sex* (Albany: State University of New York Press, 2014), 22.

57 Dworkin equated pornography with historical acts of violence, even referring to pornography as "rape" in her 1998 book *Letters from a War Zone*. See Andrea Dworkin, *Letters from a War Zone: Writings, 1976–1989* (London: Secker & Warburg, 1988).

58 Lisa Duggan, Nan D. Hunter, and Carol S. Vance, "False Promises: Feminist Anti-Pornography Legislation in the U.S.," in *Women Against Censorship*, ed. Varda Burstyn (Vancouver: Douglas & McIntyre, 1985), 130–51; and Ellen Willis, "Feminism, Moralism, and Pornography," in *Desire: The Politics of Sexuality*, eds. Ann Barr Snitow, Christine Stansell, and Sharon Thompson (London: Virago, 1984), 82–8.

59 Foreword by the editorial collective. Andrea Dworkin, "Pornography: The New Terrorism," *The Body Politic* 45, August 1978, 12.

60 Juan Carlos Mezo González, "Contested Images: Debating Nudity, Sexism, and Porn in *The Body Politic*, 1971–1987," *Left History* 23, no. 1 (Spring/Summer 2019): 47.

61 Miriam Smith, "Interview with Chris Bearchell, Lasqueti Island, 1996," *Journal of Canadian Studies* 48, no. 1 (Winter 2014): 259.

62 Mariana Valverde, "Feminism and Pornography: A Reply to Gerald Hannon," *The Body Politic* 43, May 1978, 3.

63 Mezo González, "Contested Images," 47.

64 Jackie Goodwin, "Fanning the Flames: Fire Brigade vs Red Hot," *The Body Politic* 90, January–February 1983, 10.

65 Editorial collective, "Ad News," *The Body Politic* 94, June 1983, 3.

66 David Churchill, "Personal Ad Politics: Race, Sexuality and Power at *The Body Politic*," *Left History* 8, no. 2 (2003): 115.

67 Goodwin, "Fanning the Flames," 10.

68 Stephen W. Forster, "On Mud Slinging," *The Body Politic* 56, September 1979, 4.

69 David Rayside, (volunteer at *The Body Politic*), interview by Nicholas Hrynyk, 24 March 2015, interview 1, transcript.

70 "An Interview: Dennis Altman," *The Body Politic* 13, May–June 1974, 19.

71 See Herb Spiers, Review of "Religion & Sexism: Images of Women in the Jewish and Christian Traditions," *The Body Politic* 16, November–December 1974, 22; and Herb Spiers, "Promiscuity," *The Body Politic* 31, March 1977, 7.

72 Original emphasis in bold. Jackson, "Nudity and Sexism," 12.

73 George Hislop et al., "CBC: Put Off? or Nothing to Hide?: Nothing to Show," *The Body Politic* 2, January–February 1972, 1.

74 Hislop et al., "CBC," 1.

75 Hislop et al., "CBC:," 1.

76 Marshall McLuhan, *The Medium Is the Message: An Inventory of Effects* (San Francisco: Hardwired Press, 1996 [1978]), 125.

77 Mezo González, "Contested Images," 54–5.

78 Churchill, "Personal Ad Politics," 126.
79 Mezo González, "Contested Images," 33.
80 Multiple authors, *The Body Politic* 4, MayJune 1972, 12–13; and Gerald Hannon, "Celebrate the Body! (Towards an Alternative Aesthetic)," *The Body Politic* 5, July–August 1972, 12–13.
81 "Celebrate the Body!," 12–13.
82 "Celebrate the Body!," 13.
83 Doug, "Gaylup Poll Results," *The Body Politic* 4, May–June 1972, 8.
84 Sharon Cook argues that the observer of visual culture "operates within a prescribed set of conventions and possibilities," or as Foucault would contend, a "regime of truth," a regime that mirrors patriarchal society and is composed of struggles over social power. Sharon Cook, *Sex, Lies, and Cigarettes: Canadian Women, Smoking, and Visual Culture, 1880–2000* (Montreal and Kingston: McGill-Queen's University Press, 2012), 11.
85 Advertisement: "The Club," *The Body Politic* 10, 1973, 22.
86 Cook, *Sex, Lies, and Cigarettes*, 5.
87 Bold emphasis in original. Advertisement: "Dudes: A Near Bar Nearby," *The Body Politic* 36, September 1977, 18.
88 Advertisement: "Richmond Street Health Emporium … the Busiest," *The Body Politic* 53, June 1979, 42.
89 Advertisement: "Get into It, Richmond Street Health Emporium," *The Body Politic* 61, March–April 1980, 39.
90 Robert Trow, "Diamonds in the Buff," *The Body Politic* 10, 1973, 11.
91 Trow, "Diamonds," 11.
92 Trow, "Diamonds," 11.
93 Greg Lehne, "Gay Fantasies: A Plea for Information," *The Body Politic* 9, Autumn 1973, 21.
94 Lehne, "Gay Fantasies: A Plea for Information," 21.
95 Greg Lehne, "Gay Male Fantasies: A Collage," *The Body Politic* 14, July–August 1974, 22.
96 Lehne, "Gay Male Fantasies: A Collage," 22–3.
97 Lehne, "Gay Male Fantasies: A Collage," 22.
98 Lehne, "Gay Male Fantasies: A Collage," 23.
99 Greg Lehne, "Gay Male Fantasies," *The Body Politic* 15, September–October 1974, 12.
100 "An Interview: Dennis Altman," *The Body Politic* 13, May-–une 1974, 19.
101 Joseph Interrante, "A Man's Place Is …" *The Body Politic* 64, June–July 1980, 34.

2. Pin the Macho on the Man

1 Noel Bari, "Prisoners of a Stereotype," *The Body Politic* 67, October 1980, 4.
2 Bari, "Prisoners," 4.

3 Bari, "Prisoners," 4.
4 Alice Echols, *Hot Stuff: Disco and the Remaking of American Culture* (New York: W.W. Norton & Company, 2010), 123.
5 Martin Levine, *Gay Macho: The Life and Death of the Homosexual Clone* (New York: New York University Press, 1998), 59.
6 Pamela Robertson, "What Makes the Feminist Camp?" in *Camp: Queer Aesthetics and the Performing Subject*, ed. Fabio Cleto (Ann Arbor: The University of Michigan Press, 1999), 271.
7 Roland Barthes, *The Fashion System*, trans. Matthew Ward and Richard Howard (New York: Farrar, Straus and Giroux, 1967; reprint, Berkeley: University of California Press, 1990), 135.
8 Adam Geczy and Vicki Karaminas, *Queer Style* (London: Bloomsbury Press, 2013), 86.
9 John Forbes, "Hanky Panky: Beyond the Pale & Back Again," *The Body Politic* 49, December–January 1978/9, 18.
10 Echols, *Hot Stuff*, 122.
11 From the first issue of *TBP*, the word "straight" was used to denote heterosexuals and the privileges they receive from hegemonic heterosexual culture. See Tony Metie, "Unmasquerade," *The Body Politic* 1, November–December 1971, 1; Jude, "Deconstruction of 'Sexual Identity,' *The Body Politic* 1, November–December 1971, 3; and, "A Program for Gay Liberation," *The Body Politic* 1, November–December 1971, 14.
12 Bari, "Prisoners," 4.
13 The term "sign-vehicles" lies within Erving Goffman's concept of dramaturgy. Dramaturgy suggests that individual behaviour is based on interactions with others similarly to a staged production. Sign-vehicles can be facial expressions, material goods, the context of the interaction, or other bodily means of communication from one individual to another. See Erving Goffman, *The Presentation of Self in Everyday Life* (Edinburgh: University of Edinburgh Social Sciences Research Centre, 1956), 14–15.
14 Levine, *Gay Macho*, 57.
15 Gayatri Spivak, "Displacement and the Discourse of Woman," in *Displacement: Derrida and After*, vol. 4, ed. Mark Krupnick (Bloomington: Indiana University Press, 1983), 186.
16 Adam Geczy and Vicki Karaminas contend that "[m]asculinizing gay identity cannot be seen in isolation as an impatience to the effeminized stereotype but, first, as a touchstone for opening up the possibility for different queer identities; second, to claim masculinity for gays as well as straight males; third, to internalize and embody the desire for maleness and, indeed, the desire to conquer males felt by many gays; and fourth, to recognize the complementary counterpart of the effeminate male in which the more male member is conceived as the giver and the girly boy, the receiver." Geczy and Karaminas, *Queer Style*, 87–8.

17 R.W. Connell, *Masculinities* (Berkeley and Los Angeles: University of California Press, 1995), 78. Also see Spivak, "Displacement," 178.

18 Connell, *Masculinities*, 79. Connell also contends with James Messerschmidt that "hegemonic masculinity was not assumed to be normal in the statistical sense; only a minority of men might enact it. But it was certainly normative. It embodied the currently most honored way of being a man, it required all other men to position themselves in relation to it, and it ideologically legitimated the global subordination of women to men." R.W. Connell and James Messerschmidt, "Hegemonic Masculinity: Rethinking the Concept," *Gender and Society* 19, no. 6 (December 2005): 832.

19 John Forbes, "A Drone with Cologne Is Still a Clone," *The Body Politic* 46, September 1978, 19.

20 Michael Lynch, "Young (and Old and Middle-Aged Too) Men's Cruising Associations," *The Body Politic* 55, August 1979, 39.

21 As quoted in Lynch, "Young Men's Cruising Associations," 39.

22 Levine, *Gay Macho*, 59. Levine's argument resonates with literary theorist Johnathan Goldberg's argument that "[b]ody-building is haunted by the specter of homosexuality." In his words, by putting their bodies on display, bodybuilders, such as Arnold Schwarzenegger, are the object of a sexual gaze, which "would mean that Arnold is a woman when a gay man looks at him – and this is how Arnold articulates it, equating himself with the female pinup, site of the gaze." See Johnathan Goldberg, "Recalling Totalities: The Mirrored Staged of Arnold Schwarzenegger," in *Building Bodies*, ed. Pamela L. Moore (New Brunswick, NJ: Rutgers University Press, 1997), 223.

23 Paul Martineau and Britt Salvesen, *Robert Mapplethorpe: The Photographs* (Los Angeles: Getty Publications, 2016), 273.

24 Looking at Mapplethorpe's work, Paul Martineau and Britt Salvesen argue that "Mapplethorpe's exploration of the relationship between sex and the adornment and stylization of the body is most clearly expressed in his engagement with leather and bondage." Martineau and Salvesen, *Robert Mapplethorpe*, 273.

25 David Churchill, "Personal Ad Politics: Race, Sexuality and Power at *The Body Politic*," *Left History* 8, no. 2 (2003): 125.

26 Ruth Frankenberg, "Introduction: Local Whiteness, Localizing Whiteness," in *Displacing Whiteness: Essays in Social and Cultural Criticism*, ed. Ruth Frankenberg (Durham, NC: Duke University Press, 1999), 5.

27 Rinaldo Walcott, "Blackness, Masculinity, and the Work of Queer," in *Canadian Men and Masculinities: Historical and Contemporary Perspectives*, eds. Christopher J. Greig and Wayne Martino (Toronto: Canadian Scholars' Press, 2012), 191.

28 John Yorke, "Rudeness Rejected," *The Body Politic* 71, March 1981, 6.

29 Hugh Brewster, "The Myth of the New Homosexual," *The Body Politic* 4, March–April 1972, 3.

30 Gerald Hannon, "… It's More Important to Be Nice," *The Body Politic* 11, January–February 1974, 12.

31 Hannon, "It's More Important to Be Nice," 13.

32 Hannon, "It's More Important to Be Nice," 13.

33 Susan Bordo, *The Male Body: A New Look at Men in Public and the Private* (New York: Farrar, Straus and Giroux, 1999), 45.

34 Hannon, "It's More Important to Be Nice," 13.

35 Hannon, "It's More Important to Be Nice," 13.

36 Hannon, "It's More Important to Be Nice," 13.

37 "Engineer Comes Out," *The Body Politic* 20, October 1975, 9.

38 Underlining in original. The letter to the editor was a condensed version of a letter sent directly to Connie Baillie on the same day. Trevor Mountford-Smith to The Editor, *Engineering*, 16 May 1975, File CAN 4010, Mountford-Smith, Trevor, Canadian Lesbian and Gay Archives, Toronto, Ontario.

39 "Engineer Comes Out," 9.

40 Scott Tucker, "Sex, Death, and Free Speech: The Fight to Stop Friedkin's 'Cruising,'" *The Body Politic* 58, November 1979, 26.

41 Vito Russo, "Cruising: Questions of Class and Censorship," *The Body Politic* 59, December–January 1979/80, 4.

42 Editorial collective, "Skinscapes: Photographs by Norman Hatton," *The Body Politic* 74, June 1981, 23.

43 During the 1920s and 1930s, smoking was often depicted in advertisements and Hollywood films as a sign of sophistication and independence, particularly for women. In the post-war period, smoking continued to be used as a signifier for sexiness or glamour in certain contexts, particularly in movies and other forms of popular culture. For more on sexuality and smoking, see Cook, *Sex, Lies, and Cigarettes*, 175–6.

44 In his study of tobacco choices and smoking rituals in late nineteenth- and twentieth-century Montreal, Jarrett Rudy details how men defined gender, class, and ethnic boundaries based on the hierarchy of tobacco products. In his words, "For man, what a man smoked was an expression of how he saw himself and how others interpreted his identity." Jarrett Rudy, *The Freedom to Smoke: Tobacco Consumption and Identity* (Montreal and Kingston: McGill-Queen's University Press, 2005), 46. The use of smoking in the context of Hatton's work gives the models a masculine, rugged element that seemingly liberates them from stereotypes of effeminacy, similar to the ways in which smoking was perceived as liberating women from expectations around femininity, according to Sharon Cook. Since camp plays with the assumed naturalness of gender to an extreme, Hatton's photographic collection demonstrates the ways in which sign-vehicles of

leather and cigarettes enhance the masculine nature of the figures in the photographs. Matthew Hilton, *Smoking in British Popular Culture, 1800–2000* (Manchester: Manchester University Press, 2000), 3; and Cook, *Sex, Lies, and Cigarettes*, 305.

45 Jennifer V. Evans, "Seeing Subjectivity: Erotic Photography and the Optics of Desire," *American Historical Review* 118, no. 2 (April 2013): 433.

46 Ruth Frankenberg, *White Women, Race Matters: The Social Construction of Whiteness* (Minneapolis: University of Minnesota Press, 1993), 1.

47 Editorial collective, "Skinscapes," 23.

48 Gayle Rubin, "The Miracle Mile: South of Market and Gay Male Leather, 1962–1997," in *Reclaiming San Francisco: History, Politics, Culture*, eds. James Brook, Chris Carlsson, and Nancy J. Peters (San Francisco: City Lights Books, 1998), 254.

49 Rubin, "Miracle Mile," 260.

50 Bob Batchelor, "Introduction: Creating Advertising Culture, Beginnings to 1930s," in *We Are What We Sell: How Advertising Shapes American Life and Always Has*, eds. Danielle Sarver Coombs and Bob Batchelor (Santa Barbara, CA: ABC-CLIO), xv.

51 Advertisement: "The Barracks," *The Body Politic* 15, September–October 1974, 10.

52 Advertisement: "The Barracks," 10.

53 Regarding the usage of "cycle" in *TBP*, the only other time it was referred to in the same period as The Barrack's advertisement was in a critical reading of *Time* magazine's 1969 article "The Homosexual: Newly Visible, Newly Understood" and their 1975 article "Gays on the March." It was acknowledged that Bruce Voeller (then president of the National Gay Task Force in the United States) and his partner Bill Blend were important figures in informing *Time* magazine of gay culture so that the public may "recognize the difference between a transvestite and a cycle slut." See Advertisement: "The Barracks," 10. For *Time Magazine*, see: "The Homosexual: Newly Visible, Newly Understood," *Time* (31 October 1969), 56; and "Gays on the March," *Time* (8 September 1975), 40–6.

54 Levine, *Gay Macho*, 7.

55 Advertisement: "Crowbar," *The Body Politic* 99, December 1983, 30.

56 Advertisement: "Chaps Toronto," *The Body Politic* 97, October 1983, 44.

57 Advertisement: "Custom Made Just for You. Leather Craft Ltd.," *The Body Politic* 98, November 1983, 4.

58 According to Gayle Rubin, "Among gay men, leather and its idioms of masculinity have been the main framework for gay male S/M since the late 1940s." Gayle Rubin, *Deviations: A Gayle Rubin Reader* (Durham, NC: Duke University Press, 2011), 308.

59 "Pin the Macho on the Man," *The Body Politic* 103, May 1984, 26.

60 David Vereschagin, "Buying It: Advertising and the Cult of Masculinity," *The Body Politic* 100 January–February 1984, 29.
61 Vereschagin, "Buying It," 29.
62 Vereschagin, "Buying It," 29.
63 Vereschagin, "Buying It," 29.
64 Vereschagin, "Buying It," 29.
65 "Classified Ads During the Postal Strike," 27 July 1981, Box 2, F0002–01–031, *TBP* fonds.
66 "Advertising-Classified," 1979, Box 1, F0002–01–010, *TBP* fonds.
67 "Classified Ads During the Postal Strike," 27 July 1981, Box 2, F0002–01–031, *TBP* fonds.
68 Historian David Churchill notes that since *TBP*'s early years, "[a]ds making over prohibitions such as, 'no blacks,' 'no fats,' 'no fems,' would ... not be published in the paper [*TBP*]. Churchill, "Personal Ad Politics," 116.
69 Classified ad: "Lonesome Cowboy," *The Body Politic* 16, November–December 1974, 26.
70 Classified ad: "Submissive Masculine GWM," *The Body Politic* 66, September 1980, 37.
71 Classified ad: "Shy Inexperienced 28-Year-Old," *The Body Politic* 66, September 1980, 37.
72 Advertisement: "Classified ads communicate," *The Body Politic* 44, June–July 1978, 29.
73 Advertisement: "Classified ads communicate," 29.
74 Churchill, "Personal Ad Politics," 116.
75 Classified ad: "Male 5'8, 135lbs," *The Body Politic* 10, Autumn 1973, 26. Note: Only season of the year was given to some issues early on in *TBP*'s publication.
76 Classified ad: John, "Spring Has Sprung," *The Body Politic* 14, July–August 1974, 30.
77 Classified ad: "Professional White Male," *The Body Politic* 21, December 1975, 26.
78 Classified ad: "Male 29, Professional," *The Body Politic* 21, December 1975, 26.
79 Classified ad: "W/M, Fairly Masculine," *The Body Politic* 26, September 1976, 22.
80 Tom Burke, "The New Homosexuality," *Esquire*, December 1969, 178.
81 Hugh Brewster, "The Myth of the New Homosexual," *The Body Politic* 4, March–April 1972, 3.
82 Mary Louise Adams, *The Trouble with Normal: Postwar Youth and the Making of Heterosexuality* (Toronto: University of Toronto Press, 1997), 82.
83 Brewster, "Myth," 3.
84 Brewster, "Myth," 3.
85 Michael Riordon, "Voices from the Closet (People Who Want to Have Their Cake and Eat It)," *The Body Politic* 24, June 1976, 9.

86 Sedgwick argues that "we have too much cause to know how limited a leverage any individual revelation can exercise over collectively scaled and institutionally embodied oppressions. Acknowledgement of this disproportion does not mean that the consequences of such acts as coming out can be circumscribed within *predetermined* boundaries, as if between "personal" and "political" realms, nor does it require us to deny how disproportionately powerful and disruptive such acts can be." Eve Kosofsky Sedgwick, *Epistemology of the Closet* (Berkeley and Los Angeles: University of California Press, 1990), 78.

87 John Rechy, *The Sexual Outlaw: A Documentary* (New York: Grove Press, 1977), 243.

88 Rechy, *The Sexual Outlaw*, 16.

89 Herb Spiers, "The Sexual Outlaw: A Documentary' by John Rechy," *The Body Politic* 34, June 1977, 18.

90 Rechy, *The Sexual Outlaw*, 253.

91 Spiers, "The Sexual Outlaw," 18.

92 Spiers, "The Sexual Outlaw," 18.

93 Ian Young, "An Unappetizing Spectacle," *The Body Politic* 35, July–August 1977, 2.

94 Herb Spiers, "Author Replies," *The Body Politic* 35, July–August 1977, 2.

95 Tim Guest, "Image Control," *The Body Politic* 43, May 1978, 11.

96 Peter Bowen, "So What's Wrong with Discrimination?" *The Body Politic* 77, October 1981, 6.

97 Italics in original. Bowen, "What's Wrong?," 6.

98 Jim Loveless, unnamed letter, *The Body Politic* 68, November 1980, 6.

99 Loveless, unnamed letter, 6.

100 Dan Healey, "Spiteful Bunk, Divisive Nonsense," *The Body Politic* 69, December–January 1980/1, 7.

101 John Allec, "Right on Target, but Which Target?" *The Body Politic* 95, July–August 1983, 41.

102 Echols, *Hot Stuff*, 126.

103 Sociologist Michael Kimmel has written extensively on young male identity in post-war America. His argument is that modern masculinity is in crisis because traditional anchors of male identity are receding and are becoming increasingly impossible to obtain, particularly financial independence the importance of displaying muscle. See Michael Kimmel, *Angry White Men: American Masculinity at the End of an Era* (New York: Nation Books, 2013); *Manhood in America: A Cultural History*, 3rd ed. (New York: Oxford University Press, 2012); and *Guyland: The Perilous World Where Boys Become Men* (New York: HarperCollins, 2008).

104 Alan Stewart, "Making the Truth Palatable," *The Globe and Mail*, 3 August 1985, 18.

3. Stylizing Masculinity in Urban Spaces

1 Gerald Hannon, "Kiss-In Protests Conviction of Kissers," *The Body Politic* 26, September 1976, 3; and Merv Welker, "Gay Men Organize to Make Park Safe," *The Body Politic* 26, September 1976, 3.
2 Gill Valentine and Tracey Skelton, "Finding Oneself, Losing Oneself: The Lesbian and Gay 'Scene' as a Paradoxical Space," *International Journal of Urban and Regional Research* 27, no. 4 (December 2003): 855.
3 Dick Hebdige, *Subculture: The Meaning of Style* (New York: Routledge Press, 1973 [2003]), 80.
4 Regarding terminology, I use the term "space" when referencing the material or physical landscape in Toronto, while "place" involves the shaping of space by taxonomic categories such as sexuality, gender, race, class, and the state.
5 Leif Jerram, "Space: A Useless Category of Historical Analysis?" *History and Theory* 52 (October 2013): 404.
6 Tom Warner, *Never Going Back: A History of Queer Activism in Canada* (Toronto: University of Toronto Press, 2002), 90.
7 David Newcome and Paul Pearce, "The Gay Ghetto," *The Body Politic* 2, January–February 1972, 13.
8 Ken Popert, "Our Collective Right," *The Body Politic* 47, October 1978, 19.
9 Quote originated from Kurt Hiller in 1921. *The Body Politic* 15, September–October 1974, 2.
10 Michael Riordon, "Taking Power: One of These Days," *The Body Politic* 34, June 1977, 21.
11 David Townsend, "Staying On," *The Body Politic* 92, April 1983, 29.
12 Tim McCaskell (editor for *The Body Politic*), interview by Nicholas Hrynyk, 20 March 2015, interview 1, transcript.
13 Ken Popert, "Public Sexuality and Social Space," *The Body Politic* 85, July–August 1982, 29.
14 Elizabeth Kennedy and Madeline Davis, *Boots of Leather, Slippers of Gold: This History of a Lesbian Community* (New York: Routledge Press, 1993), 150.
15 Gary Kinsman and Patrizia Gentile, *The Canadian War on Queers: National Security as Sexual Regulation* (Vancouver: University of British Columbia Press, 2010), 503.
16 LAC, RG 146, vol. 3115, file "Community Homophile Association of Toronto, Ont.," O Division, Toronto, 7 August 1973, "Re: Composite Report on the University of Toronto (U. of T.), Toronto, Ontario (Key Sectors Education)," 24.
17 See Tom Hooper, '"Enough Is Enough': The Right to Privacy Committee and Bahthouse Raids in Toronto, 1978–1983," PhD diss., York University, 2016.

18 Catherine Jean Nash, "Toronto's Gay Village (1969–1982): Plotting the Politics of Gay Identity," *The Canadian Geographer* 50, no. 1 (2006): 2.
19 Ken Popert (editor for *The Body Politic*), interview by Nicholas Hrynyk, 14 April 2015, interview 1, transcript.
20 Amerigo Marras, "Hetero-burbia," *The Body Politic* 7, Winter 1973, 25.
21 See footnote in Chauncey, *Gay New York*, 133.
22 David Newcome and Paul Pearce, "The Gay Ghetto," *The Body Politic* 2, January–February 1972, 13.
23 "Office Procedure Manual – Telephone," 1979, Box 1, F0002–01–010, *TBP* fonds.
24 John Scythes, "Toronto's Gay Spots," *The Body Politic* 7, Winter 1973, 6.
25 See "Gay Toronto," *The Body Politic* 14, July–August 1974, 19; "Montréal Gay Spots," *The Body Politic* 9, Summer 1973, 8; and Robin Hardy, Robin Metcalfe, and Kathy MacNeil, "Atlantic Travel Guide," *The Body Politic* 44, June–July 1978, 15–17.
26 Herb Spiers, "On His Way: Letters from a Small Town Youth," *The Body Politic* 12, March–April 1974, 17.
27 Herb Spiers, "On His Way," 17.
28 Classified ad: "European Male 27," *The Body Politic* 11, January–February 1974, 22.
29 Classified ad: "White male, 25," *The Body Politic* 16, November–December 1974, 26.
30 The term "social whirl" was used frequently to refer to the gay circuit, scene, or ghetto. Classified ad: Quiet, Intelligent," *The Body Politic* 18, May–June 1975, 26.
31 In total, six ads expressed distaste for gay bars, bathhouses, and spas by 1975. See ads in *The Body Politic* 21, December 1975, 26.
32 Tim (last name unknown), "Consumer Protection," *The Body Politic* 31, March 1977, 2.
33 John Scythes, "Toronto's Gay Spots," *The Body Politic* 7, Winter 1973, 6.
34 "Women in Jeans Now OK at Gay Bar," *The Body Politic* 25, August 1976, 3.
35 "Women in Jeans," 3.
36 Jack Halberstam, *Female Masculinity* (Durham, NC: Duke University Press, 1998), 273.
37 Allec and Barker, "Hot Spots," 22.
38 Also see The Barn's corresponding advertisement: "The Barn," *The Body Politic* 72, April 1981, 39.
39 See related ad for 18 East. "18 East," *The Body Politic* 72, April 1981, 39.
40 Danny Cockerline, "Out of the Closet & Out in the Cold," *The Body Politic* 110, January 1985, 32.
41 Danny Cockerline, "To the Collective," 16 December 1983, Box 2, F0002–01–036, *TBP* fonds.

42 Cockerline, "Out of the Closet," 32.
43 Cockerline, "Out of the Closet," 32.
44 Viviane Namaste, *Invisible Lives: The Erasure of Transsexual and Transgendered People* (Chicago: University of Chicago Press, 2000), 12.
45 Cockerline, "Out of the Closet," 32.
46 John Grube, "Men Looking at Men Looking at Men," *The Body Politic* 95, July–August 1983, 34.
47 Steven Maynard argues that the journey to sex was "the relationship between a man's class background and place of residence with the location of his sexual encounter." Maynard pays particular attention to aspects of the city-building process and the status of men as wage earners, both of which were important conditions for a homosexual subculture to emerge. Steven Maynard, "Through a Hole in the Lavatory Wall: Homosexual Subcultures, Police Surveillance, and the Dialectics of Discovery, Toronto, 1890–1930," *Journal of the History of Sexuality* 5, no. 2 (October 1994): 217.
48 Maynard, "Through a Hole," 209.
49 George Chauncey, *Gay New York: Gender, Urban Culture, and the Making of the Gay Male World, 1890–1940* (New York: Basic Books, 1994), 286.
50 Hugh Brewster, "The Non-Urban Gay Ghetto," *The Body Politic* 2, January–February 1972, 9.
51 Matt Houlbrook, *Queer London: Perils and Pleasures in the Sexual Metropolis, 1918–1957* (Chicago: University of Chicago Press, 2006), 76.
52 Houlbrook, *Queer London*, 210.
53 John Forbes, "Hanky Panky: Beyond the Pale and Back Again," *The Body Politic* 49, December–January 1979, 18.
54 Amy Groves, "Lesbian S&M: Valverde Roasted," *The Body Politic* 62, April 1980, 4.
55 Mariana Valverde, "Feminism Meets First-Fucking: Getting Lost in Lesbian S&M," *The Body Politic* 60, February 1980, 43.
56 As quoted in Larry Giteck, *Cruise to Win: A Guide for Gay Men* (San Francisco: Pantera Press, 1982), 11.
57 As quoted in Giteck, *Cruise to Win*, 27.
58 As stated in chapter two, the term "sign-vehicles" lies within Erving Goffman's concept of dramaturgy. Included in these sign-vehicles are bodily and facial expressions, as well as other bodily means of communication from one individual to another. See Erving Goffman, *The Presentation of Self in Everyday Life* (Edinburgh: University of Edinburgh Social Sciences Research Centre, 1956), 14–15.
59 Gerry Oxford, "Men Looking at Men Looking at Men," *The Body Politic* 95, July–August 1983, 31.
60 Brian Hickey, "Men Looking at Men Looking at Men," *The Body Politic* 95, July–August 1983, 32.

61 Emphasis in original. Michael Caplan, "Men Looking at Men Looking at Men," *The Body Politic* 95, July–August 1983, 32.
62 Ken Chaplin, "Men Looking at Men Looking at Men," *The Body Politic* 95, July–August 1983, 33.
63 Scott Tucker, "Theory and Action," *The Body Politic* 65, August 1980, 4. His response was to Ken Popert's article "Cruising and Crisis Management," *The Body Politic* 62, April 1980, 47.
64 "Meeting Minutes," 14 March 1977, Box 1, F0002–01–025, *TBP* fonds.
65 Quan Minh, "Men Looking at Men Looking at Men," *The Body Politic* 95, July–August 1983, 34.
66 George Xuereb, "Men Looking at Men Looking at Men," *The Body Politic* 95, July–August 1983, 33.
67 *The Body Politic* is not italicized in the original. "What Do You Say to a Guy After You've Blown Him in the Park?" *The Body Politic* 27, October 1976, 14.
68 Gary Kinsman and Patrizia Gentile, along with Douglas Janoff, have noted that municipal police forces and the Royal Canadian Mounted Police (RCMP) routinely performed undercover operates to locate, entrap, and persecute gay men and lesbians in the 1970s and 1980s. While the aforementioned scholars discuss the use of disguise in entrapping gay men, there has been no exploration of how such tactics were carried out on the part of police by using style to either carry out or enhance their success at entrapping gay men. See Kinsman and Gentile, *Canadian War on Queers*, 2010; Gary Kinsman, *The Regulation of Desire* (Montreal: Black Rose Books, 1996); and Douglas Janoff, *Pink Violence: Homophobic Violence in Canada* (Toronto: University of Toronto Press, 2005).
69 It is unknown how often police read *TBP*, but evidence in *TBP* suggests that police continued to respond to the knowledge of their reconnaissance by updating tactics of surveillance.
70 Dave Scott, "Police and Homosexuals Co-Operate to Stop Offences in Parks, Subways," *Toronto Daily Star*, 6 April 1972, 27.
71 Police voyeurism is another example of police performing a queerness because voyeurism is often looked upon as a perversion. The perverted nature of voyeurism does not apply to police officers in this context, however, because legitimate state "powers" encourage the police to observe and convict. Foucault argues that Bentham's panopticon is "a generalizable model of functioning; a way of defining power relations in terms of the everyday life of men." Michel Foucault, *Discipline and Punish: The Birth of the Prison*, trans. Alan Sheridan (New York: Vintage Books, 1975 [2012]), 205.
72 A glory hole is a small cut-out opening between two stalls which facilitates anonymous sexual encounters. Often, oral sex was provided using these openings, and it was considered common practice in public cruising. See "Cop Hides in Toilet for Entrapment Blitz," *The Body Politic* 54, July 1979, 15.

73 "Cop Hides in Toilet," 15.
74 Ross Irwin, "Cops Forced to Stop Entrapment at Greenwin Square Washroom," *The Body Politic* 55, August 1979, 11.
75 George Hislop, "Don't Grope Strangers (Introduce Yourself First)," *The Body Politic* 4, May–June 1972, 18.
76 As quoted in "Policemen Enticing Homosexuals, Spokesman Says," *The Globe and Mail*, 5 March 1973, 5.
77 Robin Hardy, "Guilty of Brutal Attack, 'Queerbashers' Get Jail Term," *The Body Politic* 44, June–July 1978, 5.
78 "Warning," *The Body Politic* 45, August 1978, 8.
79 Female impersonators in the army, such as the example Jackson uses of "the army's 'Kit Bags' concert party," demonstrates that even institutions considered bastions of heterosexuality contained spaces (often the stage) in which the heterosexual, masculine nature of the Canadian military was challenged. However, the drag performance in this instance is arguably non-threatening because the stage highlights the theatricality or campiness of the solder's performance – reminding heterosexual soldiers that their own sexuality is not brought into question by watching. Paul Jackson, *One of the Boys: Homosexuality in the Military During World War II* (Montreal & Kingston: McGill-Queen's University Press, 2004), 160.
80 Anne McClintock argues that "S/M performs the 'primitive irrational' as a dramatic script; a theatrical, communal performance in the heart of Western reason." Anne McClintock, *Imperial Leather: Race, Gender and Sexuality in Colonial Contest* (New York: Routledge, 1995), 143.
81 Police donning macho style or plainclothes highlights how state power can be reinvented and scripted to unconventional uniforms, revealing "that social order is unnatural, scripted and invented," according to McClintock. McClintock, *Imperial Leather*, 143.
82 Rombus Hube, "Toronto Civilian Park Patrol," *The Body Politic* 1, November–December 1971, 9.
83 "Uncovering the Enemy Within," *The Body Politic* 72, April 1981, 12.
84 Gerald Hannon, "In Gay Company," *The Body Politic* 18, May–June 1975, 20.
85 Gerald Hannon, "War on Sin Produced Gay Casualities," *The Body Politic* 20, October 1975, 8.
86 Hannon, "War on Sin," *The Body Politic* 20, October 1975, 8.
87 Editorial collective, "Olympic Crackdown," *The Body Politic* 25, August 1976, 1.
88 John Blacklock and Paul Trollope, "How a Steambath Becomes a Bawdyhouse," *The Body Politic* 38, November 1977, 7.
89 Robert Cook, "350 Demand End to Police Harassment," *The Body Politic* 33, May 1977, 1.
90 Editorial collective, "Olympic Crackdown," 17.
91 John Towndrow, "Entrapped," *The Body Politic* 25, August 1976, 9.

92 Michael Riordon, "Remember When 'Mounties' Meant the Musical Ride?" *The Body Politic* 39, December 1977–January 1978, 28.
93 Riordon, "Remember," 28.
94 Canada and the United States took on a mantle of international leadership that allowed them to flex their national muscle in the proceeding decades. Susan Faludi, *Stiffed: The Betrayal of the American Man* (New York: Harper Collins, 1999), 19.
95 Bill Lewis, "Park Pee Nets Arrest," *The Body Politic* 84, June 1982, 14.
96 Anonymous, "Letter Attachment to the Minutes of Meeting," 25 June 1982, Box 2, F0002–01–032.
97 Kinsman and Gentile note that the RCMP monitored *The Body Politic* for its coverage of the upcoming Fifth National Gay Conference held at the University of Saskatchewan from 29 June to 3 July 1977. Kinsman and Gentile, *The Canadian War on Queers*, 328.
98 Gerald Hannon, "Toronto Teacher's Home Charged as 'Bawdy House," *The Body Politic* 54, July 1979, 11.
99 Bawdy house legislation in the Criminal Code of Canada was frequently applied to gay bathhouses, even if they legitimately operated as sauna and health clubs. In November 1977, *TBP* writers John Blacklock and Paul Trollope argued that "[u]ntil the bawdy house laws are fought head-on by a courageous baths manager, owner or found-in, we will be left with precedent that the baths are bawdy houses within the meaning of the Criminal Code. Baths will continue to be raided and closed in various cities, patrons humiliated and prosecuted and their names published in the press." John Blacklock and Paul Trollope, "How a Steambath Becomes a Bawdyhouse," *The Body Politic* 38, November 1977, 7.
100 Kinsman and Gentile, *The Canadian War on Queers*, 311.
101 "A Fantasy Come True," *The Body Politic* 54, July 1979, 8.
102 "Violence at Local Gay Bar," *The Body Politic* 27, October 1976, 7.
103 After conducting interviews with two gay men on Yonge Street, journalist Ron Poramro reported to readers of the *The Globe and Mail* that many gay men, especially sex workers, were no longer being harassed by police on "the strip" (Yonge Street) because they conformed to expectations of gender. His interview with Mansie, a "blond stud" who "looked as tanned and handsome as a professional tennis player and his body was just as lean and muscular," and his partner, Michael, reinforced the idea that desirability and conservative performances of gender brought safety. When asked if police had harassed him while on Yonge Street, Mansie responded, "I know every gay on the strip and I know what's going on. The police don't hassle anybody here. They haven't bothered anyone here in the 4 ½ years I've been here." The implicit argument was that Mansie and Michael, two sex workers who embodied sexual desirability,

were safe from police harassment because they conformed to a relatively conservative standard of masculinity. Furthermore, Poramro alluded to the idea that homosexuality itself did not attract unwarranted negative attention. What attracted attention were public transgressions of gender roles because these lapses were sign-vehicles indicating homosexuality. Ron Poramro, "Police No Longer Hassle Gays on Strip, Homosexual Says," *The Globe and Mail*, 3 August 1977, 5.

104 Houlbrook, *Queer London*, 210.

105 Robin Hardy, "Overkill: Murder in Toronto-the-Good," *The Body Politic* 50, February 1979, 20.

106 Hardy, "Overkill," 20.

107 "Overkill" means that the victim is repeatedly stabbed, bludgeoned, or beaten even after death.

108 Hardy, "Overkill," 20.

109 Hardy, "Overkill," 20.

110 Hardy, "Overkill," 20.

111 Hardy, "Overkill," 20.

112 Hardy, "Overkill," 20.

113 Hardy, "Overkill," 20.

114 Hardy, "Overkill," 20.

115 Paul Trollope, "If Looks Could Kill," *The Body Politic* 51, March–April 1979, 6.

116 Hardy, "Overkill," 21.

117 In addition to restaurants, health and social services, accommodations, community dances, sporting leagues, among other categories, the collective noted nineteen bars, three bathhouses, and five discotheques, some of which, such as The Tool Box, continued to be described aesthetically as a "leather club." See "Your Summer Guide to Toronto," *The Body Politic* 105, July–August 1984, 25.

118 Gerald Hannon, "Learning to Kill," *The Body Politic* 22, February 1976, 8.

119 "Self-Defence and Self-Assurance," *The Body Politic* 61, March 1980, 41.

120 Shaun Cole, *'Don We Now Our Gay Apparel': Gay Men's Dress in the Twentieth Century* (London: Bloomsbury Press, 2000), 724.

121 This was particularly the case for the Imperial Health Club, a bodybuilding gym that was noted by *TBP* columnist Michael Lynch as not having a "toke of gay flavour in the place." In his article, he argued that "If the tension between gays and nongays here rates lower than in the Y's weightroom, it's because the gay presence here is so well hidden from the nongays." Indeed, a regular attendee interviewed by Lynch praised the Imperial Health Club as "wonderful because it's so straight." Michael Lynch, "Young (and Old and Middle-Aged Too) Men's Cruising Associations," *The Body Politic* 55, August 1979, 39.

122 Advertisement: "The Back Door," *The Body Politic* 66, September 1980, 34.
123 The first "Out in the City" section of *The Body Politic* informed readers on gay- and lesbian-friendly venues, primarily restaurants, along Yonge Street between Bloor Street and Queen Street after bars and baths closed at 1:00 a.m. Irwin Barrer, "Survival on 'The Strip' After Last Call," *The Body Politic* 47, October 1978, 35.
124 See "Out in the City: A Guide to Goings On in Toronto in the Month of April," *The Body Politic* 72, April 1981, 37.
125 "Meeting Minutes," 28 May 1979, Box 1, F0002–01–027, *TBP* fonds.
126 Lynch, "Young Men's Cruising Association," 39.
127 Lynch, "Young Men's Cruising Association," 39.
128 Lynch, "Young Men's Cruising Association," 39.
129 Ken Popert (editor for *The Body Politic*), interview by Nicholas Hrynyk, 14 April 2015, interview 1, transcript.
130 "Vancouver Gay Liberation," *The Body Politic* 1, November–December 1971, 2.
131 Ian Young, "Small Press Books," *The Body Politic* 37, October 1977, 22.
132 James Wilson, "Under Forty in the Heart of the City: Village People at Mosport," *The Body Politic* 47, October 1978, 41.
133 Popert (editor for *The Body Politic*), interview by Nicholas Hrynyk, transcript.
134 Michael Lynch, "Getting Pecs: p 39," *The Body Politic* 55, August 1979, 3.
135 While there were no explicit discussions of the lasting spatial or physical consequences of these raids, there was a report four days later that suggested the closure of lesbian bar Fly By Night Lounge on 9 February 1981 was not just a coincidence. The bar was not previously under surveillance; thus, it was believed that its closure was "a product of the same mentality" as the raids, according to Manager Pat Murphy. "'Get Lost' Says Owner and Shuts Lesbian Bar," *The Body Politic* 71, March 1981, 14.
136 George Hislop as quoted in Gerald Hannon, "Taking It to the Streets," *The Body Politic* 71, March 1981, 9. Also see Joe Hall, "Homosexuals Fear Suicides and Broken Marriages in Wake of Raids," *Toronto Star*, 7 February 1981: A7.
137 Cockerline, "Out of the Closet," 32.
138 Tom Hooper, '"Enough Is Enough': The Right to Privacy Committee and Bathhouse Raids in Toronto, 1978–1983," PhD diss., York University, 2016, 113, York Space Institutional Repository.
139 Hooper, "Enough Is Enough," 60.
140 Catherine Nash, "Consuming Sexual Liberation: Gay Business, Politics, and Toronto's Barracks Bathhouse Raids," *Journal of Canadian Studies*, 48, no. 1 (2014): 97.

141 Gerald Hannon suggested that "[s]ince the raids, there have been several media visits to the baths, all of whom recorded extensive damage, estimated by the owners at about $35,000." Hannon, "Taking It to the Streets," 11.

142 Paul Agius, "Fuming and Fighting Back," *The Body Politic* 72, April 1981, 4.

143 Susan Bordo, *Unbearable Weight: Feminism, Western Culture, and the Body* (Berkeley: University of California Press, 1993 [2003]), 38.

144 Leslie Heywood, "Muscularity Vanishing: Bodybuilding and Contemporary Culture," in *Building Bodies*, ed. Pamela L. Moore (New Brunswick, NJ: Rutgers University Press, 1997), 166. See also Kaja Silverman, *Male Subjectivity at the Margins* (New York: Routledge, 1992); and Chris Holmlund, "Masculinity as Multiple Masquerade," in *Screening the Male*, eds. Steven Cohan and Ina Rae Hark (New York: Routledge, 1993): 213–29.

145 As quoted in Gerald Hannon, "Guilty Verdict in Pisces Trial Discouraging Sign for Found-Ins," *The Body Politic* 76, September 1981, 11.

146 Hannon, "Guilty Verdict," 11.

147 Phil Shaw, "The Jock," *The Body Politic* 107, October 1984, 47.

148 Italics in original. Shaw, "The Jock," 47.

149 Classified ad: "Masculine, W/M," *The Body Politic* 80, January–February 1982, 49.

150 Classified ad: "White Masculine, Muscular," *The Body Politic* 85, July–August 1982, 42.

151 Classified ad: "GWM, 23, 158lbs," *The Body Politic* 86, September 1982, 43.

152 "Your Summer Guide to Toronto," *The Body Politic* 105, July–August 1984, 25.

153 Bold emphasis in original. Billy Schoefl, "Entrapped," *The Body Politic* 27, October 1976, 2.

154 Michael Riordon, "Voices from the Closet (People Who Want to Have Their Cake and Eat It)," *The Body Politic* 24, June 1976, 9.

155 Ken Popert, "Dangers of the Minority Game," *The Body Politic* 63, May 1980, 37.

4. "The Cowboy Hat Will Never Fit Quite Right": Intersections of Race and Masculinity

1 In his influential 1978 book *Orientalism*, Edward Said argues that "Orientalism was ultimately a political vision of reality whose structure supported the difference between the familiar (Europe, the West, 'us') and the strange (the Orient, the East, 'them')." Differentiating the exotic Orient from Europe broadly reflected in literature, theories, social descriptions, paintings, and photography, and beyond culture, came to shape

European ideas of racialized bodies. Edward W. Said, *Orientalism: Western Conceptions of the Orient* (New York: Penguin Books, 1978 [2006]), 43.

2 Said, *Orientalism*, 63.

3 See David Sealy, "'Canadianizing' Blackness: Resisting the Political" in *Rude: Contemporary Black Canadian Cultural Criticism*, ed. Rinaldo Walcott (Toronto: Insomniac Press, 2000), 91 and 98.

4 David Rayside (volunteer at *The Body Politic*), interview by Nicholas Hrynyk, 24 March 2015, interview 1, transcript.

5 In addition to Gay Asian Toronto and Zami, numerous other groups aimed at marginalized gays formed following *TBP*'s publication run. Salaam, a group dedicated at providing support for gay Muslims, was founded in 1991 in Toronto by lawyer El-Farouk Khaki. According to Aisha Geissinger, Salaam was temporarily disbanded after Khaki received death threats from "several persons claiming to belong to Islamic Jihad cells" after writing an article about gay Muslims in a student paper at the University of Toronto. It resumed operations, however, in 1998 following news that gay Muslim group Al-Fatiha formed in the United States. Aisha Geissinger, "Islam and Discourses of Same-Sex Desire," in *Queer Religion: Homosexuality in Modern Religious History*, eds. Donald L. Boisvert and James Emerson Johnson (Santa Barbara, CA: Praeger, 2012), 82–3.

6 Gay Asians of Toronto (later renamed Gay Asians Toronto) was created as a peer discussion group in 1980 by Richard Fung, Gerald Chan, Nitto Marquez, and Tony Souza to deal with racism and homophobia unique to men of colour in Toronto's community. In the words of Tom Warner, "GAT's [Gay Asians Toronto] purposes were: promoting unity and mutual support among gay Asians; organizing social, culture, educational, and recreational activities for its members; providing culturally sensitive social and support services; and advocating on issues relevant to their community's concerns." Tom Warner, *Never Going Back: A History of Queer Activism in Canada* (Toronto: University of Toronto Press, 2002), 185.

7 Warner, *Never Going Back*, 185.

8 Warner, *Never Going Back*, 186.

9 David Churchill argues that "[i]n Toronto during the 1980s and early 1990s numerous anti-racist groups sought to provide support, services, and cultural work. These groups challenged the given public culture of Toronto's lesbian and gay community by making the experience of people of colour, living in the Diaspora [*sic*] visible, recognizable, and present. Yet the institutional vitality and growth of these communities, as well as the changing demographics of Toronto, were only marginally represented in the pages of TBP, the paper remained largely the effort of white gay men." David Churchill, "Personal Ad Politics: Race, Sexuality and Power at *The Body Politic*," *Left History* 8, no. 2 (2003): 125.

10 Back cover: "Get More Definition," *The Body Politic* 95, July–August 1983, 56.
11 Fo Niemi, "Blind Narcissism," *The Body Politic* 85, July–August 1982, 5.
12 David Newcome and Paul Pearce, "The Gay Ghetto," *The Body Politic* 2, January–February 1972, 13.
13 Sean Mills, *The Empire Within: Postcolonial Thought and Political Activism in Sixties Montreal* (Kingston and Montreal: McGill-Queen's University Press, 2010), 113.
14 Mills, *The Empire Within*, 113.
15 Paul Goodman's essay "The Politics of Being Queer" was published posthumously and appeared in an edited collection entitled *Nature Heals*. See *Nature Heals: The Psychological Essays of Paul Goodman*, ed. Taylor Stoehr (New York: Free Life Editions, 1977). Originally published as "The Politics of Being Queer" in *Nature Heals*, 216–25.
16 "Paul Goodman: The Politics of Being Queer," *The Body Politic* 52, May 1979, 25.
17 In Canada, the appropriation of the N-word was done by Pierre Vallières, an intellectual leader of the Front de Liberation du Québec, and made famous in his 1967 work, *Nègres blancs d'Amérique, autobiographie précoce d'un "terroriste" Québécois* (*White Niggers of America: The Precocious Autobiography of a Quebec "Terrorist"*). The term symbolized the plight of the Québécois and the socio-economic and political pressures on people in Québéc through a racial framework that reverberated with anti-colonial and anti-capitalist sentiments throughout the world in the late 1960s. See Bryan Palmer, *Canada's 1960s: The Ironies of Identity in a Rebellious Era* (Toronto: University of Toronto Press, 2009), 339.
18 "Paul Goodman," 26.
19 Jeffrey Escoffier argues that "[t]he ideal of authenticity offered an intellectual framework with which they [homosexuals] could emancipate themselves from a culture that stigmatized homosexuality." Jeffrey Escoffier, *American Homo: Community and Perversity* (Berkeley: University of California Press, 1998), 211.
20 McCaskall further argued that "For those of us who are not white or Canadian-born, however, coming out may mean giving up far more than a closet. It may mean abandoning culture and language, cutting yourself off from a world that has made you what you are, a world not shared by your new community. And it may mean cutting yourself off from an immigrant community or family that is a major source of support and protection in an alien culture." Tim McCaskell, "You've Got a Nice Body for an Oriental," *The Body Politic* 102, April 1984, 35.
21 Canada. *Statutes of Canada: An Act Respecting Immigration, 1952*. Ottawa: SC 1 Elizabeth II, Chapter 42, 240.

22 The Canadian war on queers is laid out by Gary Kinsman and Patrizia Gentile in *The Canadian War on Queers*. Gary Kinsman and Patrizia Gentile, *The Canadian War on Queers: National Security as Sexual Regulation* (Vancouver: University of British Columbia Press, 2010), 44.
23 Franca Iacovetta describes the numerous magazines and government organizations tasked with assisting new Canadians in their acclimation to Canadian society. Magazines such as *Chatelaine* and groups such as the Canadian Association for Adult Education, made it their mission to "Canadianize" immigrants through social and cultural uplift. Recipes, exercise, homemaking, job skills, and education were all promoted as ways in which foreigners could better immerse themselves in Canadian culture. Franca Iacovetta, *Gatekeepers: Reshaping Immigrant Lives in Cold War Canada* (Toronto: Between the Lines, 2006), 10.
24 "A Minority Within a Minority," *The Body Politic* 66, September 1980, 41.
25 Escoffier, *American Homo*, 211.
26 Richard Fung, "Gay Marchers Flood Washington," *The Body Politic* 58, November 1979, 17.
27 Fung, "Gay Marchers," 17.
28 Gerald Chan, "Biases Overt and Covert," *The Body Politic* 76, September 1981, 6.
29 The article originally appeared in the *Australian National Gay Community News* 3, no. 3. Peter Jackson, "Calcutta, New Year's 1981," *The Body Politic* 80, January–February 1982, 22.
30 Jackson, "Calcutta," 22.
31 Jackson, "Calcutta," 23.
32 Jeff O'Malley, "Gay in Asia: Emotions and Exploitation," *The Body Politic* 83, May 1982, 8.
33 O'Malley, "Gay in Asia," 8.
34 Dana Collins, *The Rise and Fall of an Urban Sexual Community: Malate (Dis) Placed* (London: Palgrave Macmillan, 2016), 22. See also: Joan Nagel, *Race, Ethnicity, and Sexuality: Intimate Intersections, Forbidden Frontiers* (New York: Oxford University Press, 2003).
35 "The Rape of the Third World," *Spartacus*, April 1980, 8.
36 "Sri Lanka (Ceylon)," *Spartacus*, April 1980, 474.
37 "Third World Boy Love Attacked at Congress," *The Body Politic* 76, September 1981, 17.
38 According to gender scholar M. Jacqui Alexander, gay travel guides reinforce a "certain intransigent colonial relationship in which previously scripted colonial cartography of ownership, production, consumption, and distribution all conform to a First/Third World division in which Third World gay men get positioned as the objects of sexual consumption rather than as agents in a sexual exchange." M. Jacqui Alexander, *Pedagogies of*

Crossing: Meditations on Feminism, Sexual Politics, Memory, and the Sacred (Durham, NC: Duke University Press, 2005), 79.

39 Mrinalini Sinha argues in her book *Colonial Masculinity* that constructions of masculinity in the context of British colonial India linked white European masculinity with colonial rule and effeminacy with subjugation, establishing unique gender hierarchies within Indian society around religion, caste, class, and political positions. In her analysis, she notes that the creation of the "effeminate Bengali" was a response to political and economic shifts at the end of the nineteenth century whereby British elites reaffirmed colonial rule by embodying the patriarchal concept of the "manly Englishman." Mrinalini Sinha, *Colonial Masculinity: The "Manly Englishman" and the "Effeminate Bengali" in the Late Nineteenth Century* (Manchester: Manchester University Press, 1995), 14.

40 McCaskell, "You've Got a Nice Body for an Oriental," 36.

41 José B. Torres, V. Scott H. Solberg, and Aaron H. Carlstrom, "The Myth of Sameness Among Latino Men and Their Machismo," *American Journal of Orthopsychiatry* 72, no. 2 (2002): 164.

42 "Classified Ad," *The Body Politic* 78, November 1981, 40.

43 "Smalltown Man," *The Body Politic* 115, June 1985, 47.

44 Steve Garner argues that the "Spanish rule of blood purity, *limpieza de sangre*, which maintains a social class and racial hierarchy in Spain, was transposed as the corner stone of early colonial rule." The concept of racial or blood "purity" continued well into the nineteenth, and arguably twentieth, century and simultaneously created specific notions of racial "impurity." Garner describes the mixing of races as being the equivalent of impurity and associated with "violence, laziness, backwardness and [an] unconquered nature." Steve Garner, *Whiteness: An Introduction* (New York: Routledge, 2007), 88–9.

45 Kris Manjapra, *Colonialism in Global Perspective* (Cambridge: Cambridge University Press, 2020), 88.

46 Michael Riordon, "A Space for Ourselves," *The Body Politic* 75 (July/August 1981): 20.

47 Riordon, "A Space for Ourselves," 20.

48 Riordon, "A Space for Ourselves," 20.

49 As socio-anthropologist Stephen O. Murray argues in his widely regarded 1995 book *Latin American Male Homosexualities*, homosexuality in many Latin American cultures was not taken on as an identity, but rather the role of "gay macho" (*bujarrón*) was based on labels of *activos* (masculine inserters) and *pasivo* (feminine insertees). Murray argues that "[b] esides the *pasivo's* 'feminine insertees' stroking of male vanity, the *activo* maintains his 'stud' self-image/self-presentation by an endless stream of sexual remarks meant to signal to interlocutors an insatiable sexual

appetite. Such remarks may not signify any actual sexual expectations or even any genuine interest in the targets of the remarks, but those who are no longer *miños* (babies) and not yet *viejos* (old men) must continually exhibit an interest in phallic activity – especially if they do not have regular sexual opportunities – by talking about what they would like to do to any imaginably penetrable object." Stephen O. Murray, "Machismo, Male Culture, and Latino Culture," in *Latin American Male Homosexualities*, ed. Stephen O. Murray (Albuquerque: University of New Mexico Press, 1995), 57–8.

50 Susan Henderson and Peter Prizer, "Classified Ads Questioned," *The Body Politic* 26, September 1976, 2.

51 The Collective, "Classified Ads Questioned," *The Body Politic* 26, September 1976, 2.

52 "Orientals and Latins," *The Body Politic* 94, June 1983, 43.

53 "GBM, 26," *The Body Politic* 109, December 1984, 43.

54 Classified ad: "Sincere Male," *The Body Politic* 49, December 1978–January 1979, 44.

55 Classified ad: "Male, East Indian," *The Body Politic* 80, January–February 1982, 49.

56 Classified ad: "Educated Native Indian," *The Body Politic* 85, July–August 1982, 42.

57 "New Gay Centre Boosts Native Gays," *The Body Politic* 50, February 1979, 11. Activist groups for First Nations emerged in the 1980s largely beginning in Manitoba and Saskatchewan.

58 Scott Lauria Morgensen, *Spaces Between Us: Queer Settler Colonialism and Indigenous Decolonization* (Minneapolis: University of Minnesota Press, 2011), 78.

59 Julie Depelteau and Dalie Giroux, "LGBTQ Issues as Indigenous Politics: Two-Spirit Mobilization in Canada," in *Queer Mobilizations: Social Movement Activism and Canadian Public Policy*, ed. Manon Tremblay (Vancouver: University of British Columbia Press, 2015), 68.

60 Daniel Gawthrop, *The Rice Queen Diaries: A Memoir* (Vancouver: Arsenal Pulp Press, 2010), ix.

61 George Peterson, "Classified Ads and Racism," *The Body Politic* 27, October 1976, 2.

62 Editorial collective, "Classified Ads and Racism," *The Body Politic* 27, October 1976, 2.

63 Classified ad: "Scottish Canadian Male," *The Body Politic* 56, September 1979, 39.

64 Classified ad: "Male, White, Tall, Slim," *The Body Politic* 61, March 1980, 36.

65 David L. Eng, *Racial Castration: Managing Masculinity in Asian America* (Durham, NC: Duke University Press, 2001), 93.

66 Classified ad: "This Oriental Gay Male," *The Body Politic* 57, October 1979, 39.
67 Classified ad: "Looking for Masters," *The Body Politic* 91, March 1983, 44.
68 Fo Niemi, "Biases Overt and Covert," *The Body Politic* 76, September 1981, 5.
69 Niemi, "Biases," 5.
70 Classified ad: "Black Men Are the Best Lovers," *The Body Politic* 54, July 1979, 39.
71 Classified ad: "Want to Meet," *The Body Politic* 83, May 1982, 42.
72 Classified ad: "Generous Business Man," *The Body Politic* 100, January–February 1984, 56.
73 Neal A. Lester and Maureen Daly Goggin, "In Living Color: Politics of Desire in Heterosexual Interracial Black/White Personal Ads," in *Racialized Politics of Desire in Personal Ads*, eds. Neal A. Lester and Maureen Daly Goggin (Lanham, MD: Lexington Books, 2007), 52.
74 Shawn Taylor, *Big Black Penis: Misadventures in Race and Masculinity* (Chicago: Lawrence Hill Books, 2008 [2005]), 38.
75 Classified ad: "I Need Attention," *The Body Politic* 47, October 1978, 44.
76 Classified ad: "Young Attractive Black Male," *The Body Politic* 81, March 1982, 44.
77 Classified ad: "Attractive Black Male," *The Body Politic* 100, January–February 1984, 57.
78 John Yorke, "Overt Prejudice," *The Body Politic* 74, June 1981, 4.
79 Yorke, "Overt Prejudice," 4.
80 Churchill, "Personal Ad Politics," 116.
81 Peter Bowen, "So What's Wrong with Discrimination?" *The Body Politic* 77, October 1981, 6.
82 Lim, "GWM," *The Body Politic* 78, November 1981, 5.
83 Fo Niemi, "GWMs and Racial Stereotypes," *The Body Politic* 94, June 1983, 4.
84 Andy, "Attention Black Men," *The Body Politic* 91, March 1983, 43–4.
85 Niemi, "GWMs," 4.
86 Quan Minh, "Men Looking at Men Looking at Men," *The Body Politic* 95, July–August 1983, 34.
87 Minh, "Men Looking at Men," 34.
88 Minh believed that interracial interaction is often viewed as a symbol of upward mobility and prestige for men of colour. Minh, "Men Looking at Men," 34.
89 Looking at the "Ought To Know" series of sexology books published between 1900 and 1915, McCaskall argues that these books, which revolved around "life fluids" and abstinence of "sexual excess," perpetuated racial understandings of sexuality. He cites Michael Bliss, who notably argued that these books explained "that negroes, who were obviously short on mental ability, must have enlarged sexual inclinations by way of explanation, or compensation." McCaskell, "You've Got a Nice Body for an Oriental," 34.

90 McCaskell, "You've Got a Nice Body for an Oriental," 35.

91 McCaskell, "You've Got a Nice Body for an Oriental," 35.

92 Scott Lee, "Cloning Effects and Xenophobia," *The Body Politic* 103, May 1984, 4.

93 Richard Maddocks, "Gays and Racism: Asking Too Much?" *The Body Politic* 104, June 1984, 4.

94 Maddocks, "Gays and Racism," 4.

95 Maddocks, "Gays and Racism," 4.

96 Tim McCaskell, "Gays and Racism: Asking Too Much?" *The Body Politic* 104, June 1984, 4.

97 Emily K. Hobson *Lavender and Red: Liberation and Solidarity in the Gay and Lesbian Left* (Oakland: University of California Press, 2016), 5.

98 Ken Popert, "Race, Moustaches and Sexual Prejudice," *The Body Politic* 94, June 1983, 34.

99 Popert, "Race," 34.

100 Popert, "Race," 34.

101 Popert, "Race," 34.

102 As Christopher Oldstone-Moore argues, "facial hair has always been an important means not just to express manliness but to *be* men." Hair is an important aspect in defining masculinity because it is political. Chrisopher Oldstone-Moore, *Of Beards and Men: The Revealing History of Facial Hair* (Chicago: University of Chicago Press, 2015), 2. The politics of hair is also visibly evident in the Black Afro movement. Noliwe M. Rooks argues that hair in African American culture spoke to the political, social, and cultural landscape of the United States, particularly in the 1960s and 1970s. For instance, looking at the Afro in the 1970s, argues that "the Afro was understood to denote black pride, which became synonymous with activism and political consciousness." See Noliwe M. Rooks, *Hair Raising: Beauty, Culture, and African American Women* (New Brunswick, NJ: Rutgers University Press, 1996), 6.

103 Rebecca Aanerud, "Fictions of Whiteness: Speaking the Names of Whiteness in U.S. Literature," in *Displacing Whiteness: Essays in Racial and Cultural Criticism*, ed. Ruth Frankenberg (Durham, NC: Duke University Press, 1997), 37.

104 Richard Dyer, *White: Essays on Race and Culture* (New York: Routledge, 2013), 70.

105 Popert, "Race," 34.

106 Eng K. Ching, "Racism and Action," *The Body Politic* 96, September 1983, 6.

107 Ching, "Racism," 6.

108 Mair Morton et al., "Racism and Action," *The Body Politic* 96, September 1983, 9.

109 Morton et al., "Racism," 9.

110 See notable examples of lesbian anti-racist commitments and activism throughout Emily K. Hobson's exploration of gay and lesbian leftist activism. Hobson, *Lavender and Red*.
111 John Clifton, "Racism and Action," *The Body Politic* 96, September 1983, 8.
112 Richard Fung, "Racism and Action," *The Body Politic* 96, September 1983, 6.
113 Fung, "Racism," 6.
114 Tony Souza, "Racism and Action," *The Body Politic* 96, September 1983, 7.
115 Souza, "Racism," 7.
116 "Letter to Gays of Ottawa," 3 October 1983, Box 2, F0002–01–035, *TBP* fonds.
117 McCaskell, "You've Got a Nice Body for an Oriental," 35.
118 Escoffier, *American Homo*, 125.
119 Rayside, interview 1, transcript.
120 Popert, interview 1, transcript.
121 Classified ad: "Black Male Wanted," *The Body Politic* 111, February 1985, 44.
122 Classified ad: "Business Executive," *The Body Politic* 22, February 1976, 18.
123 The collective, "31 Words," *The Body Politic* 113, April 1985, 29.
124 Churchill, "Personal Ad Politics,"117.
125 Alan Li, "31 Words," *The Body Politic* 113, April 1985, 30.
126 Li, "31 Words," 30.
127 Churchill, "Personal Ad Politics," 118.
128 Churchill, "Personal Ad Politics," 118.
129 The collective, "31 Words," 29.
130 Ken Popert, "31 Words," *The Body Politic* 113, April 1985, 31.
131 Gerald Hannon, "31 Words," *The Body Politic* 113, April 1985, 32.
132 Several months prior, Fung had screened the video profile *Orientations*, about lesbian and gay Asians in Toronto on Thursday, 8 November 1984. Made in cooperation with Gay Asians Toronto, the film captured the racial and ethnic nuances that shape the lives of minorities within the gay community. In his review of the film, writer Philip Solanki described how subjects candidly spoke about racism, sexuality, politics, and coming out, in a sympathetic way that allowed non-Asians to "gain insight into their own unintentional biases." Philip Solanki, "Exploring a Double Identity," *The Body Politic* 110, January 1985, 23. For film screening, see "Orientations," *The Body Politic* 108, November 1984, 27.
133 Richard Fung, "31 Words," *The Body Politic* 113, April 1985, 30.
134 Brian Mossop, "The Classified Debate," *The Body Politic* 115, June 1985, 10.
135 Siong-huat Chua, "Beyond Racism," *The Body Politic* 119, October 1985, 30.
136 Chua, "Beyond Racism," 30.
137 "The Socially Handicapped," *The Body Politic* 101, March 1984, 34.
138 "Socially Handicapped," 34.
139 "Socially Handicapped," 34.

5. Stylizing Disease and Disability

1 Parts of this chapter have been published as a standalone article in *Disability Studies Quarterly*. See Nicholas Hrynyk, "'No Sorrow, No Pity': Intersections of Disability, HIV / AIDS, and Gay Male Masculinity in the 1980s," *Disability Studies Quarterly* 42, no. 2 (June 2021). https://dsq-sds.org/article/view/7148/5950.

2 Michael Lynch, "Living with Kaposi's," *The Body Politic* 88, November 1982, 33.

3 '"Gay' Cancer and Burning Flesh: The Media Didn't Investigate," *The Body Politic* 76, September 1981, 19.

4 Lynch, "Living with Kaposi's," 34.

5 Michael Lynch, "This Seeing the Sick Endears Them," *The Body Politic* 91, March 1983, 36.

6 Emphases in original. David Buchbinder, *Studying Men and Masculinities* (New York: Routledge, 2013), 144.

7 Robert Trow, "AID Disease Reported in Canada," *The Body Politic* 86, September 1982, 14.

8 A few examples include Larry Kramer, *The Normal Heart* (New York: Samuel French, Inc., 1985); Randy Shilts, *And the Band Played On: Politics, People, and the AIDS Epidemic* (New York: St. Martin's Press, 1987); Ann Silversides, *AIDS Activist: Michael Lynch and the Politics of the Community* (Toronto: Between the Lines, 2003); Jacob Juntunen, *Mainstream AIDS Theatre, the Media, and Gay Civil Rights: Making the Radical Palatable* (New York: Routledge, 2016); and Kevin Mumford, *Not Straight, Not White: Black Gay Men from the March on Washington to the AIDS Crisis* (Chapel Hill: University of North Carolina Press, 2016).

9 See Dan Royals, *To Make the Wounded Whole: The African American Struggle Against HIV/AIDS* (Chapel Hill: University of North Carolina Press, 2020).

10 For clarity, I acknowledge the alternative spelling of disability, such as "dis/ability," by disability scholars seeking to problematize disability as a term used to categorize and create hierarchies of human bodies and minds in society. In the words of Dan Goodley, dis/ability reflects the understanding that disablism and ableism "can only ever be understood simultaneously in relation to one another." However, "disability" is still widely recognized within disability studies and the wider community; thus, I use "disability" when referring to the experiences of those engaging with *TBP* through articles, classified ads, and letters to the editor. See Dan Goodley, *Dis/ability Studies: Theorising Disablism and Ableism* (New York: Routledge, 2014), xiii.

11 Ed Jackson, "Red Cross: Resisting AIDS Panic," *The Body Politic* 91, March 1983, 17.

12 This term is the same as horizontal/lateral violence, which consists of violence and/or tension that perpetuates oppression within a marginalized group. See Rebecca M. Voelkel, *Carnal Knowledge of God: Embodied Love and the Movement for Justice* (Minneapolis: Fortress Press, 2017), 110.

13 Eli Clare, *Exile and Pride: Disability, Queerness, and Liberation* (Durham, NC: Duke University Press, 1999 [2015]), 108.

14 Robert McRuer, *Crip Theory: Cultural Signs of Queerness and Disability* (New York: New York University Press, 2006), viii.

15 Rosemarie Garland-Thomson, *Extraordinary Bodies: Figuring Physical Disability in American Culture and Literature* (New York: Columbia University Press, 1997), 6.

16 Lennard J. Davis, *Enforcing Normalcy: Disability, Deafness, and the Body* (London: Verso Press, 1995), xv.

17 See Susan Schweik, *The Ugly Laws: Disability in Public* (New York: New York University Press, 2009).

18 Since the 1950s, those designated as physically or sexually non-normative were thought to bear the burden of what David Serlin terms a "double consciousness" that required medical intervention. In the post-war period, the opportunity for surgery to transform an individual's body to reflect their private identity further stigmatized disability because there were now options to thwart disability as anatomical destiny. Historian Sander Gilman contends that the ability to correct some physical "flaws" with surgery buttressed an important intersection between aesthetics, health, the body, ability, and sexuality. See David Serlin, *Replaceable You: Engineering the Body in Postwar America* (Chicago: University of Chicago Press, 2004), 10; and Sander L. Gilman, *Making the Body Beautiful: A Cultural History of Aesthetic Surgery* (Princeton, NJ: Princeton University Press, 1999), 13.

19 Goodley further argues: "[w]hile some bodies and populations are deemed more precarious than others, we are all debilitated in and by neoliberalism capitalism." Goodley, *Dis/ability Studies*, 95. See Jasbir K. Puar, "Prognosis Time: Towards a Geopolitics of Affect, Debility, and Capacity," *Women and Performance: A Journal of Feminist Theory* 19, no. 2 (2009): 161–72.

20 Fo Niemi, "Support for Disabled," *The Body Politic* 74, June 1981, 5.

21 Classified ad: Wilf Race and Chris, "Gay and Disabled," *The Body Politic* 73, May 1981, 40.

22 Classified ad: Fredericton Lesbians and Gays, "4th Atlantic Gay Association," *The Body Politic* 75, July–August, 1981, 41.

23 Gerald Hannon, "No Sorrow, No Pity," *The Body Politic* 60, February 1980, 19.

24 Hannon, "No Sorrow," 20.

25 James I. Charlton, *Nothing About Us Without Us: Disability Oppression and Empowerment* (Berkeley: University of California Press, 1998), 58.

26 Michelle Jarman, "Dismembering the Lynch Mob: Intersecting Narratives of Disability, Race, and Sexual Menace," in *Sex and Disability*, eds. Robert McRuer and Anne Mollow (Durham, NC: Duke University Press, 2012), 92.
27 Hannon, "No Sorrow," 20.
28 Tobin Siebers, "A Sexual Culture for Disabled People," in *Sex and Disability*, eds. Robert McRuer and Anne Mollow (Durham, NC: Duke University Press, 2012), 39.
29 As a term that historically encompassed "abnormal" sexual urges, Michel Foucault credits German psychiatrist Carl Friedrich Otto Westphal and his 1870 paper on "contrary sexual sensations" as the birthplace of the modern homosexual and the placement of homosexuality as a psychiatric, psychological, and medical disorder. Michel Foucault, *The History of Sexuality: An Introduction* (New York: Vintage Books, 1990 [1978]), 43.
30 Hannon, "No Sorrow," 20.
31 Benjamin Fraser, *Cognitive Disability Aesthetics: Visual Culture, Disability Representations, and the (In)visibility of Cognitive Difference* (Toronto: University of Toronto Press, 2018), 14.
32 Hannon, "No Sorrow," 22.
33 See Deborah Marks, *Disability: Controversial Debates and Psychosocial Perspectives* (London: Routledge, 1999); and Clare, *Exile and Pride*.
34 Hannon, "No Sorrow," 22.
35 Hannon, "No Sorrow," 21.
36 Don M. Fuchs, "Breaking Down Barriers: Independent Living Resource Centres for Empowering the Physically Disabled," in *Perspectives on Social Services and Social Issues*, eds. Jacqueline S. Ismael and Ray J. Thomlison (Ottawa: Canadian Council on Social Development, 1987), 193.
37 Hannon, "No Sorrow," 21.
38 "Stair Trek: Nightlife by Wheelchair," *The Body Politic* 60, February 1980, 22.
39 Hannon, "No Sorrow," 20.
40 "Stair Trek," 22.
41 Warren D. Camp, "Not Disabled," *The Body Politic* 98, November 1983, 6.
42 Camp, "Not Disabled," 6.
43 Camp, "Not Disabled," 6.
44 "Stair Trek," 22.
45 "Stair Trek," 22.
46 John Allec and Edna Barker, "Hot Spots: Toronto's Summer of 82," *The Body Politic* 85, July–August 1982, 22.
47 Name withheld, "Out of the Silent Closet," *The Body Politic* 60, February 1980, 21.
48 Name withheld, "Out of the Silent Closet," 21.

49 Classified ad: Scott, "GWM, 30, Good-Looking," *The Body Politic* 83, May 1982, 41.
50 Classified ad: Scott, "GWM, 30, Good-Looking," 41.
51 Classified ad: Richard, "Very Huggable Person," *The Body Politic* 84, June 1982, 42.
52 Hannon, "No Sorrow," 20.
53 Classified ad: "Gay Male, 23, 6′1″," *The Body Politic* 67, October 1980, 41.
54 Classified ad: Alan, "Toronto/Belleville/Ottawa," *The Body Politic* 109, December 1984, 40.
55 The fetishization of disabled bodies is partly the result of disability as spectacle in nineteenth-century American "freak shows." Rosemarie Garland-Thomson argues that nineteenth-century "[f]reak shows framed and choreographed bodily differences that we now call 'race,' 'ethnicity,' and 'disability' in a ritual that enacted the social processes of making cultural otherness from the raw materials of human physical variation." See Garland-Thomson, *Extraordinary Bodies*, 60.
56 David T. Mitchell and Sharon L. Snyder, *The Biopolitics of Disability: Neoliberalism, Abelenationalism, and Peripheral Embodiment* (Ann Arbor: University of Michigan Press, 2015), 27.
57 "'Gay' Cancer," 19
58 Lawrence K. Altman, "Rare Cancer Seen in 41 Homosexuals," *New York Times*, 3 July 1981, A20.
59 Despite a news clipping from New York in the May 1982 issue of *TBP* stating that Kaposi's sarcoma was found in nine heterosexual women, additional findings of the disease in twenty-three men in the United States helped to gender the disease as male and perpetuate the medical scrutiny of gay men's bodies. "Gay Cancer Found in Straight Men, Women," *The Body Politic* 83, May 1982, 17.
60 Robert Trow, "'Gay' Cancer Linked to Genetic Factors," *The Body Politic* 81, March 1982, 15.
61 "'Gay' Cancer," 19.
62 Lynch, "Living with Kaposi's," 35.
63 Lynch, "Living with Kaposi's," 37.
64 Bill Lewis and Randy Coates, "Moral Lessons; Fatal Cancer," *The Body Politic* 77, October 1981, 43.
65 Lewis and Coates, "Moral Lessons," 43.
66 David Rayside (volunteer at *The Body Politic*), interview by Nicholas Hrynyk, 24 March 2015, interview 1, transcript.
67 "Kaposi Research Hurt by Cutbacks," *The Body Politic* 85, July–August 1982, 16.
68 Trow, "AID Disease," 14.

69 Ed Jackson, "Murder and Other Sorts of Mayhem," *The Body Politic* 100, January–February 1984, 15.
70 Ken Popert, "Gay Recruits Needed for AIDS Research," *The Body Politic* 109, December 1984, 9.
71 Ken Popert, "Test Shows AIDS Bug Well-Established Here," *The Body Politic* 111, February 1985, 14.
72 Heather Murray, "Every Generation Has Its War," in *Gender, Health, and Popular Culture*, ed. Cheryl Krasnick Warsh (Waterloo, Ontario: Wilfred Laurier University Press, 2011), 238.
73 What is now referred to as HIV was then known as HTLV-3 in 1984. A news report from San Francisco described a California study published in the 24 August 1984 issue of *Science* magazine which found "anti-bodies to what appears to be the same virus in one-hundred percent of AIDS patients tested, 92 percent of patients with lymphadenopathy syndrome and 93 percent of sexual partners with AIDS patients." See "AIDS-Test Ambiguities Raise Concern," *The Body Politic* 107, October 1984, 17.
74 Martin Duberman, *Hold Tight Gently: Michael Callen, Essex Hemphill, and the Battlefield of AIDS* (New York: The New Press, 2014), 154.
75 *TBP* also quoted him as saying, '"Gay' triggers into the American consciousness a certain image – a white image.'" "AIDS Stat Reveal More Non-White Cases," *The Body Politic* 100, January–February 1984, 24.
76 "AIDS Stat Reveal More Non-White Cases," 24.
77 "AIDS Stat Reveal More Non-White Cases," 24.
78 Roger Bakeman, "Not Colour Specific," *The Body Politic* 124, March 1986, 11.
79 The Public Health Agency of Canada notes that data on the race of HIV/AIDS-positive individuals was not collected until 1998. See Canada, Public Health Agency of Canada, *HIV/AIDS Epidemic Updates, Chapter 8: HIV/AIDS Rates Among Aboriginal People in Canada*, Ottawa 2014, 4. www.canada.ca/en/public-health/services/hiv-aids/publications/epi-updates/chapter-8-hiv-aids-among-aboriginal-people-canada.html
80 See: Joseph Beam, *In the Life: A Black Gay Anthology* (Boston: Alyson Publications, 1986); and Essex Hemphill, *Ceremonies: Prose and Poetry* (New York City: Plume Press, 1992; Jersey City: Cleis Press, 2000).
81 Darius Bost, *Evidence of Being: The Black Gay Cultural Renaissance and the Politics of Violence* (Chicago: University of Chicago Press, 2019), 14.
82 James H. Jones, *Bad Blood: The Tuskegee Syphilis Experiment* (New York City: The Free Press, 1993), 223.
83 Daniel C. William, "AIDS: Sex, Sickness and Facts," *The Body Politic* 90, January–February 1983, 4.
84 Lawrence Mass, "AIDS: Sex, Sickness and Facts," *The Body Politic* 90, January–February 1983, 5.

85 Brian Willoughby, "AIDS: Sex, Sickness and Facts," *The Body Politic* 90, January–February 1983, 5.
86 Michael Lynch, "AIDS: Sex, Sickness and Facts (Michael Lynch Replies)," *The Body Politic* 90, January–February 1983, 6.
87 Nancy E. Stoller argues that "[g]ay male sexuality in the seventies was historically marked by less emphasis on the creation of 'family' or on sexual monogamy. The impact of gay liberation movements on gay male sexuality has recently been discussed in many venues, primarily because of the belief that patterns of sexuality among gay men have been responsible for the rapid spread of the epidemic [AIDS]." Nancy E. Stoller, "From Feminism to Polymorphous Activism: Lesbians in AIDS Organizations," in *In Changing Times: Gay Men and Lesbians Encounter HIV/AIDS*, eds. Martin P. Levine, Peter M. Nardi, and John H. Gagnon (Chicago: University of Chicago Press, 1997), 175. Aversion to monogamy for gay liberationists is also cited in numerous monographs on gay liberation. See Barry D. Adam, *The Rise of a Gay and Lesbian Movement* (New York: Twayne Publishers, 1995); and Kathleen Hull, *Same-Sex Marriage: The Cultural Politics of Love and Law* (Cambridge: Cambridge University Press, 2006).
88 Lynch, "Living with Kaposi's," 35.
89 Lynch, "Living with Kaposi's," 37.
90 Lynch, "Living with Kaposi's," 36.
91 Michael L. Callen, "AIDS: Killing Ourselves," *The Body Politic* 92, April 1983, 5.
92 Jerry Rosco from New York City was supportive of Lynch's article on AIDS. Meanwhile, Rich Grzesiak, Assistant Editor at *Philadelphia Gay News*, argued that *TBP*'s article "The Case Against Panic" in November 1982 was unfairly critical of American print media and Dr. Lawrence Mass's work. See Jerry Rosco and Rich Grzesiak, "AIDS Alternatives," *The Body Politic* 91, March 1983, 4.
93 As quoted in Rick Bébout, "Is There Safer Sex?" *The Body Politic* 99, December 1983, 33.
94 Rick Bébout, "A Day in the Media Life of Disease," *The Body Politic* 119, October 1985, 32. Originally found in Glen Allan, "The New Terror of AIDS," *Maclean's* 98, no. 32 (August 1985): 32.
95 For instance, a classified ad from Toronto in May 1981 requested someone who was "clean, ha[s] pleasant personality" while noting that the author was not into "bars, baths, drugs, liquor, poppers, big social life." Classified ad: "Toronto," *The Body Politic* 73, May 1981, 38. Another ad in December 1982 by a thirty-seven-year-old gay man in Toronto described himself as "discreet and clean" while avoiding "VD like the plague." Classified ad: "Imaginative and Sensitive Male," *The Body Politic* 89, December 1982, 40.

96 The term "polluted" draws upon a historical metaphor of disease, particularly syphilis, as a form of pollution, poison, or lack of hygiene that the ill were often viewed as having. Alison Bashford argues that pollution" held moral meaning, as it represented a polarity to "purity" and operated along gendered lines, with women's bodies coming under medical and moral scrutiny shaped by middle-class Victorian culture. Alison Bashford, *Purity and Pollution: Gender, Embodiment and Victorian Medicine* (New York: Farrar, Straus and Giroux, 1998), xii. In addition, Susan Sontag notes that sexually transmitted diseases, such as syphilis, doubly invoked stigmatization in the nineteenth century precisely because it was primarily transmitted through sexual intercourse – a "taboo" topic. See Sontag, *Illness as Metaphor and AIDS and Its Metaphors*, 39.

97 Classified ad: "Edmonton – Lonely, Mid Age GWM," *The Body Politic* 91, March 1983, 42.

98 For more on neoliberalism and sexual health, see Jonathan M. Metzl and Anna Kirkland, eds., *Against Health: How Health Became the New Morality* (New York: New York University Press, 2010).

99 Classified ad: "Versatile, Masculine Male," *The Body Politic* 100, January–February 1984, 56.

100 Michael Young, "Cruising: Not the Whole Story," *The Body Politic* 97, October 1983, 4.

101 David Palmer, "Cruising: Not the Whole Story," *The Body Politic* 97, October 1983, 4.

102 Harvey Hamburg, "AIDS: Reluctant Reporting," *The Body Politic* 97, October 1983, 7.

103 James Johnstone, "Taking Issue," *The Body Politic* 103, May 1984, 6.

104 Italics in original. Rick Bébout, "Is There Safe Sex?: Looking Behind Advice on AIDS," *The Body Politic* 99, December 1983, 36.

105 Bébout, "Is There Safe Sex?" 36.

106 Advertisement: "Anal Sex," *The Body Politic* 114, May 1985, 4.

107 Advertisement: "Anal Sex," 4.

108 Advertisement: "1 in 4," *The Body Politic* 119, October 1985, 27.

109 In particular, Kevin Orr of *TBP* reported in December 1984 that ACT educated seven gay men on how to incorporate condoms into their sexual routines. Orr noted that "[m]any gay men have never tried them before, including all of the testers. It was a new experience for them and some were more successful than others." Kevin Orr, "Condoms: Gay Men Try Them for Size," *The Body Politic* 109, December 1984, 31.

110 Gerald Hannon, "Joining the JOE Club," *The Body Politic* 114, May 1985, 51.

111 Hannon, "JOE Club," 51.

112 Hannon, "JOE Club," 51.

113 Hannon, "JOE Club," 51.

114 As quoted in Rob Joyce, "Life and Love After AIDS," *The Body Politic* 126, May 1986, 14.

115 Joyce, "Life and Love," 13.

116 Editorial collective, "The Quandary of Advice," *The Body Politic* 126, May 1986, 26.

117 In Janoff's letter, he stated that the individual with AIDS was re-diagnosed as having AIDS-related complex (ARC), which meant he could still give the AIDS virus as it was understood.

118 Douglas Janoff, "Opening Debate on Sexual Responsibility," *The Body Politic* 121, December 1985, 11.

119 Janoff, "Opening Debate," 11.

120 For more information on the purges, see Gary Kinsman and Patrizia Gentile, *The Canadian War on Queers: National Security as Sexual Regulation* (Vancouver: University of British Columbia Press, 2010).

121 Other reasons given for not publishing the article included Janoff taking an exceptionally long time to respond to the editorial collective's concerns and that he had failed to edit the article to meet *TBP*'s standards.

122 Ken Popert, "Opening Debate on Sexual Responsibility," *The Body Politic* 121, December 1985, 11.

123 The understanding of HIV/AIDS as a disability was reinforced by the Ontario government's efforts to regulate HIV-infected bodies in a similar fashion to disabled bodies by rendering them docile. In 1986, *TBP* reported on the expansion of the Ontario Human Rights Code to include people with AIDS as another way in which HIV/AIDS and disability intersected. When Borden Purcell, then chairperson of the Ontario Human Rights Commission, was specifically asked about the Act, he stated that people with AIDS were now protected under section 9(b) of the Human Rights Code (1981): "AIDS as an illness would fall within the definition of handicap." This institutional equation of AIDS as a disability only served to formalize broader understandings of AIDS as a debilitating disease and those with it as being disabled or "handicap." Ed Jackson, "Code Forbids AIDS Bias," *The Body Politic* 124, March 1986, 17.

124 Ed Jackson, "AIDS: Double Exposure," *The Body Politic* 121, December 1985, 17.

125 "Exploited for Headlines," *The Body Politic* 126, May 1986, 22.

126 Christina Simmons, "African Americans and Sexual Victorianism in the Social Hygiene Movement, 1910–1940," *Journal of the History of Sexuality* 4, no. 1 (July 1993): 53.

127 "Exploited for Headlines," 22.

128 Kathy Charmaz and Dana Rosenfeld argue that "[w]hen the body fails to function in expected ways, it changes from a disappearing entity (one of which we are unaware) to a *dysappearing* one, which means

appearing dysfunctional to ourselves and to others." Kathy Charmaz and Dana Rosenfeld, "Reflections of the Body, Images of Self: Visibility and Invisibility in Chronic Illness and Disability," in *Body/Embodiment: Symbolic Interaction and the Sociology of the Body*, ed. Phillip Vannini (New York: Routledge, 2016), 46.

129 Gerald Hannon, "Dying to Live: Reflections on the Black Death," *The Body Politic* 117, August 1985, 28.

130 Murray, "Every Generation," 245.

131 Michael Lynch, "This Seeing the Sick Endears Them," *The Body Politic* 91, March 1983, 36.

132 John De Cecco and Dawn Atkins, *Looking Queer: Body Image and Identity in Lesbian, Bisexual, Gay, and Transgender Communities* (New York: Routledge, 2012), 351.

133 Lynch, "Living with Kaposi's," 34.

134 Lynch, "Living with Kaposi's," 35.

135 Gary, "AIDS: Sex, Sickness and Facts," *The Body Politic* 90, January–February 1983, 4.

136 Bryan Teixeira, "AIDS as Metaphor," *The Body Politic* 96, September 1983, 40.

137 Broadly looking at meanings of illness in history, Sontag argues that "disease itself (once TB, cancer today) arouses thoroughly old-fashioned kinds of dread. Any disease is treated as a mystery and acutely enough feared will be felt to be morally, if not literally, contagious." Susan Sontag, *Illness as Metaphor* (New York: Farrar, Straus and Giroux, 1978), 6.

138 Sontag contends that "AIDS has a dual metaphoric genealogy. As a microprocess, it is described as cancer is: an invasion. When the focus is transmission of the disease, an older metaphor, reminiscent of syphilis, is invoked: pollution." Susan Sontag, *AIDS and Its Metaphors* (New York: Farrar, Straus and Giroux, 1989), 17.

139 Ed Jackson, "Going Public with AIDS," *The Body Politic* 97, October 1983, 28.

140 Jackson, "Going Public," 29.

141 Jackson, "Going Public," 29.

142 Jackson, "Going Public," 29.

143 Jackson, "Going Public," 28.

144 Silversides, *AIDS Activist*, 69.

145 Obituary: "Peter Evans (April 20, 1955 – January 7, 1984)," *The Body Politic* 101, March 1984, 10.

146 Murray, "Every Generation," 245.

147 Phil Shaw, "A Celluloid Valentine to the Gay Community," *The Body Politic* 127, June 1986, 32.

148 Richard Dyer, "Rock: The Last Guy You'd Have Figured?" *The Body Politic* 121, December 1985, 27.

149 Dyer, "Rock," 29.
150 Jeffrey Weeks, *Sexuality and Its Discontents: Meanings, Myths, and Modern Sexualities* (New York: Routledge, 2002 [1985]), 50.
151 The relationship between disability, aesthetics, and trauma is noted in Serlin, *Replaceable You*, 24.
152 Weeks, *Sexuality and Its Discontents*, 50.

Conclusion: Reflecting on *The Body Politic*

1 Gerald Hannon, "Sentimental Journey," *The Body Politic* 135, February 1987, 43.
2 Rick Bébout, "What Happened?" *The Body Politic* 135, February 1987, 5.
3 Bébout, "What Happened?" 4.
4 Hannon, "Sentimental Journey," 43.
5 See Tim McCaskell, *Queer Progress: From Homophobia to Homonationalism* (Toronto: Between the Lines, 2016).
6 Oral accounts have been invaluable in an exhaustive list of queer history, including but not limited to: Madeline Davis and Elizabeth Lapovsky Kennedy, *Boots of Leather, Slippers of Gold: The History of a Lesbian Community* (New York: Routledge, 1993); Nan Alamilla Boyd, *Wide-Open Town: A History of Queer San Francisco to 1965* (Berkeley: University of California Press, 2003); Michael David Franklin et al., *Queer Twin Cities: Twin Cities GLBT Oral History Project* (Minneapolis: University of Minnesota Press, 2010); Heike Bauer and Matt Cook, eds., *Queer 1950s: Rethinking Sexuality in the Postwar Years* (New York: Palgrave Macmillan, 2012); and Nan Alamilla Boyd and Horacio N. Roque Ramirez, *Bodies of Evidence: The Practice of Queer Oral History* (Oxford: Oxford University Press, 2012).
7 Gerald Hannon (editor for *The Body Politic*), interview by Nicholas Hrynyk, 17 July 2015, interview 1, transcript.
8 David Rayside, (contributor to *The Body Politic*), interview by Nicholas Hrynyk, 24 March 2015, interview 1, transcript.
9 Joan Scott, "Gender: A Useful Category of Historical Analysis," *American Historical Review* 91, no. 5 (December 1986): 1069.
10 Ken Popert (editor for *The Body Politic*), interview by Nicholas Hrynyk, 14 April 2015, interview 1, transcript.
11 Tim McCaskell (editor for *The Body Politic*), interview by Nicholas Hrynyk, 20 March 2015, interview 1, transcript.
12 Judith Butler, *Gender Trouble: Feminism and the Subversion of Identity* (New York: Routledge Press, 1999 [1990]), xv.
13 Greg Dening, *Performances* (Carlton South: Melbourne University Press, 1996), 20.
14 Rayside, interview 1, transcript.

15 John Kyper, "More Hedd," *The Body Politic* 22, February 1976, 2.
16 McCaskell, interview 1, transcript.
17 Irial Glynn and J. Olaf Kleist, "The Memory and Migration Nexus: An Overview," in *History, Memory and Migration: Perceptions of the Past and the Politics of Incorporation*, eds. Irial Glynn and J. Olaf Kleist (New York: Palgrave Macmillan, 2012), 10.
18 Alessandro Portelli, *The Death of Luigi Trastulli and Other Stories: Form and Meaning in Oral History* (Albany, NY: SUNY Press, 1991), 254.
19 Paula Hamilton, "The Oral Historian as Memorist," *The Oral History Review* 32, no. 1 (2005): 13.
20 Summerfield, "Culture and Composure," 66.
21 Rayside, interview 1, transcript.
22 Viviane Namaste argues that many others who did not conform to rigid ideals of masculinity were excluded from village life or relegated to the periphery. For example, the organizers of the 1992 Montreal Lesbian and Gay Pride Parade attempted to ban drag queens. This was because "drag queens ... exceeded 'respectable' community standards" and as such should be relegated to the stage and excluded. This material informs my discussion of representations of queer style because it both pervaded the queer community and shaped definitions of gay male masculinity, female masculinity, and fashion as it related to the negotiation between blending in and standing out in the public domain. Viviane Namaste, *Invisible Lives: The Erasure of Transsexual and Transgendered People* (Chicago: University of Chicago Press, 2000), 11.
23 Brian Fleming, "All About That Pride Body: A Painstakingly Detailed Guide to What It Takes to Look Your Best," *Fashion*, 26 June 2015.

Bibliography

Primary Sources

Altman, Lawrence K. "Rare Cancer Seen in 41 Homosexuals." *New York Times*, 3 July 1981, A20.

Burke, Tom. "The New Homosexuality." *Esquire*, December 1969, 178.

Fenwick, R. D. *The Advocate Guide to Gay Health*. New York: Dutton Press, 1978.

Fleming, Brian. "All about that Pride body: A painstakingly detailed guide to what it takes to look your best." *Fashion*, 26 June 2015. https://fashionmagazine.com/beauty-grooming/pride-body-guide/

"For Over-18s: Poll Shows 74% Approve Selling Hard-Core Porn." *Toronto Star*, 28 December 1977, A3.

Giteck, Larry. *Cruise to Win: A Guide for Gay Men*. San Francisco: Pantera Press, 1982.

Hall, Joe. "Homosexuals Fear Suicides and Broken Marriages in Wake of Raids." *Toronto Star*, 7 February 1981: A7.

Hix, Charles. *Looking Good: A Guide for Men*. Toronto: Hawthorn Books, 1977.

Merrick, Gordon. *The Lord Won't Mind*. New York: Avon Books, 1970 [1971].

– *Now Let's Talk About Music*. New York: Avon Books, 1981.

"Police Seize Rochdale Porno Films." *The Globe and Mail*, 16 November 1973, 13.

"Policemen Enticing Homosexuals, Spokesman Says." *The Globe and Mail*, 5 March 1973, 5.

Poramro, Ron. "Police No Longer Hassle Gays on Strip, Homosexual Says." *The Globe and Mail*, 3 August 1977, 5.

Rechy, John. *The Sexual Outlaw: A Documentary*. New York: Grove Press, 1977.

Scott, Scott. "Police and Homosexuals Co-Operate to Stop Offences in Parks, Subways." *Toronto Daily Star*, 6 April 1972, 27.

Stewart, Alan. "Making the Truth Palatable." *The Globe and Mail*, 3 August 1985, 18.

ArQuives

File: Assorted Vertical Files: Canada
Church-Wellesley Neighbourhood Police Advisory Committee: Toronto.
Christopher Street (1976–95).
File: Our Own Voices: Lesbian and Gay Periodicals, 1890s–2000s
Action [Right to Privacy Committee] (1979–82).
Back Chat Newsletter [Homophile Association of Toronto] (1971–6).
The Body Politic (1971–87).
Club Baths of Toronto, vertical file, undated.
Gay Archivist [Newsletter of the Canadian Gay Archives] (1977–81).
Gay Rising [Gay Alliance Toward Equality] (1975–8).
Gay Toronto (1978–9).
Gayokay [University of Toronto Homophile Association] (1971–2).
Trevor Mountford-Smith (1975) [File CAN 4010, Mountford-Smith, Trevor].

Library and Archives Canada

Canadian Broadcasting Corporation. Fonds.
RG41, file 66 (Homosexual broadcasting).
Canada. House of Commons. Standing Committee on Justice and Legal Affairs. *Minutes of Proceedings and Evidence*. Thirtieth Parliament. Issue 7. 14 February 1978.
Canada. House of Commons. Standing Committee on Justice and Legal Affairs. *Minutes of Proceedings and Evidence*. Thirtieth Parliament. Issue 15. 7 March 1978.
Canada. House of Commons. Standing Committee on Justice and Legal Affairs. *Minutes of Proceedings and Evidence*. Third session., Thirtieth Parliament. Issue 18. 22 March 1978.
Canada. *Statutes of Canada: An Act Respecting Immigration, 1952.* Ottawa: SC 1 Elizabeth II, Chapter 42.
W. Gunther Plaut. Fonds
R5917-8-6-E (Ontario Human Rights Commission).
R5917-6-2-E, vol. 87, file 12 (Social Action Committee, HBT – Gay Rights).

Interviews

Hannon, Gerald. Interview by Nicholas Hrynyk. Personal Interview. Toronto, ON, 17 July 2015.

McCaskell, Tim. Interview by Nicholas Hrynyk. Personal Interview. Ottawa, ON, 20 March 2015.

Popert, Ken. Interview by Nicholas Hrynyk. Personal Interview. Ottawa, ON, 14 April 2015.

Rayside, David. Interview by Nicholas Hrynyk. Personal Interview. Ottawa, ON, 24 March 2015.

Secondary Sources

Aanerud, Rebecca. "Fictions of Whiteness: Speaking the Names of Whiteness in U.S. Literature." In *Displacing Whiteness: Essays in Racial and Cultural Criticism*, edited by Ruth Frankenberg, 35–59. Durham: Duke University Press, 1997. https://doi.org/10.1215/9780822382270-002.

Adam, Barry D. *The Rise of a Gay and Lesbian Movement*. New York: Twayne Publishers, 1995. https://doi.org/10.2307/2074061.

Adams, Mary Louise. *The Trouble with Normal: Postwar Youth and the Making of Heterosexuality*. Toronto: University of Toronto Press, 1997. https://doi.org/10.3138/9781442682467.

– *Artistic Impressions: Figure Skating, Masculinity, and the Limits of Sport*. Toronto: University of Toronto Press, 2011. https://doi.org/10.3138/9781442695603.

Albano, Caterina. "Within the Frame: Self-Starvation and the Making of Culture." In *Framing and Imagining Disease in Cultural History*, edited by George Sebastian Rousseau, Miranda Gill, David Haycock, and Malte Herwig, 51–67. New York: Palgrave Macmillan, 2003. https://doi.org/10.1057/9780230524323_2.

Aldama, Arturo J., and Frederick Luis Aldama. *Decolonizing Latinx Masculinities*. Tucson: University of Arizona Press, 2020. https://doi.org/10.2307/j.ctv13xprdp.

Alexander, Bryant Keith. *Performing Black Masculinity: Race, Culture, and Queer Identity*. Lanham, MD: AltaMira Press, 2006.

Alexander, M. Jacqui. *Pedagogies of Crossing: Meditations on Feminism, Sexual Politics, Memory, and the Sacred*. Durham: Duke University Press, 2005. https://doi.org/10.1215/9780822386988.

Armstrong, David. *A Trumpet to Arms: Alternative Media in America*. Boston: South End Press, 1981.

Armstrong, Elizabeth A. *Forging Gay Identities: Organizing Sexuality in San Francisco, 1950–1994*. Chicago: University of Chicago Press, 2002.

Atkins, Dawn, ed. *Looking Queer: Body Image, and Identity in Lesbian, Bisexual, Gay and Transgender Communities*. New York: Haworth Press, 1998. https://doi.org/10.4324/9780203047477.

Barthes, Roland. *Image – Music – Text*. Translated by Stephen Heath. New York: Hill and Wang, 1977.

– *The Fashion System*. Translated by Matthew Ward and Richard Howard. New York: Farrar, Strauss, and Giroux, 1967. Reprint, Berkeley: University of California Press, 1990.

Bashford, Alison. *Purity and Pollution: Gender, Embodiment and Victorian Medicine*. New York: Farrar, Straus and Giroux, 1998. https://doi.org/10.1057/9780230501249.

Batchelor, Bob. "Introduction: Creating Advertising Culture, Beginnings to 1930s." In *We Are What We Sell: How Advertising Shapes American Life and Always Has*, edited by Danielle Sarver Coombs and Bob Batchelor, xi–xxi. Santa Barbara, CA: ABC-CLIO. https://doi.org/10.5040/9798216991496.

Bauer, Heike, and Matt Cook, eds. *Queer 1950s: Rethinking Sexuality in the Postwar Years*. New York: Palgrave Macmillan, 2012. https://doi.org/10.1057/9781137264718_1.

Beam, Joseph. *In the Life: A Black Gay Anthology*. Boston: Alyson Publications, 1986.

Bederman, Gail. *Manliness and Civilization: A Cultural History of Gender and Race in the United States, 1880–1917*. Chicago: University of Chicago Press, 2008. https://doi.org/10.7208/chicago/9780226041490.001.0001.

Bliss, Michael. "'Pure Books on Avoided Subjects': Pre-Freudian Sexual Ideas in Canada." *Historical Papers* 5, no. 1 (1970): 89–108. https://doi.org/10.7202/030725ar.

Bordo, Susan. *Unbearable Weight: Feminism, Western Culture, and the Body*. Berkeley: University of California Press, 1993 [2003]. https://doi.org/10.2307/jj.8441705.

– *The Male Body: A New Look at Men in Public and the Private*. New York: Farrar, Straus, and Giroux Press, 1999.

Bost, Darius. *Evidence of Being: The Black Gay Cultural Renaissance and the Politics of Violence*. Chicago: University of Chicago Press, 2019. https://doi.org/10.7208/chicago/9780226589961.003.0001.

Boyd, Nan Alamilla. *Wide-Open Town: A History of San Francisco to 1965*. Berkeley and Los Angeles: University of California Press, 2003. https://doi.org/10.1525/9780520938748.

Boyd, Nan Alamilla, and Horacio N. Roque Ramirez. *Bodies of Evidence: The Practice of Queer Oral History*. Oxford: Oxford University Press, 2012.

Bradburn, Jaime. "Historicist: I Sing *The Body Politic*." *Torontoist*, February 14, 2015. https://torontoist.com/2015/02/historicist-i-sing-the-body-politic/.

Bristow, Joseph. "Being Gay: Politics, Identity, Pleasure." *New Formations* 9 (Winter 1989): 61–82.

Brown, Elspeth. *Work! A Queer History of Modeling*. Durham: Duke University Press, 2019. https://doi.org/10.1215/9781478002147.

Browning, Frank. *The Culture of Desire: Paradox and Perversity in Gay Lives Today*. New York: Crown Publishers Inc., 1993.

Buchbinder, David. *Studying Men and Masculinities*. New York: Routledge, 2013. https://doi.org/10.4324/9780203852224.

Buring, Daneel. *Lesbian and Gay Memphis: Building Communities Behind the Magnolia Curtain*. New York: Routledge, 1997.

Butler, Judith. *Gender Trouble: Feminism and the Subversion of Identity*. New York: Routledge, 1990.

– *Bodies that Matter: On the Discursive Limits of "Sex."* New York: Routledge, 1993.

– *Undoing Gender*. New York: Routledge, 2004. https://doi.org/10.4324/9780203499627.

– *Giving an Account of Oneself*. New York: Fordham University Press, 2005. https://doi.org/10.5422/fso/9780823225033.001.0001.

Cahn, Susan K. "From the 'Muscle Moll' to the 'Butch' Ballplayer: Mannishness, Lesbianism, and Homophobia in U.S. Women's Sport." *Feminist Studies* 19 (Summer 1993): 343–68. https://doi.org/10.2307/3178373.

Campbell, Colin. *The Romantic Ethic and the Spirit of Modern Consumerism*. Oxford: Blackwell Publishers, 1987.

Caulfield, Jon. *City Form and Everyday Life: Toronto's Gentrification and Critical Social Practice*. Toronto: University of Toronto press, 1994. https://doi.org/10.3138/9781442672970.

Charlton, James I. *Nothing About Us Without Us: Disability Oppression and Empowerment*. Berkeley: University of California Press, 1998. https://doi.org/10.1525/9780520925441.

Charmaz, Kathy, and Dana Rosenfeld. "Reflections of the Body, Images of Self: Visibility and Invisibility in Chronic Illness and Disability." In *Body/Embodiment: Symbolic Interaction and the Sociology of the Body*, edited by Phillip Vannini, 42–60. New York: Routledge, 2016.

Charteris, Charlotte. *The Queer Cultures of 1930s Prose: Language, Identity and Performance in Interwar Britain*. London: Palgrave Macmillan, 2019. https://doi.org/10.1007/978-3-030-02414-7.

Chauncey, George. *Gay New York: Gender, Urban Culture, and the Making of the Gay Male World, 1890–1940*. New York: Basic Books, 1994.

Chenier, Elise. *Strangers in Our Midst: Sexual Deviancy in Postwar Ontario*. Toronto: University of Toronto Press, 2008. https://doi.org/10.3138/9781442689220.

– "Liberating Marriage: Gay Liberation and Same-Sex Marriage in Early 1970s Canada." In *We Still Demand: Redefining Resistance in Sex and Gender Struggles*, edited by Patrizia Gentile, Gary Kinsman, and L. Pauline Rankin, 29–50. Vancouver: University of British Columbia Press, 2017. https://doi.org/10.59962/9780774833363-004.

Churchill, David. "Personal Ad Politics: Race, Sexuality and Power at *The Body Politic*." *Left History* 8, no. 2 (2003): 114–34. https://doi.org/10.25071/1913-9632.5514.

– "SUPA, Selma, and Stevenson: The Politics of Solidarity in mid-1960s Toronto." *Journal of Canadian Studies* 44, no. 2 (2010): 32–69. https://doi.org/10.3138/jcs.44.2.32.

Ciarlo, David. *Advertising Empire: Race and Visual Culture in Imperial Germany*. Cambridge, MA: Harvard University Press, 2011. https://doi.org/10.2307/j.ctvjghw4v.

Clare, Eli. *Exile and Pride: Disability, Queerness, and Liberation*. Durham: Duke University Press, 1999 [2015]. https://doi.org/10.1215/9780822374879.

Cleto, Fabio. "Introduction: Queering the Camp." In *Camp: Queer Aesthetics and the Performing Subject: A Reader*, edited by Fabio Cleto. Ann Arbor: University of Michigan Press, 1999. https://doi.org/10.1515/9781474465809-003.

Cohen, Mark. *Censorship in Canadian Literature*. Kingston and Montreal: McGill-Queen's University Press, 2001. https://doi.org/10.1515/9780773569379.

Cole, Shaun. *'Don We Now Our Gay Apparel': Gay Men's Dress in the Twentieth Century*. New York: Berg, 2000. https://doi.org/10.5860/choice.38-5863.

Cole, Susan G. *Pornography and the Sex Crisis*. Toronto: Second Story Press, 1992.

Collins, Dana. *The Rise and Fall of an Urban Sexual Community: Malate (Dis) Placed*. London: Palgrave Macmillan, 2016. https://doi.org/10.1057/978-1-137-57961-4.

Conekin, Becky. "Fashioning the Playboy: Messages of Style and Masculinity in the Pages of *Playboy Magazine, 1953–1963*." *Fashion Theory* 4, no. 4 (2000): 447–66. https://doi.org/10.2752/136270400779108672.

Connell, R. W. *Masculinities*, 2nd edition. Berkeley and Los Angeles: University of California Press, 1995 [2005].

Connell, R. W., and James Messerschmidt. "Hegemonic Masculinity: Rethinking the Concept." *Gender and Society* 19, no. 6 (December 2005): 829–59. https://doi.org/10.1177/0891243205278639.

Cook, Sharon. *Sex, Lies, and Cigarettes: Canadian Women, Smoking, and Visual Culture, 1880–2000*. Montreal and Kingston: McGill-Queen's University Press, 2012. https://doi.org/10.1515/9780773587267.

Cooper, Emmanuel. *Fully Exposed: The Male Nude in Photography*. New York: Routledge, 1995.

Corber, Robert J. *Homosexuality in Cold War America: Resistance and the Crisis of Masculinity*. Durham: Duke University Press, 1997. https://doi.org/10.2307/j.ctv1198v3w.

Cossman, Brenda. *Bad Attitude/s on Trial: Pornography, Feminism, and the Butler Decision*. Toronto: University of Toronto Press, 1997. https://doi.org/10.3138/9781442671157.

Crais, Clifton C., and Pamela Scully. *Sara Baartman and the Hottentot Venus: A Ghost Story and a Biography*. Princeton: Princeton University Press, 2009.

Davis, Lennard J. *Enforcing Normalcy: Disability, Deafness, and the Body.* London: Verso Press, 1995.

Davison, J. Robert. "Turning a Blind Eye: The Historian's Use of Photographs." *BC Studies* 52 (Winter 1981–82): 16–35.

Dean, Tim. *Beyond Sexuality.* Chicago: University of Chicago Press, 2000.

De Cecco, John, and Dawn Atkins. *Looking Queer: Body Image and Identity in Lesbian, Bisexual, Gay, and Transgender Communities.* New York: Routledge, 2012. https://doi.org/10.4324/9780203047477.

Delgado, Richard, and Jean Stefancic. *Critical Race Theory: An Introduction.* New York: New York University Press, 2001.

D'Emilio, John. *Making Trouble: Essays on Gay History, Politics, and the University.* New York: Routledge, 1992.

– *Sexual Politics, Sexual Communities: The Making of a Homosexual Minority in the United States, 1940–1970,* 2nd edition. Chicago: University of Chicago Press, 1998.

D'Emilio, John, and Estelle Freedman. *Intimate Matters: A History of Sexuality in America.* New York: Harper and Row, 1988.

– *Unlimited Intimacy: Reflections on the Subculture of Barebacking.* Chicago: University of Chicago Press, 2009.

Dening, Greg. *Performances.* Carlton South: Melbourne University Press, 1996.

Depelteau Julie, and Dalie Giroux. "LGBTQ Issues as Indigenous Politics." In *Queer Mobilizations: Social Movement Activism and Canadian Public Policy,* edited by Manon Tremblay, 64–81. Vancouver: University of British Columbia Press, 2015. https://doi.org/10.59962/9780774829090-005.

Duberman, Martin. *Hold Tight Gently: Michael Callen, Essex Hemphill, and the Battlefield of AIDS.* New York: The New Press, 2014. https://doi.org/10.2307/jj.26193319.

Duder, Cameron. *Awfully Devoted Women: Lesbian Lives in Canada, 1900–65.* Vancouver: University of British Columbia Press, 2011. https://doi.org/10.59962/9780774817400.

Duggan, Lisa, Nan D. Hunter, and Carol S. Vance. "False Promises: Feminist Anti-Pornography Legislation in the U.S." In *Women Against Censorship,* edited by Varda Burstyn, 130–51. Vancouver: Douglas & McIntyre, 1985.

Dummitt, Chris. *The Manly Modern: Masculinity in Postwar Canada.* Vancouver: University of British Columbia, 2007. https://doi.org/10.59962/9780774859561.

Dworkin, Andrea. *Letters from a War Zone: Writings, 1976–1989.* London: Secker & Warburg, 1988.

Dyer, Richard. "Don't Look Now." *Screen* 23, no. 3–4 (1982): 61–73.

– *The Culture of Queers.* New York: Routledge Press, 2002.

– *White: Essays on Race and Culture.* New York: Routledge, 2013.

Echols, Alice. *Hot Stuff: Disco and the Remaking of American Culture.* New York: W.W. Norton & Company, Inc., 2010.

Edwards, Tim. *Cultures of Masculinity.* New York: Routledge Press, 2006.
– *Erotics and Politics: Gay Male Sexuality, Masculinity and Feminism.* London: Routledge, 2012.
Ehrenreich, Barbara. *The Hearts of Men: American Dreams and the Flight from Commitment.* New York: Knopf-Doubleday Press, 1983 [2011].
Eng, David L. *Racial Castration: Managing Masculinity in Asian America.* Durham: Duke University Press, 2001.
Enstad, Nan. *Ladies of Labor, Girls of Adventure: Working Women, Popular Culture, and Labor Politics at the Turn of the Twentieth Century.* New York: Columbia University Press, 1999.
Escoffier, Jeffrey. *American Homo: Community and Perversity.* Berkeley: University of California Press, 1998.
Evans, Jennifer V. "Seeing Subjectivity: Erotic Photography and the Optics of Desire." *American Historical Review* 118, no. 2 (April, 2013): 430–62. https://doi.org/10.1093/ahr/118.2.430.
Faderman, Lillian. *Odd Girls and Twilight Lovers: A History of Lesbian Life in Twentieth-Century America.* New York: Penguin Books, 1992.
Faludi, Susan. *Stiffed: The Betrayal of the American Man.* New York: Harper Collins, 1999.
Fausto-Sterling, Anne. *Sexing the Body: Gender Politics and the Construction of Sexuality.* New York: Basic Books, 2000.
Fleming, Brian. "All about that Pride Body: A Painstakingly Detailed Guide to What It Takes to Look Your Best." *Fashion,* June 26, 2015.
Foster, Gwendolyn Audrey. *Performing Whiteness: Postmodern Re/Constructions in the Cinema.* Albany: State University of New York Press, 2003.
Foucault, Michel. *The Birth of the Clinic.* New York: Routledge Press, 1963 [2012].
– *Discipline and Punish: The Birth of the Prison.* Translated by Alan Sheridan. New York: Vintage Books, 1975 [2012].
– *The History of Sexuality: Vol. 1: An Introduction.* Translated by Robert Hurley. New York: Random House, 1976 [2012].
– *Power Knowledge: Selected Interview and Other Writings, 1972–1977,* edited by Colin Gordon. New York: Pantheon Books, 1980.
Foucault, Michel, and Jay Miskowiec. "Of Other Spaces." *Diacritics* 16, no. 1 (1986): 22–7. https://doi.org/10.2307/464648.
Frank, Thomas. *The Conquest of Cool: Business Culture, Counterculture, and the Rise of Hip Consumerism.* Chicago: University of Chicago press, 1998.
Frankenberg, Ruth. "Introduction: Local Whitenesses, Localizing Whiteness." In *Displacing Whiteness: Essays in Social and Cultural Criticism,* edited by Ruth Frankenberg, 1–33. Durham: Duke University Press, 1997. https://doi.org/10.1515/9780822382270-001.
– *White Women, Race Matters: The Social Construction of Whiteness.* 7th ed. Minneapolis: University of Minnesota Press, 1999.

Franklin, Michael D., Larry Knopp, Kevin P. Murphy, Ryan Patrick Murphy, Jennifer L. Pierce, Jason Ruiz, and Alex T. Urquhart, eds. *Queer Twin Cities: Twin Cities GLBT Oral History Project*. Minneapolis: University of Minnesota Press, 2010.

Fraser, Benjamin. *Cognitive Disability Aesthetics: Visual Culture, Disability Representations, and the (In)Visibility of Cognitive Difference*. Toronto: University of Toronto Press, 2018.

Fraterrigo, Elizabeth. *Playboy and the Making of the Good Life in Modern America*. Oxford: Oxford University Press, 2009.

Fronc, Jennifer. *New York Undercover: Private Surveillance in the Progressive Era*. Chicago: University of Chicago Press, 2009.

Frosh, Paul. *The Image Factory: Consumer Culture, Photography, and the Visual Content Industry*. Oxford: Berg Press, 2003.

Fuchs, Don M. "Breaking Down Barriers: Independent Living Resource Centres for Empowering the Physically Disabled." In *Perspectives on Social Services and Social Issues*, edited by Jacqueline S. Ismael and Ray J. Thomlison, 187–200. Ottawa: Canadian Council on Social Development, 1987.

Garland-Thomson, Rosemarie. *Extraordinary Bodies: Figuring Physical Disability in American Culture and Literature*. New York: Columbia University Press, 1997.

Garner, Steve. *Whiteness: An Introduction*. New York: Routledge, 2007.

Gawthrop, Daniel. *The Rice Queen Diaries: A Memoir*. Arsenal Pulp Press, 2010.

Geczy, Adam, and Vicki Karaminas. *Queer Style*. London: Bloomsbury Press, 2013.

Geissinger, Aisha. "Islam and Discourses of Same-Sex Desire." In *Queer Religion: Homosexuality in Modern Religious History*, edited by Donald L. Boisvert and James Emerson Johnson, 69–90. Santa Barbara: Praeger, 2012.

Geller, Peter. *Northern Exposures: Photographing and Filming the Canadian North, 1920–1945*. Vancouver: University of British Columbia, 2004.

Gentile, Patrizia, and Jane Nicholas. *Contesting Bodies and Nation in Canadian History*. Toronto: University of Toronto Press, 2013.

Gilbert, James. *Men in the Middle: Searching for Masculinity in the 1950s*. Chicago: University of Chicago Press, 2005.

Gilman, Sander L. *Making the Body Beautiful: A Cultural History of Aesthetic Surgery*. Princeton: Princeton University Press, 1999.

Giteck, Larry. *Cruise to Win: A Guide for Gay Men*. San Francisco: Pantera Press, 1982.

Glynn Irial, and J. Olaf Kleis. "The Memory and Migration Nexus: An Overview." In *History, Memory and Migration: Perceptions of the Past and the Politics of Incorporation*, edited by Irial Glynn and J. Olaf Kleist, 3–29. New York: Palgrave Macmillan, 2012.

Goffman, Erving. *The Presentation of Self in Everyday Life*. Edinburgh: University of Edinburgh Social Sciences Research Centre, 1956.

Goldberg, David, ed. *Anatomy of Racism*. Minneapolis: University of Minnesota Press, 1990.

Goldberg, Johnathan. "Recalling Totalities: The Mirrored Staged of Arnold Schwarzenegger." In *Building Bodies*, edited by Pamela L. Moore, 217–48. New Brunswick: Rutgers University Press, 1997.

Goodley, Dan. *Dis/ability Studies: Theorising Disablism and Ableism*. New York: Routledge, 2014.

Goodman, Paul. "The Politics of Being Queer." In *Nature Heals*. See *Nature Heals: The Psychological Essays of Paul Goodman*, edited by Taylor Stoehr. New York: Free Life Editions, 1977.

Gordon, Colin. "Afterword to Michel Foucault." In *Power/Knowledge: Selected Interviews and Other Writings, 1972–1977*, translated by Colin Gordon, Leo Marshall, Joh Mepham, and Kate Soper; Edited by Colin Gordon, 229–60. New York: Pantheon Books, 1980.

Gould, Stephen Jay. *The Mismeasure of Man*. New York: W.W. Norton & Company, Inc., 1981.

Greenberg, Joshua M. *From Betamax to Blockbuster: Video Stores and the Invention of Movies on Video*. Cambridge: Massachusetts Institute of Technology Press, 2010.

Greig, Christopher J. *Ontario Boys: Masculinity and the Idea of Boyhood in Postwar Ontario, 1945–1960*. Waterloo: Wilfred Laurier University Press, 2014.

Halberstam, Jack. *Female Masculinity*. Durham: Duke University Press, 1998.

Hall, Stuart. *Deviancy, Politics and the Media*. Birmingham: Centre for Contemporary Cultural Studies, 1971.

Hamilton, Paula. "The Oral Historian as Memorist." *The Oral History Review* 32, no. 1 (2005): 11–18. https://doi.org/10.1525/ohr.2005.32.1.11.

Haritaworn, Jin, Ghaida Moussa, and Syrus Marcus Ware. *Marvellous Grounds: Queer of Colour Histories of Toronto*. Toronto: Between the Lines, 2018.

Harris, Daniel. *The Rise and Fall of Gay Culture*. New York: Hyperion, 1997.

Harrison, Kelby. *Sexual Deceit: The Ethics of Passing*. Plymouth: Lexington Books, 2013.

Healey, Murray. *Gay Skins: Class, Masculinity and Queer Appropriation*. London: Cassell, 1996.

Hebdige, Dick. *Subculture: The Meaning of Style*. New York: Routledge Press, 1979 [2003].

Hemphill, Essex. *Ceremonies: Prose and Poetry*. New York City: Plume Press, 1992; Jersey City, NJ: Cleis Press, 2000.

Henderson, Stuart. *Making the Scene: Yorkville and Hip Toronto in the 1960s*. Toronto: University of Toronto Press, 2011.

Hennen, Peter. *Faeries, Bears, and Leathermen: Men in Community Queering the Masculine*. Chicago: University of Chicago Press, 2008.

Hester, Helen. *Beyond Explicit: Pornography and the Displacement of Sex*. Albany: State University of New York Press, 2014.

Heywood, Leslie. "Muscularity Vanishing: Bodybuilding and Contemporary Culture." In *Building Bodies*, edited by Pamela L. Moore, 165–83. New Brunswick: Rutgers University Press, 1997.

Hilton, Matthew. *Smoking in British Popular Culture, 1800–2000*. Manchester: Manchester University Press, 2000.

Hobbs, Allyson. *A Chosen Exile: A History of Racial Passing in American Life*. Cambridge: Harvard University Press, 2014.

Hobson, Emily K. *Lavender and Red: Liberation and Solidarity in the Gay and Lesbian Left*. Oakland, CA: University of California Press, 2016.

Holmlund, Chris. "Masculinity as Multiple Masquerade." In *Screening the Male*, edited by Steven Cohan and Ina Rae Hark, 213–29. New York: Routledge, 1993.

– "Visible Differences and Flex Appeal: The Body, Sex, Sexuality, and Race in the Pumping Iron Films." In *Building Bodies*, edited by Pamela Moore, 87–102. New Brunswick: Rutgers University Press, 1997.

Hooper, Tom. "'Enough Is Enough': The Right to Privacy Committee and Bahthouse Raids in Toronto, 1978–1983," PhD diss., York University, 2016.

– "Queering '69: The Recriminalization of Homosexuality in Canada," *Canadian Historical Review* 100, no. 2 (2019): 257–73.

Horn, Marilyn J., and Lois M. Gurel. *The Second-Skin: An Interdisciplinary Study of Clothing*. Boston: Houghton Mifflin Company, 1981.

Houlbrook, Matt. *Queer London: Perils and Pleasures in the Sexual Metropolis, 1918–1957*. Chicago: University of Chicago Press, 2005.

Hrynyk, Nicholas. "Strutting like a Peacock: Masculinity, Consumerism, and Men's Fashion in Toronto, 1966–1972," *Journal of Canadian Studies* 49, no. 3 (Fall 2015): 76–110. https://doi.org/10.3138/jcs.49.3.76.

Hull, Kathleen. *Same-Sex Marriage: The Cultural Politics of Love and Law*. Cambridge: Cambridge University Press, 2006.

Hunt, Gerald Callan. "Division of Labor, Life Cycle and Democracy in Worker Co-Operatives." *Economic and Industrial Democracy* 13 (1992): 9–43.

Hutchinson Allan C., and Klaus Petersen. *Interpreting Censorship in Canada*. Toronto: University of Toronto Press, 1999.

Iacovetta, Franca. *Gatekeepers: Reshaping Immigrant Lives in Cold War Canada*. Toronto: Between the Lines, 2006.

Jackson, Paul. *One of the Boys: Homosexuality in the Military During World War II*. Montreal & Kingston: McGill-Queen's University Press, 2004.

Janoff, Douglas. *Pink Violence: Homophobic Violence in Canada*. Toronto: University of Toronto Press, 2005.

Jarman, Michelle. "Dismembering the Lynch Mob: Intersecting Narratives of Disability, Race, and Sexual Menace." In *Sex and Disability*, edited by Robert McRuer and Anne Mollow, 89–107. Durham: Duke University Press, 2012.

Jerram, Leif. "Space: A Useless Category of Historical Analysis?" *History and Theory* 52 (October 2013): 400–19. https://doi.org/10.1111/hith.10676.

Johnson, David. "Physique Pioneers: The Politics of 1960s Gay Consumer Culture." *Journal of Social History* 43, no. 4 (2010): 867–92.

– *Buying Gay: How Physique Entrepreneurs Sparked a Movement*. New York: Columbia University Press, 2019.

Johnson, Mary. "Sticks and Stones: The Language of Disability." In *The Disabled, the Media, and the Information Age*, edited by Jack Adolph Nelson, 25–44. Westport, CT: Greenwood Publishing, 1994.

Johnson, E. Patrick. *Sweet Tea: Black Gay Men of the South*. Chapel Hill: University of North Carolina Press, 2008.

Jones, James H. *Bad Blood: The Tuskegee Syphilis Experiment*. New York: The Free Press, 1981 [1993].

Jones, James J. *Alfred C. Kinsey: A Public/Private Life*. New York: W.W. Norton & Company, Inc., 1997.

Juntunen, Jacob. *Mainstream AIDS Theatre, the Media, and Gay Civil Rights: Making the Radical Palatable*. New York: Routledge, 2016.

Kasson, John F. *Houdini, Tarzan, and the Perfect Man: The White Male Body and the Challenge of Modernity in America*. New York: Hill and Wang, 2001.

Katz, Jonathan Ned. *The Invention of Heterosexuality*. New York: Dutton Press, 1995.

Kendall, Christopher, and Wayne Martino, eds. *Gendered Outcasts and Sexual Outlaws: Sexual Oppression and Gender Hierarchies in Queer Men's Lives*. New York: Harrington Park Press, 2006.

Kennedy, Elizabeth, and Madeline Davis. *Boots of Leather, Slippers of Gold: The History of a Lesbian Community*. New York: Routledge Press, 1993.

Kimmel, Michael. *Guyland: The Perilous World Where Boys Become Men*. New York: Harper Collins, 2008.

– *Manhood in America: A Cultural History*, 3rd ed. Oxford: Oxford University Press, 2012.

– *Angry White Men: American Masculinity at the End of an Era*. New York: Nation Books Press, 2013.

Kinsman, Gary. *The Regulation of Desire*. Montreal: Black Rose Books, 1996.

Kinsman, Gary, and Patrizia Gentile. *The Canadian War on Queers: National Security as Sexual Regulation*. Vancouver: University of British Columbia Press, 2010.

Klein, Alan M. *Little Big Men: Bodybuilding Subculture and Gender Construction*. Albany: State University of New York Press, 1993.

Korinek, Valerie. *Roughing It in the Suburbs: Reading Chatelaine Magazine in the Fifties and Sixties*. Toronto: University of Toronto Press, 2000.

Kramer, Larry. *The Normal Heart*. New York: Samuel French, Inc, 1985.

Lahti, Martti. "Dressing Up in Power: Tom of Finland and Gay Male Body Politics." *Journal of Homosexuality* 35, no. 3–4 (1998): 185–205. https://doi.org/10.1300/J082v35n03_08.

Larocque, Sylvain. *Gay Marriage: The Story of a Canadian Social Revolution*. Translated by Robert Chodos, Benjamin Waterhouse, and Louisa Blair. Toronto: James Lorimer & Company, 2006.

Lehman, Peter, ed. *Masculinity: Bodies, Movies, and Culture*. New York: Routledge Press, 2013.

Lester Neal A., and Maureen Daly Goggin. "In Living Color: Politics of Desire in Heterosexual Interracial Black/White Personal Ads." In *Racialized Politics of Desire in Personal Ads*, edited by Neal A. Lester and Maureen Daly Goggin, 37–76. Lanham, MD: Lexington Books, 2007.

Levine, Martin P. *Gay Macho: The Life and Death of the Homosexual Clone*. New York: New York University Press, 1998.

Lindgren, Allana C. "The National Ballet of Canada's Normative Bodies: Legitimizing and Popularizing Dance in Canada During the 1950s." In *Contesting Bodies and Nation in Canada History*, edited by Patrizia Gentile and Jane Nicholas, 180–202. Toronto: University of Toronto Press, 2013.

Lord, Alexandra M. "Models of Masculinity: Sex Education, the United States Public Health Service, and the YMCA, 1919–1924." *Journal of the History of Medicine* 58, no. 2 (2003): 123–52. https://doi.org/10.1093/jhmas/58.2.123.

Luciano, Lynn. *Looking Good: Male Body Image in Modern America*. New York: Hill and Wang, 2001.

Lupton, Deborah. *Food, the Body and the Self*. London: Sage Press, 1996.

Macías-González, Víctor M., and Anne Rubenstein, eds. *Masculinity and Sexuality in Modern Mexico*. Albuquerque: University of New Mexico: 2012.

MacKinnon, Catherine A. "Sexuality, Pornography, and Method: 'Pleasure under Patriarchy.'" *Ethics* 99, no. 2 (January 1989): 314–46.

MacKinnon, Kenneth. *Love, Tears, and the Male Spectator*. Madison: Fairleigh Dickinson University Press, 2002.

Manjapra, Kris. *Colonialism in Global Perspective*. Cambridge: Cambridge University Press, 2020.

Mann, W. E. *The Underside of Toronto*. Toronto: McClelland and Stewart Limited, 1970.

Marchand, Roland. *Advertising the American Dream: Making Way for Modernity, 1920–1940*. Berkeley: University of California Press, 1985, 238.

Marks, Deborah. *Disability: Controversial Debates and Psychosocial Perspectives*. London: Routledge, 1999.

Martineau, Paul, and Britt Salvesen. *Robert Mapplethorpe: The Photographs*. Los Angeles: Getty Publications, 2016.

Maynard, Steven. "Through a Hole in the Lavatory Wall: Homosexual Subcultures, Police Surveillance, and the Dialectics of Discovery, Toronto, 1890–1930." *Journal of the History of Sexuality* 5, no. 2 (October 1994): 207–42.

McCall, Leslie. "The Complexity of Intersectionality." *Signs* 30, no. 3 (2005): 1771–800. https://doi.org/10.1086/426800.

McCaskell, Tim. *Queer Progress: From Homophobia to Homonationalism*. Toronto: Between the Lines, 2016.

McClintock, Anne. *Imperial Leather: Race, Gender and Sexuality in Colonial Contest*. New York: Routledge, 1995.

McGowan, Todd. *Capitalism and Desire: The Psychic Cost of Free Markets*. New York: Columbia University Press, 2016.

McLeod, Donald W. *Lesbian and Gay Liberation in Canada: A Selected Annotated Chronology, 1964–1975*. Toronto: ECW Press, 1996.

McLuhan, Marshall. *The Medium is the Message: An Inventory of Effects*. San Francisco: Hardwired Press, 1978 [1996].

McRuer, Robert. *Crip Theory: Cultural Signs of Queerness and Disability*. New York: New York University Press, 2006.

Merleau-Ponty, Maurice. *Phenomenology of Perception*. New York: Routledge, 2002.

Metzl, Jonathan M., and Anna Kirkland, eds., *Against Health: How Health Became the New Morality*. New York: New York University Press, 2010.

Mezo González, Juan Carlos. "Contested Images: Debating Nudity, Sexism, and Porn in *The Body Politic*, 1971–1987." *Left History* 23, no. 1 (Spring /Summer 2019): 28–61. https://doi.org/10.25071/1913-9632.39487.

Mills, Sean. *The Empire Within: Postcolonial Thought and Political Activism in Sixties Montreal*. Montreal and Kingston: McGill-Queen's University Press, 2010.

Millward, Liz. *Making a Scene: Lesbians and Community Across Canada, 1964–84*. Vancouver: University of British Columbia Press, 2015

Mitchell, David T., and Sharon L. Snyder. *The Biopolitics of Disability: Neoliberalism, Abelenationalism, and Peripheral Embodiment*. Ann Arbor: University of Michigan Press, 2015.

Moffatt, Ken, ed. *Troubled Masculinities: Reimagining Urban Men*. Toronto: University of Toronto Press, 2012.

Mondimore, Francis Mark. *A Natural History of Homosexuality*. Baltimore: Johns Hopkins University Press, 1996.

Morgensen, Scott Lauria. *Spaces Between Us: Queer Settler Colonialism and Indigenous Decolonization*. Minneapolis: University of Minnesota Press, 2011.

Mulvey, Laura. *Visual and Other Pleasures*. New York: Palgrave Macmillan, 1989.

Mumford, Kevin. *Not Straight, Not White: Black Gay Men from the March on Washington to the AIDS Crisis*. Chapel Hill: University of North Carolina Press, 2016.

Murray, Heather. "Every Generation Has Its War." In *Gender, Health, and Popular Culture*, edited by Cheryl Krasnick Warsh, 237–57. Waterloo, Ontario: Wilfred Laurier University Press, 2011.

Murray, Stephen O., ed. *Latin American Male Homosexualities*. Albuquerque: University of New Mexico Press, 1995.

Namaste, Viviane. *Invisible Lives: The Erasure of Transsexual and Transgendered People*. Chicago: University of Chicago Press, 2000.

Nash, Catherine Jean. "Toronto's Gay Village (1969–1982): Plotting the Politics of Gay Identity." *The Canadian Geographer* 50, no. 1 (2006): 1–16. http://dx.doi.org/10.1111/j.0008-3658.2006.00123.x.

Nash, Jennifer C. "Re-thinking Intersectionality." *Feminist Review* 89 (2008): 1–15. https://doi.org/10.1057/fr.2008.4.

Nast, Heidi J. "Queer Patriarchies, Queer Racisms, International." *Antipode* 34, no. 5 (November 2002): 874–909. https://doi.org/10.1111/1467-8330.00281.

Nealon, Christopher. *Foundlings: Lesbian and Gay Historical Emotion Before Stonewall*. Durham: Duke University Press, 2001.

Nestle, Joan. *A Restricted Country*. Ithaca and New York: Firebrand Books, 1987.

Nixon, Sean. *Hard Looks: Masculinities, Spectatorship & Contemporary Consumption*. New York: St. Martin's Press, 1996.

Noble, Bobby. "Boy to the Power of Three: Toronto's Drag Kings." In *Making It Like a Man: Canadian Masculinities in Practice*, edited by Christine Ramsay, 259–80. Waterloo: Wilfred Laurier University Press, 2011.

Oldstone-Moore, Christopher. *Of Beards and Men: The Revealing History of Facial Hair*. Chicago: University of Chicago Press, 2015.

Palmer, Bryan. *Canada's 1960s: The Ironies of Identity in a Rebellious Era*. Toronto: University of Toronto Press, 2009.

Parr, Joy. *The Gender of Breadwinners: Women, Men, and Change in Two Industrial Towns, 1880–1950*. Toronto: University of Toronto Press, 1990.

Peiss, Kathy. *Hope in a Jar: The Making of America's Beauty Culture*. Philadelphia: University of Pennsylvania Press, 2011.

Penner, Penner. *Pinks, Pansies, and Punks: The Rhetoric of Masculinity in American Literary Culture*. Bloomington: Indiana University Press, 2011.

Phillip, Lyndon. "Reading Caribana 1997: Black Youth, Puff Daddy, Style, and Diaspora Transformations." In *Trinidad Carnival: The Cultural Politics of a Transnational Festival*, edited by Garth L. Green and Philip W. Scher, 102–35. Bloomington: Indiana University Press, 2007.

Pitzulo, Carrie. *Bachelors and Bunnies: The Sexual Politics of Playboy*. Chicago: University of Chicago Press, 2011.

Pon, Gordon. "Queering Asian Masculinities and Transnationalism: Implications for Anti-Oppression and Consciousness-Raising." In *Troubled Masculinities: Reimagining Urban Men*. Edited by Ken Moffatt. Toronto: University of Toronto Press, 2012.

Portelli, Alessandro. *The Death of Luigi Trastulli and Other Stories: Form and Meaning in Oral History*. Albany, NY: SUNY Press, 1991.

Potvin, John. "Vapour and Steam: The Victorian Turkish Bath, Homosocial Health, and Male Bodies on Display." *Journal of Design History* 18, no. 4 (2005): 319–33. https://doi.org/10.1093/jdh/epi051.

Pronger, Brian. *The Arena of Masculinity: Sports, Homosexuality, and the Meaning of Sex*. London: GMP Publishers, 1990.

Puar, Jasbir K. "Prognosis Time: Towards a Geopolitics of Affect, Debility, and Capacity." *Women and Performance: A Journal of Feminist Theory* 19, no. 2 (2009): 161–72. https://doi.org/10.1080/07407700903034147.

– "CODA: The Cost of Getting Better: Suicide, Sensation, Switchpoints." *GLQ* 18, no. 1 (2011): 149–58. https://doi.org/10.1215/10642684-1422179.

Ramsay, Christine, ed. *Making It Like a Man: Canadian Masculinities in Practice*. Waterloo: Wilfred Laurier University Press, 2011.

Ramussen, Birgit, Eric Klinenberg, Irene Nexica, and Matt Wray. *The Making and the Unmaking of Whiteness*. Durham: Duke University Press, 2001.

Rechy, John. *The Sexual Outlaw: A Documentary*. New York: Grove Press, 1977.

Reeser, Todd W. *Masculinities in Theory: An Introduction*. Oxford: Wiley-Blackwell, 2010.

Rich, Adrienne. "Compulsory Heterosexuality and Lesbian Existence." *Signs* 5, no. 4 (Summer 1980): 631–60. https://doi.org/10.1086/493756.

Ritchie, Donald A. *Doing Oral History*. 2002; reissued, Oxford: Oxford University Press, 2015.

Robertson, Pamela. "What Makes the Feminist Camp?" In *Camp: Queer Aesthetics and the Performing Subject*, edited by Fabio Cleto, 266–82. Ann Arbor: The University of Michigan Press, 1999.

Rooks, Noliwe M. *Hair Raising: Beauty, Culture, and African American Women*. New Brunswick, NJ: Rutger's University Press, 1996.

Ross, Becki. *The House that Jill Built: A Lesbian Nation in Formation*. Toronto: University of Toronto Press, 1995.

– *Burlesque West: Showgirls, Sex, and Sin in Postwar Vancouver*. Toronto: University of Toronto Press, 2009.

Ross, Geoffery Anquilana. *The Day of the Peacock: Style for Men, 1963–1973*. London: Victoria and Albert Publishing, 2011.

Rotundo, E. Anthony. *American Manhood: Transformations in Masculinity from the Revolution to the Modern Era*. New York: Basic Books, 1993.

Royles, Dan. *To Make the Wounded Whole: The African American Struggle Against HIV/AIDS*. Chapel Hill: University of North Carolina Press, 2020.

Rubenfeld, Jed. "The Riddle of Rape-by-Deception and the Myth of Sexual Autonomy." *Yale Law Journal* 122, no. 6 (2013): 1413–43.

Rubin, Gayle. "The Miracle Mile: South of Market and Gay Male Leather, 1962–1997." In *Reclaiming San Francisco: History, Politics, Culture,* edited by James Brook, Chris Carlsson, and Nancy J. Peters, 247–72. San Francisco: City Lights Books, 1998.

Deviations: A Gayle Rubin Reader. Durham: Duke University Press, 2011.

Rudy, Jarrett. *The Freedom to Smoke: Tobacco Consumption and Identity.* Montreal and Kingston: McGill-Queen's University Press, 2005.

Ruether, Rosemary Radford. "Misogynism and Virginal Feminism in the Fathers of the Church." In *Religion and Sexism: Images of Women in the Jewish and Christian Traditions,* edited by Rosemary Radford Ruether, 150–83. New York: Simon and Schuster, 1974.

Russo, Mary. *The Female Grotesque: Risk, Excess and Modernity.* New York: Routledge, 2012.

Said, Edward W. *Orientalism: Western Conceptions of the Orient.* New York: Penguin Books, 1978 [2006].

Schiebinger, Londa. *Nature's Body: Sexual Politics and the Making of Modern Science.* Hammersmith, London: Pandora, 1993.

Schweik, Susan. *The Ugly Laws: Disability in Public.* New York: New York University Press, 2009.

Scott, James C. *Domination and the Arts of Resistance: Hidden Transcripts.* New Haven: Yale University Press, 1990 [2008].

Scott, Joan. "Gender: A Useful Category of Historical Analysis." *American Historical Review* 91, no. 5 (December 1986): 1053–75. https://doi.org/10.2307/1864376.

Sears, James T. *Growing up Gay in the South: Race, Gender, and Journeys of the Spirit.* New York: Routledge Press, 1991.

Sedgwick, Eve. *Touching Feeling: Affect, Pedagogy, Performativity.* Durham: Duke University Press, 2002.

– *Epistemology of the Closet.* Berkeley: University of California Press, 2008.

Serlin, David. *Replaceable You: Engineering the Body in Postwar America.* Chicago: University of Chicago Press, 2004.

Shilts, Randy. *And the Band Played On: Politics, People, and the AIDS Epidemic.* New York: St. Martin's Press, 1987.

Shoemaker, Robert B. *Gender in English Society 1650–1850: The Emergence of Separate Spheres?* New York: Routledge, 1998.

Siebers, Tobin. "A Sexual Culture for Disabled People." In *Sex and Disability,* edited by Robert McRuer and Anna Mollow, 37–53. Durham: Duke University Press, 2012.

Silverman, Kaja. *Male Subjectivity at the Margins.* New York: Routledge, 1992.

Silversides, Ann. *AIDS Activist: Michael Lynch and the Politics of Community.* Toronto: Between the Lines, 2003.

Simmons, Christina. "African Americans and Sexual Victorianism in the Social Hygiene Movement, 1910–1940." *Journal of the History of Sexuality* 4, no. 1 (July 1993): 51–75.

Simpson, Mark. *It's a Queer World.* London: Vintage Press, 1996.

Sinha, Mrinalini. *Colonial Masculinity: The "Manly Englishman" and the "Effeminate Bengali" in the Late Nineteenth Century.* Manchester: Manchester University Press, 1995.

– "Giving Masculinity a History: Some Contributions from the Historiography of Colonial India." *Gender and History* 11, no. 3 (1999): 445–60. https://doi.org/10.1111/1468-0424.00155.

Smith, Miriam. *Lesbian and Gay Rights in Canada: Social Movements and Equality Seeking, 1971–1995.* Toronto: University of Toronto Press, 1999.

– "Interview with Chris Bearchell, Lasqueti Island, 1996." *Journal of Canadian Studies* 48, no. 1 (Winter 2014): 252–75. https://doi.org/10.3138/jcs.48.1.252.

Snodgrass, Mary Ellen. *World Clothing and Fashion: An Encyclopedia of History, Culture, and Social Influence.* New York: Routledge, 2015.

Somerville, Siobhan B. *Queering the Color Line: Race and the Invention of Homosexuality in American Culture.* Durham: Duke University Press, 2000.

Sontag, Susan. *Against Interpretation: And Other Essays.* New York: Farar, Straus and Giroux, 1966.

– *Illness as Metaphor.* New York: Farrar, Straus and Giroux, 1978.

– *AIDS and Its Metaphors.* New York: Farrar, Straus and Giroux, 1989.

– "Notes on 'Camp.'" In *Camp: Queer Aesthetic and the Performing Subject,* edited by Fabio Cleto, 53–65. Ann Arbor: University of Michigan Press, 1999.

– "The Image-World." In *Visual Culture: The Reader,* edited by Jessica Evans and Stuart Hall, 80–94. London: Sage Publications, 2004.

Spivak, Gayatri. "Displacement and the Discourse of Women." In *Displacement: Derrida and After,* edited by Mark Krupnick, 169–95. Bloomington: Indiana University Press, 1983.

Stein, Marc. *Rethinking the Gay and Lesbian Movement.* New York: Routledge, 2010.

Stoehr, Taylor, ed. *Nature Heals: The Psychological Essays of Paul Goodman.* New York: Free Life Editions, 1977.

Stoler, Ann Laura. "Making Empire Respectable: The Politics of Race and Sexual Morality in Twentieth-Century Colonial Cultures." In *Dangerous Liaisons: Gender, Nation, and Postcolonial Perspectives,* edited by Anne McClintock, Aamir Mufti, and Ella Shohat, 344–73. Minneapolis: University of Minnesota Press, 1997): 344–73.

Stoller, Nancy E. "From Feminism to Polymorphous Activism: Lesbians in AIDS Organizations." In *In Changing Times: Gay Men and Lesbians*

Encounter HIV/AIDS, edited by Martin P. Levine, Peter M. Nardi, and John H. Gagnon, 171–90. Chicago: University of Chicago Press, 1997.

Summerfield, Penny. "Culture and Composure: Creating Narratives of the Gendered Self in Oral History Interviews." *Culture and Social History* 1, no. 1 (2004): 65–93. https://doi.org/10.1191/1478003804cs0005oa.

Syrett, Nicholas. "Mobility, Circulation, and Correspondence: Queer White Men in the Midcentury Midwest." *GLQ* 20, no. 1–2 (2014): 75–94. https://doi.org/10.1215/10642684-2370369

Taylor, Shawn. *Big Black Penis: Misadventures in Race and Masculinity.* Chicago: Lawrence Hill Books, 2008.

Thomas, Calvin. *Masculinity, Psychoanalysis, Straight Queer Theory.* New York: Palgrave Macmillan, 2008.

Torres, José B., V. Scott H. Solberg, and Aaron H. Carlstrom. "The Myth of Sameness Among Latino Men and Their Machismo." *American Journal of Orthopsychiatry* 72, no. 2 (2002): 163–81. https://doi.org/10.1037/0002-9432.72.2.163

Tungate, Mark. *Branded Male: Marketing to Men*. Philadelphia: Kogan Page Publishers, 2008.

Turner, Mark W. *Backward Glances: Cruising the Queer Streets of New York and London*. London: Reaktion Books, 2003.

Valentine Gill, and Tracey Skelton. "Finding Oneself, Losing Oneself: The Lesbian and Gay 'Scene' as a Paradoxical Space." *International Journal of Urban and Regional Research* 27, no. 4 (December 2003): 849–66. https://doi.org/10.1111/j.0309-1317.2003.00487.x.

Valverde, Mariana. *Sex, Power and Pleasure.* Toronto: Canadian Scholar's Press, 1985.

Voelkel, Rebecca M. *Carnal Knowledge of God: Embodied Love and the Movement for Justice.* Minneapolis: Fortress Press, 2017. https://doi.org/10.2307/j.ctt1ggjhnm

Walcott, Rinaldo. "Blackness, Masculinity, and the Work of Queer." In *Canadian Men and Masculinities: Historical and Contemporary Perspectives*, edited by Christopher J. Greig and Wayne Martino, 191–204. Toronto: Canadian Scholars' Press, 2012.

Walkowitz, Judith R. *Prostitution and Victorian Society: Women, Class, and the State*. Cambridge: Cambridge University Press, 1982. https://doi.org/10.1017/CBO9780511583605

Ward, Elizabeth Jane. *Respectably Queer: Diversity Culture in LGBT Activist Organizations*. Nashville, TN: Vanderbilt University Press, 2008. https://doi.org/10.2307/j.ctv16754qs

Warner, Michael. *Publics and Counterpublics*. New York: Zone Books, 2005. https://doi.org/10.2307/j.ctv1qgnqj8.

Warner, Tom. *Never Going Back: A History of Queer Activism in Canada.* Toronto: University of Toronto Press, 2002. https://doi.org/10.3138/9781442677623

Waugh, Thomas. *Hard to Imagine: Gay Male Eroticism in Photography and Film from Their Beginnings.* New York: Columbia University Press, 1996.

– *Romance of Transgression in Canada: Queering Sexualities, Nations, Cinemas.* Montreal and Kingston: McGill-Queen's University Press, 2006. https://doi.org/10.1515/9780773576803.

Weeks, Jeffrey. *Sexuality and Its Discontents: Meanings, Myths, and Modern Sexualities.* New York: Routledge, 1985 [2002].

Weyr, Thomas. *Reaching for Paradise: The Playboy Vision of America.* New York: Times Books, 1978.

Wiegers, Yvonne. "Male Bodybuilding: The Social Construction of a Masculine Identity." *Journal of Popular Culture* 32, no. 2 (1998): 147–61. https://doi.org/10.1111/j.0022-3840.1998.00147.x.

Willis, Ellen. "Feminism, Moralism, and Pornography." In *Desire: The Politics of Sexuality,* edited by Ann Snitow, Christine Stansell, and Sharon Thompson, 82–8. London: Virago, 1984.

Index

Note: Page numbers in *italics* indicate figures.